THE SINNERS OF CRAMOND

THE SINNERS OF CRAMOND

*The Struggle to Impose Godly Behaviour
on a Scottish Community*

1651–1851

Alison Hanham

JOHN DONALD

First published in Great Britain in 2005 by
John Donald (Publisher) an imprint of
Birlinn Ltd
West Newington House
10 Newington Road
Edinburgh EH9 1QS
www.birlinn.co.uk

ISBN 10: 0 85976 6047
ISBN 13: 978 0 85976 604 3

British Library Cataloguing-in-Publication Data

A catalogue record of this book is available
on request from the British Library

Typeset by Hewer Text UK Ltd, Edinburgh
Printed and bound by Antony Rowe Ltd, Chippenham

Contents

Map. *Cramond and surrounding area*   vi

Preface   ix

 1. The Vanishing Lady   1

 2. Kirk and People   9

 3. Offenders and Discipline, 1651–1662   22

 4. The Inglorious Restoration   43

 5. Reform and Repression   66

 6. Ministerial Problems   87

 7. 'A Very Froward Generation'   112

 8. Sins and Social Changes, 1710–1730   133

 9. Victims and Delinquents, 1731–1750   156

10. Industry, an Evangelist and Disorder   178

11. Liberty, Vice, Stability 1785–1799   196

12. Surveys and Surveyors of the Parish, 1785–1794   205

13. Erring Sheep and Earnest Pastors   221

14. Cramond after the Disruption   242

Index   261

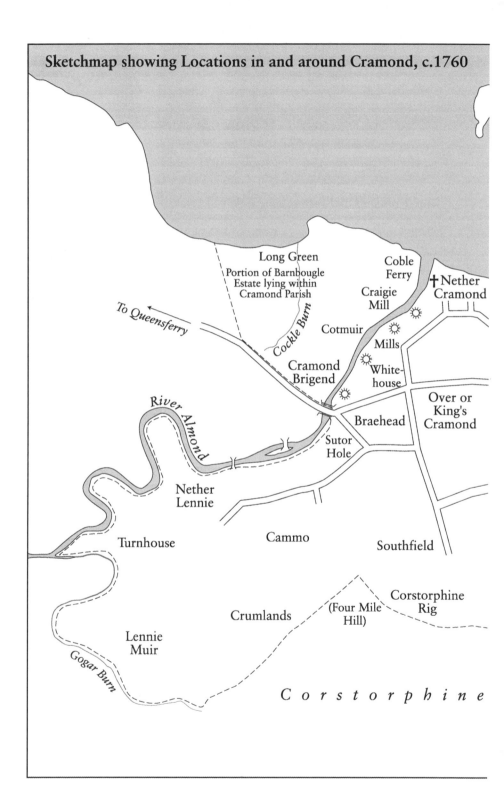

Sketchmap showing Locations in and around Cramond, c.1760

Long Green

Portion of Barnbougle
Estate lying within
Cramond Parish

Coble
Ferry

✝Nether
Cramond

Craigie
Mill

To Queensferry

Cockle Burn

Cotmuir

Mills

White-
house

Cramond
Brigend

River Almond

Over or
King's
Cramond

Braehead

Sutor
Hole

Nether
Lennie

Cammo

Southfield

Turnhouse

Corstorphine
Rig

Crumlands

(Four Mile
Hill)

Lennie
Muir

Gogar Burn

C o r s t o r p h i n e

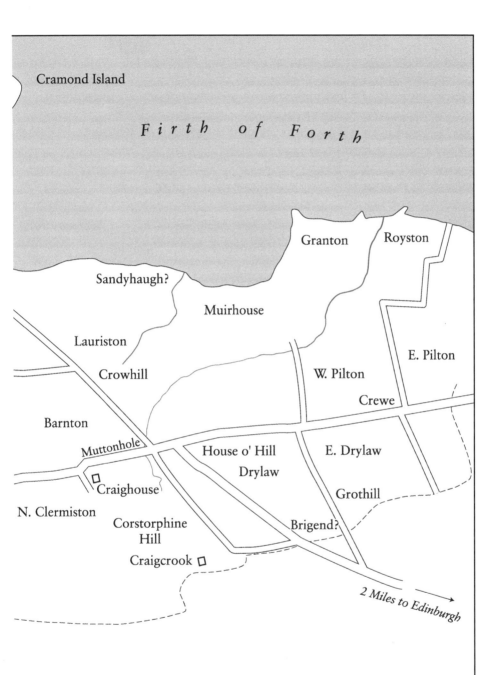

Cramond Island

Firth of Forth

Granton

Royston

Sandyhaugh?

Muirhouse

Lauriston

E. Pilton

Crowhill

W. Pilton

Crewe

Barnton

Muttonhole

House o' Hill

E. Drylaw

Drylaw

Craighouse

Grothill

N. Clermiston

Corstorphine Hill

Brigend?

Craigcrook

2 Miles to Edinburgh

Parish

Preface

I was first introduced to the Cramond Kirk Session Minutes in the 1960s and was at once fascinated by their record of the lively doings of a series of former fellow residents of the parish. Apart from sexual misdemeanours and breach of sabbath, especially by public drunkenness, offences over the years between 1651 and 1851 included cases of marital disharmony, maltreating a wife and (once) a child, exposing infants, infanticide and concealed birth, attempted abortion, escapes from custody, entertaining a member of the opposite sex behind closed doors, brawling, invented husbands, blasphemy, damaging gossip about kirk elders and lairds, poaching and theft (on the sabbath), suspected brothel-keeping, claims of rape (never accepted by session or presbytery), clandestine marriage, disturbances during a wake, maleficent cursing between neighbours and a girl's allegation that she had been sold to the captain of a ship trading to Virginia. The plights of refugees, visiting beggars and the parish's own poor and incapacitated are also illustrated.

Across time, voices come down to us from the offenders, almost all working-class, the witnesses who offered testimony against them and Cramond's ministers themselves. Some of the bolder spirits, male and female, openly objected to sessional prying into their private affairs. Such intransigence could frustrate ministerial efforts to impose godly order. So, often, did the flight of suspects.

Discontinuities in leadership also made it hard for the kirk to maintain its authority. There was a nationwide change from a Covenanting ministry to the Episcopalian regime of 1662–89 (during which a hostile element among landowners tried to have a minister ousted for sexual immorality), followed by a reversion to strict Presbyterian governance. In the eighteenth century there were two periods when Cramond had no settled minister – the first, in 1709–11, was occasioned by a disputed election, the second left the parish without effective rule for fifteen months between June 1771 and October 1776. After that there was continuity in the ministry until the Disruption of 1843, but already by the mid-eighteenth century social and economic developments were bringing changes, both to the outlook of sessions and to the make-up of the community as a whole.

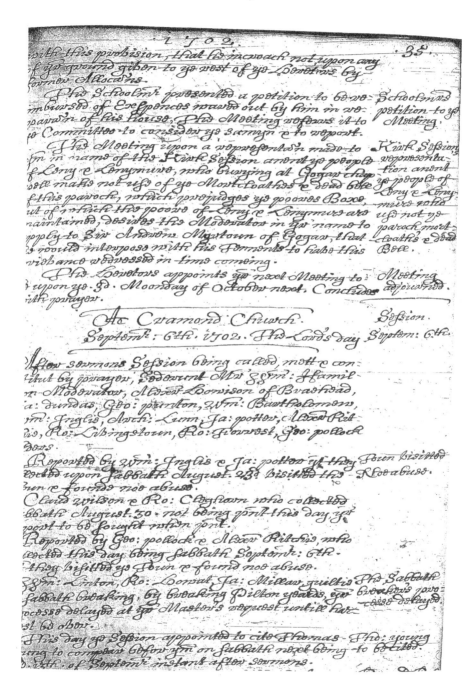

A page from the Cramond Kirk Session Minutes

Near the end of the eighteenth century the 'deaf and dumb' Cramonder, John Philp Wood, published his book, *The Antient and Modern State of the Parish of Cramond* (Edinburgh, 1794), from which I have quoted extensively. Wood's friends, the farmer and progressive agriculturist George Robertson, and the parish surgeon, elder, kirk treasurer and native of Cramond, Robert Spotswood, also left much information about Cramond and its inhabitants at their time.

For the period from September 1651 to December 1699 I have made grateful use of a photocopy of the typed transcript of the first four volumes of session minutes made in 1959 by Professor M. L. Anderson. My copy was made by permission of the Rev. C. M. Maclean. Corrections and some omissions have been supplied from the original manuscripts. I thank Massey University for a grant to purchase microfilm of the further seven volumes of session minutes, to 1878. I should also like to record my gratitude to my former colleagues in the History Department of Massey University, especially Professors J. C. Davis and Barrie Macdonald for their successive help and support. In 1989 I had the good fortune to enjoy three months as an honorary visiting fellow of the Institute for Advanced Studies in the Humanities, University of Edinburgh. This enabled me to consult further materials in the surviving papers of John Philp Wood at the National Library of Scotland (NLS), Cramond's registers of marriages and baptisms and the kirk session minutes, which by then were held at the Scottish Record Office (now the National Archives of Scotland, (NAS)), like the 'poll tax' return for Cramond of 1694. More than a routine acknowledgment is due to the staffs of these institutions. In 1989 Mr W. J. Scholes most kindly arranged for me to consult the early account books of Cramond's kirk treasurers, which were then in his keeping as clerk to Cramond session. At a later date I transcribed the enumerators' returns for Cramond in the national censuses of 1841 and 1851 from microfilm, by courtesy of the Palmerston North branch of the Church of Latter Day Saints, albeit for a purpose that my hosts had not envisaged. Boni and Jim Cron read a slightly earlier draft of the present book and I am indebted to them for their encouraging interest.

Of others who generously gave help and shared their knowledge at various times I would particularly like to mention J. A. Aitken, as editor of the *Dictionary of the Older Scottish Tongue*, and Francis Bamford, Ann Kettle of the University of St Andrews and, for permission to copy documents then in their ownership, Dr and Mrs David C. Simpson. In the 1960s I was lucky enough to attend two study-groups led by Basil C. Skinner, one of them on Cramond's industrial history as an ironworking centre. In Cramond itself I wish especially to remember Mrs Joan Aitken, Ronald and Bertha Macintosh, the Rev. Campbell Maclean and Alan and Viola Rae, members of what was then the Cramond Association.

Above all, I record my thanks to Barclay and Janet Fraser, for much hospitality over the years and for graciously encouraging a project that Barclay was far better qualified to undertake than I am. I regret enormously that he died before any draft had been written for submission to his gentle but searching criticism. As it is, this book is offered as an inadequate tribute to the man who did so much to record and preserve Cramond's historical heritage.

ONE

The Vanishing Lady

In the days when the Kirk expected to exert strict discipline over the Scottish nation the ministers of Cramond sat weekly with their elders to review the state of the parish, to receive reports of misbehaviour and to bring proven offenders to repentance. These men might well be shocked to know that the records of their deliberations are now read chiefly because they bring so many of the parish delinquents to vivid life.[1]

Certainly when the session clerk minuted the scandalous doings of one small group of Cramonders in 1690 he did not intend to inspire a sneaking admiration for the women who organised a conspiracy of silence in their village and then stood up stoutly for themselves when confronted by an irate minister.

The women's enterprise of diddling their minister was made all the sweeter in their minds by his own character and aims. Mr John Hamilton had come to Cramond in December 1689 with a mission to restore the parish to the state of Christian obedience from which it had lapsed during the final years of increasingly tenuous control by his predecessor, the last of Cramond's episcopally appointed ministers. With the ousting of James VII and II and the advent of William and Mary, a presbyterian system of church government on Covenanting principles had been reinstated. Mr Hamilton had been in voluntary exile in a charge near Belfast, where he had successfully exercised rigorous spiritual discipline over his flock. Now the troubles in Ireland had sent him back to Scotland, although – he hoped – on a temporary basis. In the meantime he had accepted the call to Cramond and set about reform, with a high-fibre diet of Calvinistic teaching washed down at need with the water of repentance.

Among those of his new parishioners who failed to respond with docility were some of the residents in the kirktoun of Nether Cramond who were veterans of earlier encounters with the kirk session and inclined to resent what they saw as unwarranted interference in their personal affairs. For instance, in 1677 Jean Smith, the village midwife, had been reported – presumably by neighbours – to have indulged in 'scandalous converse and unseemly carriage' with an unmarried man and also to have given a night's lodging to a married man from Inverkeithing. (Jean's husband, John

Harrower senior, was still alive at the time.) When all three of the suspected parties insisted that nothing wrong had occurred, the session had been forced to dismiss the accusations as unproven.

For their part, the righteous had always seen Nether Cramond as a hotbed of iniquity. (The village is situated in the north-west tip of what is now Greater Edinburgh with a small harbour on the Forth and at that time was much the largest and most closely packed settlement in the parish.) Two elders were routinely deputed to invigilate it at service time and could usually expect to catch one or more of its residents – tradesmen, artisans, innkeepers and private ale-sellers, boatowners and seamen, widows and some of the 'enrolled poor' who were supported by hand-outs from the parish poor-box – out of church and breaking the sabbath by entertaining visitors, drinking, cutting kale or drawing water from the well. Even those who dutifully attended the two long Sunday services were likely to hang around afterwards and gossip with acquaintances instead of going home for quiet religious study. Soon after his arrival Mr Hamilton took steps to curb this lack of decorum and instituted an 'evening exercise' for half-an-hour after the last service. This was to be compulsory for Nether Cramonders, intended 'for their further information and instruction and to prevent their idle communications or wandering among houses'. Those in other parts of the parish were free to attend if they wished. The scheme is not mentioned again in the session minutes and may have been among several of Mr Hamilton's less-than-successful innovations. But one feels that it cannot have endeared him to the villagers.

Nether Cramond also contained the laird's family, in the fine new house to which they had moved a few years earlier from their ancient tower-house, the manse and the schoolhouse whose dominie, Mr Thomas Forrest, was also the session clerk. Between them, laird, minister and clerk were well situated to monitor the doings of the villagers. Less subject to authoritarian overview was Cramond Island – a little way out in the Forth but accessible on foot at low tide. The island was farmed in 1690 by a single family, the Youngs. Its comparative isolation brought it to the attention of a certain Arthur Forbes, who was looking for a sanctuary in which his young protégée, Elisabeth Gordon, might give birth unmolested by the church authorities. Mr and Mrs Young proved willing to offer facilities in return for money. (Later rumour would say that this was not the first time that they had done so.) According to Robert Young's later, and largely untruthful, story, Forbes first asked if Young would receive a visitor who was 'under a consumption, that she might be the better of the air'. Forbes gave him money to buy timber for a partition to afford the lady some privacy, and Jean Smith's sons, John and James Harrower, duly erected this in the Youngs' house. The lady then paid a short visit, by boat from Leith, in order to meet Jean and to inspect and approve the arrangements for her lying-in. Before she returned again Forbes had her accommodation furnished with bedding, a barrel of beer and twenty-one bottles of ale. There were later additions of wine and sack, brought from Edinburgh.

Before dawn on Wednesday, 27 August 1690, Jean Smith was roused from her bed and hastily conveyed to Cramond Island. 'The gentlewoman' had gone into labour unexpectedly, as a result, Jean thought, of eating plums the previous evening. Before she agreed to give any professional help to a stranger a midwife was supposed to insist on being told the woman's name and marital status and the name and marital status of the child's father if he were not her husband. In the absence of such details it was automatically assumed that the case was one of adultery, with the harsh penalties which then accrued. It may be doubted whether Jean made any threat to withhold assistance from this particular client, but she did learn that the woman (whom Jean estimated to be no more than twenty years old) was named Elisabeth Gordon. The father, Elisabeth claimed, was her husband, presently serving with the Scottish forces in Ireland, but she refused to name him.

Four days after the birth the child, a girl, was secretly baptised in an irregular but valid ceremony by 'a man in a fair periwig' whom Forbes brought from Edinburgh. No doubt this was one of the many Episcopalian – or, more romantically, Jacobite – ministers 'outed' in 1689 for their refusal to switch allegiance to William and Mary. Some of them continued to offer their ministerial services to clients who would pay to bypass the proper channels for baptisms or marriages.

Although the minister, the parish clerk-cum-schoolmaster and William Ramsay the local elder lived in their midst, for a long time before the birth and for a week after it the villagers of Nether Cramond managed to keep them (and even their wives?) in the dark about these goings-on. In the meantime, gossip must have spread between neighbours and among those frequenting the various ale-houses in the village. Mrs Young's brother-in-law had been in the know from the start and she had confided in her friend Dorothy Gibson, wife of the village blacksmith. Jean Smith's sons had not only put up the partition but returned to fix a brace when the lady was in residence. The wives of William Hardy, miller at the Cockle Mill, and of the weaver James Broun had visited the baby and her mother, probably walking across to the island. Jean herself was said to have boasted to cronies 'that neither the minister nor the session nor any person else durst challenge the matter nor meddle with it'.

When the news finally reached the ears of the scandalised minister he sent the schoolmaster-clerk, Mr Thomas Forrest, across to the island. Forrest spoke to the lady and confirmed that she had given birth, but got no other satisfactory answers from her. Nor did the minister when he went there by boat on 3 September accompanied by the kirk treasurer, Alexander Howison, laird of Braehead, although he then made Mrs Young promise not to let the gentlewoman 'slip away'. John Menzies, laird of Cammo, an Edinburgh advocate and local justice of the peace, obtained an order for her arrest from the sheriff depute, and on Thursday 11 September a small posse consisting of Cammo, Braehead, the deputy treasurer, Cammo's manservant and two sheriff's officers set off to secure the lady. They were fobbed off by Arthur Forbes, who gave them his 'bond of cautionry' for the large sum of £400 Scots to produce Elisabeth before Cramond kirk session on 9 October. Three days later Forbes and the lady disappeared, leaving nought but empty bottles and the baby at nurse with Mrs Young. Subsequent efforts to trace them were unsuccessful and in October 1694, under a new minister, the session formally acknowledged that it was impossible to enforce their bond or prosecute the pair for adultery since they had fled beyond their jurisdiction into England.

In the view of the secular and ecclesiastical authorities Jean Smith and the Youngs had connived at a piece of gross immorality. Their actions posed a serious threat to good order and the spiritual and material wellbeing of the whole community. Worse still, they had broken the national covenant with an Old Testament-style God to which they had been individually and unwittingly bound by baptism as infants. From the point of view of the Cramonders the scheme had been a most profitable enterprise. Mrs Young would depone that she had been offered ten dollars quarterly if she would take the child to England and foster her there, with another £10 Scots towards the maintenance of her own children.[2] She refused, however, and eventually took the child to Forbes's house in Edinburgh and gave her to a soldier's wife who set off to England with her. For her services – and her silence – Jean was paid three dollars (about £8 8s. Scots) and the Youngs subsequently admitted to getting at least £18 Scots. (This at a time when £12 was an average yearly wage for a woman farm or domestic servant.)

When the guilty Cramonders were eventually forced to confront the minister and members of Cramond kirk session, most lied blatantly.

Jean's two sons pretended utter ignorance and a most remarkable lack of curiosity about the stranger gentlewoman encountered on the island, or the reason for their carpentry there. Without independent proof they could not be found guilty of complicity in the offence. Mr and Mrs Young each claimed to have been sent on an errand to the mainland, leaving the other to witness the baptism. (It was probably Mrs Young who told the truth on that point – it would be unusual to have a woman as witness.) While Robert Young took refuge in denials and prevarication, his wife and Jean Smith were openly truculent under ministerial questioning. Asked why she had concealed the affair, Jean retorted that 'it was soon enough when she was challenged'. Mrs Young, asked why she had broken her promise not to let the lady escape, said that once the sheriff's officers had come to take her away it was no longer any business of hers. And why hadn't she asked the name of the child's father? 'What was she concerned to do so, if she got money?'

The effective application of church discipline still depended, as it had for the old Inquisition, on obtaining the cooperation of sinners themselves. Coercion would be applied if necessary. The intention was always to bring culprits to a proper sense of guilt, resulting in full confession to minister and elders in session and 'satisfaction' to the congregation by whatever further act of penance might be judged appropriate. The essential element was repentance. Without it there was something of a stand-off. And none of those involved in this particular escapade evinced the least sign of sorrow for their misdeeds.

The Youngs held out against making any proper penitential appearance before Cramond session and the case against them dragged on without resolution for three or four years. The session's first recourse was to refer their case to the superior ecclesiastical body, Edinburgh presbytery. Among their offences was receiving a newcomer without any testimonial of good behaviour from her previous parish, although Robert Young claimed that Forbes had first promised to produce one within fifteen days. As often happened, presbytery remitted the matter back to Cramond, recommending the session to summon the Youngs before it again but to delay other action until Forbes had been located. When the couple failed to appear as summoned on 12 March 1691, Cramond cited them once more to appear before presbytery, in the vain hope that 'this session be no further troubled with that affair'. There was then a hiatus in proceedings at Cramond. Not untypically, no sessional meetings were held between 1 June and 17 September, first because the minister was in Ireland and without him session could not meet, and then because everyone was busy with the harvest. On 8 October session adopted another course. The Youngs' landlord, the new laird of Barnton, who had just recently purchased that estate, was asked to apply private pressure to make the pair obey the session's injunctions. As titular patron of the kirk he might have been expected to cooperate with the session, but he had only acquired the patronage as an adjunct to his land and was much too occupied with his own affairs to do anything about the Youngs. Besides, at a time of severe economic depression he would not wish to lose a tenant. The other common recourse of sessions – getting an employer to threaten dismissal – was not viable because as a tenant-farmer Robert Young, like Jean Smith, was self-employed.

The departure of the Reverend Mr John Hamilton to a parish in Edinburgh meant a break in the ministry and so another hiatus in sessional business between 12 February 1693 and 30 September 1694. Mrs Young died early in 1694. Robert, with a new wife, was still farming on the island in November of that year. Widowed again, he finally left Cramond early in 1713. His earlier offence had either been forgiven or forgotten, because the session then gave him the standard testimonial, certifying that he had lived in Cramond for the past twenty-four years and was of 'inoffensive carriage'.

As for Jean Smith, minister and session had to be content with the high-sounding enactment that:

> hereafter she shall bring no women strangers to bed within this parish, either married or unmarried persons, but shall presently [i.e. immediately] reveal the same either before or after to the minister or session clerk. And if she shall at any time do in the contrary, she shall be presently thrust out of this parish and get no liberty to live any longer therein.

In their fury at being hoodwinked, minister and elders perhaps over-looked the fact that Jean held her property in feu. She is one of four villagers paying hearth-tax in a list of March 1694.[3] Expulsion would have proved difficult, indeed for the past ten years sessions had been doing their utmost to eject a particularly undesirable and much less securely estab-lished man in Nether Cramond, with no success.

Six months before the event on Cramond Island Jean had probably been suspected of concealing another clandestine birth. In February 1690 the session had been told that a woman who had been in Nether Cramond for only a few weeks had given birth. Before her delivery some of the attendant women had elicited that her name was Jonet Stirlin and that the child's father was a single man in 'Saint Johnstoun' (Perth). When alerted to the case, the session refused permission for baptism until the mother found a cautioner who would furnish a bond guaranteeing that she would 'give satisfaction' (i.e. perform penance) in the parish where the sin had been committed. She promptly fled with her baby.

A year after the affair of the gentlewoman on Cramond Island Jean Smith was again in trouble with the session. She had been caught entertaining a party of friends at service time. She explained – perhaps quite truthfully – that her guests had escorted one of their number out of church when they thought that her labour pains had begun and had stayed to enjoy her hospitality when it proved to be a false alarm. Mr Hamilton was not convinced and took the opportunity to complain that Jean never entered the kirk unless to carry in a baby for christening. He also told her vengefully that 'the Lord had punished her by her own son abusing her in his drunkenness since that time, and this as the fruit of breaking the sabbath'.[4] No notice seems to have been taken of John Harrower's ill-treatment of his mother. He was a rough customer whom his neighbours addressed as 'laird' and on other occasions the session treated him with caution.

Whether their sympathies lay with the Stuart episcopalian establishment or the rebellious Covenanters, Cramond's more substantial parishioners, and above all the fifteen landowners ('heritors') of the time, liked the lower orders kept in their proper place and highly approved of Mr Hamilton and his endeavours to restore the old stringencies and social controls that their Covenanting predecessors had helped establish some two generations before. Hamilton even stood high in the opinion of Sir William Paterson of Granton, son and brother of bishops and former clerk of the Privy Council, 'a prime promoter of the cruelties inflicted on the Presbyterians during the inquisitorial reigns of Charles II and James II', as Cramond's historian, John Philp Wood, put it in 1794.[5] These parishioners probably listened with complacency when Mr Hamilton preached on one of his favourite texts: the fifth commandment ('Honour thy father and thy mother'), or more exactly its extension in the catechism to require 'The preserving the honour, and performing the duties, belonging to everyone in their several places and relations, as superiors, inferiors or equals'. But the vast majority of his hearers belonged, like Jean Smith and her women cronies, and like almost all the delinquents whose misbehaviour earned them a place in the session minutes, to some stratum of the working class. How many of these 'cottars and servants', one wonders, appreciated the minister's emphasis on proper behaviour towards their betters?

NOTES

1. *Unsourced references.* Throughout, references to the Cramond Kirk Session Minutes (KSM) are by date of meeting. The minutes are held by the National Archives of Scotland (NAS): CH2/426, vols. 1 (1651–1662), 2 (1664–1688), 3 (1689–1694), 4 (1694–1701), 5 (1701–1712), 6 (1712–1719), 7 (1719–1735), 8 (1735–1757), 9 (1757–1800) and 10 (1800–1878). Vol. 11 contains some draft minutes paralleling those in vol. 8.

2. *Money.* Of the larger silver coins commonly in use at this period, the leg dollar (so called because it featured a figure with one of his legs obscured by a shield) was worth £2 16s. Scots. The Dutch 'rex' or 'rix' dollar went for £2 18s. English crowns and half-crowns were also current. Since one penny sterling was reckoned the equivalent of twelve pence (one shilling) Scots, the half-crown was valued at £1 10s. (thirty shillings) Scots but 2s. 6d. (thirty pence) sterling. But well before union with England in 1707 the Scots used both systems of reckoning. In Cramond accounts of the 1690s small sums especially were often given in (sterling) pennies rather than Scottish shillings.

3. *Hearth Tax:* Assessments in Cramond, 7 March 1694: NAS E. 69/16 (1).

4. *God's punishment of Jean Smith.* KSM, 10 December 1691.

5. *Sir William Paterson.* John Philp Wood, *The Antient and Modern State of the Parish of Cramond*, Edinburgh 1794, pp. 19–20.

TWO

Kirk and People

THE KIRK AND THE COMMUNITY

The seventeenth-century parish of Cramond contained some 4,900 acres, all but a few hundred in farmland, growing grain or hay, or in pasture. It comprised roughly the present postal district of Edinburgh EH 4, as well as Granton and East Pilton to the east, while westwards, across the small River Almond, it had an irregularly shaped boundary with the parishes of Dalmeny and Kirkliston. By 1694, when an estimate first becomes possible, it was sparsely populated by perhaps 1,200 people.

In 1630 the area was made up of the estates or 'grounds' of twenty-one 'heritors' – designated 'of' their estate, whereas lesser persons were 'in' it. The heritors feature large in most accounts of the parish, and are treated at length, and often in entertaining detail, in John Philp Wood's *The Antient and Modern State of the Parish of Cramond* (Edinburgh, 1794). As a group they served as financial managers and civil authorities of the parish, and had joint responsibility for maintaining the fabric of church and manse, as well as providing for minister and schoolmaster. At periods when lay patronage was in force the laird of Barnton enjoyed the right (otherwise known as advowson) to nominate a new minister when a vacancy occurred.

Over time the heritors embellished Cramond with their increasingly grand houses and private pleasure grounds and some conferred a certain lustre upon it from their social standing and prominence in national affairs. But it would probably be true to say that the greater the heritor, the less his or her contact with the day-to-day life of the parish community. For almost all, a house in Cramond afforded a rural retreat conveniently close to the capital where, as lawyers, businessmen, politicians or dowager ladies, they had a townhouse and spent most of their time. When a meeting in Cramond was called for 28 March 1693, thirteen of the fifteen heritors of that date were in Edinburgh and only one attended in person. Except in summer, the 'big hooses' in Cramond were likely to stand empty or be let out. The lairds of Barnbougle (later earls of Rosebery) held land in the west of Cramond and so had the duties and privileges of heritors, but possessed no residence in the parish at all.

After attempts to control the drunken behaviour of two heritors in 1657, ministers and elders preferred to treat the manners and morals of these, their social superiors, as their own responsibility. So in a study of sinners brought before the session, few of Cramond's heritors qualify for mention. Where members of the group occupy space in the session minutes it is usually due to their frequent quarrels over the allocation of space in the kirk for private seating for them and their tenants, or else the right to add structures to church or churchyard. It is therefore appropriate that when the heritors as a body first appear in the records, in 1630, those who had been assessed for the payment of teinds (tithes) on their land were engaged in comparing their own assessments with those of the neighbours and complaining about their tenants.[1] John Moubray of Cammo wanted his valuation reduced. For one thing, his half of Cammo was no better than Patrick Hamilton's half, which was valued at much less. John Stalker of Easter Drylaw defended his low rating against criticism, saying that it was rightly less than Sir James McGill's in Wester Drylaw, because McGill had more land and got a much better yield, thanks to the money he spent on lime and the 'muck' daily brought from Edinburgh by his ten horses.[2] The John Stalker of 1630 (who died in 1638) may well be the man commemorated on a stone built into a wall in the churchyard. This reads, as it already did at Wood's time,

Here Lyes John Stalker of Easter Drylaw
An True and Lively Pattern of Piety and Probity
Wha Dyed 6 Feb.
Æta. 60. A.D. 1603

There is reason to suspect that a damaged inscription may have been 'restored' in the eighteenth century, with some of the spellings modernised and the date wrongly reproduced.

For practical purposes sessions long saw the rest of the parishioners as belonging to one of three broad socio-economic groups: farmers and 'cotters and servants'. The farmers in this classification were tenant-farmers, leasing land from their 'masters' the heritors, to whom they owed certain feudal services such as carrying stone to repair the kirk, and whose financial commitments they shared when a 'stent' was imposed to raise money for parish purposes. In 1694 twenty-six men, or their widows, held sizeable farms. Many others, including the tenants of the five mills on the Almond, each held somewhere between one and fifty acres. As a group the farmers were much the largest employers of labour and traditionally supplied the kirk with most of its elders. Some of their farm-workers were married men accommodated with a cottage and some land, including thirteen specified as the 'hinds', who were responsible for ploughing. Others were single men and women, hired for a fixed term, perhaps as little as three or six months. A proportion of these were the children of Cramonders, others were temporary incomers. At harvest time there was also an influx of casual labourers, in the form of gangs of 'shearers' (reapers).

Temporary incomers, too, were the domestic servants of heritors. These moved with their employers and it could prove difficult to bring any offenders among them to justice in Cramond. In 1694 there were 168 unmarried servants (99 men and 69 women) living in the households of their various employers. They composed twenty-two per cent of all poll-tax payers aged sixteen or over. Many were at the vulnerable stage of late adolescence to early adulthood, sometimes away from home and the influence of kinsfolk, and working in close association with people of the opposite sex. Not surprisingly, a large number of the parishioners who suffered a 'fall into fornication' belonged to this group.

'Cotters' meant simply cottagers and embraced anyone who was not a farmer or other tenant on the one hand, or a farmhand or domestic servant on the other. Inevitably it was in the two categories of 'cotters and servants' or 'cotters and those of the meaner sort' that elders expected to encounter the variety of sins that fell within their purview.

Parish kirk sessions were the ground-level unit in an organisation extending through presbyteries to synods and ultimately the General Assembly. When Cramond's extant session minutes begin in September 1651 there were thirteen elders (eight of them heritors, from whom the kirk treasurer would be chosen) and five deacons. They were picked from a leet of 'able' or 'honest' men in different parts of the parish. All were male, it goes without saying, and the majority of the non-heritors were tenant-farmers, and as such well-to-do employers. At first new appointments were supposed to be made after consultation with the congregation. In Cramond congregational approval soon became a mere formality and in time the sessioners came dangerously close to forming a self-perpetuating oligarchy. Decisions made by those attending a meeting are usually presented in the minutes as unanimous and were promulgated in the name of the whole body. Numbers were sometimes few, however, and clearly meetings were dominated by the minister. One member's discontent is recorded in 1657, when Thomas Nicoll complained that he felt his presence at meetings was pointless: no-one ever asked his opinion and the rest 'held him as a cipher'. This answer was considered highly derogatory and 'the session', says their clerk, resolved to regard him 'as a deserter of the calling of God' and so dispensed with his services.

The duties of a kirk session could be summarised as 'the overseeing of the manners of the people and punishing of scandals and looking to the wants and necessities of the poor'.[3] Looking after the poor meant primarily providing some decent, minimum, maintenance for the incapacitated, as well as occasional help to parishioners in temporary straits. In addition small sums must often be handed out to a stream of 'wandering beggars and poor strangers', many of them the victims of civil wars. Sessions of the seventeenth and early eighteenth centuries are often stigmatised as obsessed with sex. To an almost equal extent they were obsessed with money – the need to keep 'the poor's box' adequately supplied through collections, fines on sinners, charges for hiring church property such as the ornamental pall or 'mortcloth' used at funerals, for permission to put up gravestones, and the like. Any substantial surpluses or bequests were invested with a landowner, on the security of land, in return for the payment of annual interest – 'the poor's rents'.

When it came to the effort to produce a 'godly community' by overseeing the manners of the people and punishing scandals, the reformed kirk operated a remarkably efficient system of social control. (Although, as we have already seen, there were loopholes and some self-imposed restrictions, and the system was posited on the ideal that the Scots should be one people united in worship under the aegis of one national church.) When the practice of demanding testimonials from incomers was properly enforced, sessions could keep tabs on both morals and movements of a mobile population, exercising to the full that 'gift of regiment' with which elders were endowed.[4] Often, however, enforcement took more zeal and attention than Cramond sessions always attained.

The strict regulation of marriage was also in the interests of both church and state, and here the rules were carefully observed. Although matrimony was no longer a sacrament, it was a holy state to be sealed in church. Couples proposing to enter it had to give in their names to be publicly proclaimed to the congregation three times, in both churches if they lived in different parishes, in which case each had to furnish a testimonial from the relevant kirk session. They also had to deposit a 'pledge of marriage', usually money but sometimes a piece of silver plate or a gold ring or the like. All this had to be registered and the pledge was forfeit if the parties changed their minds or if, later, the premature arrival of a child showed that 'antenuptial fornication' had occurred. In the second case the parents had to perform 'satisfaction' by standing, separately and at different times, before minister and congregation for public rebuke. The unintended result of putting offenders on show could well have been to reinforce the idea that 'everyone does it'.[5] At least four of the thirty married couples in Nether Cramond in 1694 had perforce pleaded guilty to the charge and done penance. From the parish as a whole the session dealt, on average, with two such cases a year.

Intercourse 'under promise of marriage' was treated more leniently than 'fornication'. Cohabitation was naturally viewed with grave suspicion, but it seems likely that neighbours usually allowed some licence to *bona fide* courting couples. Prying eyes made it difficult to sin in privacy, but rather few such couples were brought before the session, even on the lesser charges of 'uncleanness' or 'unhandsome carriage'.

Confessed fornication, when it occurred without promise of marriage, was punished by a substantial fine – £6 for the man and £4 for the woman, whose year's wages as a servant might have been as little as £6. Besides confession to the session, while kneeling and preferably in tears, each of the pair had to make three individual appearances on 'the pillar', alias 'stool of repentance', before absolution was given and the penitent restored to full standing in the congregation. (The penalty for a relapse, with the same or another partner, was standing six times.) Since fornication was usually proved by pregnancy, it was harder for a woman to deny guilt than it was for a man. In theory men and women enjoyed equality in sin. Obviously, however, the hand of the Lord's ministers fell far more heavily upon the female culprit. Unless the sin was 'more notorious' in another parish, she would have to 'complete satisfaction' on successive Sundays in Cramond. 'Perfection' was not attained until the monetary penalty was paid, perhaps out of wages held back by her previous employer.

A woman's best chance of supporting herself and the child (if it survived) was to find employment as a wet-nurse, perhaps in Edinburgh or further afield. Unless her 'satisfaction' was postponed as a favour to her new employer and in the interests of her foster-child, she was still bound to travel back to Cramond on three Sundays, probably on foot, since it was men who controlled the means of transport. In the meantime, she had to find a 'cautioner' who would give his bond for her eventual appearance. The hardships that could be involved when a woman needed to travel some distance in order to 'satisfy' are poignantly suggested by the exceptional concession made to Jean Anderson when, on 18 February 1692, she was permitted to 'stand' both morning and afternoon on the same day, 'it being stormy weather and she great with child and not able to travel far in such snowy and frosty season'.

Adultery was prosecuted with the full rigour of biblical prohibition. It seems very probable that general opinion also condemned it, as an attack upon the concept of the nuclear family and the social status and responsibilities conferred by marriage. In 1679 and again in 1681 Bessie Rae, a single woman, bore a daughter to a soldier named David Robertson. Since Robertson had married another woman in the interval, at her second lapse Bessie had to perform the lengthy penance for adultery. She stood in sackcloth weekly for a quarter-year before she was judged sufficiently penitent. No excuse for this offence would be countenanced. Nor was any plea of rape ever accepted by Cramond sessions in the two centuries under study.

The informants who 'delated' an offender to minister or elder are rarely named, though their identity may be revealed when they are called as witnesses. It must be acknowledged that an openly censorious attitude to the activities of others is still to be encountered in Scotland. The kirk gave encouragement, in so far as the Shorter Catechism enjoined 'the preservation of our own and our neighbour's chastity, in heart, speech and behaviour'. For the neighbourly watch, barred doors immediately suggested wrongdoing within.

The kirk session was not, however, seen wholly as a prosecutory body. It could also, on occasion, serve as a cheap and accessible disputes tribunal, for instance when a parishioner brought a complaint of slander, as Agnes Simpson and her father John Simpson sought redress against two neighbours who had wronged Agnes by calling her Agnes Paterson – a taunt made obvious because women in that lower rank of society were commonly addressed by full name.[6] In its peacekeeping role, especially during the preparations leading up to the annual celebration of communion, the session also did its best to reconcile flyting neighbours and squabbling families.

Where puritanism clashed noticeably with the self-interest of the poorer, or less orderly, parishioners was on the question of sabbath or fast-day observance, which involved failure to attend one or both of the morning and afternoon services, collectively known as 'sermons'. On the one free day of the week workers might want to visit friends and relatives, perhaps in a different parish. Some better-off outsiders might wish to see the baby they had put out to nurse in Cramond, where wet-nursing was an important commercial activity for married women. Then, as now in greater numbers, Edinburgh folk might come to Nether Cramond on a fine Sunday for a sail on the Forth or a country walk. More generally, sessions never succeeded in preventing the selling of ale at service-time, and no amount of ministerial thundering could stop parishioners 'sitting at their doors after sermons, talking with their neighbours anent worldly affairs when they should be within their houses reading the scriptures, praying or religiously employed'.[7]

Provided they did not conflict with sabbath or fast-day observance, ordinary activities went on without input from the kirk, or anything other than incidental mention in the session minutes, which had no reason to refer to the herdboys' junketings at Lammas (first recorded as an old custom from the 1730s: Chapter 9), or the existence of an oyster fishery based in Cramond. Nor do the minutes record any activities that may have occurred at Hallowe'en, Fastens E'en (Shrove Tuesday), Hogmanay or the official holiday of Handsel Monday – the first Monday in the year. To their credit, ministers and sessions may have turned a deliberately blind eye to some folk-beliefs, like the magical properties of the 'Bubbling Well' near Nether Cramond or the existence of an 'ill spirit' known as a 'shelly-coat' (Chapter 6). Nor do they seem to have inquired into the precise cure employed by Hugh Murray, and his wife, who was popularly called a witch, when they were paid from the poor box for treating a 'scalled', i.e. scabby, head.[8] There are two recorded cases in which witches had been earlier associated with Cramond: one in 1597, the other in 1628 (Chapter 3). After 1651 indications occasionally emerge from the minutes of folk-belief in witchcraft and the power of curses, but Cramond sessions showed no anxiety to pursue such matters. Session blandly denied the existence of any pagan or popish superstitions, customs or charming in response to one item in a set of interrogatories sent out by presbytery in 1709. In the Age of Reason a stone built into a wall at Lauriston Castle had enough curiosity value for John Wood to have its inscription engraved for his history of the parish. It depicts the 'celestial them[e]' (otherwise natal chart) of Sir Alexander Napier, who held Lauriston in the early part of the seventeenth century.[9] For both Sir Alexander and his elder half-brother, John Napier of Merchiston, inventor of logarithms and 'Napier's bones' (a primitive forerunner of the electronic calculator), sound presbyterian principles had been entirely compatible with a scientific interest in predictive astrology.

Two rites of passage took place in the kirk and were also marked by secular celebrations. For the kirk, baptism, the only surviving sacrament besides communion, signalled entry into the company of the faithful or, in the words of the Shorter Catechism, 'doth signify and seal our ingrafting into Christ and partaking of the benefits of the Covenant of Grace'. In popular belief it was also thought necessary to the child's physical welfare. Specifically mentioned once in the session minutes is the custom of *cummering* – in modern terms 'wetting the head' of a new baby, which might be seen as a secular parallel to the church rite (Chapter 8). A wedding party, often in the form of a 'penny bridal' to which guests contributed, was the secular sequel to marriage. Again, the minutes reveal quite incidentally that it was after a marriage and its subsequent festivities on a Saturday in May 1692 that some of the wedding party, including John Johnston the parish piper, carried on drinking, piping and dancing in an inn, long after sunset, when the sabbath officially began.[10]

Wakes and funerals had been entirely secularised. Funerals became a do-it-yourself matter, conducted without benefit of clergy (but burials, Cramond sessions ordered in 1681 and again in 1682, were not to take place on Sundays at sermon-time or in the midday interval between services). Wakes were so notoriously profane, with their eating, drinking, smoking and dancing, that in 1633 the town council of Aberdeen forbade the 'reading of holy scriptures and singing of psalms' at such proceedings.[11] The public disturbances caused by one group of young people in Nether Cramond at a wake in 1702 will be described in Chapter 7. Although one entry in the kirk treasurer's accounts records that on 29 May 1685 the poor box paid for candles 'to James Reid's *laickwak*' (i.e. lyke-wake) and in May 1736 some bread and ale was provided for those who sat overnight with the body of another pauper, the kirk's usual only contributions to funerary rites were the services of the beadle as sexton and the provision for hire of a parish mortcloth to cover the coffin and, if the family could afford it, the dead- or hand-bell. They could also pay to have the church bell rung.

If the Reformers removed all odour of sanctification from death and left its associated ceremonial to the laity, they also turned the kirk into an elitist establishment, in which ordinary people were excluded from any authoritative participation. The abolition of the church gilds that formerly saw to the upkeep of altars and lights in the church, hired chantry priests to say mass before them, and raised money by such activities as church ales and the 'hoking' of members of the opposite sex after Easter, deprived both men and women of a close association with the life of the parish church and an outlet for their organisational energies. Women also lost the privileged social position of godmother – were reduced, one might say, from godparents to gossips. Indeed, for a long time it was only in exceptional circumstances that a mother sponsored her own child at baptism. This role was usually reserved for the father or some other male relative. Nor, at this earlier period, did women often act as witnesses at marriages.

It has been said that the common people of Scotland were christianised for the first time after the Reformation.[12] At the same time it could be argued that much of common life was dechristianised and the numinous removed from mundane activities. For instance, the invocation of saintly intercession, so readily resorted to in earlier times, was swept away as superstitious. But if christianisation means assiduous instruction in approved theological doctrine, the claim may be true enough. Preaching, at great length and of course extempore, was seen as the most important part of a minister's duties, and his abilities in that direction formed the chief criterion in choosing a new incumbent. The better-educated and more serious-minded members of a congregation undoubtedly found intellectual stimulation, and nourished a delight in legal argument, in following a preacher's 'heads' and 'proofs'. Among those who sat more passively there must always have been some 'too stupid and ignorant' (or in the terms of a later age, mentally disadvantaged) to take in much at all. Unknowable is just how many others, faced with extensive sermonising in particular and in general the dreich sabbath, to be wholly and uninterruptedly devoted to 'the public and private exercise of God's worship', would have shared the view of the people castigated in Malachy 1:13 (and quoted in the Shorter Catechism) as saying, 'Behold, what a weariness is it!' Nevertheless, whatever individuals may have felt about them, the services in the parish kirk performed one important social function: they brought together the people of the scattered habitations to meet as a united community.

THE COVENANTING ASCENDANCY IN CRAMOND

Thanks largely to the system of lay patronage, during the turbulent years between 1597 and 1643 Cramond became a pocket parish of the revolutionary movement that led to the signing of the National Covenant in 1638, to the (temporary) abolition of lay patronage and to the 'second period of compulsory puritanism'.[13] In 1597 the patronage of the parish had been relinquished by the bishop of Dunkeld and conveyed by the king to Sir James Elphinstone, in respect of his holding of the estate of Upper Barnton in Cramond.[14] Elphinstone became Secretary of State for Scotland in the following year, and in 1604 baron of Balmerino in Fife. The minister at that time was Michael Cranstoun (?1590–1631), who was something of a popular hero of the opposition to James VI and his government.[15] Although entrusting the choice of a minister to laymen was vehemently opposed by the Scottish reformers, John Elphinstone, second Baron Balmerino, put it to good use. He was a prominent member of the revolutionary movement that opposed Scotland's existing episcopal establishment and its headpiece and mainstay, Charles I, and after the deaths of Michael Cranstoun and his successor he took care to install more ministers of the correct reforming views in the manse. In 1634 the famous Covenanting ideologist and propagandist Samuel Rutherford was tempted by the offer of Cramond, but accepted the charge of a group of parishes in the harder ground of Galloway, 'where the labourers are few and the harvest great'. Instead, Lord Balmerino's close friend and protégé William Colvill became minister from 1635 to 1639. He was then caught and imprisoned for attempting to take a message from Balmerino and other Covenanters to the king of France, seeking support against Charles I. His successor at Cramond was the Reverend William Dalgleish, a colleague of Samuel Rutherford in Galloway, where the bishop had deposed him for nonconformity in 1635–7. In 1638 he was a member of the reforming General Assembly that abjured episcopacy.[16] Dalgleish would remain minister of Cramond until 1662, when he would once more be deposed for nonconformity with a ruling establishment.

In 1635 John Lord Balmerino himself had been convicted of treason for possessing a copy of a supplication protesting against the Church Acts of Charles I. Although the death penalty was subsequently remitted, his continued opposition to the royal policies for the church caused the king to label him 'one of the chief contrivers and most malicious prosecutors of this wicked covenant made against us and our authority'.[17] Balmerino and his son, who succeeded him as third baron early in 1649,[18] were not the only landowners in Cramond with strong Covenanting sympathies. Another was Sir Thomas Hope of Craighall, who became a heritor of the parish when he bought the estate of West Granton in 1619. He became Lord Advocate in 1626 and gave his legal support to the Covenant in 1637–8, having previously served Charles I by prosecuting Balmerino. His prosperous legal career had started in 1606 with his brave defence of the six ministers convicted of high treason for denying the royal authority in ecclesiastical affairs.[19] Cramond's historian, John Philp Wood, wrote that to Sir Thomas's 'sound counsel the firm establishment of the Presbyterian mode of worship in this kingdom is in a great measure due'.[20] The Edinburgh merchant James Inglis, who in 1622 bought Nether Cramond and the old tower-house of the bishops of Dunkeld, of which part still exists, was succeeded in 1637 by his son John, who had strong presbyterian persuasions. So did Sir John Smith, nominated one of the supervisors of the Covenant in 1640, who acquired the lands of Grotthill (now called Groathill) while Lord Provost of Edinburgh in 1642–3.

These ardent presbyterians would certainly have ensured that a comparatively wealthy parish like Cramond was in the forefront of the drive to organise society along the lines set down by the early Scottish reformers. This would mean an adequate ministerial stipend,[21] a large and active kirk session of minister, elders and deacons, a kirk treasurer and sub-treasurer and a school, largely devoted to religious indoctrination, under an accredited master who would also act as clerk to the session and the heritors, keep registers of marriages and baptisms and, as precentor (or 'reader'), conduct part of the kirk services and lead the congregation, line by line, in thumping out the psalms in the Scottish metrical version.[22] If the church had not already been remodelled as a building suitable for presbyterian worship, the work was surely undertaken at this time, when Sir Thomas Hope paid in 1635 for the making of his private aisle and entrance-way. The accepted date of 1656 for the seventeenth-century nucleus of the present church is self-evidently too late.[23]

The kirk treasurer's account books are extant from 1636. But in 1643 religio-political zeal caused Cramond's leading heritors to plunder the parish's funds. That year, 'at the beginning of this great work', they borrowed 'the whole treasure of [Cramond's] kirk and the poor's money', amounting to £2,000 Scots.[24] The 'great work' was evidently that resolved on by the General Assembly of August 1643 (at which Sir Thomas Hope nominally represented the king as Lord High Commissioner).[25] This was the project of forcing the new 'Solemn League and Covenant' upon England, with the aid of an English parliamentary army. The money was taken on the security of Balmerino's land, and for the next fifty years and more the parish would struggle to obtain, at the very least, the promised annual interest.

In one of those extraordinary twists in Scottish affairs, the English parliamentary army on which Lord Balmerino and other proponents of the Solemn League and Covenant had relied in 1643–4 instituted a triumphant invasion of Scotland in 1650. Although Cramond's account book was preserved, the kirk session minute book disappeared, along with the registers of marriage and baptism – used, perhaps, to light fires by English soldiers occupying the village from which the inhabitants, including the schoolmaster-clerk, had fled. Not even the second Lord Balmerino remained unscathed: his recently interred body is said to have been disturbed when Cromwell's soldiers broke into his burial vault at Restalrig looking for lead coffins to melt down into bullets.[26]

NOTES

1. *Heritors* 1630. John Philp Wood, The *Antient and Modern State of the Parish of Cramond*, Edinburgh 1794, pp. 95–9.
2. *Lime and muck.* Carters daily brought loads of ashes, stable dung and street sweepings from Edinburgh for the 'gooding' of land. Cramond's home gardeners today can unearth broken clay tobacco pipes from these sweepings. The quantities of cockle and oyster shells that they also find were spread on the fields to provide lime.
3. *Sessional duties.* Minister John Somerville at his first session, 5 Sept. 1675.
4. *Gift of regiment.* Quoted by James Kirk, ed., *The Second Book of Discipline, with Introduction and Commentary*, Edinburgh 1980, p. 89.
5. *Intercourse before marriage.* Perhaps it still needs to be said this was not, as myth sometimes has it, a test of a woman's fertility.
6. *Insulting use of wrong surname.* 30 June, 7 July 1657.
7. *Sitting at their doors talking.* 14 Jan. 1692.
8. *Scalled head.* KSM, 5 Nov. 1676; Compt Bk, 19 March 1693.
9. *Sir Alexander Napier's celestial theme.* Wood, *Cramond*, p. 41 and Plate 1, facing p. 56.
10. *The piper.* The previous mention of such a functionary comes from 1635, when 'the piper of Cramond, called Fleggum', caught the plague just as it was thought to be dying out there. He 'smittit' his two brothers, both of whom died, and unluckily travelled about the countryside for fourteen days, probably spreading the infection: Sir William Fraser, *Memoirs of the Maxwells of Pollok*, Edinburgh 1863, vol. 1, p. 441. Did Fleggum have any successor during the Puritan years that followed?
11. *Wakes.* Prohibition by Aberdeen Town Council quoted in the *Dictionary of the Older Scottish Tongue* under Lyk(e)wake.
12. *Has been said . . . christianised.* By Christina Larner in *Enemies of God: the Witch-Hunt in Scotland*, 1981.
13. *'Compulsory Puritanism'.* T. C. Smout, *A History of the Scottish People* 1560–1830, 1969, p. 79.
14. *Patronage.* Wood, *Cramond*, pp. 266–7. In feudal style, the patronage was vested, not so much in Elphinstone and his heirs as in the land itself. This meant that when the estate of Barnton changed hands, so would the rights of patronage.
15. *Sir James Elphinstone and Michael Cranstoun.* Ibid., p. 79. Wood relates that Cranstoun's preaching in Edinburgh in December 1596 inflamed rioters against James VI and a group of royal councillors, who included Sir James Elphinstone–Scottish history can be very complicated. Wood implies, however, that Cranstoun may later have been bribed to support the establishment of episcopacy in 1610.
16. *Cramond and the Covenanters. Letters of the Rev. Samuel Rutherford*, ed. Thomas Smith, Edinburgh 1875; imprisonment of Colvill: Wood, *Cramond*, pp. 79–80; *Fasti Ecclesiae Scoticanae*, ed. Hew Scott, 2nd edn., Edinburgh 1915, *sub* Cramond.
17. *Charles I on Balmerino.* 'A Large Declaration Concerning the Late Tumult in Scotland', quoted Wood, *Cramond*, p. 274. The first Lord Balmerino had similarly been sentenced to death, then reprieved, when James VI made him a scapegoat in 1607: Rosalind Mitchison, *Lordship to Patronage, Scotland 1603–1745*, 1983, p. 11.

18. *Third Baron Balmerino.* One cannot resist quoting Wood (*Cramond*, p. 276). His father and mother had no children for many years, 'but at last, when she was near fifty, and had been under a course of medicine for the dropsy, owing to the physicians mistaking her case, she was delivered of a son'.

19. *Six ministers.* Cramond's minister Michael Cranstoun was one of those who visited them with comfort in prison: *Ibid.*, p. 79.

20. *Sir Thomas Hope.* Wood, *Cramond*, pp. 56, 121 and (at length) 132–9, and *Dictionary of National. Biography.*

21. *Ministerial Stipend.* The minister had a glebe of about six acres and, from 1631, a stipend of 8 bolls of wheat, 24 of bere (a form of barley), 24 of oats, 8 of meal and 420 marks in money: Wood, *Cramond*, p. 78 n. In 1649, when Mr Dalgleish complained of the expense of living so close to Edinburgh, his annual stipend in cash was increased to 800 marks. Neither he nor his successors were ever to crave any kind of further augmentation 'at any time hereafter'(!): *Acts of the Parliaments of Scotland* (12 vols. 1814–75), VI (ii) 421a.

22. *Schoolmaster's salary.* Like the minister, the schoolmaster was paid in a mixture of cash and kind, with assessments on particular pieces of land. In addition he collected the fees from his pupils and payments for registering baptisms and marriages. Schooling was not free, and the basic curriculum consisted of learning the catechism and acquiring sufficient ability to read from the bible, in its alien English dialect. Writing (it would seem), arithmetic and Latin were extras, embarked upon by relatively few.

23. *Craighall aisle.* Diary of Sir Thomas Hope, November 1635. The date of 1656 for building the kirk apparently depends on a misunderstanding of the entry in the KSM for 2 March 1656. This records that 'the session, taking to consideration the ruinousness of the kirk and that the time of year meet for the building of the same draweth nigh, think fit that [the heritors should meet] to consult about the building of the same'. 'Building', however, often meant no more than 'repairing' or 'altering', and the work at that time apparently involved re-roofing and some interior reconstruction. Over the years the church underwent a series of modifications. One (after 1664?) led a heritor in May 1678 to speak of erecting seats 'in this new church' to replace those she had inherited in 'the old' one.

24. *Borrowed poor's money. Acts of the Parliaments*, VI (ii) 420b–421a, referring to 1649. In that year the 2nd Baron Balmerino died impoverished and Cramond's interest had been unpaid for 4½ years. By September 1682 arrears of interest on the £2,000 came to £2,340 and continued to mount thereafter. Only a small part of the principal and almost none of the interest was ever recovered from the inheritors of the debt, with whom an unsatisfactory accommodation was finally made in 1696.

25. *Hope as Commissioner.* Wood, *Cramond*, p. 137.

26. *Balmerino's body. Ibid.*, p. 276.

THREE

Offenders and Discipline, 1651–1662

The Scots – or more precisely some of their leaders – having surrendered the Stuart king Charles I to the mercies of English parliamentarians, had then proclaimed his son as Charles II of Scotland. But on 3 September 1650, at Dunbar, a Scottish army was disastrously defeated by English troops under Cromwell. The Cromwellian army proceeded to occupy Scotland and then abolish the monarchy and incorporate Scotland in a commonwealth with England and Ireland.

The invaders might represent an 'Army of God', but the people of Cramond fled at their approach. Not only did they lose their parish records, but the kirk bell was removed by the invaders and only recovered in 1658 after prolonged negotiations with the military governor of Leith. The imposition of a form of military government by English 'puritans' did not, however, bring any substantial changes at parish level, and Cramond's minister since 1639, the Reverend William Dalgleish, now aged fifty-two, was left undisturbed. Cromwell was not likely to force those great bugbears of the Covenanters–bishops, patronage and a prayer-book – upon the Scottish kirk.

It was therefore business as usual when, on Sunday 7 September 1651, after the people of Cramond 'were returned from the several places where they were scattered', Dalgleish, four elders and three deacons met in session. (Three days, as it happened, after the final defeat of Charles II and a Scottish army at Worcester, where at least one Cramond man, John Stalker junior, had fought and been taken prisoner.)

At that first meeting the minister made it his priority to ask the size of the day's collections for the poor, to charge the deacons with distributing the money to those in most urgent need, and to ensure that receipts and payments were recorded in the parish account book. He also gave his usual injunction to the members to enquire carefully in their respective bounds for people living 'scandalously' and either admonish them in private or 'delate' them to the session. The deacons were to look diligently into the needs of the poor and report on any who required assistance.

There was one piece of outstanding business to deal with: 'fornicators' must not remain unpunished, and a pair of confessed sinners were ordered to make separate 'public satisfaction'. On 16 November Christian Duncan was summoned before the session, probably at the request of the session of Inverkeithing, where she was required to answer a charge of 'falling in fornication' with a certain Galloway man, a soldier in Massie's regiment, while she was a servant in the house of one of the baillies of Inverkeithing. Her brother bound himself in an obligation of £20 Scots to ensure that Christian would appear before that session when summoned. This was standard practice, and so too was the cooperation between the sessions of the two parishes. In the case at issue, Cramond session could hope to avoid spreading scandal by not putting Christian on public display in their own church, but they also lost the money that formed part of the penalty and would go into the poor box.

As far as the kirk session minutes go to show, the people of Cramond were singularly quiet and law-abiding for a whole thirty-three months from September 1651 to June 1654, and regularly (according to the clerk) the elders had no delinquencies among their charges to report at weekly sessions, apart from one case of drunkenness in January 1653, for which the culprit appeared once before the congregation. Possibly folk were occupied with restoring their affairs to order after they had been driven from their homes and workplaces. It is equally likely that the members of the session were similarly engrossed and had little time to investigate the doings of their charges.

Occasional meetings of the session were, however, occupied with important business on behalf of the parish. In September 1653 arrangements had to be made to appoint a new parish schoolmaster, and in February 1654 a new church officer (alias beadle or bellman) was installed. His multitudinous duties included summoning delinquents whom the session wished to interview, as well as any witnesses whose testimony was necessary if an accused person was obdurate and refused to make voluntary confession to the session.

Early in 1654, in a concerted effort to tighten discipline before communion was held on 9 July, Mr William Dalgleish started a series of exhortations to his session. In March he bade them 'take notice' of anyone who cursed or swore, and in April they were told to bring before the session persons 'overtaken with drink'. In May he warned them to ensure that incomers to the parish brought proper testimonials of good behaviour from their previous parish. And having had so few 'abuses' reported by the elders from their own quarters, he seems to have given a specific direction that on the sabbath they should take turns to invigilate their bounds.

Further prompting by an Act of the General Assembly, and the prospect of a visit from the brethren of Edinburgh presbytery, then encouraged closer policing by the elders. Sabbath observance became a particular concern and a special effort was made to ensure that harvesting did not stop people attending church. All the same, the elders who patrolled the parish at service-time found William Anderson away from church on 6 August, and on 20 August the schoolmaster was instructed to punish a young boy who was caught playing at sermon-time. On 27 August an elder reported that on his rounds in Nether Cramond he had seen Thomas Moubray and his wife Elspeth McGowan laying out peas to dry when they should have been at church. Moubray excused himself by saying that it was his wife's idea and she, in a standard formula, undertook to perform public penance if she committed a similar fault again. On 24 September Alexander Morison in Lauriston admitted being drunk and was warned that he would be seriously dealt with, in accordance with an Act of the General Assembly, if it happened again.

William Anderson had also made promises never to absent himself from church in future, and explained that on the Sunday in question he had attended the West Kirk in Edinburgh because he wanted to visit a brother there, who was very ill. Anderson was one of the relatively few people at this period who failed to appear promptly when summoned to attend the session – the beadle had had to deliver a second citation before he appeared. That was on 27 August. On 24 September Anderson was again delated to a sessional meeting, now for being drunk on the sabbath, and this time it took three summonses before he appeared on 15 October and confessed his fault, tearfully persuading the session of his repentance and promising not to succumb to temptation again. Next month another man, David Broun, denied his guilt when accused of a similar offence. As it happens, this is the first denial recorded in the minutes. When such a thing occurred – when, as the minutes put it, an offender was perceived 'to be in no way sensible of his fault' – it was necessary to work upon him to obtain an admission of guilt and the signs of repentance that must precede forgiveness. Broun was told to return in a week's time and meanwhile the minister undertook to speak to him privately. Broun disobeyed this and a further summons, but Dalgleish's ministrations evidently bore fruit because he eventually confessed to the session and promised, with God's help, to strive against the sin ever afterwards.

Drunkenness among the parishioners was a major preoccupation of Cramond kirk session at this particular period. The reference to an Act of the General Assembly suggests that this reflected a common concern over an offence that led too easily to the heinous sin of blasphemy and to other forms of unchristian conduct like quarrelling with the neighbours and wife-beating. Most of the offenders were men, although Janet Kennedy confessed and promised reform in April 1657 and on 5 June 1659

Margaret Ker admitted to the session that when she had vomited in church in May she had been drunk and not ill, as she had previously maintained. She was made to acknowledge her sin before the congregation who had been thus incommoded. The session were more lenient with James Flookheart who was sharply rebuked for excessive drinking 'and blaspheming in his furious passion' and warned that next time he would be made an example of, and when James Batherston confessed on his knees before the session to being drunk and striking his wife, he was admonished and dismissed after professing himself 'unfeignedly grieved for his said scandalous carriage' and promising 'through the Lord's grace not to fall in the like again'.[1] In December 1657 Robert Moubray was summoned for drinking in Nether Cramond all the time of the afternoon sermon and 'carrying himself unably and indiscreetly at the drink', and three weeks later Thomas Millar in Nether Cramond appeared, to be sharply rebuked for his unsober carriage in 'ordinar tippling and drinking excessively' and warned that next time he would be made a public example and a warning to others. He was, however, 'deprehendit very drunk' in July 1660. Thomas Wilson was threatened with ostracism in April 1657: if he were seen drunk again, 'all the congregation shall be publicly admonished from the pulpit not to keep company with him'.

Rebuke might be efficacious for a time, but was insufficient to deter alcoholics. Alexander Morison in Lauriston, who had (on the third occasion) been convicted of habitual drunkenness and found still insensible of his sin in February 1658, was called before the session in May after informing the minister that he wished to perform penance for 'his scandalous carriage' and was sharply rebuked for his previous habitual drunkenness and obstinacy. The passage conveys something of Mr Dalgleish's style – and suggests that the culprit had been well coached in the expected answers:

> And being interrogat what sense he had of his bygone miscarriage, and also what he resolved to be for time to come, he answered that he was heartily grieved for his unchristian carriage in his sinning against God and in giving evil example to others by his excessive drinking and stubborn obstinacy, and resolved through the Lord's grace to walk in time to come as becometh a Christian. The session having thought fit to continue him till some further evidence of his repentance appear, he being by the minister very much exhorted to lay his sin to heart and to study sincerely reformation of life in time to come, was dismissed till the session think fit to cause cite him again.

The availability of ale to those tempted to 'slight the preaching' by drinking at sermon-time was, naturally, seen as a prime cause of such profaning of the sabbath, but the session could do little to curb sales at improper times, beyond paying special attention to suspect premises during the general visitations that were carried out during services. On 1 April 1655 'the minister earnestly exhorteth the elders and deacons to be careful in their several quarters to visit the ale-houses and to delate such as they shall find drinking within the same after sermon', and on 27 May 'all the elders are exhorted to visit their several quarters when they go home [after the Sunday services], especially the ale-houses'. This would become an almost annual charge, often issued in late spring because it was during the warmer months that parishioners felt tempted to make the most of the one day in the week that was free from work by straying abroad to slake their thirst in congenial company. According to the session minutes, on only three occasions between September 1651 and January 1662 were ale-sellers actually caught breaking the sabbath. On one of these the elders who invigilated Nether Cramond reported that Margaret Scugall, servant of John Beg and Rachel Cochran, had carried a half-gallon barrel of ale to Jonet Fairholm's house 'in time of preaching'.[2] Despite the excuse that this was a work of necessity, drink being required for Jonet's sick husband, Rachel Cochran, who enjoyed some status in the community as one of the heirs of certain small properties, 'the Corstons' lands', took the responsibility for an act of 'scandalous carriage' and salved her respectability by undertaking that if she should ever be found committing the same offence again she would submit to any censure the session pleased, and volunteered that if any ale was again seen to be taken from her house on the sabbath, the session might confiscate it for the use of the poor.

In many such cases, drinking came to sessional notice only because it constituted breach of sabbath or fast day. Breach of sabbath, in one form or another, was the commonest manifestation of 'indiscipline' in Cramond during the period 1651 to 1662 because it included mere failure to attend one or both of the Sunday services. Among those delated for the latter offence were Margaret Scugall, Rachel Cochran's servant, who promised to attend 'if sickness hinder her not', and David Berry, who explained that he was aged and weak and unable to make the journey to the church in winter, but promised to come every Sunday as soon as 'the day waxes long and the weather fair'.[3] Some boys caught playing on the ice on 24 December that year had a different reason for non-attendance in winter, but apparently reformed after the schoolmaster beat them on the session's instructions. But sabbatarian zeal was taken to excessive lengths in May 1655 when the two invigilators in Nether Cramond reported young Alexander Shedd for playing at home at sermon time. The minister, after diligent enquiry, learned that the boy had in fact been sick that day and had been dressing himself sedately while some other children, presumably below the age of responsibility, played in the room around him.

A wide range of activities incurred censure because of their timing, as when James Raeburn fought with his servant on an inappropriately sacred day.[4] Often fishing (i.e. poaching salmon in the Almond, and so an offence against Lord and laird together?) was the temptation. Margaret Faape set a fishing net (and was also accused of drunkenness) on a Sunday,[5] and Robert Moubray in the Brig End took fish at sermon-time the same day. John Inglis in Over Cramond similarly profaned the sabbath by fishing in May 1658 and expressed penitence on his knees before the session, although at first he claimed that all he had done was cross the river to fetch a fork that he had hidden in a bush the night before. It was not true (he first said) that he had then used the fork to strike at a fish. A third case of fishing on the sabbath in July 1658 moved the minister to inveigh against

> the great dishonour done against God through the base and scanda-lous carriage of several by fishing on the sabbath day, and most earnestly desiring that such gross unchristian carriage may be pre-vented for the time to come, does appoint intimation publicly to be made upon sabbath next that whatsoever person in this congregation shall be found at any time hereafter to commit such lewdness by profaning the Lord's day in that kind, they shall be caused to make their repentance publicly and shall be referred to the civil magistrate for their further punishment.

Harvest time was a particularly challenging occasion for those who wished to enforce regular church attendance on all members of the community. Not only would the rural inhabitants of Cramond be under pressure to take advantage of a chance fine day, Sunday or not, to get in their crops, but they would be employing an influx of temporary hands from outside the parish. The session conceived it their duty to ensure that all these souls were gathered in. On 26 August 1655 two of the elders were enjoined 'to see that those in the remotest parts of the parish keep the sabbath day in time of harvest'. To this end they were to visit the families in their respective areas before and after the services and 'exhort all such as are able, whether parishioners or strangers, to come to the kirk'. On 31 August next year two other elders were to see 'that no hired shearers [reapers] within the parish stay from the kirk in the time of harvest'. But the harvest was so important that in 1658, when bad and tempestuous weather affected work, the annual communion was delayed 'till the corns be cutted down', and on 22 August the weekday sermon was cancelled for the same period. The harvest was finally in by 26 September and the 'lecture' resumed. Next year the weather in August was again 'unseasonable and tempestuous' and presbytery ordered a fast day to be held to try and improve matters. Seed-time in February to March was another important season in the rural year, and the weekly sermon was cancelled 'in regard of the season', or 'till the seed-time be ended', on 13 February 1659 and again in 1661.

The reluctance of some people to put churchgoing before business or pleasure is understandable, especially when they were required to attend two lengthy services of reading and preaching on Sundays and another every Tuesday, not to mention the less frequent fast days and the sermons of examination and preparation for the parish communion. But to some extent rebels were setting themselves apart from their community. They were also likely to arouse the condemnation (and envy?) of their more virtuous neighbours, and it may not always have been the invigilating elders and deacons who 'delated' backsliders.

It behoved members of a Christian community to live at peace with their neighbours. The 'scolding' of Christian Court and Agnes Squire in Nether Cramond brought them before the session in October 1659, as did the cursing and blaspheming of Humphrey Kent and his daughter 'Barra' (Barbara) in Lennie Muir. Especially before communion time, the session took under avisement any notable cases of domestic discord. In June 1654 Jean Cranston and Margaret Corston were delated to the session for scolding. When they appeared each brought a written paper containing accusations against the other, with 'much injurious language'. This was a domestic squabble between mother-and daughter-in-law. Margaret's husband, Matthew Barton, was away at sea and until he returned (and, one assumes, took steps to keep his wife and mother in order) the session contented themselves with debarring both women from the forthcoming communion. Two couples were summoned before them in January 1655 and each made to promise to live peaceably together. The action was ineffective in one case, as seven weeks later the man was called in and sharply rebuked for his 'unchristian carriage to his wife'.

In April 1657 the session summoned John Beg and Rachel Cochran, who had been married in 1652, to explain why they did not live in the harmony expected of husband and wife. Rachel complained that John was a jealous husband who had long held unjustified suspicions about her. The session, discreetly deciding (at the minister's suggestion?) that to intervene further would be 'ane difficile and dangerous matter', contented themselves with an exhortation to live peaceably and christianly together in time coming. A year later Rachel complained to the minister that she had been unjustly slandered by Jonet Anderson, who had said that her husband, John Lindsay, was keeping company with Rachel in an unseemly and suspicious manner. Mr Dalgleish told the session that he had put much effort into putting the scandal to rest and removing any cause for more jealousy. As a result, Jonet Anderson was summoned before the meeting, and kneeling in tears declared 'her hearty grief and sorrow for any groundless, passionate expressions of that kind that had escaped her'. She was dismissed after being told 'to resist the devil and to walk watchfully and circumspectly as becometh a Christian' and warned about the consequences of a repetition. In December 1660 two of their neighbours in Nether Cramond, Thomas Millar and his wife, admitted 'unchristian brawling and striking one another'. Yet another resident in the village, John Duncan, had previously been before the session, accused of frequent tippling and drinking. Perhaps he had some excuse, as the session then noted 'how greatly God was dishonoured by the continual contention which is betwixt the said John's mother and wife'.[6] All three were rebuked with a warning, after undertaking to submit to the sharpest censure if they quarrelled again. When Katherine Stuart was accused of flyting with Elisabeth Auchinleck, wife of John Stuart – and probably therefore her sister-in-law – the session thankfully handed the case over to Dalmeny session, since Stuart and his wife lived in that parish. It is worth remarking that both parishes included Stuart among the offenders, presumably because he was held responsible for his wife's behaviour.

The sessions also dealt with accusations of breach of promise. When John Kincaid asked to have his banns read for marriage with Agnes Millar, Jonet Adamson objected. Kincaid told the session that Jonet had in fact quitted him of his earlier promise to marry her, before three witnesses. These all said that Kincaid had 'transacted' with her, buying her off with £20. The session then permitted John to be 'proclaimed' with Agnes Millar, but because only two of the three witnesses testified to hearing Jonet say that she freely 'quitted him', they resolved to 'try for further clearing' before allowing the marriage to take place. Kincaid and Agnes seem to have been duly married some three months later, in December 1661.

The session were equally careful to ensure that there was no impediment to the marriage between John Lumsdale and Margaret Lowdon. Since Lumsdale was an incomer, he required a testimonial from his previous parish of residence. He had been a servant of the Earl Marshall and objected that the distance from Cramond was so great that he was unable to go and fetch one. Instead he offered to obtain two credible witnesses to swear on oath that he was unmarried.[7] Cramond referred the problem to the next meeting of presbytery, which permitted them to take sworn evidence in the matter.

Still greater problems arose when a woman was faced with proving the death of her husband 'on active service'. On 1 March 1652 the session conducted an enquiry to establish whether the death of Alison Hill's husband, John Meane, left her free to remarry. A formal interrogation was administered to a witness, Isobel Chapman, whose own former husband, Robert Carson, had been a fellow-soldier with Meane as Scottish volunteers in the army raised by General Robert Monro in the early 1640s to assist Ulster settlers under attack by the native Irish. Isobel had accompanied her husband to Ulster and had known Meane when he lived in Dinboge, about two miles from Coleraine. In 'the second summer after the Scots army went over to Ireland' (1643) Meane and Carson were among those sent to besiege Charlemont. Many of the company were killed, and when Isobel's husband returned he told her that John Meane was among the casualties, having been shot through the head. Carson himself had buried him 'under a fald dyke' (i.e. a wall enclosing a fold for sheep or cattle).

This evidence, admittedly hearsay, was not deemed sufficient: Alison needed to produce either a formal certificate or two witnesses to the death, and Cramond session referred the matter to Edinburgh presbytery, as they always did in any case of slight difficulty. The presbytery minutes are lost and nothing more is recorded until on 14 October 1655 a certain John Marshall gave in a supplication to the session confessing sorrow for the 'disorderly marriage' he had contracted with the late Alison Hill. He was referred to presbytery and ordered to make public satisfaction before the congregation of Cramond. His disorderly marriage would have taken place outside the parish and without any banns being read there. One cannot blame Alison Hill and John Marshall for taking matters into their own hands when ecclesiastical authorities were so fussy and proof that a soldier had been killed was so hard to come by. In June 1659 Catherine Steinson was also faced with the need to prove the death of a previous husband who, 'for anything she knew', had been among the Scots killed in the Cromwellian victory at Dunbar in 1650. The session told her to collect what evidence she could and presbytery eventually gave permission for her marriage to go forward.

During these last ten years of William Dalgleish's ministry rather few cases of 'antenuptial fornication' are noted in the session minutes. In February 1655 Thomas Cleghorn junior, member of a leading tenant family, and his wife were ordered to make public satisfaction for their sin.

In February 1660 Elspeth Steinson confessed that she had been pregnant when she married James Millar, and their pledge at proclamation, of £5 16s. Scots, was confiscated for the benefit of the poor, and on 2 December 1660 the session, 'understanding that Alexander Flookheart in Nether Cramond and his wife [Isobel Corston] was delivered of a child upon November last and that thereby it was evident that they had fallen in fornication before their marriage', condemned them to make the usual public satisfaction and surrender their pledge.[8]

Whether the parishioners of Cramond observed a stricter sexual ethic at this time than they were soon to do, or whether minister and elders were less zealous than their successors in detecting sexual laxity is a question that cannot be resolved. Possibly a measure of restraint among the general populace was induced by strongly 'puritanical' preaching and precept from those in authority, allied with the tighter controls, both civil and ecclesiastical, that the Cromwellian administration is credited with introducing to Scotland. Certainly sinners were induced to express their penitence before Dalgleish's session with an overwrought emotionalism. Already by 1660, however, sexual restraint was less obvious among those of the people who were little inclined to self-discipline by temperament, education or economic and social circumstances.

Like the antenuptial variety, fornication usually came to sessional notice when the girl gave birth or was obviously pregnant. Thus in March 1655 Jean Hastings confessed, perforce, that she had had a child and named the father as John Inglis, lately servitor to Mr John Inglis, laird of Nether Cramond. The father was now in London and the session, in view of the distance, told Jean to produce a letter from him acknowledging the child, within four or five weeks – an indication of the difficulties of communication. This was duly done and after paying her penalty Jean was permitted to begin her 'public satisfaction', appeared in the place of public repentance on the statutory three Sundays and was received back into the congregation, after giving 'great evidence of her sorrow'. Her fellow-sinner, however, was out of reach.

A sad case was considered by a special committee of the session in 1658. Under questioning from the minister Margaret Alison in Muirhouse admitted that nearly three years previously she had borne a child to William Duncan, a month after his death in May 1655. Immediately after the birth she had strangled the child with a string and placed the body in a chest in her room, where it had remained until recently found. Asked whether she had taken any drink in an attempt to procure an abortion, she said that on 2 February 1655 she obtained two drinks for the purpose from a gardener in Muirhouse, although without telling him why she required the concoctions. She then, of her own accord, confessed that in 1651, when she was living in the West Port in Edinburgh, an English soldier who was quartered in the same house had lain 'in whoredom with her' for a year, but she had now forgotten his name. She was no doubt handed over to the civil arm as a murderess.

At the hiring season of Martinmas 1658 Marion Wauchop left Cramond for a post in Edinburgh, and in April next year she came to Cramond session to ask for a testimonial of good conduct during her time in that parish. Some of the sessioners were reminded that when she was in Cramond her behaviour had been 'scandalous-like' with her fellow-servant Alexander Wilson, and she was questioned about a report that she and Alexander had twice spent a night alone together. This she denied. Alexander, when summoned, denied impropriety but admitted that on two nights Marion had 'steekit' the other servantwoman, Jonet Young, out of their shared room, which lay next to his, so that Marion and he had been alone on that particular side of the close. He claimed, however, that on both nights he had gone to bed before Marion barred Jonet out and it was not till the next morning that he knew that Marion had slept there alone. The session had him removed and Marion recalled. At first she 'shamelessly denied' being alone with him behind locked doors, but then agreed with Alex's account, including his denial of sexual intercourse. Since physical proof to the contrary was lacking and both denied wrongdoing, they were dismissed with a prohibition on keeping company together on pain of being treated as fornicators.

But on 10 May Marion Wauchop again appeared before Cramond session and was sent back to the North West Kirk in Edinburgh because Cramond had been told that she was 'under process' there on suspicion of taking some drink 'to wrong, as is thought, the child in her belly'. The other session then wrote to Cramond that Marion, 'after her oft denial, backed with an insolent and uncivil carriage', had at last confessed to being pregnant by Alexander Wilson. It appears from the parish compt book that Wilson paid the financial part of his penalty on 15 February 1660.

After giving birth, Marion went as wet-nurse to the laird of Houston in Strathbrok (Uphall). On his behalf the minister there wrote to the minister of Cramond expressing Marion's willingness to return to Cramond and do public penance, but begging that she might delay until her charge was weaned because 'the child, being weak, might be wronged' while she was absent. A year later Cramond's clerk again wrote to the minister to have Marion summoned without further delay. He replied with an earnest request for postponement because Marion was still breastfeeding the laird's child. Marion was finally received into good odour at Cramond, after professing repentance, on 17 July 1664. Later that month Alexander Wilson was delated at Cramond for a new fornication, and it was learned that he was being prosecuted in Edinburgh for a third.

The Reverend William Dalgleish and his session had two notably recalcitrant men to deal with at different times. On 7 December 1656 James Gray and Katherine Barton were accused as relapsed adulterers, having, as they admitted, eaten and drunk together in Edinburgh and Leith and returned to Cramond in company, 'only they both deny carnal copulation'. Referred to Edinburgh presbytery, Katherine admitted to them that the pair had in fact had intercourse. Subsequently James confirmed this and presbytery recommended that they should be reported to the civil magistrate. The two constables (and elders) accordingly did this, whereupon James fled from Cramond.

Pending his reappearance, the session dealt with a woman who had accompanied the pair on their trip to Edinburgh and back and failed to report their misbehaviour. Worse still, Jean Cranston and her daughter, also named Katherine Barton, were revealed to have acted as go-betweens, 'trysting' James and Katherine Barton 1 to meet together. Mother and daughter were summoned before presbytery and condemned to do public penance in sackcloth. Jean was made to stand at the church door in sackcloth between nine and ten am on two sabbaths and then sit in public view in the church until the service was over. Her daughter, however, was permitted the lesser penalty of sitting in a place of penitence for one day only, and without wearing sackcloth.

Three years later Cramond session received a letter from Dalmeny session to say that James Gray was now in the Colt (or Coat) Muir there, together with his wife. Cramond session recommended their minister to send for him, 'to see how the said James is affected with his frequent scandalous adulteries'.[9] Dalgleish had to report that he could find no evidence of repentance, but would take further pains with Gray, and the session decided to ask the minister of Dalmeny to add his own endeavours to bring him 'to some real sense of his horrid iniquity'. Although Katherine may not have been married, she still counted as an adulteress if she had relations with a married man, and the two were regarded as 'trelapse in adultery', apparently meaning that they had had relations with each other at three separate periods.

The efforts of the two ministers were successful in bringing James before Cramond session, when, in June, he humbly asked to make public satisfaction, confessing on his knees to his threefold adultery with Kather-

ine and professing himself truly sorry. He was then sent a little way off
while Katherine was called in. She renewed her confession, and then
revealed of her own accord that James had told her (perhaps to make her
jealous) that on the night of the wake held for James Moubray he had lain
all night with Blanch (spelt Blench) Little, that Blanch had fetched them a
quart of ale and that 'Blanch had a bed which would allure any man to lie
in it'. The session were well aware of earlier rumours about a connection
between James Gray and Blanch and, expressing their delight 'that God in
his providence had at this time unexpectedly brought a new presumption
to light', recalled James and confronted him with this new development.
James stoutly denied ever saying anything of the sort to Katherine, while
she maintained to his face that she was telling the truth. The minister then
earnestly entreated him 'to glorify God by a clear and ingenuous confession
of that adultery with Blanch Little', since it was now plain to all that he had
been guilty. Unless he did so it would be impossible to allow him to do
penance for his adultery with Katherine Barton. James refused to confess,
although at the sudden turn of events he was 'so dashed in countenance
that . . . scarcely could he use any words to deny or excuse himself'.

A week later James had recovered sufficiently to deny 'obstinately and
impudently' that he had ever had intercourse with Blanch, and the session,
finding him more and more obdurate despite the evidence against him,
'laid him by' as one who could not be admitted to repentance. On 5
August, still 'obdured', he was referred to presbytery and disappears from
Cramond records, unless indeed he was the smith of that name living in
the Colt Muir in 1676. Blanch of the alluring bed also disappears until, an
aged and blind woman, she was enrolled among the ordinary poor on 7
January 1683. The mortcloth (pall) was hired for her burial in May
the same year. One of the Katherine Bartons was similarly enrolled among
the parish poor by December 1687 and the mortcloth was hired for
another in March 1685.

For several years before August 1661 the session had tried to make Robert
Bowie, a married man, keep away from the house of David Boag and his wife
at Cramond Brig End, where the attraction was their daughter Isobel Boag. It
would seem that the scandal reached its height after David and his wife fell
out with Bowie in June 1661 and both sides indulged in some public
slanging of each other: for instance Robert Bowie maliciously spread it about
that Isobel had parted with (i.e. aborted) two children by him 'and that he
would cause her to wear the sack-gown'. David Boag, his wife and daughter
were summoned before the session and David, rebuked for harbouring

'such a scandalous person' as Bowie despite previous prohibition, expressed his grief but claimed that Bowie had always come to his house against his will and that he had been unable to get rid of him. David and his wife agreed that Bowie had made the threat about the sack-gown, but denied all knowledge of any tokens exchanged between him and their daughter.

Isobel herself totally denied that she had committed adultery with Bowie, or that he had tempted her to. In response to a pointed question, she also denied that she had ever conversed alone with him in 'an unseemly, suspect manner'. In reply to further questions from the minister, who was clearly well-informed about the couple's doings, she agreed that one afternoon the previous winter 'about daylight going' she and others had come upon Robert Bowie as he lay behind the House of the Hill, 'his horse in his hand'. Seeing Isobel, he immediately took her up behind him on his horse and they rode away from her companions. She also admitted that on 29 May she had ridden behind him from the toun (Nether Cramond) to her father's house, and had been alone with him since.

At the next session meeting Robert Bowie also denied adultery, and said that he had not spoken to Isobel since quarrelling with her parents about a month before. He agreed that he had 'horsed from Edinburgh several times' and had twice drunk with Isobel in Edinburgh, but alleged that her parents were present. He was promptly caught out in a lie about not seeing Isobel since June, as he had to admit that about 1 August he had drunk four Scots pints of ale (almost two English gallons) with her in a house where her sister lived in Mary Wynd in Edinburgh, but claimed he left Isobel there and came away alone. As to the tokens that had formed an item of gossip, he had given Isobel a pair of gloves, but this was because she had made his bed when he stayed with the family, and once when he was drinking in her father's house he had asked her for a token and she had given him a plait of her hair. It was true that he had said he would cause her to wear the sack-gown, but he was in a passion at the time.

Isobel next obstinately denied receiving any token from Bowie, and when the pair of gloves was mentioned first swore stoutly that she had been given none, and then alleged that they were in repayment for some tobacco. She also denied the plaited hair, and would say only that her sister might have given him some loose combings, or else Bowie himself 'had taken some such loose hair of hers out of the wall'.

The session still failed to believe Isobel, and she and Bowie were confronted on 8 September with their conflicting stories. Bowie maintained that the gloves were for making his bed and not in return for tobacco. He also affirmed, in her presence, that she had clipped a plait of her hair with a pair of shears and given it to him as a token. Isobel continued to contradict this. Asked why he, a married man, had asked for a plait of her hair, Bowie could make no reply. Having consulted presbytery, the session strictly forbade Bowie to haunt either Isobel's company or her father's house any longer. Both Bowie and her father willingly agreed, as also to abstain from all godless and unchristian scolding of each other. If Bowie broke the prohibition it was understood that he and Isobel would be held guilty of adultery. On presbytery's advice the process was then left in abeyance until (Isobel being sick) they saw 'whether God in his providence would bring any more to light there anent'. It seems that God failed to respond.

In another case, gossip was not substantiated. On 2 May 1658 the session were told that Marjorie Waker or Walker, who had left the previous Martinmas to take service in Kilbucho, had now been found to be pregnant. The supposed father was David Hutton who had been her fellow-servant in Cramond. David's present whereabouts were not known for sure, but it was arranged that Mr Dalgleish should enquire for him when he met the minister of Kilbucho at the forthcoming synod meeting – a centre of the 'ministerial network'.

Marjorie came to Cramond and appeared before the session on 30 May, denying fornication with Hutton and offering to purge herself by oath. The session were unwilling to accept this, since it was said that she and Hutton had been in bed together on occasion. Marjorie said that Hutton had indeed twice come to her bed. The first time she immediately arose, and the second time she was asleep but a young man was also present in the house with them and remained until Hutton left. The session thought the circumstances suspicious but shelved the matter in the hope that further evidence might appear. They then made more enquiries. On 20 June Marjorie again made the journey to Cramond to ask the session to put an end to the groundless gossip about her, and they gave her a testimonial to say that, as far as they could judge, she had been innocent of any blame while living in Cramond.

Sessions were usually inclined to assume the guilt of any person brought before them, though scrupulous not to condemn without proof. They had some justification for their attitude, because, as in the cases of James Gray and Robert Bowie, evidence had often been collected and sifted before the accused was confronted with it. In the face of close questioning by the minister, and perhaps testimony privately obtained from witnesses, at this period few offenders managed to sustain a denial for very long. Robert Moubray at Cramond Brig End, charged with taking a fish at sermon-time in June 1657, challenged the session to produce witnesses. Eye witnesses in fact existed and gave their evidence to the elder of the bound, and Moubray's next recourse was simply to ignore further summonses.

In an attempt to keep some control over their parishioners, in May 1654 the session ordered that no incomers were to be taken in without a testimonial from the previous parish of residence. On 26 December 1658 they further instructed their clerk to enter details in the minute book of all testimonials issued to people leaving the parish or received from those entering it. Rather few such entries were in fact made, after the three for that same day which recorded that Marjorie Crie had left at Martinmas 1657, and that one male servitor (senior servant) of Lord Balmerino and one of James Dundas's had brought testimonials from Largo and the North West parish of Edinburgh respectively. Both employers, significantly, were members of the session. More often employers, landlords and servants or tenants alike worried about obtaining testimonials only when exigency demanded.

One major problem that faced the Cramond kirk session in the 1650s was how to deal with two delinquent heritors. A comparable situation would arise only once again, in 1700, when there were similar difficulties about enforcing public penance, and equal standards, upon a locally powerful and respected personage. It was also awkward in 1657 that many lesser parishioners were being brought to book for just the same offence – public drunkenness. But heritors were kittle cattle. Both sides were extremely conscious of the deference due to rank, and often enough the session could bring a heritor's servant to book only with the agreement of his employer. In fact the heritor concerned might well be the 'master' of one or more of the elders (what at other times and places would be termed a feudal lord), and he was one of the men upon whom the kirk depended to pay minister and schoolmaster and meet building costs. The heritor also had the advantage that he was often absent from the parish on his lawful affairs. Consequently, it is likely that Cramond session would have turned a blind eye to the doings of these three men, had not their activities been forced upon their notice.

James Primrose of Whitehouse, one of the 'honest men' who had been present by invitation at the sessional meeting to choose a leet of elders on 17 October 1652, caused offence by public drunkenness and swearing at a burial in May 1657. The minister and two elders were deputed to speak to him. Primrose refused to make a formal confession to the session, although he was willing to do so to the minister and just two or three of the elders. The session considered that a private confession of that sort was insufficient for so public an offence, and ordered the beadle to cite Primrose to their next meeting. In his place Primrose sent Mr David Heriot, probably a lawyer, who obtained a delay, and meanwhile the minister and some of the elders were to confer further with Primrose. The matter rested there until Primrose was rash enough to compound his offence and be seen drunk in Nether Cramond on the night of 29 May, the eve of a solemn fast. On 28 July the minister told the session that he, James Howison of Braehead and two other elders had spoken to Primrose and received his frank acknowledgment of sincere sorrow for his drinking and blaspheming. He would not do it again. On this occasion the session seem to have happily abrogated responsibility and left it to the minister to deal further with the culprit as he saw fit, and admit him to communion if he chose.

On 16 August 1657, and while James Primrose's case was still under discussion, the session ordered that Mr Robert Adamson of Craigcrook should be cited to their next meeting 'for his excess in drinking'. Adamson, who was at the time the largest landowner in Cramond, sent a letter saying that he was unable to attend on that date but humbly acknowledged his fault and asked them to pass over it this time, on condition that if it happened again he would submit to any censure they chose to inflict. The session felt that he ought to appear before them in person and delegated the minister and Mr James Balfour, indweller in Craigcrook, to indicate this. They reported that they had spoken to him and found him 'sensible of his fault'. Since he was about to go to Bute, his sister had asked them not to construe this absence as disobedience. Alas, on 6 September Adamson was reported to have relapsed and been seen drunk in Corstorphine parish on the night of Sunday 30 August – the very day that Cramond session had received the report from Dalgleish and Balfour.

No prosecution was pursued until the parish communion was over, and on 25 October the session continued the delay while they considered what to do. Adamson headed the list to be dealt with, and on 8 November the minister reported that he had been told on Adamson's behalf that he was willing to appear before the session. Next week the message was that he would come some day that week to talk with the minister. He seems not to have come and on 29 November the minister undertook to speak to him when making a formal visit to the relevant part of the parish. Adamson then promised to attend the session by 14 November at latest. It was in fact 20 December when at last he turned up, acknowledged 'his miscarriage by excessive drinking' and promised not to do it again. He was rebuked and admonished 'to walk more circumspectly' and so dismissed without further penalty. In the circumstances, 'circumspectly' was a good word, since the hope was probably that in future the laird of Craigcrook would at least stay home when intoxicated.

While it seems unlikely that no Cramond heritor ever succumbed again to the influence of drink, any who did so in future were more discreet about it, or else no complaint reached the session with sufficient force to require official action.

Accusations of witchcraft could still be taken very seriously, both in Scotland and England, and there would be a recrudescence of Scottish trials in 1661–2. When the epithet 'witch' was bandied between flyting women, however, a sensible session might pay little attention. On 23 October 1659 the session received a complaint from a woman in Wardie, alleging slander against Agnes Johnston in Nether Cramond after Agnes had met her in Wardie one Sunday, called her a witch and affirmed that she could prove her one. As the alleged slander had occurred in the West Kirk parish, Cramond session ordered Agnes to answer to the session there.

In the past Cramond had been involved in two witchcraft cases. In 1597 an accusation was brought against one Jonet Stewart in the Canongate, alleging that she had passed a wife of Cramond through 'the girth of woodbine' nine times, 'for curing of her disease' (i.e. discomfort). She had also taken Bessie Henderson down the backside of Nether Cramond, taken up nine sops of salt water, put them into a stoup and used them, with invocation of [Saint?] Giles, to wash a sick woman by the name of Uchiltrie, from the crown of her head to the sole of her foot while the patient was held up between two sisters. Nine was a traditional magical number, and passing through woodbine was probably meant to ease a difficult childbirth. Jonet seems to have been no more than a practitioner of folk medicine, with less lethal effect than the foxglove leaves that various women boldly prescribed 'to end or mend' a sickly child in Tyninghame in 1634. A second suspected Cramond witch was a certain Margaret Burges. All that seems to be known about her is that a commission to try her was issued to John, Lord Balmerino, and others in 1628.[10]

So there were potentially serious implications in a quarrel between Isobel Wallace and her neighbour in Nether Cramond, Margaret Corston, in July 1660. Margaret, the wife of Matthew Barton, who had troubled the session in 1654 by trading insults with her mother-in-law Jean Cranston, complained to the session that 'Isbell' had called her a witch, a runnagate and a blackened bitch. Isobel counterclaimed that Margaret had first called her a drunken harlot and loun. Moreover, Margaret had told her darkly that although everything could not be done in an instant, she would still take revenge on her, even if her own child was dead and Isobel's living. Questioned about Isobel's statements, Margaret would admit only to calling her a drunken loun. But she explained that when Isobel was with her, Isobel's child had come into the house, and Margaret could not help weeping, because, she said, her own daughter had died a few days after Isobel had cursed her. Isobel for her part admitted that when Margaret called her a drunken loun she had retaliated with 'blackened blade', and when Margaret made her remark about how she hoped to be revenged, she had replied (with some pertinence) that Margaret was as good as acknowledging that she was adept in witchcraft ('that that was as much as the said Margaret kythed herself a witch').

James Waker, called as a witness, supported Isobel to the extent that he had not heard her call Margaret a witch and had merely noted some reference to witchcraft in the course of their flyting. The session ignored this aspect of the matter, and finding from their own admissions that Margaret and Isobel had unchristianly slandered each other, ordered them to be reconciled before appearing at the next meeting. Margaret Corston, however, was then found to be persisting 'in her obstinate, malicious humour' and the session resolved to ask presbytery what to do with her. Finally they decided that 'the petty debates' between the two women were a matter for a civil magistrate and arranged for John Inglis of Nether Cramond to put an end to their controversy. Appeal might be freely made to the session, but if a case was not proven a penalty could be exacted, and Margaret and Isobel Wallace each had to pay 12s. 'for not proving their bill'.

Relief of the poor was one of the duties of a godly community, strictly enjoined by the Reformed Kirk. Thus in February 1654 'the great necessity of some sick persons' was reported to the session and the subtreasurer was asked to see to them. In July of that year £37 was distributed among necessitous poor of the parish, and in October meal, donated by 'Lady Drylaw', widow of James Loch of Drylaw, was given out in various proportions to twenty-four people in need. On 3 January 1658 the session carefully considered the poor and distressful condition of Thomas Wilson and his wife. The elder of the bound was instructed to buy them a firlot (quarter boll) of oatmeal to be going on with, as well as giving them a daily chopine (nearly an English quart or about one litre) of ale, the costs to be met from the poor box. In the meantime the session would 'think upon the best way for supplying [their needs] in time to come'. In November 1659 one couple were allotted 40s. monthly for the winter months from November to March. If all went well, the kirk treasurer kept the aged and sick poor from outright starvation and still had a reasonable surplus in the box when he gave in his annual accounts. In 1656, for example, James Howison of Braehead showed the session's committee of audit that he had received a total of £669 17s. 8d. and spent £587 13s.4d. The treasurer expected that his available funds would include the 'annual rents' (interest) on capital sums that had been lent to notable lairds on the security of land. This interest was needed to provide a healthy balance to meet emergencies or provide the cash that might be borrowed from the poor box when, for instance, the church needed repair, or rebuilding in 1656, and the heritors were slow to meet their obligations to raise the sum required. When a new schoolmaster and clerk was appointed in 1657 the heritors apportioned payment of part of his salary among themselves. There was trouble immediately: several failed to pay at Whitsun 1658 and the threat had to be made to distrain on their tenants.[11]

After a period of enforced and unwelcome toleration had been introduced by Cromwell's Edict of Toleration in 1657, the strict presbyterians of Cramond probably welcomed, on 15 October 1659, their minister's recitation from the pulpit of the 'most seasonable testimony against a toleration of soul-murdering and deluding sects' that Edinburgh presbytery had unanimously issued. Tolerance of dissenting opinion is seldom a notable characteristic of either revolutionaries or religious zealots. Moreover, for the Covenanters uniformity of dogma and worship was essential to their vision of a special relationship between God and nation. In 1651 Charles II had been recognised as king of Scotland on the understanding that he supported the Covenant of 1638 and the Solemn League of 1643. When, through the efforts of General Monck, he was recalled to England on 29 May 1660, the Scots generally welcomed his restoration to the thrones of both countries. The dissolution of the Commonwealth also returned independence to Scotland. So far, so good. But from a monarchical point of view kingship necessarily involved control, and over the previous thirty years or more power had fallen disastrously into the hands of a seditious group of religious fanatics. Reasserting due control meant restoring a measure of authority over the religious establishments in both countries. In England, an Act of Uniformity obliged clergy to conform to Anglicanism – and many refused and lost their parishes. In Scotland, early in 1661, a royalist parliament passed an 'Act Rescissory' that put the clock back to 1633 by rescinding all intervening legislation. At one swoop this overturned the triumphant achievements of the Covenanters. In particular the Act restored the episcopal system of church government that had been abolished, against royal wishes, in 1640 and returned patronage to lay hands – in Cramond to the third Lord Balmerino, who still held Barnton. Mr William Dalgleish presided over his last sessional meeting on 5 January 1662. All but one of the ministers of Edinburgh presbytery similarly resigned their charges, feeling it impossible to remain under the new disposition.[12] Replacements were found, however, among qualified men who felt less strongly about receiving nomination from a layman, seeking collation from a bishop and swearing allegiance to the king.

NOTES

1. *Excessive drinking.* Flookheart, Nov. 1657; Batherston, 19 Sept. 1658. Spelling of names is normalised as far as possible. Flookheart is also spelt Flockheart, Flueker and Flucker. A later clerk never decided whether one of the elders was surnamed Bartleman or Bartholomew, and it is not improbable that with time Cramond's Swine family turned into Swans.
2. *Carrying ale.* 27 Jan. 1661.
3. *Absentees.* Scugall, 2 March 1656, Berry, 12 Dec. 1654.
4. *Fighting with servant.* 29 April 1655.
5. *Setting net.* 14 June 1657.
6. *Mother and wife contending.* 28 Feb., 7 March 1658.
7. *Oath in lieu of testimonial.* 22 July 1660.
8. *Antenuptial fornication.* Two further cases appear in the compt bk in 1660 and 1661.
9. *Gray's frequent scandalous adulteries.* 15 Jan. 1660.
10. *Witchcraft.* Jonet Stewart (1597): Robert Pitcairn, *Criminal Trials in Scotland from A.D. 1488 to A.D. 1624,* Bannatyne Club, 1833, vol. 2, p. 28. Women in Tyninghame (1634): Grant G. Simpson, *Scottish Handwriting 1150–1650: An Introduction to the Reading of Documents,* East Linton, 1998, No. 27. Margaret Burges (1628): *Register of the Privy Council,* 2nd ser. vol. 2, p. 494; George F. Black, *A Calendar of Cases of Witchcraft in Scotland, 1510–1727,* Bulletin of the New York Public Library, 1937+, p. 84 B. In the small number of accusations reported in Cramond's KSM, accuser and supposed witch are invariably of the same socio-economic status. They do not support the idea that the 'typical' victim of a charge of witchcraft was a disadvantaged woman who had uttered curses against someone better off.
11. *Heritors and clerk's salary.* 13 Feb. 1659.
12. *Resignations in Edinburgh Presbytery.* Rosalind Mitchison, *A History of Scotland,* 1970, p. 251.

FOUR

The Inglorious Restoration

The first few pages of the second volume of kirk session minutes are now lost or badly damaged by wear, and the extant legible record starts in July 1664, during the brief ministry of the Reverend Alexander Young. Young, who would leave about September 1665 to become archdeacon of St Andrews and subsequently (1671) bishop of Edinburgh and (1679) bishop of Ross, was not the first appointment of the new dispensation, but his predecessor, John Hamilton, regent in St Leonard's College, St Andrews, seems to have moved on before he was even formally installed at Cramond. Young was succeeded in April 1666 by another regent in St Leonard's College, David Falconer, who remained at Cramond for nearly eight years, up to March 1674. He then returned to St Andrews as professor of divinity. In August 1675 he was succeeded by John Somerville, another minister who had enjoyed a series of rapid promotions: Cramond would be his sixth parish in some twelve years.[1]

There is nothing to suggest that these ministers were any less conscientious than their predecessors, and the episcopal administration had very little impact at parish level. The new nonconformists were not quiescent, however. During the long gaps between ministers they even held services in the kirk itself. In July 1674 John Inglis of Nether Cramond admitted to the Privy Council that on six occasions he had attended illicit conventicles in Cramond parish church. He was imprisoned and fined one quarter of the valued rents of his lands – nominally at least: in practice the full amount of such penalties was not always collected. Like Lord Balmerino, Inglis had already, in 1662, been heavily fined for nonconformity with the new order. He remained resistant until his death in 1684. Sir Alexander Hope of Granton, a son of that Sir Thomas who had prominently supported the Covenant, showed his own disapproval of Cramond's episcopalian clergy by blocking the passage in his private aisle in the church by which ministers had formerly reached the pulpit.[2]

For Cramond kirk sessions business continued as usual. They passed resolutions that the parish should be invigilated on Sundays at harvest time, 'till the corns shall be cut down', so as to correct 'anything amiss' among inhabitants or temporary workers. The deacons who collected at the church door at service time were, as usual, to visit Nether Cramond and report any offenders. And, 'finding that many withdraws from the afternoon's sermon upon vain and frivolous pretexts', they ordered that any caught absent without good reason 'shall be censured as sabbath breakers and contemners of the ordinance'.[3] There were, however, very few prosecutions for breach of sabbath, drunkenness or non-attendance at church. One couple in Nether Cramond were caught drinking at sermon-time in July 1667 and three others were netted the following month. In the previous year Jonet Reed, also in Nether Cramond, was sharply rebuked before the session for 'giving some irreverent words to some of the session for bidding her come to the kirk at the ringing of the last bell'.

In 1664 a session that was still, perhaps, influenced by puritanical strictness refused to accept David Anderson's plea that shoeing a horse on the sabbath had been a work of necessity because the son of the earl of Wigton was posting home to his sick wife and compelled him to shoe the horse against his will. At any rate, the session did not believe his assertions and were unfavourably impressed when he broke into invective against those who had brought the accusation – whether neighbours or some of the session themselves is not stated. At David Falconer's first sessional meeting, on 22 April 1666, Robert Annand in Nether Cramond was reported for gross profanation of the sabbath in flaying a horse in full sight of those assembling for the morning service. He had to make public confession before the congregation next Sunday, but James Lees in Nether Cramond, who had ordered him to do it, suffered only a sharp ministerial rebuke before the session, once he had been brought to admit guilt 'after much pains taken on him', on 19 August. Similar rebukes were administered to two men who had carried home coal on the sabbath and to a married couple who carried barrels of ale on horseback.

If sessions were now coming down less stringently on certain forms of delinquency, they cannot be accused of turning a blind eye to sexual misdemeanours. Throughout the Restoration period (and beyond) a monotonous procession of fornicators appeared before ministers and sessions. Much of the problem was attributed to employers who failed to demand testimonials when they hired servants from outside the parish. In May 1665, for instance, 'taking to their serious consideration the enormities of several servants received into the parish without testimonials', the session had it proclaimed from the pulpit that 'no servant flitting to this parish shall be received without a testimonial'. Not, of course, that a certificate of previous good behaviour was a necessary guarantee of future virtue. Something was eventually done to enforce requirements in September 1675, when it was once more ordered that all testimonials issued or received were to be entered in the session minute book. This would be efficiently done by the admirable Mr Thomas Forrest, appointed school-master and clerk under Mr Falconer's aegis in June 1673.

It was indeed among 'servants' – whether incomers or native Cramon-ders – that sexual licence commonly occurred. On 4 September 1664 Thomas Shedd and Marion Gillies confessed fornication and were 'ex-horted by the minister to lay their sin to heart', told to speak with him further within the next week and 'ordained to separate presently [im-mediately] from one another's company and not to dwell longer in one family'. Their son was baptised on 2 December, but the couple did not marry until June 1667. In due course they produced a daughter, Agnes, who would feature in a scandal of her own (Chapter 6).

In May 1665 Jonet Smith in Lennie Mure was reported to be with child and named the father as her fellow-servant James Sharp. Sharp 'absolutely denied that ever he had any carnal dealing with the said Jonet', so the minister, Mr Young, interviewed their employers, James Anderson and his wife. These said that they had found Jonet in their barn with another man 'in a scandalous manner', but knew nothing of any relationship with Sharp. Sharp continued to deny his guilt and on 7 October next year was 'laid by' until Jonet, who had fled the parish, could be found. In August 1665 she was reported to have given birth to twins and to be in the West Kirk parish in Edinburgh. Two years later there came news that she was lodging in the Cowgate with a certain Bessie Ritchison, but she then fled thence and Cramond seems to have given up the case.

Flight, temporary or permanent, was a frequent response to sessional accusations. Minister and elders would devote a great deal of time and effort to tracking down offenders, but sometimes gave up in despair, as happened in the case of Nicolas Gilchrist who was wanted in July 1664 for fornication 'long ago' while the church was vacant and with a man whose name was no longer recollected. Edinburgh ministers enquired for her from their pulpits, but by March 1665, when the investigation proved fruitless, the session resolved 'not to trouble themselves any further with such a vagabond'.

Persistence paid better when David Pride and Helen Gibb flitted from Cramond, where they had been proclaimed for marriage in November 1665 but had fallen under suspicion of fornication. At the time the church was again vacant pending the appointment of a new minister. Elders did not forget the matter and when, in April 1666, it was learned that the pair were in Torryburn, the new minister, David Falconer, undertook to write to his counterpart there. When no reply had been received by 19 August, he wrote again to Torryburn and also to the minister of Abercorn, where Helen now was. It was not until 21 April 1667 that the pair, now married, expressed penitence and were 'received' at Cramond.

'Processes' were frequently long-drawn-out. Sometimes sinners simply dragged their feet when cited to appear before the session. Alexander Wilson, formerly fornicator with Marion Wauchop (Chapter 3), who was now accused of a relapse with Margaret Inglis, was in the churchyard when the beadle first summoned him, ignored two further citations and left the parish.[4] Concern for the beadle's fruitless efforts in chasing up such people would lead the session in June 1682 to impose a charge of 6s. Scots for his benefit on those found guilty of any scandal. On 11 September the session learned that Wilson was under suspicion of another scandal in Edinburgh and 'thinks fit to lay him by as a scandalous, impenitent person till both he clear himself of the said scandal in Edinburgh and till some evidence of his repentance appear'. It seems not to have done.

Occasionally culprits had their penitential appearance delayed for substantial reasons – when a woman had a sickly baby at breast, for instance. In two cases the demands of a heritor were paramount. Robert Kilgour, guilty of fornication, had his penance delayed when his employer, James Primrose of Whitehouse, said that he was 'necessitated to keep [him] at home for a time every sabbath lest his yard should be broken'.[5] William Weems, who had admitted to indulging in premarital sex in early 1663, was a servant of Lord Balmerino and heavily engaged in his master's affairs – an excuse for non-attendance that the session accepted as very 'just'. Weems eventually stood on the pillar once, on 28 December 1664, and was then dismissed 'because he could not possibly win again through the throng and multitude of his master's business, which he must wait on'.

On the other hand Sir Alexander Hope's coachman, John McDonald, acted of his own accord in May 1669 when two Cramond women accused him of fathering their children and he was being prosecuted for a third such offence in Duddingston. As 'an infamous person' he was ordered by presbytery to stand before the congregation in sackcloth at his first penitential appearance in Cramond, but refused to do so and fled the parish.

The man's rapid disappearance left Elisabeth Binks alone to face an accusation of fornication with John McClelland in Drylaw in September 1668. Whether or not truly, but certainly unsuccessfully, she pleaded rape. As she was coming home to Crowhill from Edinburgh, she said, carrying a load on her back, McClelland had 'gripped' and 'forced' her. Asked why she had not shouted for help, she said she was unable to do so because her load was tied around her neck and she was almost strangled by it. She persisted in her story. Presbytery was appealed to and recommended that Elisabeth must do penance as a fornicator, 'it being most improbable-like that the man forced her upon a high street', and she accordingly, with some reluctance, stood two days on the pillar. For several weeks she failed to 'stand' a third time, but finally completed her penance and was 'received' on 5 December 1669.

Denial did not constitute perjury unless falsely made under oath, but was one reason for lengthy processes. Stout denials and recanted confessions meant that it took two years to resolve Margaret Duncan's accusation of paternity against John Robison. First, in April 1665, Margaret fled after obeying an order to speak with the minister. Robison was excused from attending before the session because he was unwell, while an elder was commissioned to make enquiries for Margaret among her relatives in Upper Cramond. On 28 May Robison declared that he could deny on oath that 'ever he knew the said Margaret by carnally dealing'. On 18 June the minister told the session that Margaret had come to him and retracted the whole of her previous confession, so that it was unnecessary to take Robison's oath. Evidently Margaret's change of heart was not believed, however, as Robison continued to be summoned before the session, finally appearing and reiterating his denial on 27 August. Since six months then elapsed before a new minister was installed, matters remained there until the case was reopened on 29 April next year, after Robison was overheard to say that 'he would take Margaret Duncan's child if it came to time' and had also admitted that one night he had 'struggled' with her when he came drunk from Leith. In private conversation, the minister (now David Falconer) failed to induce a confession and Robison was referred to presbytery. A year later still Mr Falconer reported that Robison had finally admitted his guilt to presbytery. On 5 May Robison then 'most impudently' reverted to denials and Cramond further consulted presbytery. At last, on 19 May 1667, Robison made his confession before session.

Bessie Broun, on the other hand, seems to have been cheerfully frank about her various admirers. In August 1669 she confessed to fornication with her fellow-servant John Haliday, who had 'lain carnally in her bed' at Martinmas (11 November) 1668, on the night when he went to take a new hire in the Braehead of Muirhouse. Haliday at first denied Bessie's accusation, even before presbytery, but finally admitted its truth to Cramond session on 2 January 1670 and was 'sharply rebuked for troubling the session so long by his obstinate denial'. Each of the pair stood on two sabbaths, but neither was permitted to complete the penance by standing before the congregation a third time until they paid their monetary penalties. Neither of them paid, and in February 1671 Bessie was questioned about a new pregnancy, whereupon she confessed that both Patrick Chisholm in Cammo and James Robison in Royston had slept with her. She then left the parish for a time and was reported to be sick 'some place near Edinburgh'. Patrick and James both admitted sleeping with her. Patrick remembered the date because it was the night that farmer Archibald Wilson in Royston got in his winter grain, and James said his offence took place on 21 October, on the day when George Hodge in Muirhouse was married. Both, however, denied paternity. On 2 July the session was informed that Bessie's child had been born, that Bessie had now returned and that Patrick owned that the child was his. Bessie, now 'trelapse' in fornication, was enjoined by presbytery to satisfy in sackcloth, for an indefinite period. She was in fact received back into grace on the fourth occasion on which she stood, and the child was given baptism, on the understanding that Patrick would satisfy thereafter. By 7 January 1672, when Patrick and James had each stood twice, both men were declared fugitive.

None of the men involved with Bessie was married. Indeed, adultery was rarely recorded at this particular period. But gossip about a case involving a married man was reported to Mr Falconer in February 1667, probably after the story was spread around by the alleged eye-witness, fifteen-year-old James Flookheart. When the minister heard about it he privately questioned young Flookheart and also, on two occasions, Grissell Waker, who admitted the charge of adultery with John Rae. Grissell, Rae and James Flookheart had gone to spend the night in one of the mills, or perhaps rather its kiln-lodge. According to James, after the candle had been blown out, Rae relit it and held it to the boy's face to see if he was asleep, then lay with Grissell before the fire. James affirmed that he then saw them 'in the Act'. The minister related all this to the session at their next meeting and then questioned Rae, who utterly denied the charge of adultery, and young James, who reiterated his story. Grissell meanwhile had fled. In her absence Rae continued to maintain his innocence to both session and presbytery, and all that the session were able to learn of Grissell was that she had been living, pregnant, in Blackfriars Wynd in Edinburgh for a time. She then disappeared entirely from their ken, not surprisingly in view of the harsh penalties inflicted for adultery on a single woman who had been involved with a married man.

James Flookheart was old enough to be accepted as a witness. Sessions usually had misgivings about taking the evidence of younger children. In

December 1671 Helen Thomson had complained to the session that her employer, Elspeth Lithgow, had slandered her by calling her a thief and, on Jonet Baptie's evidence, a 'loun' because Jonet, 'a little lass' in the same household, claimed to have seen her lying with her fellow-servant James Millar. James and Helen could not be shaken in their denial and presbytery declared that the bare assertion of a child was insufficient grounds for putting them to the oath by which people were now being permitted to exculpate themselves.[6]

There were some very unusual features about another case in which the session rejected the unsupported evidence of a juvenile. In October 1673 Jonet Ramsay, a young girl of about twelve, had been brought from prison in Leith to produce an accusation against James Given or Giffin, a resident in Cramond. Her story was that recently, when she was in Given's service, he had thrice lain with her in adultery, and then to conceal it had sold her to a 'Virginia captain' (i.e. bound her as indentured servant to the captain of a ship trading to Virginia?). Given had probably had her imprisoned on a charge of defamation. Given and the girl were confronted with each other at the sessional meeting of 19 October, when she confidently asserted her accusation and he strongly denied it. The session, 'taking to consideration that she was but a witless young lass, about twelve years of age, as some there showed, could not lay much hold on her speech', and resorted as usual to presbytery for advice. Meanwhile, at Given's request, Jonet was told to find cautioners to ensure her appearance before session and presbytery when called, and obtained her two brothers as guarantors. That, unfortunately, is the end of the story. There is nothing further about it in the Cramond minutes and there are no extant presbytery minutes for the period in question. James Given, who had married in 1672 and had a daughter baptised in July 1673, may have left Cramond shortly afterwards.

Whereas Mr William Dalgleish's utterances were sometimes reported at length in the minutes, neither Thomas Forrest nor his two predecessors, Robert McKynnell and the son who took over for a time after Robert's death, say anything about any views that the Restoration clergy may have expressed about the general behaviour of their flock, and the only recorded proclamations from the pulpit emanated from the Privy Council. It may or may not be due to different emphases by different session clerks that the session minutes now cease to record that penitents wept before the sessioners or made emotional recantations from the pillar. But it seems quite likely that a certain reticence on the part of these particular clerks reflects their wish to distance themselves personally from the episcopalian regime. Before his appointment as clerk and schoolmaster Forrest was 'chaplain', i.e. tutor, in the household of Sir Alexander Hope and probably shared Hope's presbyterian views. He may, indeed, have been a minister manqué. Young candidates for the ministry often took up a position as private tutor while awaiting a call from a parish.

The kirk treasurers found money tight, and in June 1665 the session, 'finding it impossible to supply the wants of so many poor ones' without the 'annual rents' due from their invested funds, decided to 'pursue' the 6th earl of Cassilis legally for the payment of principal and accrued interest. In August they also voted to pursue Lord Balmerino, whose bond they held for £700. A third debtor was John Inglis of Nether Cramond. Ten years later he owed £400 in principal and interest unpaid since Candlemas 1671.[7] Quite why these funds were in his hands is unclear, but one possibility is that the money had been borrowed from the poor box to pay for work on the church building. In 1682 his son was asked to give the heritors his father's accounts from such an operation. Although Inglis had been hard hit by fines and, like the other two, failed to meet Cramond's requests for repayment, even when legal action was taken against him, he was still able to buy more lands in Cramond in 1676, and it is believed that it was about 1680 that he built himself his new house, the original nucleus of the present Cramond House, standing not far from the kirk.[8] Nor did his heir, James Inglis, balk at obtaining a baronetcy from James VII and II in 1687.

At the last meeting presided over by Mr David Falconer, on 15 March 1674, session and heritors allocated a vacant space in the church to James Hunter, an advocate who had now bought the estate of Muirhouse and wished to build more seating for himself and his tenants. This seemingly harmless agreement would lead in time to a bitter row between some of the heritors, in which Mr Falconer's luckless successor, Mr John Somerville, became embroiled. It was not Somerville's only trouble as the Covenanting backlash increased in strength and as Charles II, and still more his brother James, contrived to lose support, taking with them the 'episcopalian' church and its ministers.

Bishops were, in any case, anathema to dedicated Covenanters, who had always seen them as instruments of royal control over the kirk. Perhaps, too, it was seen as an affront to the authority of Cramond session when the bishop of Edinburgh issued a warrant for the marriage of Elisabeth Higgins, gentlewoman servitrix to Sir Alexander Hope of Granton's lady, and George Braithwit, iron-founder and burgess of Edinburgh in October 1677, and when, in August 1683, two Highlanders in the service of Sir George Mackenzie of Tarbat and Royston were married by order of the bishop of St Andrews. In 1665 the competent authority to judge a case of breach of promise had been acknowledged to be, not the session or presbytery but the commissioner of Dunkeld, who permitted the defendant to clear himself on his unsupported oath.

More obviously, in a renewed quarrel over the allocation of seating between heritors, James Hunter of Muirhouse, a tricky lawyer, aroused ill will by appealing to the bishop of Dunkeld over the heads of session and heritors. When the bishop undertook to act as arbiter Mr Somerville had to withdraw his support for the two local lairds, Sir John Young of Lennie and Hugh McCulloch of Pilton, who had previously been chosen to adjudicate in the matter. As a result, some of the heritors refused to pay their share of costs for repairing the wall of Somerville's yard and Young and McCulloch stalked out of the meeting when Somerville again asked for reimbursement in March 1679. The £112 was paid only years later, to Somerville's widow.

Between them, James Hunter of Muirhouse and James Loch of Drylaw shouldered most of the work of kirk treasurer at this period, which presumably indicates that they supported the minister. But the minutes reveal nothing about the religious and political affiliations of individual heritors. Sir Alexander Hope died early in 1680, followed by John Inglis in 1684. Balmerino and his son, and Sir John Smith and his son, eventually sold their lands in Cramond. At least two of the estates in Cramond were acquired by prominent supporters of the ruling régime: in 1683 Royston became a country seat for Sir George Mackenzie of Tarbat, chief minister of the king in Scotland from 1682–1688, who was created Viscount Tarbat by James II in 1685. Then in 1687 Granton was bought by Sir William Paterson, eldest son of a bishop of Ross and brother of the last archbishop of Glasgow and for some time Clerk of the Privy Council, in which role, according to J. P. Wood, he 'distinguished himself by uncommon asperity against the Covenanters'.[9] At this period neither man, however, played a conspicuous role in the parish life of Cramond.

For upholders of Scotland's proud presbyterian traditions the crunch came in 1681 when a Scottish parliament at which James duke of York was commissioner passed a Test Act that required allegiance to the king and his heirs and acceptance of the existing settlement in church and state. It also made clear that the king was supreme head of the church. A Succession Act confirmed James as Charles's heir. Since James was a committed Catholic, the virtual certainty was that a papist would be king of Scotland and enjoy

power over the Scottish kirk. This extraordinary prospect fuelled Covenanting fires and attracted more adherents to the cause. Significantly,
perhaps, the first indication of falling numbers in the session minutes is the
complaint in September 1682 that the usual parish collections for the poor
in Cramond were falling off, because the deacons were not taking their
proper turns as collectors at the church door. Those who failed either to
officiate or obtain a substitute were ordered to pay a fine for each absence.

About the same time, perhaps, Somerville had his own position
threatened. Character assassination (as well as murder itself – notably
the killing of the archbishop of St Andrews in 1679) was a favourite
technique of Covenanters anxious to unseat episcopalian ministers. In line
with the preoccupations of the period, accusations of sexual immorality
were frequently the method of choice. And indications are that Somerville
was a target. If the session minutes of the time made any reference to the
subject, it would have to have been in the missing pages that covered the
dates between 4 November 1683 and ?29 June 1684. One clue to the affair
does occur later, on 2 June 1690, where it is noted that Alexander Young
(a brother of Sir John Young of Lennie) is still owed £34 by some heritors
as their share of the cost of the dinner he had provided 'some years ago' for
some heritors and the ministers of Edinburgh presbytery 'when they had
kept presbytery here about Mr John Somervell late incumbent here his
scandal'.

The mythology of 'Covenanters good, Episcopalians bad' was thor-
oughly established when Wood described Somerville as deprived in 1689
for refusing to pray for William and Mary (which meant breaking his oath
of allegiance to James VII and II), and, as was then alleged, 'on account of
his former way of converse among the congregation not having been so
harmless and blameless, as the carriage of a minister ought to be among his
people'. This was a little disingenuous: in a footnote Wood made further
reference to 'a process of scandal between Mr Sommervell and his maidservant' noted in Fountainhall's *Decisions*, I. 232. In his unpublished notes
Wood recorded the fuller story.[10] This was that on 9 April 1683 John
Somerville brought a criminal prosecution against a former, unnamed,
woman servant of his, who had defamed him by telling presbytery that
while she was in his service he had 'five or six times attempted to debauch
and lie with her, and told her it was not such a sin as it was represented'.
She took care to add that her virtue had nevertheless stood firm against the
reverend gentleman's lustful advances. There is something about these 'five
or six times' and the complacent assertion 'that she had always resisted
him' that fails to ring true. If this was a dirty tricks campaign, it failed of its

purpose. Somerville remained as minister and continued to deal faithfully with offenders among his charges, except that even fewer absentees from church were now being called to account.

Between 1675 and 1688 most of those delated for drinking had compounded their offence. Two men in Nether Cramond had also beaten their wives. One, James Waker, was 'caused sit down upon his knees and beg pardon of God'. James Dick was delated for drunkenness, swearing and fighting, for which he was condemned to lie in the stocks for two hours, and five women from one family – the disorderly Millars in Upper Cramond – were accused to the session of drunkenness and 'unhandsome carriage among themselves', but dismissed with an admonition when no sufficient proof was adduced. In April 1683 one of the wife-beaters was again found drunk and confessed to public swearing and abuse, but was let off with a rebuke and warning after professing penitence. John Tailor in Nether Cramond was summoned before the session as 'a notable person of a drunkensome and profane carriage' who had moved to Cramond from Larbert after doing penance there for adultery and incest with his wife's bastard brother's daughter. When he appeared the minister rebuked him for his frequent drunkenness and striking his wife.[11]

Once or twice drink brought out latent hostility against elders and betters. Archibald Rae got drunk and abused the family of his late employer, the laird of Drylaw, on several Sundays in 1687. James Donaldson was asking for trouble when called before the session on suspicion of 'unseemly carriage' with a neighbour's wife. He challenged the sessioners to prove it and was generally 'outrageous in the face of the session'. The affronted elders judged that he was drunk, counted his behaviour as an abuse of the sabbath, since the meeting was being held on a Sunday, and had him set in the stocks forthwith. (Creating public entertainment of this sort was evidently not considered any breach of the sabbath calm.) It is noteworthy that both Donaldson and Dick were punished in this way; not, as would have happened earlier, made to receive a ministerial rebuke in front of the congregation at service time. Punishment for some offenders had become both harsher and more secular in nature.

Those people who came before the session for sabbath-breaking at this period had invited public comment much more obviously than the old man who, in 1697, would be caught reading his bible and looking after the house while his daughter was at church. In August 1681 Isobel Boag (the former associate of Robert Bowie with his tokens of gloves and plait of hair?) was rebuked for selling six or seven Scots pints of ale – well over two English gallons – on the Lord's day. John Lindsay, junior, acknowledged that he had worked at his trade of tailoring on a fast day in December 1678, not, he claimed, 'in contempt of authority, but out of necessity'.

Rebukes were evidently formulaic and many people must have regarded the threat of one as small deterrent. Four men and two girls 'profaned the sabbath' by going out to sea in a boat one fine Sunday in May 1682, and in September 1684 Margaret Paton and Jonet Anderson were fined £1 each for breaking Widow Squire's fruit tree on a fast day. It was the profanation of the day, not wilful damage to property, that concerned the session. In July 1687 John Johnston the piper, his wife and his niece Isobel Dobie committed a 'great abuse' by flyting and fighting and 'bloodying' each other. They failed to answer the sessional summons and session referred it to the two local Justices of the Peace 'to take order with them'. This resort to the civil powers to reinforce the authority of the session was an important feature of parish government at the time. The JPs in question were two of the active heritors, men who were almost automatically invited to become elders and took their turn as kirk treasurer.

While most of the cases of antenuptial fornication were detected where the session expected to find them – among the lower socio-economic group – one or two children of tenant-farmers (the class from which elders were mainly recruited) failed to conceal premarital indiscretion. So far from making a public example of them, the session were inclined to be lenient. Thus in October 1685 Alexander Wilson in Royston, son of the late elder Archibald Wilson, confessed to antenuptial fornication with Jean Cleghorn. The session, considering the scandal 'not very public', arranged to let them off with a private sessional rebuke and a payment of one dollar over and above the usual pledge of marriage. The pair failed to appear until 7 February, when Alex came alone, his wife being in childbed (their son Claud was baptised in March). The session then permitted Jean to receive private absolution from the minister, at her own house, if she should be in danger of dying. But such concessions were not made to Alexander's brother John, who was relapse in fornication in 1680 with a Bessie Broun – the one who appeared in the previous chapter? He had to stand six days on the pillar and pay £12 – double the usual penalty – 'for terror to others'. Two months later one of the elders had to tell him to enter the pillar 'for obediencing of his repentance'. He never completed his penance because he was 'removed by death' and buried on 31 July 1681.

Highly exceptional circumstances meant that in June 1684 the session was willing to accept private 'satisfaction' from John Gloag, who operated the ferry near the mouth of the Almond, for his antenuptial fornication with his first wife, 'it being hitherto forgotten by reason of her sudden death in childbirth, and that he could not be brought in public for it'. The circumstances are revealed in the parish compt book: on 5 June 1683 the kirk treasurer had paid £8 14s. Scots 'to Mr Edgar, surgeon, who took away John Gloag's wife's child from her' – by caesarian section? Neither mother nor baby survived. Gloag failed to meet his first appointment with the session and was fined 20s. for that intransigence and also a breach of fast day when he was duly induced to kneel and express penitence.

'Restoration' sessions were no less zealous than their predecessors in investigating the activities of persons whose behaviour gave grounds for suspicion. But as when Jean Smith was accused of 'scandalous converse and unseemly carriage' with two separate men (Chapter 1), there was sometimes 'insufficient probation' of sin. On 10 April 1681 William Bartan and Elisabeth Robison were delated for 'uncleanness'. Bartan confessed 'that he did strive to lie with her in drink, but was hindered'. She admitted only that he had struggled with her. Three witnesses, John Ramsay, John Taylor and William Hardy (all, it is carefully added, 'of age'), saw them 'in unhandsome posture together viz. that the said William was lying above her, but whether they were actually guilty of the sin of uncleanness they could not tell'. The session found the pair at least guilty of unhandsome and unchristian carriage and ordered them to appear on the pillar next Sunday.

In July the previous year John Sim, tailor, an incomer from Methven, and Bessie Johnston were accused of flyting and abusing their neighbours in Nether Cramond, and, as well, scandalously living together in one house although not married. They admitted scolding their neighbours but denied fornication, and were given the lesser penance of sitting before the pulpit next sabbath and expressing public sorrow for 'unchristian converse'. They were, in fact, proclaimed for marriage together shortly afterwards. John Johnston, also in Nether Cramond, whose banns with Elisabeth Anderson had been first proclaimed on 2 October 1686 and then suspended for a time, was reported on 4 December to have been alone with her in her house for three weeks. He denied any carnal dealings with her, and said that on all but two nights he had shared his bed there with the twelve-year-old son of John Sim. John and Elisabeth were told to cease cohabiting until married and John had to oblige himself to pay all penalties if 'anything shall be found out of this scandal hereafter'. They were married on 9 December. Presumably no 'scandal' did come to light, and the marriage pledge was returned to them on 7 August 1687.

Recourse was had to the JPs in difficult cases. Agnes Kello confessed fornication with Andrew Tailor in October 1684, and when Andrew refused to meet the session after frequent summons, Sir John Young of Lennie was asked, as JP, either to make him come or put him in prison. In March 1682 the session paid £9 4s. 7d. for imprisoning Robert McKie or Mackie as 'disobedient to the discipline of the church'. McKie, a mason in Drylaw, had been accused of fornication with Elisabeth Wilson on 4 September 1681. He was evidently undeterred by sessional retribution and in June 1683 Margaret Swan and her brother obliged themselves under the usual large penalty of £100 Scots that Margaret would come and satisfy for her fornication with the late Robert McKie, formerly servant in Grotthill. Thomas Parke, gardener in Drylaw, who was about to take employment elsewhere in Scotland, had his wages and any other dues arrested by the Cramond JPs to ensure that he performed his penance and paid his penalty. He must also find a cautioner, on pain of imprisonment, to guarantee that he played his part in maintaining his child by Jonet Drummond.[12]

Usually the stoutest denials finally crumbled after a lot of trouble had been caused the session. One especially annoying offender was a seaman, Robert Boag in Cramond Brig End, who appeared on the pillar on the afternoon of Sunday 17 December 1682 and had been dispensed from a third appearance before being absolved because he was about to go to sea. Having knelt and been formally exhorted to repentance, Boag then, in front of the congregation, retracted his previous confession of fornication. Not surprisingly, the disconcerted minister, who had been about to absolve him, pronounced him hardened in sin and ordered him to do further penance. At the next sessional meeting Boag came, admitted his guilt and expressed sorrow for his misbehaviour on the pillar, and was ordered to make another appearance there next Sunday.

According to the woman involved, Peggy's Mill was the scene of an act of adultery between William Broun, one of the millers, and Jean Lauriston in August 1684. Again the minister first elicited evidence from the parties in private and later rehearsed it to the session. Jean told him that on the Saturday night three weeks before Broun had shut the doors of the mill and 'lain carnally' with her. Asked why she did not at once tell her mother and the rest of the family, Jean said she did not wish to upset her mother. On Sunday morning, however, she told fifteen-year-old George Ochiltree when they were out herding the cows together, and on Monday, 'being pressed in her mind with the guilt of so heinous a sin', she revealed to her parents what had happened. On Monday, too, she went to Broun as he was drying oats in the kiln and told him that she feared she was pregnant by him. He had answered that she need not worry, there was no chance of it.

The two were then brought face to face before the session, and Jean maintained her story, asking why she should tell lies about Broun, or slander herself untruthfully? Broun hotly denied the story, saying that he had never had a thought of that kind, 'far less the deed'. Asked whether Jean had come to him at the kiln on the Monday and spoken as she said, he replied that he could not remember having any sort of work about the kiln on that day, and had dried no grain since harvesting until the day before yesterday. Both were told to come back in a month, when Jean should know whether or not she was pregnant.

When they returned, on 5 October, Broun said he could swear on the bible that the thought of committing adultery with Jean had never entered his head, and the devil must have stirred her up to lie about him. Clearly, though, Jean's story was believed rather than his, and the minister urged him to consider the nature of such an oath and not add perjury to sin.

In reply to questioning, Jean said she thought she was not pregnant, that she was telling the truth and would swear to it, and that Broun had never tempted her or lain with her before or since that time. When at the next meeting each stood by their story, the session relinquished the case to presbytery. It may be supposed that this Jean was not the same Jean Lauriston who had stood on the pillar on six Sundays between October 1679 and January 1680 for double fornication.

Katherine Doe fell under censure for adultery when she admitted, in July 1678, that she was with child to Robert Kneelands, who had married Isobel Rankin in 1674. The session immediately ordered a sack-gown to be made and Katherine suffered the usual penance of standing at the church door in sackcloth between the second and third bells for service, going thence to the pillar in the same garb, and continuing this at the session's pleasure until they 'discerned some signs of repentance in her'. Robert Kneelands was similarly sentenced on 11 August, when Katherine stood for the first time. The idea was apparently that Katherine should complete her penance before Robert underwent his, but he took her place on 22 September because she had fallen ill. It was Katherine's turn again on 29 September, then she must have been ill again, because Robert stood the next Sunday and on 13 October gave way to two penitent fornicators who were about to leave Cramond at Martinmas for work elsewhere. Robert next stood in sackcloth on 22 December. On 2 March 1679, to speed the absolution of the pair, Robert was allowed to stand each Sunday morning and Katherine each afternoon. On 4 May both asked for absolution and were referred to presbytery. Katherine's daughter had been baptised in January, sponsored by Robert's father-in-law, William Rankin (!), and Katherine now pleaded that she was in great need and wished to earn some livelihood for herself and the child. On 1 June both offenders were ordered to be absolved after a further visit to the presbytery, and Robert was indeed absolved on 28 September 1679. Katherine stood twice more at the church door in January 1680 and sat, rather than stood, on the pillar, but fell dangerously ill again. She was not finally absolved and 'received from the pillar' until 20 June 1680. The session certainly exacted the full penalty in this case, but it was Katherine's sickness that spread the affair over two years.

On one day in March 1683 the session had two cases of insolence to deal with. Thomas Callendar had abused one of their number, and James Donaldson came drunk and aggressive when they were taking evidence about his alleged 'unseemly carriage' with Isobel Matthie, wife of a neighbour in Nether Cramond. Donaldson's wife, Christian Lawrence, admitted that she had heard several reports of their behaviour, but loyally protested that she had never seen any sign of it herself. Three of her other neighbours contradicted this testimony, however. Agnes Johnston said on oath that about a month before, when she and Christian were coming home from Edinburgh, Christian had told her in confidence that her husband often drank with Isobel Matthie, and one night after they had been drinking together she overheard Isobel invite him to go out into John Bell's yard. Christian had followed them and seen them lying together 'in the act of uncleanness'. To prove that she had seen them she took away the snuffbox lying in her husband's bonnet. Next morning she returned it 'and lamented sore [and] he desired her to hold her peace' and promised not to frequent Isobel's company again. Christian had also told two other women that 'she got . . . her husband and Isobel Matthie lying together one night in John Bell's yard'.

It was not Kirsty Lawrence who brought this affair to sessional notice (the session were simply 'informed of a scandal raised' about Donaldson and Matthie). At least three aggrieved persons brought complaints to the session, however. Marion Leichman had her fellow-servant George Story summoned for damaging her good name by accusing her of stealing oats and bere from their employer, the goodwife of Grotthill, and selling them to a third servant. Marion's complaint rebounded because both she and Story were found guilty of purloining (also called 'pickery'), and had to pay half-a-crown (30s. Scots) each to the poor box. Elisabeth Batherston complained about Jonet Charity, also for calling her a thief. Charity admitted doing so from malice. And Isobel Matthie, the lady who later allured James Donaldson, asked for redress against John McMath, who had proposed marriage to her. Isobel had then discovered that he was married already because his wife arrived in Cramond and claimed him. John had to appear once on the pillar and pay a fine for his attempted bigamy.[13]

Two babies, one alive the other dead, were found in the parish and caused a good deal of excitement in the winters of 1682 and 1688 respectively. In November 1682 a child was found laid down near the smithy in Barnton and the minister asked from the pulpit that enquiries should be made for the mother. On 4 March next year one of the session announced that the mother, a Dutchwoman named Katherine Walmser, wife of a soldier, was living in the Canongate, Edinburgh. She told a remarkable story. She had given her child to her sister-in-law Katherine Anderson, now servitrix to the laird of Liberton, to take to her father-in-law, who lived at Loch Tay. She supposed that this had been done. The infant was restored to her and, noted the parish clerk, 'she took it away from us very willingly'. After much exhortation by the minister, and several prevarications, the sister-in-law confessed that of her own accord and without anyone's knowledge, but for unexplained reasons, she had laid the child down near Barnton Park Dyke. For the 'unchristian intentional murder' she was sent to Edinburgh in the care of Sir John Young of Lennie, to be punished by a quorum of JPs, while Cramond charged her cautioner £12 for their own expenses over the matter.

To the modern mind, when, towards the end of Somerville's ministry, Jonet Millar was exonerated of child murder, minister, session, and even the King's Advocate for Scotland relied on a nonsensical superstition and a barbaric ritual in place of hard evidence. About 1 January 1688 a dead child was found in Cramond Muir, near the 'toun' of Upper Cramond, and on the authority of Drylaw, JP, searches were conducted throughout Cramond and Corstorphine to find any woman who had recently given birth and could not account for the child. The search was unsuccessful, but the minister subsequently learned that one Jonet Millar, the sister of Daniel Millar in Upper Cramond, had gone from her brother's house to Comrie on the day that the child was found, and that common gossip identified her as the mother. Her brother was dispatched to Comrie to fetch her, under a bond of £100 Scots, and Jonet accordingly came before the session 'to offer herself to a trial'. Because the body of a murder victim was supposed to bleed when touched by the murderer, the child, by then three weeks dead, was exhumed from the grave and carried in, and Jonet was made to handle it before the session and 'a confluence of people, but no tokens of blood kythed [manifested] at all'.

The minister then interrogated Jonet about her movements in the six months before Martinmas, and she said she had then been in the service of the young laird of Muirhouse (Alexander Hunter). At Martinmas she had gone to service with Deacon Andrew Ker, glover in Edinburgh, but stayed there only a short time, because her father in Comrie had sent for her to be married to a man whom she had known there. So she stayed four or five weeks with her brother Daniel until he had been married (at Ratho on 30 December 1687), and then went to Comrie. She could clearly prove all this, and if she had heard of any dead child being found before she went to Comrie she would never have gone so soon. Jonet was 'examined several ways and no clearness therein', so the case was referred to the King's Advocate. It is not said whether the examination involved any investigation by parish midwives to see whether Jonet showed signs of recent childbirth. The Advocate declared that the evidence presented to him 'did fasten no guilt upon her', Deacon Ker provided her with a testimonial for the short time she had spent in his service, and Jonet and her fiancé Donald Stalker were married at Cramond, after the banns had been read only twice, after sermons on Sunday 11 March.

In addition to 'overseeing the manners of the people and punishing of scandals', Cramond sessions had plenty of work in their third area of duty, 'looking to the wants and necessities of the poor'. In November 1675 there were seven people enrolled as 'ordinary poor' with monthly pensions, all but one living in Nether Cramond. On 7 July 1678, when the cheapness of food led to a temporary reduction in payments, eleven were already listed and four more were added. On 4 December 1687 there were twenty-two 'ordinary poor', thirteen women and nine men, fourteen of whom lived in Nether Cramond.

Two of those on permanent parish assistance in 1678 were somewhat colourful, as well as unfortunate, members of the community. James Stuart in Craigie had been in trouble already in 1655 for his addiction to swearing, and in 1660 for his 'scolding and reviling speeches against John Purgillies [alias Pargillies] at Brigend'. In May 1676 he was expunged from the poor roll because of his insobriety and for foolishly 'scolding on some of the members of the session', but after craving pardon was restored to his pension of 20s. a month. In September 1678, after having his whole household plenishing destroyed by fire, he was given a special payment of two rex dollars (£5 16s.). Next month the session granted him a testimonial to enable him to get help by begging around the countryside, and in June 1683 he was given 4s. as fee for presenting a foundling for baptism.

On 7 March 1686 his widow was granted 40s. to help defray the costs of his burial.

Jean Allen, in the House of the Hill, was left with five small children and another on the way at the death of her husband, James Hume, in 1676. James had been a man of some standing in the parish, since he was among the 'able men' considered for election as elders and deacons in August 1654. Being 'in great necessity', Jean was given 12s. on 5 November and enrolled among the ordinary poor on 1 January 1677, at a pension of 30s. a month. On 1 April, when in childbed, she was given an extra rex dollar (£2 18s. Scots). In March 1678 her need was thought to be less and her pension was reduced to 20s., and in November she lost it altogether: among other things she was taking in as lodgers 'vagabond strangers without testimonials'. 'Present necessity', however, earned her a one-off payment of 20s. on 11 January 1680. The session paid 13s. 4d. for a pair of shoes for her son, Alex Hume, then aged ten-and-a-half, in January 1682. The session were meeting half his fees as a 'poor scholar' by the end of that year. In February 1683 when Jean petitioned that she could not maintain him at school, she was granted 20s. per month for his assistance, provided she kept him to his lessons.

Misfortune did not sweeten Jean's temper, and in August 1683 four of her respectable neighbours complained to the session that she frequently abused them, their wives and families, calling the men warlocks and reprobates and falsely charging them with breach of the sabbath. They challenged her either to prove her assertions or make amends for the offence. Jean admitted abuse and calumny, but said she had been provoked by them. It was not her first such offence: it had previously been recorded in the sheriff books that she must leave the parish the very next time her neighbours complained. The session accordingly resolved to obtain an order from the sheriff to put her out if she did not leave voluntarily. As so often, threatening to expel someone from the parish was very different from achieving that end, especially if, as seems probable, Jean's husband had held his property in feu. In 1686 Jean Allen was again reported to be harbouring 'profane women' in her house, still at House o'Hill, and the two Cramond JPs were asked to remove, not Jean but her lodgers. Her unappreciated efforts at self-help gave her small margin for emergencies, and in January 1687 she asked for assistance to buy herself coal 'in this storm' and was given money enough for half a boll.

In a very few cases, parishioners were permitted to eke out a living for themselves by begging. James Charity, like James Stuart, was encouraged to seek help from neighbouring parishes in 1687, because his house, along with that of Thomas Crauford, had been first robbed by soldiers in September 1682, and then burnt in an accidental fire. Robert Wauchop, 'an old servant in Drylaw', was given £1 8s. in February 1684, and then became a licensed beggar or 'bluegown'. In April 1690 he was recorded to be lying sick in House o' Hill and received something from the Cramond poor box.

The kirk treasurer and sub-treasurer made many such emergency payments to deserving cases. In July 1676 William Boag at Cramond Brig End, 'having his head overgrown with a scall', asked the session to arrange treatment and Hugh Murray was entrusted with the case and given an initial half-crown to buy drugs. Hugh, besides being knowledgeable in medical matters, was 'in strait' and the further £6 13s. 4d. paid him in November represented both his fee and a means of assistance. Nothing could be done for Jonet Kidd, who had a cancer in her head 'and in so sad a disease cannot live long', but she was given a rex dollar for financial help. In February next year her widower petitioned successfully for help in the poverty occasioned by her long illness and then the funeral expenses. Robert Wilson in Nether Cramond, who had a cancer in his lip, asked the session for aid and they agreed to give him three dollars 'to pay any who could cure him'. Later he had half-a-crown, being 'in strait and sick'. John Matthie, one of the ordinary poor, whose leg had been broken, got £5 14s. James Forrest was given another half-crown 'for the present help of his dumb child' in April 1685, and in May the session, 'considering the sad case of Bessie Robison, lying sick and swollen', increased her pension from 20s. to 30s. a month. Payments were also made to the mother of a child sick of the smallpox, a woman 'sick of the Axes', i.e. ague, and a man suffering from a rupture.[14]

At need, parish funds were drawn upon to meet burial expenses for the parish's own poor and for indigent strangers. For strangers a special bier was made in 1675, with iron bands and 'snecks' furnished by James Flookheart the smith. In 1687 William Neilson in Nether Cramond and his wife died and were buried together, leaving no money to cover the cost, which would include making the grave, the coffins and the statutory linen winding sheets. One of the latter is specifically described in the compt book for 1676 when four ells of small harden (narrow coarse linen) were bought for a winding-sheet for Thomas Millar. Exceptionally, when James Reid, who had made the strangers' bier, died in 1685 the treasurer not only paid for making his grave but gave 2s. for candles at the wake.

Besides caring for their own poor, Cramond session were expected to assist a wide variety of 'strangers' like the 'seven broken [shipwrecked] seamen, being Dutchmen' who were given 18s. in February 1681, or a poor woman with a testimonial from St Cuthbert's parish who was looking for her husband, 'who went from her in a fit of distraction'.[15] The exotic 'Augustus Rodolphus Wibert ane Hungarian distressed gentleman with many recommendations' was given £2 2s. in November 1683, whereas John Clark, 'a sea broken man', got only 14s. Cramond also extended charity to such people as John Oxon, 'an English stranger, a scholar', Thomas Etrick, a poor stranger from Glasgow, three old soldiers, and a stranger suffering from palsy. Some excitement must have been caused by the appearance in January 1686 of a 'distempered young woman' who was lodged with John Young for two nights and supplied with drink and a pair of shoes.

Some people were regular visitors. Jacob Tennant, a distressed schoolmaster with a family, was given some assistance in July 1681 and again in September 1683 and August 1688, while his wife was given a donation in December of that year. Jean Guthrie, a cripple, was given 8s. in June 1683, when James Johnston was paid 6s. to carry her into the neighbouring parish of Dalmeny. In September she cost Cramond 10s. in donation and transport. She was back (deposited in Cramond by some adjacent parish) in September 1685, March 1686 and April 1687 when, for the first time, she is described as 'a minister's daughter, being "creeple" '. Other such crippled people sometimes came with itinerant harvest workers and were shunted from door to door in a parish to receive charity before being reclaimed by their companions. They were usually carted about in barrows, and in 1684 Cramond paid 10s. for a barrow to take a 'creeplewoman' in Over Cramond out of the parish.

The accession of James VII and II in 1685 seems to have brought to a head the difficulties faced by Cramond's minister and session, and the minutes begin to make plain that parishioners increasingly deserted to the nonconformist 'meeting-houses'. It proved hard to recruit suitable elders: on 2 January 1687 John Wells in Peggy's Mill flatly refused to join the session and those present at the meeting referred him to a JP. William Ramsay in Nether Cramond evidently held similar objections but more cravenly claimed to be too sick to attend as an elder at present. On 16 October 1687 Somerville told the three sessioners present at his meeting that all but four of the deacons had deserted the parish church for meeting-houses, and he asked each of the heritors to nominate an additional person from among his tenants. Nothing at all seems to have come of this proposal. Collections had also seriously diminished because the money was 'being abstracted' by the meeting-houses, and when James Loch of Drylaw gave in his account as kirk treasurer on 24 October it showed that he was out of pocket to the tune of 5s. although he also had a surplus of £4 19s. 8d. which he 'conceived' to be part of the poor fund that he had handled and which he had ready to pass on to the next treasurer. Even the enrolled poor, dependent on subsidies from the established kirk and session, had to be summoned together in November and warned that if they failed to attend church diligently, or went to meeting-houses, they would lose one month's pension for the first offence and be removed altogether from the roll on a second. On 2 June 1689 it would be reported that the enrolled poor had not received their pensions for the months of March and April owing to the smallness of collections when so few people attended the church, 'and the poor's annual rents could not be getten in neither'. That the problems were not peculiar to Cramond is shown by the Council's decree proclaimed on 1 January 1688 that parish clerks were to receive their dues for registering the marriages and baptisms of persons who deserted the church for the meeting-houses.

The Council's request, on 28 December 1678, 'that prayers might be put up to God for the preservation of the King and Protestant religion from subversion by the late hellish damnable plot and contrivance of the Papists against his Majesty's life, and our Reformed religion established in the kingdoms' may well have been loyally observed. But Mr Thomas Forrest reports tight-lipped later propagandist decrees enjoining the celebration of events like the anniversaries of James's birth and 'the restoration of the government' on 29 May 1660. Least of all can presbyterians have joined enthusiastically on Sunday 29 January 1688 in the decreed national thanksgiving for the Catholic queen's pregnancy.

More on English than Scottish initiative, William and Mary replaced James II in November 1688, and on 11 April 1689 episcopal church government, 'so grievous to this church and nation and so disagreeable to the disposition of the people', was again abolished in Scotland. For refusing to read the proclamation or pray for King William and Queen Mary Somerville was deposed, in common with over 650 other non-juring Scottish ministers, on 2 May. It was the turn of Episcopalians to form a breakaway movement, and some of the dispossessed clergy notoriously made themselves available to perform marriages and baptisms for any who wished to bypass the legalities of the established kirk.

Many in Cramond would welcome the reintroduction – or attempted reintroduction – of sound parish discipline after what was perceived as the laxity of the Restoration years. As Chapter 1 perhaps demonstrated, others were less anxious to accept the return of puritanical dictates. It could be argued that their stance was partly encouraged because the meeting-houses had, ironically, helped to discredit traditional spheres of authority.

NOTES

1. *Ministerial appointments. Fasti Ecclesiae Scoticanae* I and Wood, *Cramond*, pp. 80–81.
2. *Blocking the way to the pulpit.* 16 April 1691.
3. *Contemners of the ordinance.* Nov. 1666.
4. *Ignoring summons from the beadle.* July-Aug. 1664.
5. *Robert Kilgour.* 1 Sept. 1667. A few months later Kilgour was in trouble for antenuptial fornication (both he and his wife having previously been guilty with a different partner): April – July 1668.
6. *Accusation by the child Jonet Baptie.* 24 Dec. 1671–2 June 1672. Ministers usually disliked putting suspects to an oath, fearing that it might lead to perjury.
7. *Candlemas.* 2 February. It seems odd that such dates retained their 'papistical' designations but those were too deeply entrenched in both popular and legal use to be abandoned. Yule, however, sometimes substituted for 'Christmas'.
8. *Cramond's new house.* It is, of course, possible that the money came from his wife or his son's wife, Ann Houston, who married James on 31 October 1682.
9. *William Paterson.* Wood, *Cramond*, p. 20.
10. *Mr Somerville's process. Ibid.,* p. 81, quoting the complaint rehearsed to the Committee of Estates in April 1689 by 'some of the parish': KSM vol. 3, 6 Dec. 1689, and Wood MSS, NLS MS 9885, p. 53. I am grateful to Ann Kettle, University of St Andrews, for ascertaining for me that Fountainhall gave no more details than Wood reports.
11. *Drunkards.* Wife-beaters: March 1677, 22 Dec. 1678; James Dicke: April 1681; Millar women: April 1682; John Tailor: Sept. 1686.
12. *Parke the gardener.* 21 Nov. 1686.
13. *Complaints to session.* Leichman: 16 July, 5 Nov. 1676, Compt Bk. 12 Nov. 1676 (the goodwife, the widowed tenant-farmer Margaret Wright, commonly had difficulty dealing with her servants); Batherston: 12 Dec. 1680; Matthie 18, 25 Feb. 1677.
14. *Medical treatment.* Kidd: Sept. 1678; Wilson: March 1685; Matthie: April 1684; smallpox: Dec. 1685; axes: 1 Feb. 1681; rupture: 1 May 1687.
15. *Fit of Distraction.* Compt Bk, Sept. 1681.

FIVE

Reform and Repression

On 9 May 1689, as Thomas Forrest approvingly recorded, a national thanksgiving was held for the deliverance of Scotland and England 'from an arbitrary and despotical government which had reduced the lands into slavery, and from Popery which was quickly overspreading these kingdoms'. Cramond then remained without a minister of its own for seven months. Among the visiting preachers was Mr John Hamilton, who had been exiled from his charge at Cumber in County Down near Belfast, as a result of the civil upheavals in Ireland. Originally, it seems, he had moved to Ireland as a refugee from the episcopal régime in Scotland.[1] Some of the leading parishioners in Cramond had already been impressed by Mr Hamilton's preaching in Edinburgh churches and, as a result, in November a call was sent to him in Ireland inviting him to become Cramond's new minister. He accepted, on condition that he must be free to return to Cumber if it ever became possible.

John Hamilton was a man of strong personality and managerial bent. He remained at Cramond for under four years but undoubtedly made his mark in the parish. He held his first formal meeting with the kirk session on 6 December 1689, and immediately set about restoring good discipline and organising the parish along the lines that he was accustomed to in Ireland. The first step was to reconstitute the session from existing elders, with the temporary assistance of 'some honest, sober and godly men, so esteemed to be by their neighbours', until new members could be formally instituted and a full session installed so that 'vice may be curbed and there may be the face of a judiciary in the parish for restraining impious courses of atheism, profanity or scandal, and for encouraging piety and setting up the worship of God in families'. Additions would include William Ramsay in Nether Cramond, who had avoided joining Mr Somerville's session.

The next piece of business at the first sessional meeting was to arrange for minister and sessioners to visit all the families in the parish, collect names and organise a catechising and examination, an exercise that had apparently lapsed during the latter part of Somerville's ministration. The parishioners were to assemble variously in a conveniently large house in each of six districts, where the minister would preach to each group and then exhort them to observe their general duty as Christians and the particular obligations attending their station in life. This exercise was completed on 27 December, and the minister then began holding his annual 'diets of examination'.

One innovation for Cramond was Hamilton's custom of holding a monthly meeting 'for mutual conference and prayer' between minister and sessioners. In April 1691 he also instituted the practice of 'privy censures' for session and session clerk, which involved sessioners withdrawing two at a time while their conduct was discussed by the rest. And, as was already mentioned, he began thirty minutes of 'evening exercise' for Nether Cramonders after the two regular Sunday preachings.

The reaction to some of these practices was disappointing. Hamilton's first Monday meeting for prayer and conference with the sessioners was attended by five people, including the clerk, and few of the elders ever showed great enthusiasm for devoting one working morning a month to extra religious exercises. It was just as difficult to get adequate attendance at the weekly sessional meetings. At one on 24 July 1690, just after a new leet of twelve elders had been formally admitted to office, the minister and those present 'regretted the frequent paucity of the session members', a complaint monotonously renewed. On 14 May 1691 Hamilton reproved several members for absenting themselves from both the Monday meetings and the sessions, and warned that they would be named and censured if they did not amend their ways. In December he told them that the habitual absentees would be noticed when presbytery visited Cramond. Two of the chief offenders, neither of whom attended the 'privy censures' held in June 1692, were John and Thomas Wells, and Thomas was singled out on this occasion for ceasing to take his turn collecting for the poor at services. He made the excuse that he had no-one to share the duty with him. Hamilton also reproved the session for not coming to the monthly meetings: 'he supposed', he said plaintively on 3 December 1691, 'that it might tend to their mutual edification'. On the previous Sunday he had exhorted parishioners in general to attend the sermons more assiduously–as it was, 'there was scarcely the face [appearance, shape] of a congregation to be seen in the church' on Thursdays.

To improve attendance at sessions, those present at the meeting of 3 December 1691 voted that anyone absent without a valid excuse would be fined 6s. Scots for each occasion. All the same, they were again 'ill satisfied' at their fewness on 31 December, and only four members were present on 28 January 1692. On 6 June the minister added to his usual reproaches the accusation that elders were not visiting their bounds more often, and did not accompany him when he went there to conduct his annual examinations. The business of harvest actually caused three elders to break a Fast Day in August 1690. William Johnston and his brother and fellow-elder John were sharply rebuked before the others for allowing their corn to be cut that day, and made the excuse that it was not their own servants who were involved: it was hired shearers who had insisted on working, presumably because they were paid by piecework. The Johnstons were judged to share the guilt for not preventing it. John Wells at Peggy's Mill was similarly charged for allowing his mill to grind on the same day, and all were warned that they would be dismissed from office if they did it again. In the same month James Aikman was suspended briefly after some of the elders of the West Kirk parish wrote to say that he had been seen in the West Port, Edinburgh, 'overtaken with drink scandalously'. A promising candidate for eldership, James Kay in Grotthill, had been 'laid by' as 'unfit' at present, for unstated reasons, in July that year.

Already before Mr Somerville's departure the poor box had been empty. All the same, parishioners took up a generous special collection of £5 sterling (£60 Scots) for French (Huguenot) and Irish protestants in May. From October 1689 onwards the treasurer's accounts show an overwhelming stream of poverty-stricken 'strangers' passing through Cramond, many of them refugees from Ireland and threatened, in the words of a proclamation issued by the royal Council, by 'the sword of a barbarous enemy in the present distress of Ireland by the prevailing of an antichristian party there'. It is impossible to tell whether any of the Irish exiles actually settled in Cramond, although in August 1690 Matthew Young was given some money, 'having the burden of his three sisters from Ireland', and the family of Moses Cherry, who attended Cramond school as a 'poor [subsidised] scholar' in 1690, had come from Ireland and returned there about November 1694. Four people for whom a collection was made on presbytery's recommendation on 16 January 1690 were two students of philosophy, 'Mr David Thomson, a conformist recanted' and Mr Tolin, an Irishman disinherited by his parents for turning protestant. John Wilson, 'an aged stranger and a great sufferer' (from religious persecution is understood), was given 14s. from the poor box on 14 January 1692.

Besides the refugees from Ireland the stream of unfortunates included war-widows, like 'a woman stranger from Holland with four children' whose husband had been killed at Atholl in the army of William of Orange, Mary Stewart whose husband had been killed at Derry, another whose husband had been killed at Bothwell Bridge when, in June 1679, Monmouth and English troops had defeated an army of Covenanters, and several women widowed at the battle of Killiecrankie, where 'Bonnie Dundee' and his Highlanders had won a bloody but ineffective victory for the Jacobites on 27 July 1689. Charity was also given to various soldiers, like John Robison, 'a soldier under the surgeon's hand of his wounds received at Killiecrankie'. Other victims were an old man and, on another occasion, a merchant, robbed by the Highlanders. The sick included people afflicted by palsy, blindness, 'the crewels' (scrofula) and a child who needed to be 'cut for the gravel' (kidney or gall-stones). These were, in addition to the usual parade of distressed gentlefolk, widows with small children, 'Mr Donald Fashion, a poor schoolmaster', 'sea-broken men' and even a stranger from Jersey, and Cramond's own 'extraordinary' poor, like Robert Wauchop the blue-gown, 'lying sick in the House of the Hill'.

While old loans and the interest on them remained unpaid and the current heritors took money from the poor's fund to meet their obligations over repairs, sessions did their best to find cash where they could. To combat the expectation that couples found guilty of antenuptial fornica-tion would get back at least half their 'pledge of marriage' after they made satisfaction for their lapse, they enacted in 1690 that the whole pledge would be confiscated for the poor unless the parties gave in a written petition pleading poverty, when their case would be judged on its merits. Of subsequent applicants, only one – a shoemaker – was turned down. They also enacted that parishioners who chose to marry in other parishes must pay a 'gratification' amounting to half-a-dollar (28s. Scots) for farmers and their children, and 14s. for servants and cotters. The same, or more, might be charged to anyone who wished to be married on a day other than the regular Thursday 'preaching day'.

On 26 December 1689 sessional attention had also been drawn to the loss of income when parishioners of other places brought their dead to be buried at Cramond, using their own mortcloth instead of hiring Cra-mond's. If the pall of another parish was used in the procession, the session declared, it must either be removed from the coffin at the kirk stile or the mourners pay half-a-crown to Cramond poor box. In the latter case, the beadle was empowered 'to seize upon their mortcloth and keep the same aye and till they pay the same', and must explain the rules when asked to make a grave for any non-parishioner. Did any unseemly tussles occur over the corpse in such circumstances?

Restrictions (much resented) were placed upon the 'ordinary poor' in April 1691: if any married, their pension was not to be increased but rather decreased, 'especially if their marriage be to their advantage', and when any died after being maintained from the poor box for a year or more, any goods or plenishing they left were to be sold for the benefit of the box. Further, none was to have a pension increased without making specific, personal, petition to the session.

Naturally, proper sabbath observance once more became an object of prime concern for sessions. The habitually unruly Daniel Millar notably caused scandal in June 1692 when he bought a loaf of bread in Nether Cramond from the parish's sole baker after the Sunday services and openly carried it through the churchyard in sight of the dispersing congregation. Sunday invigilations were, of course, renewed and caught people drawing water from wells, gathering kale, carrying tools from Edinburgh, drinking in the Nether Cramond inn or cutting a child's hair. Two women strangers were found at the time of afternoon sermon in John Young's house (inn?) 'and meat roasting at the fire'. Similar breaches occurred on fast days when parishioners took salmon and Jean Smith's daughter Jean Harrower was delated for 'knocking of beir', i.e. cracking barley for the pot.[2] Helen Hutson, seen taking kale from her yard, confessed to the minister and was allowed to receive a private rebuke from two elders when she said that if she had to face the whole session 'it would turn her light in mind as she had been formerly'. The sessioners duly gave regular reports on such habitual absentees as the Gloag family in the Shoreside (whose men sometimes made the excuse that they had to stay home to row the ferry), the Gellon brothers, who were market gardeners, the midwife Jean Smith, who never entered the church unless she had to bring a child for baptism, and Margaret Wright, 'the goodwife of Grotthill', who explained that she was aged and often sickly, but promised to come now and then when able.[3]

Drinking, such as frequently tempted the pensioner sisters Elisabeth and Marjorie Crie, was naturally a continuing target, especially on the sabbath. On the holiday of Handsel Monday – which fell on 1 January in 1691 – John Ballantyn and his wife (the former adulteress Bessie Rae), Henry Millar and his wife (Margaret Carle) and William Carle were seen drunk and fighting in Nether Cramond. Next January the session enacted that hereafter nobody must sell ale at service time on Sundays, or drink at home or in 'the hostler houses'. Among offenders caught by invigilating elders in Nether Cramond was Thomas Johnston, son of James Johnston and Rebecca Mungell, who was seen on 27 November 1692 carrying a ten-pint barrel of ale from Agnes Fairholm's house through the Green. When challenged, he took it back to Fairholm's house.

For the third time Jean Smith outfaced minister and session. On Sunday 20 December 1691 the two elders inspecting Nether Cramond at service time saw her carrying a stoup of ale into her house and hastily closing the door behind her. When one 'chapped' at the door Jean refused to open it. The elders then cunningly went to church, came out before the sermon had ended, and Jean, her son John Harrower and several other people were found drinking. Jean's story to the session was that the wife of John Knight, gardener in Lauriston, had felt ill in church and been helped to Jean's house by Harrower and two women. William Waddell had followed, thinking that it was his own wife who had been taken ill. (She was due to give birth very shortly.) Few of the session believed this tale of emergency medical attention, but they were unable to refute it, and Mr Hamilton had to be content with upbraiding Jean for breach of sabbath and for her habitual failure to attend church. It was at this time that he attributed her son's violence towards her as a 'judgement'.

The minister's various visitations of the parish regularly brought up cases of 'scandals and variances'. In December 1691 during his visit to the Drylaw area some of those present at his examination passed on gossip about relations between John Smith and Eupham Story. Initial questioning produced no material evidence on the subject, but Mr John Hamilton did not give up easily. When Smith was about to leave his service at Whitsun next year, his employer, Lady Drylaw, was asked to retain his wages 'until the scandalous reports of him be afterwards tried'. A month after that Smith and Story came before the session. It appeared that a whole group of people had attended the secular bridal at Pilton for the new marriage of Jean Taylor, widow of John Nimmo, tenant there. After the party Eupham, Smith, the sisters Helen and Mary Howat and the piper John Johnston had gone to Cleickhim Inn and drunk there in the house of John Davidson until late. (Davidson's wife was also present, 'in childbed'.) Eupham then slept the night with Margaret Renny in Lady Drylaw's house but 'no evil was done by them'. The session forbade Story to keep company with Smith, whose wages were to be detained further in case 'any scandal should be made out against him', and told Margaret Renny 'to carry herself more warily'. Apparently nothing more did emerge to John Smith's discredit, and Eupham Story married someone else, moved to the Dean and was convicted, on her husband's admission, of antenuptial fornication in December the same year.

These examinations were also an occasion for peacemaking endeavours. On 12 June 1690 Margaret Anderson complained that before witnesses among her neighbours in Nether Cramond Margaret Johnston had called her a 'ridden witch'. Margaret admitted this, but said that Anderson had been so called by others twenty years before. Moreover, Anderson had called her a 'loun'. On the session's orders, Johnston knelt and asked forgiveness from God and from Margaret Anderson for slandering her, and offered to be reconciled, but Anderson refused to forgive her. The session told them to make up, threatening that if they heard any more of it they would have them publicly rebuked and also 'scrapped out of the poor roll'.

After a period of quiescence Rachel Cochran was at loggerheads with her neighbours in Nether Cramond, Margaret Gibson and Agnes Henry. On 14 May 1691 the elder James Dundas was asked to speak to Rachel and reconcile the parties. Next year Rachel brought a complaint against Alison Mason, who had abused her good name, both to her face and behind her back, by calling her Rachel Henderson. When Alison was asked why she had slandered Rachel, and Rachel's deceased parents, in this way, she could only say that she had heard several other people miscall Rachel thus before she did. She was told either to produce some of those responsible, or else face punishment for originating the slander herself.

At the same time as Rachel's first variance was dealt with, the elders of the bound reported a long and irreconcilable quarrel between John Wilson, his brother-in-law Daniel Millar and Dan's brother John Millar, all in Upper Cramond, and six people in Nether Lennie were to be debarred from communion or made to perform penance if they did not reach amity. The women of the Millar family were twice involved in flyting with neighbours and threatened with expulsion for any repetition, and in November 1691 John Hodge was reported for drunkenness and irreverent carriage towards his father William Hodge. The Hodges did not answer their second summons. Three elders, told to rebuke them privately, reported that they had promised with God's grace not to be found in the like again. On that assurance, and more particularly 'because the said William is crackbrained', the session forbore to inflict any further censure.

In June 1692 another visitation of the parish brought the report that Bessie Johnston, wife of the Nether Cramond tailor John Sim, and Margaret Carle were 'in variance' and the recently married William Burnton or Brunton and his wife 'contentious' – they were rebuked for fighting each other. Bessie Johnston then came before the session on 23 June and complained in person that Margaret Carle, now married to Henry Millar, had called her 'bitch' and 'whore'. The previous March a complaint made directly to the elder of the bound, John Aikman, came from Margaret Wright the goodwife of Grotthill, who accused two of her own servantmen of miscalling her and one of her women servants witches and whores and cursing and fighting. The session simply told Aikman to pass on their advice to Margaret to 'thrust' the offenders out of her service.

'Examining of scandals' was avowedly a prime aim of session meetings. Informants were often anonymous, but censorious neighbours may be suspected. Who complained when, before her marriage to (and antenuptial fornication with) Henry Millar, Margaret Carle was accused of 'scandalous carriage' in sleeping habitually in the house of her widowed father with nobody else there? She asserted that she went there only in the daytime to help him bandage his sore arm, and spent nights in Thomas Rankin's house. Disbelieving this, the session forbade her to stay with her father at night unless she took another woman to lie with her. Certainly the Carle family had a bad reputation. Evidently more was also suspected than recorded when James Broun the slater was told to desist from his 'scandalous' occupancy of Margaret Kello's bed while she slept with the woman next door, or when the session noted a long-standing scandal occasioned by Thomas Adamson in Nether Cramond and his wife Helen Baxter entertaining Alexander Grinton in their house, 'both night and day'. Helen Baxter was a natural target for gossip, with two fornications in her past, the second with Adamson before their marriage.[4]

When not quarrelling among themselves or abusing their mistress, the goodwife of Grotthill's servants kept a close eye on the activities of Margaret Drummond. The ensuing story may be told in the words of the minutes for the three sessional meetings of 22 and 29 May and 12 June 1690. On 22 May there was cited

> Margaret Drummond in Grotthill, spouse to Richard Johnstoun, being delated for her scandalous carriage in her husband's absence, being seen by James Angus and Jean Scot, servants to the goodwife of Grotthill, upon sabbath last at night to have opened her door about 10 o'clock at night to John Johnstoun, ane unmarried person living in the Dean, and immediately she closed her door again and entertained him all night in her house, her own husband not being at home and seldom comes home by reason of variance betwixt him and her. And when challenged by one of the members of session she confessed the same, but denied that she had committed wickedness with him. As also, being challenged, she confessed that she had entertained a man who came out of her country from the Castle of Drummond two nights about Yule last, her husband being from home, and no other person being in the house with her.

On 29 May Margaret appeared before the session

and being enquired at by the minister why she carried herself so scandalously on sabbath night was eight days . . . she answered that Adam Johnstoun in Newhaven, and Adam, Andrew, James and John Johnstouns his sons, also his daughter and good-son, had trysted to meet at the Dean that sabbath with Richard Johnstoun her husband, and that he had mistrysted them that day and gone to Borrowstouness. And when the foresaid persons had been at the Dean that day and not found him, they came to her house at Grotthill before the forenoon sermon and that she conveyed them to the Crew, and went in with them to Thomas Gray's house there, and helped them to drink a quart of ale, and then left them and presently returned home. And that the same sabbath night about 9 o'clock at night the said John Johnstoun came to her house . . . and chapped at the door and she opened to him. And that the door fell to of its own accord, as it ordinarily does. And that he sat down and lighted a pipe of tobacco and then rose and stood in the floor a little and craved from her some money that she owed to him. And immediately went away. And that he stayed not in her house all night, nor so much as a quarter of an hour.

'And why then came not these witnesses who had informed against her to the door at that time and challenged her?' The minister also challenged the said Margaret Drummond why she had entertained a young man at Yule last in her house two nights? To which she answered, that it was true she had done so – she had kept the said young man called John Clemat in her house two nights and that she could not refuse him lodging, seeing he came out of that country from whence she came and she knew his parents, and especially when the goodwife of Grotthill and James Kay had refused him lodging in a rainy night. And that he was seeking threshing or any other week's work but could have none. The minister asked her why she took not in one of the goodwife of Grotthill's servant men to lie with him, or one of her women to lie with her? She answered she could get none of them.

This day James Angus, servant to the goodwife of Grotthill, one of the witnesses, . . . declared that upon that sabbath night when he and Jean Scot, servitrix to the goodwife of Grotthill, were sitting at the door taking off their clothes for going to their beds, he saw John Johnstoun go to Margaret Drummond's door and enter the house, and that the door falls not to of its own accord as she affirmeth, but he durst not go to challenge them, fearing her husband Richard Johnstoun, who is a malicious, ill-set person and had broken a whip-staff over his head upon the account of that business since. But that he saw Jean Scot go to the door and he left them and went to his bed. But also he saw the foresaid Adam Johnstoun and his sons at her house that same sabbath day in the forenoon, and that the said Margaret Drummond went away with them to the Crew.

Jean Scot also saw Adam and his sons there and added that Margaret returned from the Crew before the morning sermon was over:

And that night about 9 o'clock she saw John Johnstoun go to Margaret Drummond's door and chap three times, and immediately the door was closed upon them, and that she went to the door and saw that it was locked, for she discerned the bolt of the door to be locked, and that forthwith she went in and told the goodwife of Grotthill, her landlady, and her son, and desired them to rise out of their beds and challenge the matter and they would not.

Faced with the testimony of both neighbours, Margaret made the damning admission that her door did not in fact close of itself. The session then ordered that Margaret and all the Johnstons should be cited to appear before them in two weeks' time. On 12 June John Johnston came to the session:

requiring from them a testimonial from his infancy to Martinmas last, at which time he went from this parish. The session refused to give him one until he were cleared of that scandal. And being examined by the minister in face of the session, where he was all night on Saturday before that sabbath [that] he came to Margaret Drummond's house, he answered that he was in his master's house in the Dean all that night. And having his chest and clothes stolen out of the stable where he lay, his father, Adam Johnstoun in Newhaven, and his brethren and sister came tomorrow, being the sabbath, to the Dean by an appointment to visit him and comfort him, and then he and they all went together unto Blackhall, where they drank three chopins of ale, and then to Grotthill to Margaret Drummond's house and took her along with them to the Crew at 11 o'clock that sabbath and drank a quart of ale there in Thomas Gray's house, and then went to his father's house in Newhaven and dined there. And at night [he] returned to Margaret Drummond's house in Grotthill and chapped at her door and went in before the gloaming, and lighted a pipe of tobacco and then went away. The minister asked him what his errand was to Margaret Drummond. . . . He answered to crave some money from her which she owed to him. The minister told him there were six days of the week in which he should crave his debts and not on the sabbath day, and challenged him why he was not rather at the church, for he had spent that sabbath ill by prophaning it exceedingly. . . .

Adam Johnston also appeared

and confessed that he and his sons were all together that sabbath at Dean, Blackhall, Grotthill and Crew and drank there three pints of ale. The minister sharply reproved him for prophaning the sabbath day and giving ill example to his children and said he would inform the minister of their parish of Leith of their abuse of the sabbath. . . . [He also] reported that he had challenged Thomas Gray in Crew and his spouse for selling ale to the foresaid persons on the sabbath in time of sermon and assured them if they should be found guilty of the like hereafter they should be brought to public censure, and they promised never to do the like hereafter.

Margaret's husband seems not to have answered the summons. He might be on bad terms with his wife, but still thrashed her officious neighbour, Angus. Margaret herself subsequently fled Cramond. No testimonial was to be given to her until 'purgation' of the scandal occurred.

There was still less privacy available in Nether Cramond. In January 1691 John Tailor, the man with a past record for 'incest' in Larbert and for habitual drunkenness and disorderly behaviour in Cramond, made a drunken public declaration in the house of the smith Francis Wilson that he could prove that James Reid had committed adultery with Agnes Crauford.[5] Investigation produced a number of witnesses who gave some support to Tailor's allegations. Margaret Bishop said she had seen James Reid lying in the foreside of Agnes Crauford's bed with his feet hanging over. When she reproved him he came out of the bed and broke down the curtain, then asked her for a 'prin' (pin) to mend it with, which she refused. William Mylne had then come in and accused James of lying in bed beside Agnes, 'that was drunk'. James was supposed to have been in the bed with her 'as long as one might have gone to the head of the town and returned'. Tailor, subsequently challenged to produce more than hearsay evidence, could only add that about two years before Agnes Cowan had come to his house and said to his wife, 'Jonet Cuthell, will you go down and see a sport? James Reid with Agnes Crauford even now!' Whereupon Jonet Cuthell went down to Agnes Crauford's house, and saw her alone with James Reid, who was sitting on her bedside.

John Young in Nether Cramond, cited as a further witness, said that he knew Agnes and James 'together often and late enough in Agnes Crauford's house, but he would never meddle in that business'. He was willing to add that he often heard them talking through the thin partition between the two houses, and that the tailor lad looked through a hole and saw them kissing each other several times. For himself, however, he 'never saw anything himself, nor would meddle the least in that affair'. Although Tailor was formally discredited as a drunken tale-bearer, never to be accepted as a witness again, the evidence seemed sufficient to get Agnes and James discharged from conversing together, under the pain of being esteemed guilty of the crime of adultery.

Elisabeth Crie subsequently reported that on 21 April at night James Reid had come down to Agnes Crauford's house, very drunk, and had sent out John White, Agnes's husband, to fetch two chopins (about two English quarts) of ale, 'and fell asleep there in the seat'. The tinker's wife then came in and led James out of the house, claiming that she was taking him to Elisabeth Ker's house to give him a pint of ale. When he had gone, John White went to bed, whereupon his wife followed Reid out of the house. And then next night Reid went again to Agnes's house, and when he saw Elisabeth Crie there he kicked her ('struck her with his feet'). Elisabeth told the minister that she had often seen Reid sitting alone with Agnes, and within the last week she had seen them conversing twice or thrice in the same day, but 'never saw any unseemly carriage betwixt them'.

The next thing was that the couple were seen together in Edinburgh, and returning home in company with each other. And on the night of a congregational Fast William Ramsay, the elder, and the session clerk were told that James Reid and Agnes were alone in her house, took two witnesses and found them together. Agnes said she couldn't prevent James coming ('he would not for her refrain his coming thither'), and when Mr Forrest asked him why he contravened the order of the session, James said rudely that 'he would not be hindered by the session or any of its members to converse with her when he pleased, and he hoped ere it were long they should get other things should trouble them more'. The session decided that if the pair didn't abstain from each other's company in future they would have to be tried by presbytery. Agnes Crauford and Margaret Kello were both objects of a sessional act of 29 January 1691 forbidding any private school to operate within a mile of the parish school, because children were being 'spoiled in their learning' and the parish schoolmaster deprived of fees. Apart from being almost certainly unable to write so much as her name, Agnes was hardly a good mentor for youth.[6] In November 1696 the telltale Tailor, possibly to the general relief, was 'intending for London anent his civil affairs' and the session first gave him a rex dollar and then, because he had no means of getting there, lent him another.

Some others of those who bore witness against their neighbours had not themselves enjoyed a blameless reputation. On Thursday 4 June 1690 a wedding was taking place in Nether Cramond. Marion Gillies, who had been watching from her window, went to Isobel Pratts' house and invited Isobel and Dorothy Gibson, the smith's wife, to look out. They then saw Jonet McMath come to the yard where William More was lying overtaken with drink, and watched Jonet lead him into a ruinous house, where the couple lay down together and William, 'as they apprehended, committed fornication with her in their sight'. Dorothy then 'went through several houses seeking Jonet McMath's mother to set her on them'. The women may well have been suspicious of the pair to begin with, since it was subsequently admitted that they had first had relations twelve months before. But an interesting feature of the case is that Marion Gillies had produced a child by Thomas Shedd some years before they married, and at this same sessional hearing on 12 June Isobel Pratts brought her testimonial of satisfaction for fornication with a man in the New Kirk parish, Edinburgh. Had these women 'internalised' the ethical teaching of the kirk, or was their attitude 'I didn't get away with it, so why should she?'

Sometimes stories were not believed, however careful their details. In late 1689 Jonet Bleckie, who had been in service in the Canongate in Edinburgh, returned to her father in Nether Cramond, where she gave birth. Questioned on 23 January 1690 Jonet alleged that she had been married 'by Father Dumbar, a popish priest', to a soldier-servant of the duke of Gordon when he was stationed in Edinburgh Castle. Her husband 'was long gone since to the North Highlands', like one of the witnesses, John Macintosh. The other witness was 'Anna Bane, a taverner young woman, who lived with Mr Irvin, a changer above the Canongate Tolbooth'. The session thought Jonet was not married at all, and she had to confess that she had become pregnant before the alleged wedding. (In fact it emerges much later that this had been her second 'fall'.) She was told that she must 'satisfy' either in the parish of the Canongate or in Cramond, 'where the whoredom is most notour'. On 29 May Andrew McFarlane, himself in trouble for threatening and abusing his neighbours and soon to be threatened with dismissal from his employment if he failed to bring a testimonial, asserted that Jonet had lain with a soldier between

Leith and Granton. She admitted that a soldier had 'conveyed' her towards Granton, but denied any unseemly carriage between them. McFarlane failed to bring his promised witnesses to the contrary and, like John Tailor, was convicted of 'unjust and unnecessary false witnessing', told he would never be accepted as a witness in future and would be severely punished if he did anything of the sort again. Jonet, however, was 'exhorted to carry herself more warily'.

A woman whose misbehaviour had been publicised might well be seen as easy prey. Jean Anderson had been allowed to stay in Cramond in November 1691 on condition that she performed penance for a 'fall' in Edinburgh. She was in the habit of going to a garden in Drylaw to get kale, and one afternoon George Wilson, who worked there, had taken her to the backyard, locked the door (he said that was his practice with anyone who came in), threw her down and, forcibly stopping her mouth, held her arm beneath her head, and lay carnally with her. This, Jean said, was all due to the fact that Wilson had been present earlier when John Frazer and Laurence Wright had taunted her by saying, 'Jean, you would not refuse a man'. When Jean later saw Frazer and his wife she said ironically to him, 'I thank you, John, for your speeches formerly!', adding, 'George Wilson has tried me too surely now'.

Frazer's wife gave evidence that Jean had said to John, in front of several other people, 'Woe worth you, John Frazer!' He asked if George Wilson had been 'trying her', and she answered 'By her faith, he had, and that too surely'. Eventually Wilson admitted his guilt, although he claimed that Jean had deliberately gone to the garden on a number of occasions and tempted him. Apparently she herself had admitted putting his hands into her hair on one such visit. Mr Hamilton told Jean that she was most to blame for her provocative behaviour and 'having played the whore before', and she was ordered to go to the West Kirk and satisfy for her previous fornication there, before doing her penance in Cramond.

For a time before Whitsun 1689 Jean McBaith had worked as wet-nurse for William Inglis in Craigcrook, one of the most substantial farmers in the parish. In late December she returned to Cramond and gave birth in a house there. To two of the women who attended her delivery she said that while in Inglis's service she was coming back from Edinburgh in the twilight one evening when, on the highway at a place on the border of the parish called the Cocklers' Rest, she was forced by a man who alighted from his horse and lay with her. She asked his name and he said it was Finlaw Martin and he was unmarried. She had never seen him before or since. When this was repeated to the session they viewed the story with suspicion, not least because Jean had previously been accused of fornication in both Edinburgh and Corstorphine. Furthermore, no such 'Finlaw Martin' ever came to light. (It is still more suspicious that there was a man of that distinctive name living in Nether Cramond but nobody suggested that he was the person meant.) Reading between the lines, it looks as though the real suspect was William Inglis. His wife certainly seems to have thought so.

On 23 January 1690 Jean came before the session with her child, asking to have it baptised. Permission was refused until Inglis agreed to become cautioner for Jean and to help find 'Finlaw Martin'. Failing such undertakings, no baptism would be allowed. He therefore gave his bond for £200 and agreed to pay Jean's penalty of £12. The child was then baptised, sponsored by Inglis's servant Thomas Rankin. Inglis asked the session to admit Jean to penance at once, and offered to pay her penalty out of hand, so that she could be admitted to service 'for she had nothing to live upon', but they refused until Jean brought testimonials showing that she had completed penance in her previous parishes. On 15 February, however, they agreed to allow her to delay her penance in Cramond until Candlemas 1691, when she should have finished her engagement to nurse a gentleman's child in Edinburgh. Meanwhile, on 10 July 1690, Inglis again went to the session, again asking to pay Jean's monetary penalty and be relieved of his bond. This time they agreed and expressed willingness to accept any different cautioner that could be found, 'considering that his cautionry for her was the cause of dispeace between him and his wife'.

Refusing to absolve a penitent before the fine was duly paid could create an awkward trap. Early in January 1692 Jean Forbes, 'who is scandalised with James Sim', was being sought at her previous lodging in the Dean Village on the Water of Leith. On 18 February the clerk reported that both of them had taken service with Mr William Gordon, laird of Jean's home in Easter Pencaitland and kirk treasurer of that parish. Both of the pair confessed their fornication to Cramond kirk session and Jean began her penance on the pillar, but said she had no money to pay her penalty because when the laird of Easter Pencaitland received a letter about her from the minister of Cramond he promptly 'thrust her from his service' and detained the wages due to her to cover the £4 of the fine. Jean therefore asked Cramond session to write and get the money from him. Unhappily for her, in July the session delegated this to John Menzies of Cammo, their own kirk treasurer and a very dilatory gentleman. On 1 December it was noted that Jean had neither paid nor made her third appearance on the pillar, although Sim had done both and was absolved on 22 December.

Jean's case was carried over on 5 January 1693, when Cammo had evidently done nothing about getting her money, and not surprisingly, when her name next came up before the session, on 7 October 1694, she was found to be fugitive, 'having fled from the exercise of discipline'.

Repenting a betrothal could also prove expensive. Margaret More and John Gilcrise were twice 'proclaimed' in February 1690 before calling the marriage off (she 'quatt' him and he 'passed from her'). They had laid a rex dollar and a leg dollar in pledge, and she had the rex dollar returned but the other was confiscated. A year later, however, after she had married John Lachlan the other dollar was restored to him for present relief in his poverty.

In 1690 Eupham Spotswood gave in her name to marry John Young in Currie. When William Waddell (alias Weddell or Warden, son of the Helen Hutson who feared for her sanity if she had to face the full session) heard of it he went to the minister and asked for the banns to be stopped. He told the session that he and Eupham had kept company and communing together since last bere-seed time, and were fully resolved to be married, but had decided to wait until next Whitsun. In the meantime they had fee'd themselves in service for the next half-year. Then just lately, as they stood before Mistress Corse's gate in Whitehouse, Eupham had given him her hand of her own accord and promised that she should never have another man. When Eupham was told this, she agreed that she and William had discussed marriage at the date mentioned, but she denied ever making any promise to him. Moreover, the previous Friday before giving in her name for proclamation with John Young she had sent for William and given him over because her father had not consented to his suit. William had to admit that no sworn promises had been exchanged, and said he was now willing to 'quit' Eupham, so her banns were allowed to go ahead. But, 'thinking that the said Eupham had not dealt fair with William Waddell', the session asked the minister to rebuke her sharply, and fine her if he thought fit. Waddell soon found himself another wife, and anticipated marriage with her by two months.

Once more minister and session went to great lengths to find the mother of an abandoned child when, on the night of Monday 30 November 1691, one was found at the door of the first house in Nether Cramond 'toun'. The minister was told and at once sent horsemen out in search of a stranger woman. A certain Elisabeth Leslie, with two other children, was discovered and brought to him but denied that the child was hers. In the meantime it was looked after by Andrew Henderson's wife, and the putative mother put under guard, at a cost of 8s. 6d. paid from the poor box to the two men who watched her all night. In the morning, 'after much pains taken upon her', she finally admitted being the mother, whereupon the minister gave her 5s. sterling (£3 Scots) and had her and her family removed from the parish bounds.

However strict the parish discipline, there were always likely to be difficulties about enforcement. Sessions were scrupulous to obtain either spontaneous confession or proof of accusations. When in February 1690 William Gray and Anna Waterston were suspected of premarital intercourse, William was reported to have 'bragged before company that he had lain carnally with her', but nothing could be done because both parties denied all accusations and no witnesses to William's boast came forward.

James Reid, the persistent companion of Agnes Crauford, was not the only person to resent sessional interference in his personal life. On 18 September 1690 when the minister was told that John Johnston and his wife Elisabeth Anderson in Nether Cramond were sheltering Elisabeth's pregnant niece Jonet Anderson, Jonet failed to obey a summons and the beadle was sent to fetch her aunt instead. Elisabeth, who answered the session's questions 'haughtily and impertinently', was assured that if she let her niece leave Cramond without appearing before them they would punish her for 'resetting' Jonet. Also, her present intransigent behaviour towards them would not be forgotten. John Gibson, accused of fornication with Margaret Duncan, demanded that she be brought to confront him and in another 'haughty and dubious' answer insisted that 'he was not to be his own accuser'. When some sabbath visitors were found in William Hardy's house and challenged for being out of the church, they gave the Nether Cramond invigilators 'rough and harsh answers'. William More eventually obeyed a summons to the session for fornication with Jonet McMath, but refused to do public penance until Jonet had completed hers, although under threat of dismissal from service he did enter the pillar next Sunday. James Cumin, too, was eventually made to appear to answer a charge of breach of sabbath by carrying his carpenter's tools from Edinburgh, but ignored the first three summonses. As a result of much similar disobedience the fee that those summoned had to pay the beadle was doubled in 1692.[7]

In November 1692 infants arrived too early in the marriages of John Howison and his wife Jonet Cleghorn and the beadle's son John Elder junior and his wife Mary McCullie or McCulloch. Both couples were told to appear on the pillar next Thursday, to be absolved after paying their fines. They were warned that contempt of the session in failing to do so would mean appearing on the pillar on three sabbaths as ordinary fornicators. Elder and his wife appeared on 1 December. Howison and his wife did not, and were told that after a third summons they would be called before presbytery and made to stand thrice each. After the third such summons had been carefully delivered to Howison in person at his house, the couple were publicly called thrice at the church door. Not only did they continue to ignore these summonses but they stated plainly that they refused to perform penance.

Their child had been allowed baptism on a joint undertaking by John Howison and his father that John would perform his penance, and an angry session now ruled that the couple should 'have no benefit of sealing ordinances to themselves or their [future] children in this parish' until they made satisfaction. The clerk was to notify this to neighbouring parishes and any parish to which John might move. John was probably kin to the heritor Alexander Howison of Braehead and emboldened to defy the session for that reason. For that reason, too, the session were determined to make an example of him, lest others be 'hardened' in sin by seeing him go unpunished, and they therefore determined to refer the case to presbytery. The minister offered Howison a last chance by holding back the appeal until presbytery next met. But it was not until 12 February 1693 that Howison and his wife appeared on the pillar – together and for a single time, after all – and were absolved. The session, or their clerk of his own accord, then recorded triumphantly 'and this as the good fruit of the reference from the session to the presbytery given in on 1 February [when] they, being cited to answer the presbytery, came and satisfied the church censure of the session of Cramond'. But whether it was eventually punished or not, such stubbornness, like antenuptial fornication itself, would be widely noted and help to undermine the authority of minister and session.

As ever, employers were often remiss in seeing that new servants brought a testimonial, and people could have been settled some time in Cramond before the session noted the lack. When one *was* produced it might be inadequate, like Andrew McFarlane's two lines from the laird of Hallyards covering the quarter-year spent in his service, or well out of date, like one issued by Cramond to a native of the parish who had left some sixteen years earlier, or that shown by an aged stranger-woman from the parish she had left six years previously.[8]

That woman left promptly when told to get a testimonial for the six months preceding her arrival. The removal of some other undesirables was easier to demand than achieve. Heritors agreed to cooperate but did little in practice, so that on 5 January 1693 the hope was expressed that 'the heritors' Act made against scandalous and disorderly persons' in October 1691 and renewed in August 1692 might be 'made practicable'. William Carle, who had come from somewhere up north and was asked for a testimonial on 15 February 1690, said that 'some years ago' he had given one to Mr John Somerville, then minister. The session asked either to see it or to have a written receipt from Somerville. Carle produced neither and on 1 June 1691 and again on 8 October that year Lady Cramond or her baron court was asked to expel him from Nether Cramond. In July 1692 he was sentenced by her court to be committed to the House of Correction if he did not leave by Lammas (1 August). On 15 December Carle, Andrew McFarlane and Elisabeth Harrower (a daughter of Jean Smith who had fled and was wanted for failing to obey a summons to the session and for suspected theft in Currie, where she had deserted her husband) were referred once more to her court and Lady Cramond was to be asked bluntly to 'cause thrust them out of her ground. And the Lady Cramond and her court are desired to be more careful in putting Acts into execution, that vice may be curbed and piety may be more countenanced and advanced' – and, by implication, the session receive some backing.

The act of January 1693 was inspired by the failure of presbytery to take action against James Hill, a servant of the elder John Wells in Peggy's Mill, whose disorderly marriage by an outed minister had first come to the session's attention in July 1692. Cammo, as a Justice of the Peace, was now asked to get him expelled from the parish. Hill's offence of clandestine marriage was seen to be compounded when a woman arrived in Cramond with the child she accused him of fathering while he had lived in Fife.

William Carle resisted all efforts to expel him and was eventually enrolled among the ordinary poor of Cramond. Andrew McFarlane also remained in the parish, which had already given him money when he was sick in November 1690, provided a winding sheet and coffin for a son who died in October 1691, would contribute school fees for his son John in January 1694 and pay for Andrew's own coffin when he died in November 1694, after which the parish supported his widow.

Sir William Paterson of Granton, that former persecutor of Covenanters, agreed in April 1691 to reopen the passageway previously stopped up by Sir Alexander Hope, out of personal regard for John Hamilton.[9] He is the only heritor on record at the time as taking an effective interest in the morals of his tenants and servants, in so far as he wrote once to the minister to say that his gardener had fathered a child by one of the women servants. Paterson undertook to see that the man did penance and was granted 'a line to have the child baptised'. During Hamilton's ministry, indeed, the parish heritors bulk large in the session minutes for two reasons only: their renewed squabbling over their rights to private seating in the church, and their persistent failure to meet their obligations over the needed repairs to church, manse, various offices, schoolmaster's house and churchyard walls.

By this time there was very little space left for erecting permanent seats for heritors and their tenants along the sides of the church. (The common people were accommodated on movable forms in the body of the church.) Viscount Tarbat, for one, had fulminated from time to time about his unjust treatment over seating and made it a ground for refusing to pay dues. After much negotiation, and mediation by Sir William Paterson, during 1691–2 matters were temporarily adjusted between Tarbat, Muir-house, Cammo and the dowager Ladies Lauriston and Drylaw, though at one point Muirhouse, tricky as ever, tried to support his claims by producing a falsified extract from earlier session minutes.[10] Any improvements that were authorised and made by one heritor tended, of course, to raise new objections from others who found that their light or view was now obstructed

Another acrimonious dispute occurred when Ann Houston, the widowed 'Lady Cramond',[11] enlarged the family seat and blocked one of the entry-ways enjoyed by George Hamilton of Barnton. At a heritors' meeting on 15 August 1692 Ann's lawyer criticised the Reverend John Hamilton for officiously and improperly trying to settle the matter himself 'in compliance with Barnton's inportunity [sic]'. When the matter came up again under John Hamilton's successor, the young William Hamilton, he declined to adjudicate, saying tactfully that he was too ignorant of hereditary rights in Cramond.

On that same 15 August 1692 John Hamilton received a call from Edinburgh presbytery. Cramond had previously fought off demands that he return to his charge in Ireland, and now spent much energy in unsuccessful resistance to this new takeover threat. It had earlier been said that the whole parish was unanimous in its support for him and would not be so loyal to any substitute. (The latter proved untrue, in the event.) Once Cramond had accepted that they could not prevent Edinburgh poaching their minister, on 28 December 1693 Barnton led heritors and elders – the two groups who now enjoyed rights of nomination – in a unanimous call to Mr Henry Hamilton, minister at Currie, 'to take the care and oversight of their souls' as next minister. This, however, was frustrated by presbytery, after hearing 'Cramond's reasons for [his] transportation and Currie's answers returned and Cramond's duplies and Currie's replies'. Four newly licensed preachers were reported to be available, and after hearing them the heritors and session voted unanimously to call the probationer Mr William Hamilton. ('Hamilton' was almost an occupational name for ministers at the time!)

William Hamilton turned out to be a great success as a pastor, combining personal popularity with, on the whole, little diminution of his predecessor's efforts to uphold godly discipline among the community. It was not to be his fault that examples of disorderly and irresponsible behaviour, already common enough despite the authoritarian rule of John Hamilton, would not lessen among some sections.

NOTES

1. *Hamilton's move to Ireland.* He had then stipulated that he should be free to return to Scotland whenever its church became 'free' once more: 23 Aug. 1692.
2. *Breaches of Sabbath.* Drawing water: 1 Oct. 1691; gathering kale: 17 Sept. 1691; carrying tools: 1 Oct. 1691; drinking: 1 Dec. 1692; hair-cutting: 10 Dec. 1691; roasting meat: 6 Nov. 1691; cracking barley: 17 Sept. 1691.
3. *Margaret Wright.* 6 June, 7 July 1692. She was in fact aged 55.
4. *Scandals.* Margaret Carle: 27 Feb. 1690; Margaret Kello: 5 Feb. 1691; Adamsons: 8 Oct. 1691.
5. *James Reid.* This was possibly the 'James Red' in Nether Cramond whose wife was paid £2 18s. 'upon the accompt of chirurgery upon some of the ordinar poor' on 29 Oct. 1691. Does this mean that Reid's wife (Christian Steill) herself practised as a surgeon?
6. *Private Schools.* Two more were being run by men: Archibald Logan in Upper Cramond and James Waker in Lauriston. Waker was aged and had no other means of support and was enrolled among the parish paupers on condition that he ceased teaching.
7. *Intransigence.* Gibson: 6 Nov. 1690; Hardy's visitors: 6 Nov. 1691; William More: 28 Jan. 1692. (Jonet McMath created a stir by standing up and leaving the pillar on her first appearance, but had the excuse accepted that she had thought that no sermon was to follow the 'lecture' – the part of the service conducted by the clerk as 'reader'); Cumin: 5 Nov. 1691.
8. *Inadequate Testimonials.* 17 July 1690; 6 Dec. 1689; 12 Nov. 1691.
9. *Unblocking passageway.* On 29 Nov. 1696, in return for a concession and in wording irresistibly reminiscent of the last act of *Don Giovanni*, Paterson also agreed 'to let the Lord Hopetoun's effigy come into his aisle' in the kirk.
10. *Falsified extract from the minutes.* 12 Nov. 1691.
11. *Lady Cramond.* Ann Houston had been left with a son, Sir John, born 23 September 1683, and four daughters when her husband, Sir James Inglis, died aged 28 in 1689.

SIX

Ministerial Problems, 1694–1709

The Reverend William Hamilton came to Cramond in September 1694 as the parish's second choice. A member of a family of noted Covenanting views, he had been baptised when young at one of the Covenanters' conventicles, and was a fitting person to continue the reformist policies of the Reverend John Hamilton. Cramond was his first ministerial charge: while awaiting a parish he had been 'governor' (i.e. tutor) to the earl of Dundonald at Paisley.[1]

Twenty-one years earlier his session clerk, precentor and parish school-master, Mr Thomas Forrest, had come to Cramond from a similar position. His long experience as an active participant in parish affairs must have been of great assistance to the new young incumbent. Hamilton also inherited a group of long-serving elders. In particular Alexander Howison of Braehead and James Dundas in Southfield, with their long service as treasurers and ruling elders (delegates to presbytery), lived for another eight years, while John Menzies of Cammo continued to serve the parish in the dual role of elder and Justice of the Peace throughout Hamilton's ministry.[2] At least two of those added to the session during this time were what the 1694 poll tax return called 'tradesmen' and not tenant-farmers: George Pollock was one of the parish's fifteen weavers and John Potter a mason.

Early in William Hamilton's ministry, on the other hand, three elders had their services dispensed with. In July 1695 the session noted that they did not 'incline to insist any further in pressing their attendance' upon George Linn and Thomas Wells, who had long distanced themselves from sessional activity, and on the same day the minister mentioned that John Aikman was generally known to have fallen (for the second time) 'into the sin of drunkenness, which was become notour and had given offence to the congregation'. He was deposed in August.

Personally, Hamilton seems to have been a merciful man, and well liked by his flock. There was, however, no question of departing from the rigid system of parish discipline that had been reinstated in 1689. Jean Gribb had sinned with a fellow-servant in the service of the elder, Baillie William Inglis in Nether Cramond. The father made one public appearance and had the child baptised before disappearing to Newcastle. Jean went to her mother in Kirkliston. On the morning of 22 February 1702 she called privately on the minister, who summoned two elders and the clerk to interview her. She was then permitted to 'stand' at that morning's service, because she lived at a distance and had difficulty in attending, her partner had already been convicted and partially censured, and her child was sick and likely to die. All the same, Jean had to make two further sabbath appearances. Upholding morality was more important than the welfare of mother and child: William Inglis, who had retained the wages due to her, pleaded her great poverty on 27 March 1703, but only to the extent that her monetary penalty was reduced from £4 to £3 Scots. Jean's child in fact lived to become a burden on Jean's mother in 1707, Jean herself having died in the meantime and no support being obtainable from the father.

Great care was taken to trace people, or to check doubtful details about their stories. Margaret Baverage, wanted for fornication in April 1699, was reported to be in Kinglassie. The minister there eventually replied to enquiries to say that she had fled, and Cramond then heard that she was in Abbotshall. Since the church there was vacant, Hamilton arranged to write to one of the ministers of the presbytery of Kirkcaldy. He applied to the minister of the Wemyss, and the woman finally returned from Kinglassie and was allowed to make her first two public appearances on one day, because she was living at such a distance. The next Sunday she stood the third time and was given a testimonial for her time in Cramond.[3]

When Christian Wright came to the parish with a child in 1698 and furnished a testimonial of good behaviour for the four years that she had lived in Mr James Webster's parish in Edinburgh, Hamilton had consulted Webster, who was evidently unaware that she had been guilty of fornication during that time. The testimonial was confiscated.

A woman who was brought to bed in Hugh Nimmo's change-house in August 1704 was interrogated by Thomas Forrest the clerk, who had called there on other affairs. She was the wife of a soldier, presently in Holland, and lived in Tarves, Aberdeenshire, but had come to Edinburgh to transact some business, hoping to complete the long journey home again in time for the birth. She had the proper documents, including a letter from her husband, and a watchmaker in Holyrood also confirmed her marriage.

Equally careful enquiries were made about the foster children of Cramond women. Margaret Carle, asked to identify the parents of the nurseling she took in after the death of one of her own children in 1704, could report that it had been born in fornication to the son of a Lord of the Session. In April of the same year Rebecca Nisbet, living in the Gladstone, told the session that the father of the child she was nursing was a Lieutenant Gilbert Broun, presently quartered at Longniddry. The child had been begotten in Corstorphine, the parents had satisfied church censure and Mrs Margaret Seatoun was paying the quarterly fee for nursing.

This enquiry brought to attention the fact that Rebecca had produced no testimonials from her previous residences, and she was told to bring them within a month. When she gave three testimonials from former employers she was told to take them back to the relevant parishes and get testimonials from the kirks there. She pleaded poverty and the session said they would defray her expenses. They then learned that Rebecca was housing her sister, Anne Nisbet, guilty of adultery in Edinburgh, and another pregnant stranger. Under pressure from the session and Rebecca's landlord, Archibald Lunn, they all left at Martinmas. About a year later Rebecca came wanting a testimonial for the two years she had spent in Cramond. The request was refused until she brought the testimonials she still owed. She then furnished one from Corstorphine and obtained Cramond's, after being rebuked for 'entertaining scandalous persons'.[4]

Early in 1696 when Alexander Linn produced a certificate of marriage from Mr John Murray, minister at Tynron in Nithsdale, Hamilton was asked by the session to write to Murray questioning its authenticity and asking whether it was known in Tynron that the couple had indulged in the antenuptial fornication to which they now confessed. In August, after Linn had drawn further attention to himself by fishing on the sabbath, Hamilton showed the testimonial to Murray's father, a minister in Edinburgh, who verified his son's signature and confirmed that the scandal had not been notorious in Tynron. Linn and his wife therefore performed their penance in Cramond.

A 'disorderly marriage' took place between Daniel McKenzie and Margaret Jackson, servitrix to the countess of Argyll in Pilton. On 6 February 1702 Daniel produced 'a sort of a testimonial' under the hand of Mr Samuel Mowat, 'sometime curate in Cranford John, but very confused and informally written, without the writer's name and subscription of witnesses'.[5] One of the witnesses remembered only that the marriage had taken place in the middle of the day. It was a market day, therefore Wednesday. He could not give the date, but thought that he would recognise the house again. The second witness, clearly a kinsman of the groom, was Colin McKenzie, a twenty-year-old apprentice to Mr Andrew Murray, surgeon in Edinburgh. He had witnessed the marriage in an Edinburgh tavern – identified as Scott's House in the Bishop's Land – on the previous 11 June. The couple were married, he knew, by a Mr

Mowat, who was unknown to him but he heard people say that he was a minister. Nine or ten other people were present, but he knew only two further McKenzies, Murdo and Donald. Donald lived in the north of Scotland. Although the 'disorderliness' of such casual affairs was obvious, the chance to bypass the time-consuming, cumbersome and expensive parish process would seem steadily more attractive in time to come.

The threat of refusing a testimonial when one was desired was used in October 1697 against the hind James Kay, who tried to avoid an appearance before Cramond session by claiming to be a parishioner of Corstorphine. When he died two years later, however, it was Cramond that undertook the maintenance of his orphan. The other threat, expulsion, successfully frightened at least one of Cramond's inhabitants. After Hamilton had left to become a professor at Edinburgh University, it emerged that Cramond had harboured a family of crypto-Catholics during his ministry. The father, George Clark, explained on 24 December 1710 that he had attended the kirk (and, indeed, had a daughter baptised there in July 1700), for fear that Hamilton would 'thrust him out of the parish' if the truth came out. The concealment was so successful that on 1 April 1709 Cramond had told presbytery that there were no papists in the parish.

Breach of sabbath and, increasingly, 'slighting the ordinances', i.e. failure to attend church, continued to be a major concern of sessions, and a minor battlefield between minister and elders on the one side and the less docile of their charges on the other. Great efforts were made to patrol the parish (especially, as always, Nether Cramond) at service time, in order to catch offenders and intimidate others into attending the sabbath sermonising. On 25 December 1695 it was agreed that elders would be best to vary the times of their invigilation. On 11 April 1697 the 'visitors' were again told to vary their times because Nether Cramonders simply hid ('keep themselves quiet in their houses') when the patrol was expected. As a result, in Nether Cramond there were found at home James Reid, Henry Millar and his wife Margaret Carle, Elisabeth Crie, William Marshall, Isobel Gloag (wife of the innkeeper Robert Mitchell) and Elisabeth Raeburn (wife of Thomas Crie, also an ale-seller); in Lauriston, Marion Hume and the gardener John Knight and his wife; in Muttonhole the innkeeper James Lees; in Cleickhim Inn James Tailor; in Crewe John Gilbert (an ale-seller); in Shoreside the ferryman and persistent absentee John Gloag. All were delated for frequent absenting, and any pensioners among them were to lose their next month's pay. On 17 April 1702 it was noted that 'several in the parish absent themselves from the public ordinances on the Lord's days'. The sub-treasurer, Dundas, should stay away from church and search Upper Cramond next Sunday, while on some Sundays others might search Nether Cramond 'privately', in addition to the invigilation by the collectors.

When Agnes Mitchell, wife of Robert Bowie, was accused of non-attendance at church somebody – was it one of the session? – alleged that one Sunday the invigilating elders had found her in Margaret Couper's house, 'hiding herself under a board' (i.e. table). This, however, proved to be a calumny (or at any rate unproven) when the clerk discovered no such incident recorded in the sessional minutes.[6] On the other hand, when, in May 1696, two elders found her husband in bed at service time, Alexander Gibson's wife in Muirhouse 'entreated the session to admonish him to frequent the public ordinances better'.

In March 1704 Agnes Haistie cheerfully admitted that she had stayed at home all one Sunday, keeping company with a young man, who was, she said, 'in suit of her for marriage'. She was a native of Cramond but before returning she had lived for several years in Edinburgh and had one child by a sailor there and another by the servant of a man in the Guards. When haled before Cramond session for her breach of sabbath, she said roundly that 'her staying at home was offensive to God and not to man'. This confused venture into theology deeply shocked the minister, who rebuked her for her haughty and foolish behaviour and answers, and exhorted her to humility and not to think highly of herself.

Absenteeism was, of course, frequently conjoined with drinking at service time, and in summer even those who had attended both services on the sabbath had to be told to refrain 'from their old profanation by gathering together at their doors or in the fields for worldly discourse'. No such gossippers were actually brought before the session for rebuke, but a variety of other unallowable Sunday activities earned censure. Invigilators in Nether Cramond found John Ramsay and his wife and four strangers taking their dinner in time of the afternoon's service, Charles Short, a miller at the Cockle Mill, and his wife staying home and drinking in sermon time, and John Gloag rowing some Edinburgh folk across in the coble to see 'a fish [stranded whale?] that came in on the other side'. The minister was recommended to deliver a private rebuke after the two mills of Fairafar and Peggy's Mill kept operating too long one Saturday night, even though careful enquiry revealed that it was an oversight, one of the millers having fallen asleep and those at the other mill having been deceived by the example of their neighbours into thinking that the sabbath had not yet started.[7]

It seems to have been as much the activity as the timing that puzzled the session so that they had to consult presbytery both when Jonet Linn and David Pillans sat drinking and arranging a foster-mother for their child during the afternoon service one Sunday, and the previous year when John Lachlan and Jonet McMath met with friends 'after sermons' in Robert Mitchell's inn to make a match between them. (See further Chapter 7, for both couples.) Presbytery ruled that matchmaking on the sabbath deserved a sessional rebuke.

The ubiquitous inns (or change-houses) and the informal establishments of ale-sellers appear time after time in accusations of excessive drinking. On 8 March 1700 James Waker junior and Alexander Millar (also junior?) in Upper Cramond were delated for excessive drinking 'from house to house', swearing and fighting. Alexander Millar tried to extenuate himself. After he and his neighbour, John Frazer, came from the kiln (at Peggy's Mill) he accompanied Frazer home and then happened to meet James Waker, so they went together to Millar's house and drank just one pint of ale, and then went to Daniel Millar's house and drank two pints and then turned towards Waker's but Waker pressed him to go to Edward Moubray's house. Alexander refused, saying that Edward and his wife would be in their bed, but Waker insisted and chapped hard at Moubray's door until Moubray rose and let them in. (It was then about 10 o'clock.) Putting together the accounts of Millar, Waker and Moubray, it seems that they got a pint of ale, and when a second had been filled for them Waker asked Millar whether it was true, as he had heard, that Millar had a shelly coat. Millar said that 'he desired him to forbear and not to liken him to an ill spirit'. But Waker called him that a second time, Millar threatened to throw the stoup at him and they began wrestling around the floor. According to both Waker and Moubray, Millar did throw the cup at Waker. Moubray had to get out of bed again and separate them. Moubray claimed that his guests were not drunk and he heard no swearing from them, but when he 'put them both to the door' he heard Alexander Millar say to James Waker that 'he thought the devil was in him'.

The proprietors of these informal ale-houses (Edward Moubray was a tailor by trade) could expect cavalier behaviour from their customers. On an earlier occasion David Martin, after a rough wooing of the widow Jonet Wilson, went to Moubray's house about sunrise to ask for a bed. The 'public room' in such houses probably contained the family beds, so that John Davidson's wife, who was lying in childbed, must have been close beside those who came one night in 1691 to drink and dance to the piper.

James Lees' change-house at Muttonhole came to sessional notice on several occasions. On 19 April 1700, in one of the catch-all enquiries held before the parish communion, accusations of 'scandalous carriage' and excessive drinking were made against a group of people belonging to the minor tenant-class who had variously drunk for three hours there on two successive Wednesdays. The moderator (i.e. the minister) and three elders were deputed to make enquiries. Mr Hamilton and the elder Robert Cleghorn went first to Hugh Nimmo's house and questioned Hugh's wife Agnes Bell, one of the gathering at James Lees' (Lees was probably married to her sister). Agnes related that James Ormiston and his wife (Susannah Smith), Robert Pratts and his wife, James Loury, Andrew Chrystie and herself had all been drinking there, some having come at 10 am and remained until 1 pm, while some came at 1 pm and stayed until nearly night. But in the time that she was there she had seen nobody drunk, 'only James Ormiston's wife, who was last in coming, fell unwell'. At the inn the investigators got the same account. Alexander Ritchie, the recently appointed elder who had first looked into the scandal, was clearly discomfited at the outcome and 'says they have not told the verity, but he cannot get it proven'. The participants probably resented such interference in their private affairs on a weekday, and moreover felt themselves the social equals of the complaining Ritchie.

In August 1704, according to the session, Hugh Nimmo gave great offence to his neighbours, the whole parish and even neighbouring parishes when he emerged in a drunken rage from James Lees' premises, cursing and blaspheming at his wife. When one of the company piously remonstrated, saying 'Do you not care what become of your soul?', Hugh had made the awful response that he was so provoked by his wife 'that he cared not what became of either his soul or body, providing he were revenged of her'. The minister asked whether Hugh's wife was saying anything at the time to annoy him, but Hugh had forbidden her to speak and, provokingly enough, she complied. The quarrel was serious enough for Mrs Nimmo to leave home briefly, but she agreed to return after church on the day of the sessional meeting.

Since the session often now met in the kirk on Sundays, their own staid sabbaths were frequently enlivened by investigating 'scandals'. Concern for morals led them to examine such rumours as that Patrick Stewart, who had recently come to dwell in Cramond, had 'a woman which he calls his niece stay[ing] under roof with him in the night time', and that the widowed William Pargillies and Margaret Kello were living together under one roof and must be told to stop. (They were married two months later.[8])

On 18 July 1701 Jonet Wilson, who was the widow of William Daingill or Dingwall, a servantman of James Lees in November 1694, and had been left with three young children at his death, came before the session and acknowledged that a man had come to her house at twilight on Sunday 29 June. His name was David Martin and he 'had wrought lately with the laird of Upper Cramond'. Only her children were also present. He had remained nearly an hour. In answer to further questions she said Martin had not been in drink, had never been to her house before and she did not know why he had come, except that 'he sat down and spake to her and desired promise of marriage of her'. He offered her no ill. No, she was not in bed and the door was 'put to' but Martin shut it up. Questioned still further as to how Martin could have proposed marriage if he had not 'offered ill to her first', Jonet contradicted her first statement. She was removed and, 'considering her hesitating answers and thinking her guilty, but not having sufficient probation', the sessioners sent one of their number to consult Jonet's sole accuser, Thomas Edie, who had eavesdropped on 'base discourse' between the pair.

Possibly some family concern, as well as prurient curiosity, was involved, since Edie's wife was a Jean Wilson. Certainly Edie gave evidence against Jonet with the sanctimoniousness common to those who are constituted their brother's – and more particularly sister's – keeper. 'It was so base discourse that he thought shame to express it', he said, but was pressed by the minister to give the actual words alleged. (If he did, the clerk did not inscribe them.) He testified that between 11 and 12 pm, at which late hour he was going to Peggy's Mill, he heard voices, listened at Jonet's door 'and knew David Martin's tongue and heard him speaking filthy language'. After a period of quiet he heard Jonet say, 'Rise!' and add 'filthy expressions not fit to be rehearsed'. Next morning he told her what he had heard and she forbade him to say anything about it, and threatened that 'if he should speak of it, that she should curse him as long as she lived, and cause her young child curse him'. (This – perhaps arising from the biblical injunction against offending little ones and evidently seen as a particularly potent curse – Jonet admitted.)

Edie also claimed that he overheard Jonet accuse Martin of being drunk, and Martin say that he had been drinking at the West Port, Blackhall and Muttonhole. He cited Margaret Logan (the wife of John Wells, tenant of Peggy's Mill) as witness to the fact that Jonet subsequently told him that she had after all been in bed and was going to deny that Martin was in the house. When Edie told her that 'she had done that which could not be mended', Jonet replied 'that she trusted in God, no'. Some of the elders then reported the evidence of the ale-house keeper Edward Moubray that David Martin had come to his house about sunrise on the Monday morning, asked for a bed, lay down and 'desired his shoes to be laid out of sight'.

At length Jonet was persuaded to admit that she had had intercourse with Martin that night and that he had promised to marry her, 'but she said she would never marry him, though she should never be married'. Nor had she kept company with him at any time before.

On 8 August, however, David Martin gave evidence to the session, saying that he was a widower, his wife having died at Yule the previous year, and he had come to Cramond about May. On the Sunday in question he had drunk in James Lees' house in Muttonhole and then called for a chopin of ale at David Reid's in Upper Cramond, and then after sunset had gone to Jonet Wilson's, where, he maintained, he stayed not so much as a quarter-hour. He had no particular errand there, but Jonet had come to William McCrabbie's house, 'where he quartered', and 'told that he was dear there, and that she would fetch a peck of meal out of Edinburgh and bake it to him' ('dear' apparently meaning that he was living at great expense). That was all he had had to do with her. Then, confronted with Jonet's confession and Edie's evidence, Martin was reduced to saying that 'he could not tell what passed between [the two of them], nor what he said to her, or she to him, he was so overtaken with drink'. But if she turned out to be pregnant he would acknowledge the child as his. He was next reported to have fled to Aberdour, whence he had come. Jonet stood before the congregation for the third time on 23 November and was rebuked, but Mr Hamilton told those in church that he could not declare her absolved 'because of her hardness of heart, ignorance and stupidity'. On 5 December 1707 Jonet admitted that she was expecting a child by John Davidson, coachman to the duchess of Gordon at the time that the child was begotten 'in the Canongate, [in a house?] beneath the cross'. She was rebuked for her wickedness and also her former 'obduredness in sin'.

On another sabbath the sessional meeting was regaled with the details of how Agnes Bryce, servitrix to the elder Claud Wilson, had been observed with a male servant, Samuel Johnston, in the fields on a Sunday afternoon. The couple would admit only that as they were walking back from a drinking party in Edinburgh Agnes sat down to examine her sore foot, whereupon he kissed her. George Mure, aged over sixty, and Cornelius Kay were walking past, however, and at 'the Blue Gate' Kay's dog started barking, and Mure looked up and saw, he said, Agnes 'concerned with drink and vomiting'. The couple were sitting by the side of the highway 'about a stone's cast' from Mure and Kay, and Mure saw Samuel 'between her legs, and then he lifted up her clothes and was lying above her. He was not long above her: he pulled her up again and could not get her kept up, she was so in drink'. Mure then said to Kay, 'What is yon? It is a man lying with a woman!' Kay stood up and at first was unable to see the woman, 'but at length saw him sitting on his knees between her legs, and . . . saw him roll up her coats and lie down above her'. At that Kay got Mure to shout at them, 'to hinder them to commit sin'. Mure shouted twice, but they took no notice until two other men came along the road, and then the pair went away together, 'she leaning on his arm', 'and caused fill a chopin of ale at Jean Aikin's door at Cleckhim In'. Cornelius Kay was another of those who were more tender of others' morals than their own, having confessed to fornication with his woman servant the previous year.

A former Cramonder, Agnes Shedd, daughter of the Marion Gillies who had avidly watched the activities of William More and Jonet McMath in 1690, had left Cramond at the age of twenty-one. Six years later she returned home pregnant after working in the north of England. Her story went that she had been in service in the parish of Easington, twelve miles south of Newcastle. There she had been married by the minister to George Mosse of that parish, but her husband had then been pressed as a 'land soldier'. Unluckily for Agnes, there was a regular sea traffic with Newcastle, and the Reverend William Hamilton gave Skipper Robert Punton of Cramond a letter for a Mr Low, 'who preaches in a meeting house at Newcastle'. Low replied that Agnes had not told the truth: the parish clerk of Easington declared that she had not been married there and the man suspected of fathering her child was George Giffard, 'a profligate man, of whom it was reported that he had married two women in England and one in Scotland'. Agnes had been seen with him in Newcastle.

When she had recovered from childbirth, Agnes came before the session and stuck to her story. Asked what witnesses were present at her supposed marriage, she answered 'a great many', but could give no names. She also contradicted her statement that she had left her husband in prison, pressed for the army, because she now said that he had promised to follow her by Christmas. Later she acknowledged that he was called George Giffard, but she had been advised to give a different name, because at Newcastle his foster-brother told her that Giffard was married to a woman in Linton called Jonet Broun. When, on her way back to Cramond, Agnes 'came the length of Dalkeith', this was confirmed by her uncle, whose wife was a relation of Jonet Broun's and knew that Jonet was still alive. Agnes added that when she came away the authorities had Giffard in custody, because he had no place of settlement. Finally, on 30 April 1708 she admitted that she was neither married nor proclaimed for marriage.

Agnes then went to foster a child for a wright in South Leith, who promised to let the session know before she left him. He refused, however, to oblige himself to ensure that she made satisfaction, so Agnes and her mother promised that she would compear when called. Her widowed mother, who had been on the poor roll since 1697, also undertook to keep the session free of any trouble and expense in maintaining her grandchild and had this agreement recorded in the presence of the session on 4 February 1709. On presbytery's advice, Agnes was sentenced to the lesser excommunication until she gave evidence of repentance and reformation, but should not be brought more than once before the congregation before then, since the affair had occurred in England. She had finished weaning the child she was nursing and was back in her mother's house by 1 May 1709. On 27 July she appeared on the pillar and the minister informed the congregation of what she had done, and notified that she was excommunicated until she gave evidence of repentance. Nothing further seems to be recorded of this not over-bright member of a very poor family.

Most people realistically accepted the session's domination over their personal affairs as a fact of life. Resistance was usually passive, and prohibitions were quietly ignored rather than overtly questioned. Archibald Johnston, wanted to account for his failure to attend church in November 1699, 'always absents himself when the minister enquires for him'. Offenders continued to ignore summonses as long as possible before appearing before the session, might take refuge in flight elsewhere or join the army, and a man with some money might try to conceal fornication by establishing the woman in a rented chamber in Edinburgh. Thomas Martin, son of a cotter and probably another of the employees at Peggy's Mill, was a particularly recalcitrant offender. On 29 November 1696 Margaret Arthur answered a summons to the session and confessed fornication with Thomas, the sin having been committed in his father's house about Lammas near night when she was a servant there. She cited as witnesses Thomas's mother, Margaret Wells, who had come upon them then, and George Wight's man, who had later seen them together in a close in Edinburgh. Mrs Martin told the session that all she knew was that Margaret Arthur had been lying in bed with one of the children after gloaming. Hearing the child 'greeting', she had missed Margaret and gone into the yard to look for her. When she called, Margaret answered, but she did not see her. When Margaret returned to the house she asked where she had been and Margaret said she was sewing in the moonlight. A little later Thomas came back in. His mother had never seen the two together, but declared that 'she had her suspicions of them, and that she was troubled very much about it'. Next Sunday (6 December) Thomas had Margaret's confession read to him and the minister urged him to confess and 'not harden himself by continuing in denial . . . yet he persisted in a stiff and obstinate denial of guilt'.

Asked why Margaret had been dismissed by the family, Thomas said it was because 'she would not go shear ["reap"] where his parents bade her' and alleged that her accusation arose from malice. Subsequently it was reported that he had forbidden Margaret to attend further sessional meetings and told her that he would take a chamber for her in Edinburgh. A long series of attempts to bring him to repentance would follow. His uncle, John Wells of Peggy's Mill, was asked to work on his conscience. On 25 December the beadle certified that he had personally cited Thomas to answer the session, in front of Alexander Millar and Andrew Johnston, millers at Peggy's Mill, and it was decreed that if Thomas did not appear he would be referred to a JP 'as contumacious and disobedient to church discipline'. He did 'confess judicially' on 3 January 1697. On 11 April his third penitential appearance was delayed because he was failing to give sufficient evidence of repentance. On 3 October he promised to 'complete satisfaction' the next Sunday but did not. Various elders tried in vain to speak with him and on 7 January 1698 he was reported to have left the area. Meanwhile, on 12 September 1697 Alexander Millar, a widower, was delated for dwelling together with 'Margaret Arthur, a young woman' – presumably the same Margaret. He promised to put her away when two elders intervened.

Although Agnes Haistie was unusual in telling the session to mind their own business, individual elders were sometimes abused: when an elder spoke to James Kay about better attendance at church, Kay 'stormed and was very angry at him', and William Boag was 'very rude' when approached by another. Boag had created offence by his gesture of defiance in sitting with his head covered on his first appearance before the congregation for fornication.[9] The migratory William Sawers lost his temper when he arrived late after making the journey from Dalmeny and, finding that he was not permitted to 'enter the pillar' to begin his penance, flounced off, saying 'They shall seek me ere I seek them'. The session, 'ill satisfied with his carriage', forbade him to start satisfaction until he appeared before them and produced testimonials.[10] John Ladley, who was about to marry an Edinburgh woman, was asked at a private gathering in Edinburgh why his banns were being read in Corstorphine rather than Cramond, where he was presently living. In the presence of John and Jean Harrower and the gardener William Chisholm, he boasted that he 'cared not a fig' for Cramond session, and had this reported back to them.[11] On 19 April 1700 Margaret Anderson, one of the ordinary poor, was delated for cursing the family of an unnamed elder at his door as they were at their evening devotions. Her pension was suspended until she came before the session and acknowledged her fault, but by 21 June Mr Hamilton had to report that he 'could not prevail with her but that she continued most ignorant and obstinate'. When she appeared on 5 July the session decided that there would be no edification in having her admonished in public, 'she being so very stupid'.

Occasionally an aggrieved parishioner came to the minister for redress. On 15 September 1695 John Knight, gardener in Lauriston, complained about his neighbours James Baptie and his wife Margaret Thomson. On two successive Sundays, while Knight's wife, Isobel Broun, was keeping the cows on the Knights' own grass, Margaret had come 'swearing and cursing and using imprecations upon her and the kine', and one of them 'swelled and died that night'. Also Baptie came to their door cursing and threatening him, to which Mary Purvis and Thomas Ballantyn would testify. Baptie denied cursing but admitted that he had thrown Isobel down, and his wife also denied cursing and swearing but agreed that she had accused Isobel of feeding the cows too close to her corn 'and confessed she banned that they should not eat there'. Mary Purvis said that she saw Baptie throw Isobel down and that she heard his wife say 'If John Knight call me a witch for his cow's death, he should have her malison as long as she lived'. While Mrs Baptie was evidently willing to take advantage of any imputation of uncanny powers, the farmers among the sessioners probably recognised that the dead cow had become bloated by an unusually lavish diet. The neighbours may have taken revenge on the Knights in October 1697. On a Saturday the Knights had brought home a cloth (a 'web'), perhaps from the waulk-mill, and set it to dry in the quarry behind their house. There it lay forgotten all Sunday. Isobel was then accused, significantly, not only of this heinous breach of sabbath but also of cursing and scolding her neighbours. Margaret Thomson and Mary Purvis both affirmed, in Mary's words, 'that Isobel Broun did always curse horribly'.

An outsider, Helen Strachan in Inverkeithing, made many complaints to Hamilton about his parishioner Daniel Millar, and on 10 September 1709 told the session that when she was travelling to Edinburgh along the highway Daniel came off the land where he was weeding corn and struck her. Daniel counterclaimed that Helen called him a robber and shouted at him, so he took her by the arm to take her to Lord Charles Ker, JP and laird of King's Cramond, to get her punished. She fell down, but he denied hitting her. He had two male witnesses who agreed with this and said that Helen had called Daniel an adulterous dog and a robber dog. Helen admitted to 'adulterous dog'. Her woman witness declared that she had seen Daniel strike Helen and throw her down. Both parties were rebuked.

Although the originator of a 'delation' is not usually stated (was it Mrs Baptie who reported that the Knights had left out the cloth one Sunday morning?), the complainant was clearly an elder in person when John Wells on his Sunday visitation in September 1696 found Robert Broun at home 'pulling John Wells his peas'.

Broun may have been actuated by hunger rather than malice against an elder: about the same time William Mylne stole fruit from the laird of Braehead's yard. During the troubled years at the end of the century pensions had to be augmented because of 'the starving condition of the ordinar poor in this dearth',[12] and the record of mortcloth hirings reflects a notable increase in deaths from the 'fever' that ran through the nation in the autumn of 1699. The situation was summed up when, on 28 March 1700, a solemn national fast day was observed on account of 'The continued pinching dearth, the great and unusual sickness and mortality of late through all the land (and doth yet in part continue), the disappointing of the African Indian Company's colony in America [the Darien Scheme] . . . and for the stupendous burning of so considerable part of Edinburgh within these few days'.

In October 1699 there had been a meeting appointed by the Commissioners of Supply of the shire, attended by the two heritors of Cammo and Braehead, a number of elders and sixteen nominated male 'heads of families' representing the various areas of the parish. They had to decide whether a 'stent' of £600 Scots per annum should be raised to care for the parish poor, the alternative being to issue them with badges and allow them to beg within Cramond. The great majority voted for the stent, which was to be levied on heritors' estates according to valuation, with the tenants bearing half.

The session shepherded its resources very carefully, and one of the duties of an elder was to report, and substantiate, cases of dire need within his bounds. Providing orphans with the minimum of necessary clothing was one recurrent charge on the poor box. For instance, on 18 December 1701 Hugh Millar was to be bought two shirts and a 'weillie-[under-]coat' and twice £3 Scots was spent on clothes for William Shedd, 'a poor boy at Cramond Brig End', on the second occasion (22 May 1702) 'upon the condition that he come to the school and learn'.

Younger children might have to be put out to nurse at parish expense. When James Kirkcaldie in Nether Cramond and his wife, who had come to the parish six months earlier, lay sick of a fever in July 1699, 'having a young child sucking', the session arranged for the infant to be given out to a foster mother for six weeks until the mother recovered. On his wife's death James Thomson, the smith in the House of the Hill, was left with two children, and it was agreed on 7 June 1706 that the youngest should be 'set out', and a foster mother found as cheaply as possible. A month later a woman agreed to take the infant for half-a-crown a month. But in the meantime Thomson's sister, one of those married aunts who often felt an obligation to care for orphans, had taken the child away without the session's knowledge, wanted them to pay her for keeping it, and was asking more than the half-crown. The session remained adamant that that was their best offer. When an abandoned child had been found in the parish in August 1702, James Murdo's wife made a much better bargain: the session agreed to pay £10 Scots a quarter as she and her husband were poor, 'but of a good and Christian behaviour and would do a conscientious duty to the child'. However, the mother was found and sent with her child to the minister of Linlithgow, where they belonged.

Another child had been found exposed after gloaming on 11 December 1696. It belonged to an Andrew Peacock, who had formerly lived in Cramond with his wife. Earlier in the day Peacock had visited Thomas Cowan's house at Cramond Brig, with a 'lass' and a young child. Mrs Cowan helped him place the young child on his back and heard him say that his wife had died as they were on their way to Ireland. He was now going to Braehead (the kirk treasurer) to seek some support, 'and if he got it not he would lay down the child'. Subsequently the minister of Carriden reported that Peacock had left his parish a few days earlier, and would be sent to Cramond when he returned. It is not noted that he did so, and the widow Elisabeth Robison eventually cared for his abandoned daughter.[13]

One foundling, who had been given the name Jonet Cramond, had an unsettling childhood, being passed from hand to hand as she grew up. In December 1702 she was being kept by James Marr and his wife, and was badly in need of clothes. In June 1704 she was examined by the session but 'thought too young to do for herself', so her maintenance was continued. Two years later she went from the care of Alison Mason into that of Thomas Anderson, who had a poor family to support and after two months wanted arrears of payment. Four months later he was again asking for fees, and there was an argument over the amount: he and his wife would not take less than 30s. a month, and in the meantime Jonet was 'naked' (meaning ill-clad). Clothes were bought for her, but on 3 January 1707 'the session considering that she hath been burdensome to the box these several years appoints that she go off at Candlemas [2 February] next and payment to be made for her entertainment this month and no more'.

Among other disadvantaged people who received parish assistance were John Pollock, blind son of the dead William Pollock, who was enrolled on 12 August 1698, and Margaret Kenlay, 'a young woman distempered', who, in December 1702, had to be provided with a man 'to wait upon her'. On 31 December next year she was said to be 'distracted' and enquiries were made of the goodman of the Correction House in Edinburgh to see whether he would take her, and if so, what he would charge weekly. Meanwhile her parents were given some money towards her help. The goodman, however, refused to take her without an order from a magistrate in Edinburgh, and would also want the session to pay twenty shillings sterling monthly. The session thought it fitter (i.e. more convenient and much cheaper) to give her parents twenty pence (20s. Scots) monthly, 'as long as she is in any measure sober, and more when she is furious'. But they also suggested that if the elder Alexander Ritchie happened to go to Linlithgow he should speak to Alexander Crauford, 'who useth to help furious folk', and ask what he would charge to undertake her care. In the event, the unhappy woman died some months later, and the treasurer paid out on 20 August 1704 for her coffin and grave-making.

Other objects of occasional charity were Margaret Paton, given £4 to buy a plaid so that she could attend church; William Hill, who was 'lying of a sore leg' and was in great strait because he and his wife (Jean Harrower) had no means of reaping their corn; Katherine Couper, who was given half-a-crown to take her nurseling to its grandfather in Dollar after the father, a workman in Edinburgh, left his job and disappeared; John Johnston in Nether Cramond (the piper?), 'being troubled both with the gut and gravel', and Thomas Adamson, who petitioned for help 'of his age and having his oats burnt lately upon the kiln, for which he had wrought these twelve months past, and that he had nothing to maintain himself'. The session, 'pitying his distressed case', gave him £12 Scots for supply.[14]

Two lame soldiers were also succoured in the parish. One was given money in January and February 1695, but on 7 March the beadle was paid 6s. 8d. for making a grave for him. The other, who had come from Flanders, was reported to be staying in Nether Cramond on 27 September 1696 and the session arranged for him to receive two rolls and two mutchkins of ale each day 'until he recover his health some better'. On 23 October they combined two charitable deeds by giving John Baxter in Nether Cramond the price of a firlot of coals in return for taking the soldier into his house 'for warmness, in order to his recovery'.

Later, in October 1709, Cramond contributed to the expenses in Edinburgh of Mr Alexander Buchan, catechist and missionary to the

Island of St Kilda, who was exhibiting two of the island children 'to testify his pains amongst them'. Is it unfair to suggest that in the eyes of Lowland Scots the inhabitants of St Kilda were much on a par with the savages of the South Seas?

Less generosity was shown to some other classes of strangers. In December 1691 one of the acts that the session wanted passed in the laird's court obliged his tenants to take turns 'to help away cripples out of this toun, that the [poor] box be no more burdened in paying for carrying them away'. In December 1703 a stranger woman who had 'lost the power of her body from the middle downward' was brought to Cramond on a barrow, having been put out of the Canongate. She claimed to have been born in Cramond and to have lived there when young. But the session arranged for women to visit her to see whether she was in a fit state to be carried away again. And in August 1697 the treasurer paid £1 4s. 'to two men who kept away the beggars at the communion'. (Eighteen such beggars had received largesse from the poor box on the Monday after communion in 1692.)

In general, sessions looked after their own poor with a mixture of paternal care and stringent attention to both economy and morals. The case of Jean Allen displayed, over time, both aspects. (For her earlier history, see Chapter 4 above.) As a widow with six young children, she had been subsidised from the poor box, but her behaviour frequently got her into trouble with the session. Proposals to remove her from Cramond had no effect. She was again in her house in the House of the Hill and received some monetary assistance in October and December 1689, 'having her daughter lying sick', while in January 1690 she was allowed a testimonial, 'bearing only that she is an object of charity and hath her daughter lying sick on her hand'.

Subsequently she returned to Cramond, was enrolled among the ordinary poor and, along with Barbara Tuedy, on 14 August 1696 had her pension suspended for scolding and flyting. Then in May 1702, when Jean was at church hearing the preparation sermons before communion, 'it pleased God to tryst her with the sad affliction to have her house burnt to ashes with all her household plenishing'. She gave in a petition (written in elaborate form, by the schoolmaster?) about how it was 'the laudable custom of this present government to take special care and inspection of those who, by God's providence, are trysted to be under such sad circumstances', and the elders undertook to collect money on her behalf. Jonet Wallace, who lived in a house belonging to Jean and had also lost everything in the fire, was to be given £2 Scots out of the £21 17s. 6d.

collected for Jean. Not all the money was handed to Jean at once, however: the treasurer was still husbanding most of it five months later when, in December, Jean received news from London that her son Alexander, who served as a soldier in the English fleet, was dead. She asked for a certificate that she was his mother so that she could have the arrears of pay sent to her, and was also ordered to receive the rest of the money collected for her. For a short time she left the parish again, and was put out of the poor roll, but soon returned 'in strait' and was restored.

The ability to withhold pensions gave the session powers of discipline over their enrolled poor. If physically able, they were expected to attend the weekday sermon, especially that at which the money was distributed, on the first Friday of the month. 'Slighting the ordinances' caused Elisabeth Millar to be suspended in April 1700, although two months later three other absentees from church, Christian Rae, William Barton and William Carle, were merely rebuked by the sub-treasurer before receiving their month's money, 'these persons being so brutishly ignorant as to be incapable of more public admonition'. Barton, however, had his pension withdrawn next year 'for horrid swearing and cursing'.

The elderly Elisabeth Crie was frequently in disgrace. On 31 September 1696 she was accused of frequent drunkenness and absence from the previous Sunday's service and had a month's pension withheld. She would admit only to a single case of drunkenness and lost the next month's pension as well. On 5 April 1700 she was suspended 'for her disorderly carriage by drunkenness and theft', and on 19 April was rebuked for frequent drunkenness and cursing and told that next time she would not only forfeit all charity from the poor box but be thrust out of the parish. Apparently this was one of those empty threats: at the distribution on 2 April 1703 'nothing was given to Elisabeth Crie because she drank the last month's pension'. Margaret Couper was put out of the roll in March 1703 'for keeping too much drinking in her house both sabbath day and week day', and at the same time a single payment of 15s. was made to the wife of the drunkard Edward Turner, 'and to be given her without her husband's knowledge'.

With some justice, the session often thought little of the intelligence or strength of character of their poorer constituents. While they encouraged self-help, and were willing in principle to give James Thomson in the House of the Hill the £20 Scots that he wanted to help him buy a house in 1704, they pointed out that he had no means of maintaining one, and instead gave him £4 Scots 'for present supply'. John Millar in Nether Cramond asked to be given a lump sum with which to trade in victuals, rather than being enrolled among the poor at 24s. Scots per month. The experiment had, however, been tried the previous year, and when asked how he had employed his former trading stock, Millar replied that he had lived on it, as well as paying his house rent of £4. It was decided in June 1705 to give him nothing for the past six months but enrol him now. The reason for the reluctance emerges when, three months later, Millar was delated for being 'exceeding drunk within these few days'. A month after that, John Millar and Robert Bowie, ordinary poor, were reported to the session as being very drunk the last night and cursing one another, and were suspended until rebuked.

That the poor were expected to be not only deserving but obedient to the designs of their betters was made clear when, on 4 August 1704, the session stopped Elisabeth Millar's month's pension, 'until she mean herself to them again'. She had offended by withdrawing her son from service with the elder Claud Wilson and giving him bedclothes so that he could go to sea with the Dutch men-of-war.

Although Cramond session dutifully reported to their equivalents in the West Kirk parish that the latter's pre-communion fast day in June 1696 had been 'profaned' when a married couple from Inverleith Mains had drunk in Cramond and two other men spent all day fishing there, they were not always best pleased to receive similar referrals from outside. Two such were produced at the meeting of 22 February 1702. One, from the North-East parish of Edinburgh, concerned a couple who had confessed to antenuptial fornication in Royston park. Cramond session remitted the case back, saying that no-one in Cramond had any knowledge of the event or the persons and they thought it 'no way for edification to take notice of the said persons here, which would raise a scandal where there is none'. They tried to take the same line when informed that John Pickens, drummajor to the Scots Guards, had reported himself to Cramond's minister for fornication in the fields at Cramond with a woman who was also unknown to the session. In this case, however (which turned out to be a matter of adultery, not fornication), Edinburgh presbytery eventually insisted that Pickens should perform penance in Cramond, and two-and-a-half years later he was ordered to begin weekly appearances in sackcloth on 31 December 1704. His penance continued into March 1705 – a pointless exercise as far as the congregation of Cramond were concerned.

An earlier referral from the North-East parish of Edinburgh had faced the young Mr William Hamilton with a major challenge to his authority. In

February 1700 one Mary Miller was brought from Edinburgh to appear before Cramond session. She had given birth to a child in November 1699 and named as father Sir William Paterson of Granton. If the Cramond minister and session felt any impulse to overlook this accusation against one of their leading heritors, the fact that they were informed of it by another session would make such a course impossible.

J.P. Wood saw Sir William Paterson as a former persecutor of Covenanters, 'a conduct certainly not proceeding from purity of principle, the session records of this parish bearing ample testimony to the scandalousness of his carriage, even at an advanced period of life'.[15] An observer untrammelled by lingering sectarian loyalties might see the incident less as an example of Sir William's general moral depravity and more as the sad surrender to temptation of a retired and infirm widower. It was the sadder because he had given the youthful minister and his session the same cooperation that he had extended to the Reverend John Hamilton, recommending to their assistance a man with two young children in Granton, putting some pressure on his gardener, Archibald Adamson, to answer sessional enquiries about his 'disorderly' marriage, 'partying' the session in ensuring that one of his domestic servants ceased to sleep under the same roof as a groom of Lord Tarbat's, and threatening to expel a man with no testimonial.[16] If Mary Miller was the same as the Mary Miller who was one of Sir William's maidservants in November 1694, the affair could have had roots in the past. On the other hand, in Sir William's favour it can be stressed that Mary's lapse of 1699 was not her first: she had previously committed fornication with a man in the parish of Newlands, Tweeddale, and performed penance for it.

Mary's undisputed account was that in 'the week before Fastens Even' 1699 Sir William had left his family in Edinburgh and spent four or five days with her at Granton House. The only other occupant of the house had been Paterson's servant boy, although the gardener Adamson and his wife were living within the close of Granton House and knew that they were there.

When the Reverend William Hamilton questioned him privately, Paterson made no bones about confessing his guilt and avowed that he was willing to accept what censure the session thought fit to inflict, although he hoped that 'they would deal discreetly with him, and have in consideration his old age and character'.[17] His case was held over until Mary had finished her six statutory appearances as a relapsed fornicator, which she did on 7 April 1700. In the event, getting Sir William to appear before the session, let alone the congregation, took a great deal longer. Cammo was first asked to speak to him 'anent his removing of the scandal of fornication' on 28 March. On 5 July the minister reported that he had been to Granton House but found it inconvenient to approach the laird because he had visitors, and that now he had heard that Paterson had gone back to Edinburgh, sick. (He is, however, listed as present at a heritors' meeting on 12 August.) After Sir William had obtained a further delay, on 6 December Hamilton reported that he had found him lying dangerously ill and could not trouble him.

On 3 January 1701 the session were told by Claud Wilson (the elder for Granton and Paterson's tenant) that Paterson had recovered, whereupon the minister tried unsuccessfully to find him. The session had now become impatient, and on 31 January asked the minister to write and summon Paterson to satisfy, on pain of being publicly cited. He should also demand a reply to his letter. Some ten days later Hamilton visited Paterson in his lodging in Edinburgh, where he was 'lying in his naked bed of rheumatic pains'. Paterson requested another month's delay. When the month was up, the minister received a stately letter which he read to the session:

> Reverend Sir, I am extremely sensible of the worthy gentlemen that compass your session their tenderness to me in this unlucky particular, and must beg it as a further favour from you to give [them] my hearty thanks and to show them how sensible I am of their goodness to me, and withall to assure them that my delaying to wait on you and them is not pretence but real sickness. For since I came to Town, which was in the beginning of October, I was not in a condition to go the length of Granton, if were to save my life, and have been worse of late than ever (I mean since you did me the favour to see me). However, this is to assure you and them that how soon I dare venture abroad I shall wait on you and give you all the reasonable satisfaction you can desire. And though I expect from you, and my noble, worthy and kind neighbours, that this unworthy business may be taken away in as private a manner as you conveniently may, yet I leave the method of it entirely to your own discretion and kindness, and shall study to approve myself worthy of any favour I meet with from you and them. And in the meantime I continue, reverend and dear sir, your faithful and obliged servant Willm Paterson.

The session seem to have been unmoved by this epistle and suggested that Paterson should be approached by 'some of the heritors who have influence upon him'. If Paterson would just make one appearance before them the session would then decide how to act. Paterson, however, continued ill for the next few months. On 11 July 1701 the minister heard that he was better in health and travelling back and forth between

Granton and Edinburgh, but there was more delay while Paterson visited 'the bathing wells' (Bath or Buxton?) in England. When he returned, the minister again tried to see him at his house but 'had not the conveniency of speaking with him'. After receiving a letter in the name of the session, Paterson promised to attend on 7 November, but wrote the day before to say that he was expecting his neighbour Lord Tarbat to dine at the crucial date and must stay at home. He would instead 'wait on' the session next Friday, 14 November. At last he then kept this humiliating appointment and was suspended from the 'sealing ordinances' of the church until the scandal was removed by due appearances before the congregation, a penance to be completed before the first Sunday of January 1702.

The kirk session minutes do not reveal whether this satisfaction was performed or not, possibly because a new volume of minutes was started on Friday 2 January and when the clerk came to enter his draft notes in it there were plenty of other scandals to occupy his pages. Alternatively, the session may have been reluctant to have a permanent record of their heritor's disgrace, or privately made this concession to him. Probably Sir William did comply with their demand. If so, his public appearances could have been discreetly managed, in the way implied in a sessional resolution of April 1702 that henceforth when 'scandalous persons' made their final public appearance they must sit before the pulpit so that the minister and congregation might clearly hear their profession of repentance. In Sir William's case, a mumbled apology from his own secluded seat may have been accepted as adequate.

There was a sequel to the story three years later. On 5 November 1704 Sir William's gardener, Archibald Adamson, came to the session with a formal complaint against John Young in Nether Cramond and his wife Katherine Couper for slandering Adamson's wife, Jean Hogg. They had spread it around that Sir William had been caught in bed with Mrs Adamson and publicly removed by his son. On 17 November the son, John Paterson, sent a letter asking the minister to investigate the origin of the story and punish those responsible, and Mrs Adamson also came asking for justice. The witnesses who were called before the meeting were the Nether Cramonders Jean Smith the midwife, her daughter Jean Harrower, William Charley, Robert Millar and the smith Francis Wilson.

Gossip, once started, had gained force: not just because of Sir William Paterson's previous conviction but also from Jean Hogg's earlier reputation and the circumstance that her marriage to Archibald Adamson had been 'disorderly', and the more notorious when the couple initially refused to have it legitimated by the minister of Cramond.

The first witness, Katherine Couper, said she had heard from Jean Harrower that as Jean was going past Granton House she saw a group of people gathered at Archibald Adamson's door. They had told her that 'the lady' (Margaret Elliot, who had married John Paterson in September 1703) had gone to get her husband 'to fetch the old laird out of [the] house, for he had been long in the house with Jean Hogg, Archibald Adamson's wife, and they knew not what ill might be betwixt them'. Jean Harrower, however, now denied to the session that she ever said any such thing. Nor did anyone else admit to witnessing the interesting scene.

Nevertheless, having come into possession of the tale, Katherine Couper gleefully passed it on to her husband, John Young, who evidently took more interest in the affairs of his neighbours than he had pretended in 1691 when he disclaimed any desire to meddle with the doings of Agnes Crauford and James Reid (Chapter 5 above). When the couple met William Charley and some other neighbours, Katherine said that her husband had a 'ploy' to tell. When Charley asked what ploy, Young replied that Charley had formerly scolded him for calling Jean Hogg a whore. Now he could call her one and prove it too. Charley asked 'what way would he prove it?' and Young recounted that last Saturday night the young laird of Granton had taken his father out of Jean Hogg's bed, and that Robert Millar had been there at the time and subsequently told the story in the presence of Francis Wilson. Millar, however, told the session that he heard the story only when Young told it to Charley, and Francis Wilson said that he learned it when Charley passed it on to Andrew Hill (who was Adamson's brother-in-law).

After Jean Hogg had declared herself satisfied with having this chain of ill-supported gossip elucidated, the process was halted temporarily because many of those involved, including the Adamsons, were afflicted by smallpox. On 8 December Sir William Paterson himself wrote asking the minister to have Young and his wife rebuked as soon as possible, even though it was difficult to get a full meeting of the session. Accordingly, Hamilton called the culprits before some of the witnesses and elders and Katherine Couper expressed her sorrow on her knees and was told never to spread such gossip again. Her husband then acknowledged his rashness in repeating what she had told him and expressed heartfelt repentance. For our part, we have no grounds for rejecting the session's implied exculpation of the laird of Granton.

On 20 August 1709 the heritors and members of session were asked to stay behind after the sermon to discuss Edinburgh presbytery's intention of 'transporting' their minister to become professor of divinity in the University of Edinburgh. As with his predecessor, they made strenuous but ineffective objections to losing him. Hamilton preached his farewell sermon on 30 October, on the eminently Calvinist text from Acts 20.32, 'And now, brethren, I commend you to God, and to the word of his grace, which is able to build you up, and to give you an inheritance among all them which are sanctified'. Exhorting the people to live in the fear of God, to read the scriptures, to 'frequent the ordinances' and keep holy the sabbath day, and to pray much, he asked their prayers, 'as he should not be forgetful in praying for them', and declared, with evident sincerity, that he had enjoyed 'great respect and kindness from all persons of this parish, high and low'. Speaking subsequently to the session, he thanked the elders for their kind and respectful carriage to him as their pastor, and promised 'all the service and kindness he could do for them and the parish'. Indeed, 'the professor' continued to keep in touch with Cramond and moderated sessional meetings for some time while the manse was vacant. 'Highly distinguished for piety, learning, and moderation',[18] he became Principal of Edinburgh University a few months before his death in 1732. Two of his sons would later follow him into the manse at Cramond.

Meanwhile, the choice of William Hamilton's successor occasioned a battle royal among the heritors and anyone else who could claim a vote under the rules that continued in force until the parliament of the United Kingdom, as constituted in 1707, effectively restored Barnton's sole right to nominate.[19] As a result, the manse remained vacant for some fifteen months. At this point, therefore, there is an opportunity to rehearse more of the stories of some members of William Hamilton's flock and, ignoring chronological restrictions, pursue a few individual histories further.

NOTES

1. *William Hamilton.* Henry Sefton, 'Neu-lights and Preachers Legall': Some Observations on the Beginnings of Moderatism in the Church of Scotland', in Norman Macdougall, ed., *Church, Politics and Society in Scotland 1408–1929* (Edinburgh 1983), p. 188, and Cramond Poll Tax return 1694. Five months after his institution at Cramond, presbytery sent him to the north for three months, for reasons unexplained in the session minutes, so that no sessional meetings were held between 3 March and 23 June 1695.

2. *Menzies of Cammo.* He built himself a fine new house at Cammo (which was later renamed New Saughton), 'but his affairs becoming involved', as Wood put it, 'he was obliged to retire to the more humble mansion of Whitehouse, and to dispose of Cammo' in 1710 to Sir John Clerk of Penicuik: Wood, *Cramond*, p. 65.

3. *Margaret Baverage.* 28 April, 19 May, 9, 11 June 1699.
4. *Nisbet.* 5 Oct. 1704, 1, 15 March 1705.
5. *Cranford John.* This must be Cranford St John, near Kettering, Northants.
6. *Hiding under table.* 11 April, 2 May 1701.
7. *Unallowable sabbath activities.* Worldly discourse: 4 April 1701; dinner party: 18 Mar. 1705; Charles Short: 19 July 1695; Gloag: 8, 22 Oct. 1699; mills: 20 June 1697.
8. *Cohabitation.* Niece: 4 July 1701; widowed couple: 30 Oct. 1702.
9. *Abusing elders.* Kay: 19 Sept. 1697; Boag: 15 Nov., 6 Dec. 1706.
10. *Sawers.* 5 March 1703. Sawers eventually (30 Jan. 1704) gave the session his complete life-story to date. Born in the parish of Denny, Stirlingshire, he left at the age of two. Subsequently he stayed four years in Cardross, on the Clyde, before returning to Denny for six months. He then went, at the age of twelve, and probably to his first paid employment, to St Ninians. After two years there he moved to Falkirk, then Kinneil in the parish of Bo'ness, where he lived with an employer for five-and-a-half years before spending six months in Tillicoultry. After that he moved to Dalmeny and lived with Robert Harrower for six months, until at Martinmas 1701 he went to Craigie in Cramond parish and became involved with a widow there. He then took service in Leuchold in Dalmeny. From Whitsun till 30 September 1703 he served a man in Midlaw, Dunfermline, then went to the West Kirk parish in Edinburgh, stayed twenty days with John Grieve in the Dean, and was then reported to be in service in Ratho Byres. On 24 March 1704 Sawers was said to be in the parish of Uphall.
11. *Cared not a fig.* 3 Nov. 1699.
12. *Stealing and dearth.* 27 Sept. 1696; 8 June 1696.
13. *Peacock.* Two children are in the baptismal register, born in 1689 and 1691. For fostering by Elisabeth Robison: 29 Aug. 1700, 7 Nov. 1701.
14. *Occasional charity.* Paton: 28 Oct. 1700 (lack of clothing was a popular reason for non-attendance at church); Hill: 16 Aug. 1702; Couper: 5 July 1706; Johnston: 6 June 1707; Adamson: 4 Sept. 1709.
15. *Ample testimony of Sir William Paterson's depravity.* Wood, *Cramond*, p. 20.
16. *Assisting session.* Man in Granton: 16 Dec. 1698; groom: 4 March 1698.
17. *Paterson's Confession of guilt.* 1 March 1700.
18. *Wood on Revd William Hamilton. Cramond*, p. 81.
19. *Act of Union, 1707.* Lord Rosebery promptly took to the House of Lords his long-standing dispute with Sir John Inglis over fishing rights in the Almond, and gained a decision that deprived Inglis of his half-share. In compensation, Inglis was given half of Rosebery's gallery in Cramond church: *Ibid.*, pp. 93–4

SEVEN

'A Very Froward Generation'

The third period of puritanical rigour, instituted by the Reverend Mr John Hamilton and carried on by his more congenial successor, Mr William Hamilton, may have served to polarise attitudes to ecclesiastical discipline and further emphasise the distinction between respectable conformists and the unconstrained. A majority of Cramonders – silent as far as the session minutes are concerned – evidently accepted sessional controls. During William Hamilton's ministry a more rebellious mood becomes discernible among some of those born after 1670, especially to families with a history of 'meddling' from minister and elders.

Sessional meetings therefore had plenty to occupy their attention and the clerk (still Mr Thomas Forrest) was assiduous in recording evidence. Gratifyingly, it is sometimes people's own words that come down to us. Witnesses were now being required to sign their testimony. Few – almost none of the women – could in fact write their names, so that minister or clerk had to sign on their behalf and they authenticated the signature by first touching his pen. The carelessly repeated statement that basic education in Scotland included writing is plainly wrong. But the attention to due legal form means that the sessional records of the time can bring people and circumstances vividly to life for a moment.

That the young farm-servant Jonet Linn was pregnant when she married David Pillans some time in June 1696 is not sufficiently unusual to hold great interest. Nor is it especially remarkable that in April Jonet vehemently denied to the session that she was carrying a child, and offered to support her denial on oath. This was, however, the second time that neighbours had suspected her condition and the session began an investigation into rumours that Jonet had suffered (or perhaps procured) a miscarriage the previous November. Her association with David Pillans may have gone back to November 1694 when Jonet, then aged nearly seventeen, was working for Archibald Nimmo's family in Lauriston, while David was employed by John Nimmo and his wife Barbara Pillans nearby, in Muirhouse. When her time of hire was up, Jonet moved to work for that family. David may have been born outside the parish, or at some time during the months between July and December 1677, when pages are lost from the baptismal register, so his relationship, if any, to Barbara Pillans is not known. The name, however, seems significant because it was Barbara's evidence as Jonet's employer in 1695 that obtained a sessional verdict of 'not proven'. (It may not be without importance, either, that Barbara's husband John Nimmo was added to the session in November 1695.)

When the story of the alleged miscarriage of 1695 finally came before the session, witnesses testified that 'the voice of the country' had been that Jonet was with child: 'all the country knew that she was big bellied'. More specifically, Jonet Aire, wife of the mason James Charity, said that she and Jonet had been reaping for John Nimmo at harvest time and she had seen Jonet 'after she had taken her pottage at breakfast turn sick and vomit her breakfast three days together'.

Mrs Nimmo, however, said that she had had no grounds to suspect that Jonet was pregnant. She described how Jonet had taken 'a great colic' one evening before Martinmas when the tailor James Muir was working in the house (doubtless making winter clothes for the family). After giving Jonet a warm drink they had lain her in her bed – which was evidently in the one family room – and she recovered again. Muir testified that he had been in the house until supper time, when his wife (Mary Purvis) came to fetch him, and Mary said she then saw Jonet lying quietly in bed but did not speak to her. At a later interrogation, on 15 May, she added that her husband had told her that Jonet had not for an instant been out of his sight or that of the Nimmo family, all the time he was there. Apparently on the basis of that hearsay evidence, and the testimony of an elder's wife, the session finally found that Jonet's past guilt could not be proven, despite the damaging evidence produced as an afterthought by the neighbour Grissell Broun, that on the night in question one of the Nimmo boys had been sent to fetch her, saying 'We think Jonet Linn be crying [i.e. in labour], but my mother can get nothing out of her'. Grissell had answered that summons and saw that Jonet was 'unweel', but (discreetly, perhaps) asked her no questions.

On 6 December 1696 the session heard that Jonet had given birth to a son twenty-one weeks after marriage. She and David subsequently compounded their offences by drinking on Sunday 28 February 1697 in the house of Margaret Naper in Muirhouse Hauch and setting the boy to be fostered by the wife of William Waddell, who had had a daughter baptised the previous March. Jonet then nursed a child of Robert Cairns. Her own son died ten months later.[1]

Another scene shows a neighbourhood watch in action in Nether Cramond and throws light on the character and reputation of Jean Smith's son, John

Harrower. It emerges that he was addressed by the villagers as 'laird', a nickname implying a degree of deference but not necessarily esteem. It may well suggest, too, that Nether Cramonders associated arrogant manners with heritors as a class. On at least one occasion Harrower had physically assaulted his mother when drunk and the session themselves may have been somewhat leery of him. When in June 1702 he submitted his account for making coffins for some of the parish paupers, his entries did not tally with those in the kirk treasurer's book, 'but because he had served the session cheaper than any other wright would do, they appointed to give him four pounds Scots, that he might not be complainous of them'.

One afternoon in July 1700 Harrower had gone to Agnes Adamson's house asking for her lodger, Ann Millar. Agnes later told the session that when Ann appeared, Harrower said to her 'I am owing you the working of a pair of stockings. Go, and I will pay you'. Ann demurred, saying 'May you not pay me here, laird?', to which he replied 'No, but [just] go to our stair-foot and I will pay you'. Suspicious, Agnes went to her gavel window to watch them, and saw them standing at Harrower's door while he made water. She promptly went to her own door, but before she got there they had both gone into Harrower's house and shut the door upon themselves. Her neighbour Ann Alexander then came out of her own house and sat down at the stairfoot hard by Harrower's door. About an hour later she got up and knocked at the door and the window, watched by Agnes Adamson and the teenaged sisters Cecile and Marion Johnston, who had joined her by that time. When Harrower opened the door, he was observed to be wearing nothing but shirt and breeches. Ann Anderson said to him, 'They say, laird, you have a woman in the house with you'. This he denied, so she made him open the window in the back of the house to let her see in. Pushing through, Marion Johnston saw Ann Millar's foot sticking out from under the bed. John Harrower then locked his door and went to Thomas Crie's ale-house. While he was away, Marion heard Ann come to the window and 'cry to be out'. In the meantime, Ann's sister Isobel Millar, aged about sixteen, had gone to fetch Harrower from the ale-house. When he returned he tried to 'stick' his door after him, and aimed a kick at Cecile Johnston, but Isobel thrust past and pulled out her sister, who was reluctant to emerge because of the onlookers who had collected.

Ann Millar subsequently denied to the session that she had either been alone in the house or hidden under the bed. She also said that the door had never been shut, and indeed had no lock. She and Harrower agreed that he had 'tempted her to sin' but said that she did not yield to him, although Harrower had previously told the session that he was too drunk to remember whether he had denied to the neighbours that he had a woman in the house.[2] Both were found guilty of scandalous behaviour tending towards fornication. Ann Millar did, however, succumb to temptation later, giving birth to a child in June 1703 'in the gardener's house of Pilrig' in West Kirk parish. The father was John McCleish, a writer, i.e. clerk. At the time of the affair Ann had been in service to Mr Fulton in Blackfriar Wynd, but was dismissed by Mrs Fulton 'because she used to go forth in the night-time'. She had been twice guilty with McCleish, once in the Fultons' house and then about twenty days later 'in the fields as she was coming from the Wolmet' (in Corstorphine?). Having returned to Cramond to live with her sick father, John Millar, by March 1704, Ann was told by Cramond session to produce evidence that she had offered to give satisfaction in the West Kirk parish, or else the magistrate would be asked to 'extrude' her from Cramond.

Like Marion Gillies and Isobel Pratts, who gave evidence against William More and Jonet McMath in 1690 (Chapter 5), Agnes Adamson and Ann Alexander showed a rather surprising concern for morality when they attempted to rescue Ann Millar from Harrower's clutches. Both were young married women who had produced untimely children. Ann Alexander and her husband William Crie had been found guilty of prenuptial fornication in August 1699. Agnes, the daughter of Thomas Adamson and Helen Baxter (who figured in their own scandals in Chapter 5), was pregnant by another man when she married Andrew Hill. The child was baptised as Hill's in September 1698.[3] At the sessional hearing into his misconduct John Harrower claimed that Agnes Adamson had acted from malice. Dislike of him may well have entered into it. But possibly of equal concern to the women was the fact that he was thirty-eight and probably much older than Millar.

The villagers of Nether Cramond lived in close contact, clustered mainly about the village green below the kirkyard wall. They were few enough for everyone to know everybody's business – in November 1694 there cannot have been more than 130 people over the age of fifteen. In addition, many were related. Families might quarrel among themselves, but solidarity was the order of the day when one member came into conflict with someone outside the group.

It is nowhere explained just why William Carle and his daughter Margaret were regarded with animosity by neighbours and sessioners alike, so that for years there had been fruitless attempts to expel William. Both, however, appear in a sufficiently unattractive light in an incident that brought all the participants before the session in October 1702. It apparently started with a quarrel between Carle and his fellow-pensioner Margaret Couper, during which he claimed that she had been a whore these twenty years. (It was not only sessions who were obsessed with sex – the standard insult to a woman implied either promiscuity or dealings in witchcraft.) Doubtless Margaret Couper responded in kind, but no witnesses testified before the session in support of the Carles. Hearing the shouting, Christian Lawrence 'came up the toun' and Alison Ramsay, Margaret Couper's daughter, went down to fetch her brother but was intercepted by Carle's daughter Margaret, who said to her jeeringly, 'Good day to you, maiden! Forgive me if I lie!' Again, Margaret was no model of rectitude – she and her husband Henry Millar had done penance for antenuptial fornication. When Margaret went on to call her 'an impudent and a prompted [ready?] whore', Alison started weeping and was taunted with 'Why weep you, for any beggar's gait?' Christian Lawrence then joined in and struck Margaret Carle on the cheek. When William Carle called Margaret Couper 'a soulless loun' and her daughter a whore, Couper seized his 'stilt' (crutch), which got broken in the ensuing scuffle. Carle retaliated by snatching the 'toy' (small bonnet) from her head and put it up in his plaid. After that he pursued her into her house and refused to leave. His daughter, enraged at the destruction of her father's staff, then fetched a pitchfork.

Or so the sequence seems to have gone, from the confused and self-exonerating accounts that the participants later gave the session. When the minister reproved Carle for stealing Margaret Couper's bonnet, found in his plaid, Carle declared that if he had been near a fire he would have burnt it. Of the three outside witnesses whose evidence was called for, two said they saw nothing and the third, the laird's officer James Broun, said that all he saw was the fork in Margaret Carle's hand, which he took from her. It seems unlikely that the row in the street drew no more of an audience. Did the neighbours prefer to keep out of other people's quarrels? Were they anxious not to antagonise the Carles, or simply reluctant to incriminate Margaret Couper and her supporters? Despite general hostility, father and daughter remained. The session particularly blamed the Carles for this affray and asked for the laird's court to expel them, 'they are of so wicked, turbulent and unchristian behaviour'. As usual, Cramond Court took no effective action.

The wake held for Agnes Johnston of Nether Cramond on the night of Sunday 2 August 1702 achieved the distinction of attracting sessional notice because of the disturbances caused by a youthful group among the mourners who 'went through the town . . . troubling the town in the night time'. Barbara Reid, Christian Robison and Cecile Johnston heaped stones against Thomas Hastie's door, William Temple, Marion Johnston and

Mary Garvie stood on top of the minister's dyke and took cherries off his tree and David Pillans, Robert Millar, Cecile Johnston and Christian Robison went to Andrew Henderson's house and threw stones at a cat on the tiles. Moreover, David Pillans and Robert Millar 'hurled' Cecile and Marion Johnston up and down the green of Nether Cramond in a 'hurle [wheel-] barrow' – with much nocturnal shrieking, one imagines. Most of the culprits, who admitted drinking at the wake but denied being drunk, were rebuked for their light behaviour and dismissed. The Johnston girls, however, were found not 'sensible' of their bad behaviour and summoned to appear again at the next session to be further dealt with. Apart from David Pillans, who has appeared already in this chapter as the eventual husband of Jonet Linn and was given a special ministerial reminder that he was a married person and should have been 'minding death' that night, the ascertained ages of the group ranged from almost twenty-two in the case of William Temple to Mary Garvie's fifteen (she was 'going in her sixteenth year'). Five of them featured in some capacity in other incidents that came before the session between 1700 and 1709, so that the wake provides a link between them and their stories. The Reid, Millar and Kneelands families were well known to the session. Cecile (or Sicilia) and Marion Johnston have already been mentioned as witnessing John Harrower's advances to Ann Millar. Christian (the name is sometimes spelt Kirstin and was doubtless pronounced Kirsty) Robison was the illegitimate daughter of Bessie Rae and the by-then-married soldier David Robison, born in 1681 (Chapter 2). In March 1702 she had married her exact contemporary in Nether Cramond, Patrick Donaldson, son of Christian Lawrence who had caught his father, James Donaldson, with Isobel Matthie and confiscated his snuffbox (Chapter 4).

Cecile and Marion Johnston were nieces of Agnes Johnston, daughters of her brother James Johnston. Ten days after the wake their elder sister Jonet had been brought to bed, at the age of thirty and having successfully concealed pregnancy up to that point: she confessed to fornication with a former fellow-servant. William Temple was Agnes Johnston's nephew, son of her sister Margaret and the seaman John Temple, and Mary Garvie was Agnes's granddaughter, apparently orphaned before January 1695 when Mary, 'a poor child in Nether Cramond', was bought a pair of shoes from parish funds. These relationships, not in themselves important, are out-lined in Figure 1. Other members of the extensive Johnston clan have been mentioned in previous chapters. They included the Adam Johnston, then living in Newhaven, who went with his family one Sunday in 1690 to visit and drink with Margaret Drummond, estranged wife of his ill-tempered son Richard (Chapter 5), Bessie Johnston, who married the tailor John Sim in 1680, after cohabiting with him, and possibly John Johnston, the Cramond piper.[4] Some of the group of young and wayward people whose light behaviour will be described in the rest of this chapter therefore shared a family tradition of disorderly conduct. Most were second- or third-generation Nether Cramonders from less than well-to-do backgrounds who had grown up together, attended the parish school together and suffered under the dominie's discipline.

Fig. 1.   Some family connections in Chapter 7

1.   JOHNSTONS

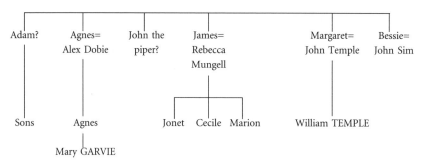

2.   McMATHS

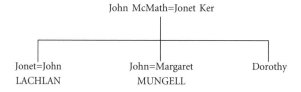

3.   DONALDSON–ROBISON

Agnes Johnston herself seems to have lived most of her life in Nether Cramond. She had married on 1 April 1662, and so was most probably born in the early 1640s, at a time when Covenanting fervour was at its height. She then lived through a series of unsettling changes of government in church and state: the loss of national independence while Scotland suffered an uneasy coexistence with an occupying power, then a quarter-century of restored episcopal and monarchic rule, accompanied by orchestrated dissent, and finally a new puritanical reaction.

In the course of her adult life Agnes had had occasional minor brushes with ministers and sessions. In 1659 she was accused of charging a woman in Wardie with practising witchcraft. About February 1683 she received Christian Lawrence's confidences about the infidelity of Christian's husband James Donaldson. In 1695 Agnes and Jonet Ker, Mrs John McMath, had a heated exchange of insults and on 9 August they were induced to promise cautiously 'to endeavour to refrain from scolding one another'. Probably both shared the sentiments expressed next month by Thomas Cowan, wright at Cramond Brig End, who was reported to the minister for abusing John Gray in front of witnesses. Cowan 'acknowledged he was in the wrong to John Gray' but added firmly that Gray 'was also in the wrong to him'. In January 1700 Agnes was 'delated' for carrying home water from the well in sermon-time. On 26 December 1701 the session approved the purchase of five ells of 'pladden' to make her a coat, and in her last illness they bought drink for her and paid a woman to wait upon her. Interestingly, none of her family undertook that charge. Perhaps they could not afford to do so.

Before Agnes's wake her nephew William Temple had already come to sessional notice on two occasions, in association with lads of like age and background. These included Andrew Baverage, son of the deceased Andrew Baverage senior, who had been educated as a 'poor scholar' between 1694 and 1697, at the same time as Mary Garvie was receiving parish support. The Margaret Baverage who had been brought back to Cramond to perform penance for her fornication in 1697 (Chapter 6) may have been his elder sister. John Kneelands was probably the son of the tailor James Kneelands and a nephew of the Robert Kneelands who had stood lengthily in sackcloth for his adultery with Katherine Doe in 1678 (Chapter 4). A third crony was Patrick Donaldson.

One Sunday in March 1701 William Temple had been dutifully in church for the morning sermon, but after the service the sixteen-year-old boys John Hardy and Andrew Baverage, who had been down at the Cocklemill turning malt for John's father William Hardy, 'brought up word to the town [of Nether Cramond] that a beggar young woman and a young man were lying together in the kiln lodge'.[5] When the last bell was ringing to the afternoon's sermon, Temple went off to see for himself, accompanied by John Kneelands.

Looking into the lodge, the two young men saw the beggar-man lying naked (meaning sparsely clad) with the woman, 'who had no clothes on her but pladden sleeves and a shirt'. She was 'clapping' (patting) his head, and said the young man was her brother. William and John denied doing any ill to the woman, but John 'lifted her shirt and offered her 12d. Scots [1d. sterling] to let him handle her nakedness'. She refused, however, either to permit this or to take the money. The Cramond lads remained there about half an hour, and then escorted the two beggars, and two other beggar lads who were with them, out of the mill 'logie'. The party of beggars then ran away.

Temple and John Kneelands were summoned to appear at the next meeting of session. John promptly joined the army instead, and when the beadle took a written citation to his parents' house, John's mother defiantly 'refused to send it to him, and said she would burn it'. In August, before he had done penance for his previous breach of the sabbath, William Temple was delated with Andrew Baverage, Richard Ramsay and Patrick Donaldson for another case of sabbath-breaking. The four of them had taken a yawl from Cramond over to Dalgety in order to transport Donaldson across to Fife. The three others then stole some pieces of coal from the shore there and gave them to Margaret Couper, the one who came off worst in a slanging match with William Carle. She was probably Richard Ramsay's grandmother and her house had recently been broken into and all her possessions stolen.[6] These offences were really the result of youthful high spirits: Baverage was sixteen and Ramsay just seventeen. On 2 January 1702 William Temple confessed his two breaches of the sabbath, and was shown that he deserved public rebuke, 'but because of his young age' (he was 21!), they 'delayed his public appearance, until he should be more sensible of his fault'. He failed to compear when he was next called, was cited in writing and warned that if he failed to come he would be cited from the pulpit, and finally made satisfaction with a public appearance before the congregation on 29 March. The next year, the elders who visited Nether Cramond on Sunday 21 March found William at home with his father at the time of morning sermon.

David Pillans, last seen here at Agnes Johnston's wake and before that in his premarital relations with Jonet Linn, was accused in January 1703 of 'a scandalous behaviour flagrant in people's mouths'. The complaint came from William Etrick and his wife, Margaret Forbes, who alleged that David had attempted to rape her as a little group of seven Nether Cramonders were walking home from Edinburgh on Saturday 16 January. The group included Cecile Johnston, Cecile's mother Rebecca Mungell, the wife of the Nether Cramond elder, William Ramsay, and two men besides David

Pillans: William Stewart and James Clelands. Mrs Etrick's story was that near Muttonhole she had taken a short cut, branching off on her own on the road leading to Lauriston. 'And when she had gone a piece of that way she heard William Etrick cry on her, and she answered that she was coming'. Looking behind her, she saw that she was being followed by David Pillans, 'who came up to her immediately and struggled with her, and threw her to the ground. And she resisted and said the curse of God would pursue him, and she cried and struggled. And when she took him by the hair of the head then he did forbear struggling with her and sat down upon a rigg-side over against her, but he got her not wronged'. After he had called to her, her husband had gone on home. David, said Margaret, accompanied her there 'and she durst not speak to him by the way, for fear he had killed her'.

Her husband supplied the information that he had met David 'at the head of the minister's riggs, and his wife a piece behind him' and then, 'not finding that David Pillans was come home', went again to look for Margaret, who told him what had happened. On the following Friday he had 'challenged' David after he came home from the plough, and David had struck him on the head with his whip-staff. It might seem that Etrick had some suspicions about his wife, because, apparently in answer to his questions, she assured him that she had never been in David's company before, 'nor never drank with him in [one] cup'.

The testimony given the session by Etrick and his wife did not tally exactly. There were no witnesses to the alleged incident itself, and David denied throwing Margaret down. His story was that Margaret had herself come to him 'at the Bluegown's lodge', had taken him by the arm and had hung on to him from there to Lauriston Loan, saying 'We shall not part until we come to Cramond'. He denied that he had struggled with her, or that she 'either cried or roared by the way'. The group had not kept together consistently. William Stewart said he had gone in company with David and Margaret along the highway from the Cleickhim Inn to 'the head of the new causeway'. After that he saw no more of them. He met William Ramsay and William Etrick at Loury's Knowe as they came looking for their wives, and heard Etrick call Margaret, but not any answer from her. Mrs Ramsay agreed with his evidence. James Clelands, interviewed in the absence of the other witnesses, said he had seen Margaret at the West Kirk, 'came the length of the Dean with her' and left her there. He then met David Pillans and the two of them stopped for refreshment at the strategically situated Cleickhim Inn and drank two chopins of ale. As they emerged from the ale-house (both, he admitted, the worse for drink) the rest of the company, including Margaret Forbes, came up. Evidently they too had been drinking.

Rebecca Mungell, who lost sight of David after she came past 'the castle' (of Lauriston?), deposed that Margaret 'got a fall by the way', though she was 'not in drink'. Her daughter, Cecile Johnston, could not confirm the fall but said that Margaret 'had gotten a sup' but was less drunk than David. David, recalled on 5 February, again denied 'struggling' and said that Margaret 'hung on his arms' and that 'she was in drink as well as himself was'. Margaret, recalled to clarify the timing, said that David had 'set upon her' a little while after her husband had called to her on the second occasion. As so often, minister and the session had difficulty in making out any clear case, apart from David's confessed drunkenness. It may or may not be relevant that Margaret would be the victim of a drunken beating from her husband in February 1706.

Pursuing events in chronological order, it was again the turn of Cecile Johnston's cousin William Temple to come before the session in October 1703. William and his friends plainly felt that the commandment to keep holy the sabbath applied, if at all, to the attendance at services on which the kirk insisted. One Sunday evening he was involved with a group who went drinking in ale-houses in Nether Cramond. The central figure in the subsequent scandal was not William and not one of the previous set of villagers but John Harvie, son of John Harvie and Elisabeth Robison in Lauriston, who may have been younger than the rest of the party because he had only recently turned seventeen. After sermon-time Harvie had shared a chopin of ale (about an imperial quart) with Richard Ramsay – one of those who stole coal at Dalgety – in Elisabeth Ker's house.[7] Harvie then met another friend from Lauriston, James Nimmo, who was utilising free time on a Sunday to find John Sim and arrange to have some tailoring done. Nimmo and Harvie then met William Temple at Jonet Ker's house, where the attraction was her daughter Dorothy McMath. Dorothy, the sister of Jonet McMath and daughter of the John McMath who had disgracefully proposed marriage to the alluring Isobel Matthie despite being married already (Chapter 4), was just eighteen. Nimmo and Temple each bought a pint of ale and Harvie and Dorothy jointly paid for a third, Dorothy fetching all the drink. After finishing their ale the three young men left. But John Harvie, who, Nimmo said, was drunk 'but spake good enough sense', ran back again. Nimmo and William Temple followed him and peered in at the window, when they overheard John Harvie say, 'I love you, Dorothy, better than both your father and mother, and better than both my own father and mother'. Temple also heard Dorothy say, 'you may lie here all night, for you will not win in to your father this night'. Dorothy and her mother then invited Harvie to lie with them in their own bed, rather than a second one that was also in the room, and he took off his clothes and lay on the outside, next to Dorothy. Meanwhile William Temple ran to fetch John's parents.

After Harvie had lain in bed for a period that witnesses estimated variously as thirty minutes and two-and-a-half hours, his parents arrived and 'cried in' to Jonet Ker, asking if their son was in her house. She swore ('banned') he was not, saying 'the devil be in the house he was in'. But when the door was opened, they found John's clothes lying and John himself sitting naked, hiding himself behind the bed among some whins. James Nimmo also testified that the day before the sessional hearing he had been in Muttonhole and heard Harvie say 'that he would do it over again, though he should take the long sands for it' (i.e. be disinherited). Harvie agreed about this and most of the other evidence.

Before the session enquired into the matter Sir John Inglis (himself barely twenty) had carried out his own investigations and 'done his part as civil magistrate' by having John Harvie (the youth's father?) scourge Dorothy and her mother through the toun of Nether Cramond. It seems that the pair were already suspected of keeping a disorderly house and James Nimmo was thought to have been a previous client, though James said only that 'he lay in [Jonet's] house a piece of a night when he was unweel, and that she and her daughter rose out of the bed and sat at the fireside, and he lay down in their bed, but did not cast off his clothes', which the minister told him was scandalous, 'the door being closed on them'. Dorothy herself was unable to attend the sessional meeting of 24 October (as a result of the whipping?). To prevent collusion, her mother was kept from going home and the minister, the clerk and three elders, apparently accompanied by John Harvie junior, went to the house to take her testimony. The case afforded them some difficulty, especially about censuring people who had already been punished by a magistrate. A sub-committee of the session recommended that the laird's baillie should be asked to fine people who sold or drank ale at sermon-time, 'or after sermons to excess', and in December presbytery authorised the session to impose the sentence of the lesser excommunication on the two women in 'the scandal in Cramond'. When Mr Hamilton tried to convince them of their sin, he reported on 28 January 1704, mother and daughter remained 'obdurate and insensible of their fault'.

About a year later, William Temple was once more cited before the session after interested observers had reported his activities. On Handsel Monday (which was New Year's Day) 1705 he had crossed by the ferry to the Dalmeny side of the Almond, perhaps to join those playing golf on the seaside links there. He was then 'seen in ane unseemly manner in the fields' with a local girl, twenty-two-year-old Isobel Ramsay. When the minister called him in privately, William confessed that he had been with Isobel in the Cockleburn. When she went to leave he conveyed her 'a piece of her way' and they sat down together at the side of a whin bush. He denied, however, that there was any improper behaviour between them. Isobel confirmed this. But one John Reid had come up to them and said to William, 'Knave, what are you doing there with a lass?', to which William replied that he was troubling her for a kiss. Isobel had refused to give him one. At the time, William said, 'both he and she were lying on their broadside'. Other observers, however, said he was on top of her. According to another, nine-year-old, witness, Reid wagged his staff at William and 'said he should garr him smart for it'. William impertinently rejoined 'What! What!' (perhaps the clerk's anglicisation of 'Hoot! Hoot!'?). A little later William was seen tying up his breeches. A second boy with Reid also saw William lying above Isobel, after which he 'rose and went over the burn and hid himself among the whins, and a little after returned to the links to those who were playing at the golf'.

The session found William guilty of scandalous carriage and he and Isobel had each to make one appearance in the public place of repentance. He may have left Cramond thereafter. In December 1707 Isobel, by then living again with her mother in the Cockleburn, was reported to be with child to a maltman in Leith. She had already appeared thrice before the session of South Leith, and also before the presbytery. Presbytery charged Cramond session to ensure that (as was usual in such cases) the midwife and the women in the Cockleburn who attended her in childbirth made her name the father of her child before the midwife 'should lay her hand on her'.

While it was a party of young men who had desecrated the sabbath by drinking in Nether Cramond in October 1703, a company predominantly of young women disgraced themselves in April 1708. Agnes Johnston's granddaughter Mary Garvie, now about twenty-one years old, was the member most seriously affected by the prolonged drinking bout that would occupy much of the elders' attention between April and June 1708. On 9 April the minister reported to the session that Mary Garvie and Elisabeth Alvis, her fellow-servant in the household of John Howison in Bridge Mill, Dalmeny, had broken the sabbath by drinking in Cramond. Mary Garvie said that she had been sick on the Saturday, and during the morning service on Sunday had sat alone in Christian Robison's house. Between sermons Mary was joined by Christian, Marion Fairholm, David Ormiston and Jonet Millar, and they drank a pint of ale, obtained from Elisabeth Raeburn (Mrs Thomas Crie).

Of these participants, Christian Robison had been another of the unruly mourners at Agnes Johnston's wake. Jonet Millar was probably a sister of Isobel and the Ann who had been censured for indecent behaviour with John Harrower in 1700. If so, Jonet was also twenty-one at this time. David Ormiston, possibly a cousin of Marion Fairholm, had been angrily reported by the West Kirk session in May 1706 as being 'found so beastly drunk in this church on sabbath 17th March that [he] abominably vomited in time of divine worship, which raised a great disorder in the congregation' – not surprisingly. David, who was then servant to George Linn in Granton Mains, had insisted to Cramond session that he was not intoxicated, and 'none could say that he was given to drinking'. He had been 'unwell in his health some days before that sabbath', and on the Sunday morning went to a certain Robert McClaren 'to get blood let', taking a fellow-servant along for company. There they drank with McClaren's two servants just two pints of ale, one warm and the other cold, and then went to hear the morning sermon at the West Kirk, and in kirk David had found himself unwell.

Evidence was that on the Sunday in 1708, after the afternoon sermon in Cramond, Mary Garvie, Christian Robison, Elisabeth Alvis, Jonet Millar and some bairns who were with them drank a quantity of ale, which was fetched by Christian Robison. Mary contributed a bawbee (6d. Scots, a half-penny sterling) and Alvis nothing. Christian confessed to obtaining three chopins from Isobel Gloag (wife of the inn-keeper Robert Mitchell). They had consumed no more than that (i.e. something like one English gallon in total) and were not drunk. Jonet Millar agreed, and supported Mary Garvie's statement that Mary had been sick that morning, although she had attended the afternoon sermon.

Mary's fellow-servant Elisabeth Alvis, however, failed to uphold her claims. Instead she said flatly that Mary had not been sick, whether on Saturday, Sunday or the next day, but performed her usual work. Moreover, Mary was so drunk on the Sunday that 'she had a great trouble in helping her home . . . by the way, and taking her home that night. Which other people saw, and those of John Howison's family. And that [Mary] went straight to her bed when she got her home'. This unfriendly testimony was confirmed by the minister himself, who met Mary on the way home, very drunk and being assisted by Elisabeth Alvis. Faced with this, Mary eventually admitted the facts. On 25 June Elisabeth, also cited for drunkenness, failed to compear to answer for herself, and gave 'slighting answers' when summoned. (On 14 May she had denied 'reproaching' some of the sessioners.)

Mary Garvie's future history will be recounted later, along with that of others. On 25 June 1708, when the session were again questioning Christian Robison about her sabbath drinking with Garvie and Alvis, the moderator challenged her about a scandalous carriage on the previous Friday. Christian – illegitimate daughter of Bessie Rae, it may be remembered – had spent a merry twenty-four hours, with a freedom altogether unbecoming to a matron. Her husband Patrick Donaldson, the young man who had helped take the yawl across to Dalgety on a Sunday in 1701, was evidently away from home at the time of his wife's escapade and may have been at sea.

On Friday 19 June William Haddan, a drummer at Edinburgh Castle, married and living in the Castle Wynd, had trysted two men to meet him at Cramond, but they failed to arrive. As he rode along the highway from Edinburgh, at Craigcrook Dyke William overtook Christian Robison and some other young women, including Cecile Johnston, Elisabeth Raeburn (the supplier of ale), and Jonet Millar, who had also drunk with Christian and Mary Garvie in that earlier incident. While William was to deny that he already knew Christian or had had any converse with her apart from buying and selling, it seems that they were acquaintances. They all went on together, William obligingly carrying Jonet's wool in front of him on his horse. At Muttonhole they all shared three chopins of ale at Hugh Nimmo's ale-house, and when they reached Nether Cramond they drank a quart of ale and a gill of brandy at the house of Elisabeth Raeburn and Thomas Crie.[8] Christian then went home briefly, and William and the other women were joined by Alexander Ronald and – making a short reappearance in these stories – John Harrower. The company then sent for Christian to rejoin them, over another quart of ale.

Two hours before sunset the party broke up. William, Christian and Jonet Millar 'went down the backside' and drank a chopin of ale in John Elder's, and then visited the Bubbling Well, near the shore of the Forth, north-east of the village. On the way back they drank another chopin in Elder's, and then returned to Elisabeth Raeburn's 'by the back way'. By then Elisabeth was in bed, but they roused her up and consumed another four chopins of ale. Finally William and Christian repaired to the house of Christian's widowed mother Bessie Rae[9] where they sat up all night. Capacity was shrinking by now and they 'drank only a pint of ale, which was fetched from Elisabeth Raeburn's'. Meanwhile, William's horse 'stayed in Christian Robison's house all night', doubtless fuelling local scandal.

Next morning – an hour before the sun, Christian said – she left her mother's, paid a short visit to Jonet Sim, and then joined William at her own house, where he collected his horse. According to William, whose private clock never synchronised with Christian's, it was then between two and three in the morning. They went together to Gogar, where Christian had arranged to visit her recently married contemporary Jean Fairholm. At Jean's house at Gogar Mill they drank two or three pints of ale in company with Jean, her husband and his sister. At 10 am William went off to see to some fighting cocks that he had at the Cat Stone.[10] Thence he made his way to Colinton Mains and then Corstorphine. At the West End of Corstorphine he alighted to get a chopin of ale and met up again with Christian, who 'got a share' of his ale and 'came with him the length of the road that goes up the hill'. They parted about 12 o'clock by her timetable and between 10 and 11 by his. (It is worth mentioning these discrepancies to show how, in the virtual absence of clocks, people commonly made their own estimates of time.)

After parting from Haddan, Christian went to Marion Fairholm's and heard that gossip was being spread about her relations with William. Jonet Millar, when examined as a witness, said she had never seen William Haddan before that Friday, but had previously heard that his wife was jealous of his acquaintance with Christian. On 25 June 1708 Haddan received a ministerial rebuke for drunkenness and 'offensive converse' with Christian, while the two of them were forbidden to talk together in future.

By 1709 John Temple, father of William, and Rebecca Mungell, mother of Cecile and Marion Johnston, were among the ordinary poor of the parish and 'in strait'. In November 1713 Rebecca had her pension increased, being old, blind and unable to do anything for herself. Old age was not easy for the poor: no wonder their juniors took their pleasure where and when they could.

David Pillans seems to have kept out of trouble after Margaret Forbes's accusation. He must have earned relatively good wages as a skilled ploughman, but on 8 January 1710 it was reported that he was lying sick, and the elder of the bound was deputed to find out what was needed for him and his family. On 29 August 1714 his wife Jonet Linn was 'lying in of twins' and given half-a-crown from the poor box. In October she tried to persuade the session either to pay for one child to be fostered, or to give her the equivalent wage, in which case she would keep both. The session refused this disingenuous bargain, but promised to give support when necessary. In September 1718 'Janet' Linn, now widowed, was given

25s. sterling for the immediate needs of her family of several small children, and on 3 June 1720 she applied to be entrolled among the poor, but, not being thought a suitable applicant on economic grounds, she was given a single payment of 12d. In September 1728 the session proposed to ask 'Janet Lind' to share accommodation with Agnes Waker, in a much-resisted scheme to put elderly pensioners together.

Margaret Forbes and her husband William Etrick were given a testimonial on 26 April 1713, attesting their sixteen years' residence in Cramond. Margaret, probably now widowed, was back before October 1719, when she was enrolled among the ordinary poor.

Cecile Johnston's further history, as it emerges in the parish records, is faintly disreputable but unadventurous. Like many of her contemporaries in Nether Cramond she remained in the village, marrying local men. She is probably the Sicill Johnston who married 'John Gloag younger in the Shoreside' on 16 May 1707 and in December had to pay the penalty for antenuptial fornication. A son, John Gloag junior, who died in 1784 aged seventy, and a daughter were baptised in Cramond. There is no reason to suppose that she was not the Cecile who subsequently married a John Miller, son to James Miller, gardener in Cramond, in 1719. After being once proclaimed with him, she had faced opposition from Agnes Mordoch, who said that she had had the promise of marriage from John, 'and that with solemn oaths'. Agnes failed, however, to pursue her complaint. Two daughters were born of that marriage, in 1722 and 1724. Since John Miller was a common name, it would be unsafe to make an identification with any of the delinquents of that time. On 7 April 1728 Cecile hired the best mortcloth for him, on her promise to pay, which she honoured on 19 May.[11] On 9 September 1730, when she was forty-seven years old, she made an irregular marriage in Edinburgh with William Elder, sailor in Cramond. In May of the previous year a Cecile Johnston was also called before the minister and the elders of Nether Cramond on a complaint by the church officer that she had abused him 'in a most opprobrious manner, using such expressions as are not decent to be named', and acknowledged that in the heat of her passion she had used such language, without just ground.

Two years after the drinking-session of 1708, in December 1710, Elisabeth Alvis was rebuked by the minister of her parish of Dalmeny for her sabbath drinking at Cramond and for fornication with David Howison, a son of the house.[12] Ten years further on (10 July 1720) David Howison asked for a child to be baptised in Cramond, and was told that since he had never purged his premarital fornication he must obtain a sponsor 'free of public scandal' to hold up his child to baptism. In

December 1723 'Elspeth' Alvis, spouse to David Howison, was seen and rebuked for carrying kale through the street in sermon-time, and in February 1729 David made the excuse that he could not attend church because he lacked shoes. He was enrolled among the parish poor in 1740, aged sixty-two, and was still receiving a pension in February 1744.

In September 1720 Christian Robison, a married woman in Cramond parish, was convicted by the West Kirk session of scandalous carriage with a man in the fields. Cramond session decided, however, that it was none of their business.

Dorothy McMath, while still under excommunication as the seducer of young John Harvie in 1703, was reported in 1708 to be with child in fornication with a William Johnston, who had lain with her in a house at Ratho and also in Cramond.[13] On 4 March 1709 Cramond session heard that William was 'turned a soldier', leaving Dorothy to face the wrath of session and presbytery, which was of opinion that 'she does not deserve the countenance of any sober Christians', and should be referred for punishment to the civil magistrate. This was to be publicly intimated to the congregation. The magistrate (John Menzies of Cammo) was also asked in August to search for Johnston, who had lately gone to Holland with the recruits but had now returned to the Canongate, where he was working at his trade. When found, he should be given 'to some of the Flanders captains, he being under church censure for fornication and being also a thief'. On 16 October session was informed that Dorothy had 'within this fortnight' gone off to the Canongate and married Johnston, paying one of her Cramond neighbours to accompany her, without telling her the purpose. The marriage was performed in his own house by that Mr John Barclay who was such a thorn in the side of presbytery and local sessions.[14] What happened to Dorothy thereafter is unknown to me.

Two years after her affair with William More in 1690 Dorothy's elder sister Jonet McMath had been proclaimed for marriage with a soldier but no marriage took place and the entry in Cramond register was cancelled. In October 1694 she confessed to a 'relapse in fornication' with another man in Edinburgh, for which she had performed due penance. In September 1697 Jonet and John Lachlan, then a widower with two small children, were reported to have drunk together in Robert Mitchell's inn after Sunday sermons, arranging marriage between them. Both admitted to drinking on the sabbath, but insisted that there had been no talk of marrying. This was supported by witnesses, among them Margaret Mungell, who was married to Jonet's brother. Lo! On 31 October their banns were accepted for proclamation and Jonet and John were married on 19 November. They then had several children, including twins in 1709. After John's death Jonet took up with the Alexander Ronald who had helped William Haddan and Christian Robison with some of their drinking in 1708 and had witnessed the baptism of Jonet's son, John Lachlan junior, in 1698. In December 1710 the impoverished Alexander and Jonet were cited for disorderly marriage. They said they had been married in Edinburgh on 2 December and produced a testificate of marriage, 'very informal', which the renegade, Episcopalian, minister Mr John Barclay was alleged to have issued. Their story was that some acquaintances had taken them to a house at the head of the Canongate, and sent for Mr Barclay to come and marry them.

Unfortunately, the acting moderator at the session on 7 January 1711 said he knew Mr Barclay's hand very well, and this was not written by him. When asked the names of the witnesses, Alexander could name none. He and Jonet were therefore forbidden to cohabit in the meantime and were referred to the Justices of the Peace. In May it was reported that Alexander Ronald had been 'put away to the soldier trade to Flanders'. On 17 June Jonet was again affirming that she was married. This time the moderator was Mr William Hamilton, who had recently left Cramond in order to become Professor in Edinburgh, and he said that he had consulted Barclay, who denied marrying the pair. In January 1712 Jonet was ordered to 'satisfy as a scandalous person' and appear on the pillar once or twice. She was then to be left unpurged until presbytery advised what to do with her. In December the session arranged to pay George Punton the 'house maill' (house-rent) that Jonet owed him at Martinmas, and he promised that he would put her out of his property before Whitsun. In June 1716, however, 'Janet McMaath' was allowed 40d. for keeping in her house a poor woman 'who brought forth a child as she was travelling to her own country'. On 6 June 1717 a George Baxter was accused of breach of sabbath in 'cursing, swearing and beating of Janet McMaath to the effusion of blood' during a drinking session. Jonet was still in Cramond and had still not been 'purged of the scandal she has lain so long under' so as to be 'received again into the communion of the church' in April 1727, but by then was being given occasional monetary assistance, which had started in July 1726 when she was unable to work owing to a sore arm. On 19 May 1728 she was given 12d., 'being in distress', and on 24 May 1731 she was named one of four people who lived by begging within the parish. In order to stop this practice, it was ordered that if she was unable to earn her living she must be paid from the poor box.

Agnes Johnston's granddaughter Mary Garvie kept out of the session minutes, apart from one uninformative citation to Dalmeny session on 3

March 1720, and payment from Cramond session of one shilling to wait on Andrew Henderson in March 1724, until, aged forty-five or so, she caused a scandal by her 'too familiar' connection with the blind William Anderson on Monday 1 January 1733. William, whose words are recorded almost verbatim by the clerk of the time, said that near the smithy he was met by someone whom he took to be Mary, and she said, 'Will, you go and I will give you a chapin of ale'. As they were going to William's house, his father-in-law said, 'Will! Rather come into my house!', but Mary said 'No, no!' In William's house William and Mary had a pint of ale, and then, he said, 'she fell on the floor and asked my hand to lift her up, and . . . I being blind, and also drunk, fell above her'. The door was not locked. According to Mary, in striving to take a kiss William had thrown her over a stool and then fallen above her.

William Crie, tailor in Nether Cramond, declared that two boys had come to him and said 'Come here and see a braw sight!', so he looked in and saw William Anderson and Mary Garvie 'in an indecent posture upon a chest'. He rushed off to summon some neighbours, including Anderson's father-in-law John Clerk. The door, he said, had been locked hard and fast before it was opened at Clerk's arrival. Both accused persisted in their denials of guilt. Anderson was cited before the presbytery, but in January 1734 proved contumacious about making any public appearance before the congregation of Cramond. On 29 April 1733 Mary was reported to have left Cramond and 'gone a-begging through the country'. This is the last we hear of her. Like so many of her contemporaries in this group of Nether Cramonders, Mary seems never to have broken successfully out of the poverty into which she had been born. Many of the group, however, displayed in their delinquencies that stubborn independence often identified as a component of the Scottish character. Who is to say that an authoritarian kirk had not helped to nurture this trait, at the same time as it positively encouraged a censorious interest in the doings of others?

NOTES

1. *Fostering.* Cramond women were in demand as foster mothers, helped by Cramond's reputation as a fine healthy place, and its closeness to Edinburgh. But the 'good air' of the district was not always enough to see an infant safely through its first months of life, and the accounts for the hire of mortcloths contain numerous references to unnamed infants who died while in the care of foster parents in Cramond, such as 'John Knight's foster' (8 June 1684), 'Helen Baxter's foster' (8 January 1688), 'Francis

Wilson's foster' (19 May 1689), and Margaret Couper's (15 May 1696). When a child survived, however, close links might be established between the fostering family and the natural parents. One woman who had allegedly come from Edinburgh to 'get the air because she was unweel' was recommended to Henry Bartleman's wife by her sister, whose child Mrs Bartleman had fostered previously: 1 Aug. 1703.

2. *Accusation and denial in Harrower case.* 9, 25, 29 Aug. 1700.

3. *Agnes Adamson's child.* 17 June 1698 and baptismal register.

4. *The Johnston family.* Because the parish registers of marriage and baptism before September 1651 are lost, some relationships between members of Agnes Johnston's generation have to be tentatively deduced from the names of those who recur as witnesses to later marriages and baptisms. Thus an Adam Johnston (father or brother?) witnessed Agnes's marriage to Alexander Dobie from Corstorphine on 1 April 1662. James Johnston and John Temple, husband of Agnes's sister Margaret, witnessed several marriages and baptisms among the clan.

5. *Kiln lodge.* The kiln must have been of the variety known as a 'cockle', hence the mill's name.

6. *Theft of coal, etc.* 8, 15 Aug., 7 Nov. 1701.

7. *Elisabeth Ker's house.* This formed a dividing point when Nether Cramond was split into two 'bounds' for such purposes as examining the inhabitants before communion day. It seems possible that it was the inn also said to be run by either Robert Mitchell (whose mother was an Elisabeth Ker) or Robert's wife Isobel Gloag. In his tax return of 1694 Mr Forrest described Mitchell as tenant in Nether Cramond, adding as an afterthought 'he selling ale' – the only person in Cramond so specified in the document.

8. *House of Elisabeth Raeburn.* There is some seeming contradiction between testimonies because the women termed this ale-house 'Elisabeth Raeburn's' whereas William Haddan thought of it as belonging to her husband.

9. *Bessie Rae.* She had married John Ballantyn, a widower with small children, in 1683 and had a further family by him.

10. *The Cat Stone.* A locally famous antiquity. Sir James Young Simpson (1811–1870) deduced that it marked the burial-place of the grandfather of the legendary Anglo-Saxon heroes Hengist and Horsa. Sir James, however, is now celebrated more for his pioneering use of chloroform in childbirth than for his expertise in archaeology.

11. *Promise to pay.* Recorded payments for mortcloth hire therefore do not always indicate date of death with much accuracy.

12. *David Howison.* Baptised March 1678, Alexander Howison, laird of Braehead, being a witness.

13. *William Johnston.* Was he the William who, caught at home by the Nether Cramond invigilators in April 1703, 'ran to the bed and hid himself'?

14. *Rev. John Barclay.* Formerly minister at Cockburnspath. Presbytery was reported, on 16 September 1711, to have had many complaints that he 'does in an irregular and clandestine manner marry persons sometimes within the forbidden degrees, as also married men which had their wives alive at the time. And many are married by him without the knowledge or consent of their parents or proclamation of banns. As also he gives false testimonials to cover the sin of uncleanness and refuses to compear but when compelled by a civil magistrate'.

EIGHT

Sins and Social Changes, 1710–1730

Since the great reforming days of the 1630s–40s the assorted heritors in Cramond had seldom acted harmoniously together for the good of the parish. When, in 1709, it came to choosing a successor to the beloved William Hamilton, there was an irreconcilable split between two factions. By the rules introduced in 1690 some thirty-six elders, feuars and portioners of the parish also had a voice in the selection. So the fourteen elders who were tenants or tradesmen, and people like Jean Smith, her son John Harrower and Margaret Kello could have played a decisive part in the election of the new minister. In the event, however, all the non-heritors voted with their 'masters' and feudal superiors.

Each of the rival parties tried to recruit as many supporters as possible. Votes were claimed on one side, opposed by the other, for three elders, one (William Ramsay) ill and long inactive and two who had moved to other parishes – one all of seven years before. Lawyers found something to dispute about the qualifications of almost everyone who claimed a vote.[1] Among the electors were, however, George Mackenzie of Tarbat, earl of Cromarty, whose son now held Royston, and William Law, goldsmith in Edinburgh, who voted on behalf of his brother John of Lauriston, in exile and gambling his way around Europe.[2] Perhaps most bizarre of all was the Edinburgh writer to the signet who obtained a vote as owner of the tiny island of Inchmickery in the Firth of Forth, inhabited by seabirds and perhaps a couple of sheep which needed no spiritual and little pastoral care.

An initial leet of four possible candidates was eventually reduced to two, one of whom obtained 34 votes and the other 26. Wisely, presbytery set aside this election and called for a new one. From a new leet of Mr James Smith, minister at Morham (one of the rejected candidates in the previous list), Mr James Dickson, minister at South Leith, and Mr Robert Mutter, probationer, Mutter was unanimously called on 6 March 1711. He refused the call, however, and on 17 June the twice-passed-over James Smith 'being mentioned as a fit person, it was thought proper to write to the earl of Ruglen [in London] to have his concurrence'. A third leet, consisting of Smith and a further probationer, was put up and eventually, in July, Smith was unanimously chosen. He was inducted in January 1712, after the manse had remained vacant for some fifteen months.

Whatever the doctrinal or political divisions behind the dispute, the voting lists suggest that in 1710 the heritors split between an 'old guard' and a smaller group of 'new men'. The latter were headed by Lord Charles Ker, second son of the marquis of Lothian, who had bought King's Cramond in 1707, Sir John Inglis of Nether Cramond, John's father-in-law (and current stepfather) Adam Cockburn of Ormiston, Lord Justice Clerk, who himself voted in right of his wife, Ann Houstoun[3] and whose daughter Sir John had married in June 1708, and George Loch of Drylaw and his mother (Isobel Foulis). On the majority side were notably the earl of Rosebery and the proprietor of Barnton, Lord John Hamilton, earl of Ruglen (and later earl of Selkirk), whose rights as sole patron would be restored in 1712, thanks to the English Tories in Westminster. The increasingly impoverished John Menzies of Cammo supported them, but his son, Dr John Menzies, sided with the Inglis faction – despite a legal objection that since his vote cancelled his father's he ought to be disqualified!

The Inglis family connection in the parish was further extended when John Clerk of Penicuik, who had married Sir John Inglis's sister Janet in February 1709, bought Cammo from old Menzies. Clerk, who became an elder along with Lord Charles Ker in November 1712 and played his part in Cramond affairs until he moved to Penicuik in 1726 on his father's death, was a model gentleman of 'the Augustan age' – much-travelled, a noted amateur antiquarian and patron of the arts. Another ornament of the age who spent time in Cramond was Robert Dundas of Arniston, Solicitor-General for Scotland (1717–20) and then Lord Advocate. He had married the eldest daughter of Robert Watson of Muirhouse in 1712 and for a time lived, when in Cramond, in the substantial house of King's Cramond. Like Ker, Clerk and Ruglen, he served his turn as ruling elder for Cramond and occasionally acted as treasurer. In March 1723 Inglis's father-in-law, Adam Cockburn, was also residing in Cramond when the law courts were not sitting. He was an elder in another parish, but was invited 'to honour this session with meeting with them and giving his advice and assistance in the affairs of this session as occasion shall offer'.

At the Dundas seat at Arniston a great scheme of beautification was in train. The house, fashionably, would shortly be rebuilt to a design by William Adam. Sir John Clerk similarly remade his house at Penicuik and at Ormiston John Cockburn (1685–1758) would become known as a great 'improver' and arboriculturist. The new minister, James Smith, had been a tutor in the family of Robert Dundas and would not have felt out of place in such cultured and elegant surroundings. He was remembered in the 1780s as 'a person of fine natural parts, improven by a good education in polite letters both at home and abroad', a man of eloquence and the possessor of 'a great measure of prudence, charity and moderation'.[4] In 1730 he would, like his predecessor, leave to become professor of divinity in the university of Edinburgh, shortly succeeding him as principal. He does not, however, seem to have left any special individual mark upon the minutes of Cramond kirk session meetings.

Since Dundas and Cockburn occupied but did not own residences in Cramond, they counted as 'gentlemen not being heritors'. Although this was not a new distinction, it marks an increasing breakdown in the old class divisions of 'heritors, farmers, cotters and servants'. At a different level, the English practice of describing a married woman as 'Mrs So-and-So' was being adopted to distinguish women of some respectable standing, like Janet Mercer or Macer, wife of William Inglis in Nether Cramond, whose husband was the leading elder, feuar of seventeen acres of land in the village, and baron baillie to Sir John Inglis.[5]

With hindsight, it is possible to detect the steady growth at this period of what must be called a 'middle class' in Cramond – a group at any rate who might or might not be perceived as 'gentlefolk' but were decidedly not to be lumped with 'the common people'. Two Edinburgh 'gentlemen' who came under suspicion in Cramond were given good characters by their own ministers,[6] and when, in October 1730, the West Kirk session enquired about a baby being nursed by Elisabeth Anderson in Cramond, she related that Mistress Christian Paterson, wife of Mr Frazer, one of the officers of the Excise, had sent for her some ten months earlier and told her that she had a child to put out to nurse, which belonged to a poor relation who was going to the south country for a time. Would Elisabeth nurse it? Elisabeth was quite sure that 'the daughter of so worthy a man would not recommend any child to her but what was right' and agreed to take it. (It was hastily removed again when enquiries began.) Men designated as merchants lived in the parish, at least two sons of farmers were sent to the university and in due course made careers as surgeons, and in the 1720s excise officers were stationed at Nether Cramond.[7]

Almost all the elders were still tenant-farmers, but William Livingston, son of the elder Robert Livingston, was also a brewer in King's Cramond and would be succeeded as elder and brewer there by William Dawling, who married a Howison of Braehead. Dowie's Mill possibly took its name from Livingston's fellow-elder, John Dowie, or his successor Charles in

Sutor Hole. Archibald Lunn bought Craigie Mill, where his family had been tenants, rose to the status of heritor thereby and rejoiced in the lairdly title 'Craigiemiln'. Robert Mitchell, the innkeeper in Nether Cramond, was another who became prosperous. According to later, possibly malicious, stories, in 1708 when he was leasing maltbarns, a kiln and some houses in Nether Cramond from Archibald Lunn, Lunn delegated him to buy the 'Temple Lands' from Menzies of Cammo. Instead Mitchell bought them for himself. Subsequently he also purchased Lunn's properties in the village.[8]

These people, of rising importance in their own spheres, might have agreed with a later member of the middle classes, Sir Walter Scott, whose father would be factor for Lauriston in the 1760s and '70s, and for a time a minor heritor, when Scott wrote in *The Heart of Midlothian* that the superior gentry at this period 'were at once idle, haughty, fierce, divided by faction, and addicted to intemperance'. One is also reminded of the minister of Ratho's pregnant commendation of an earl of Lauderdale in the 1790s, 'who was remarkable, *in his rank,* for religious decency, and for his regular attendance on public ordinances'.[9] The thriving members of this amorphous middle class, often tolerant of the failings of their own sort, were careful to distance themselves from 'the common people'. And a certain cultural divide between the better- and the less-educated is illustrated by an entry in the register for May 1730 when the schoolmaster registered the baptism of 'Phoebe' Henderson and then, presumably on her father's insistence, changed the name to 'Feve'.

To John Philp Wood and his friends in the 1780s some aspects of Cramond life at this period would seem almost as culturally remote as the Middle Ages. As a piece of 'oral history', one of them took down an old man's rambling reminiscences of youthful exploits and the quaint customs of half a century before.[10] Perhaps the unnamed informant was a carter like Alex Gillespie in Fairafar, because he remembered how, before the coming of toll roads, the Cramond carriers of coal and lime had their own organisation, 'the union of whipmen', into which boys between the ages of twelve and fourteen were initiated once they could drive a plough.[11] On admittance they gave a whipman's 'bond' which obliged them to assist one another and to carry in their bonnets the emergency repair kit of knife, leather-worker's awl and thick thread.[12] (Were they also given the secret 'horseman's word' of 'Baith in Ane'?) Union meetings were held at roadside public houses and at the AGM in summer a piper was hired and there was much merrymaking in the afternoon. Sometimes the servant girls living nearby would come, 'and the young lads and them would have danced together'. In the winter, he also mentioned, horns were blown at every farmer's house about 8 pm 'when they suppered the horses and cows'.

But what this informant most vividly remembered were the pre-1758 Lammas games between two rival groups of herd-boys and their supporters, from both Cramond and Corstorphine parishes. The herds from the west end of the Clermiston – Lennie area met on Lennie Hill and those from the east on Clermiston Hill. The day started for each side with a feast of sweet cream, butter and cheese around an earthen tower up to twelve feet high, topped with a pole and a banner decorated with ribbons lent by the young lasses of the area. After their dinner, shared with any poor boys who joined them, the herds from the west side marched down the hill to Lennie Port, blowing their horns and led by a piper and their 'ancient' (standard-bearer). There they were joined by a group of 'young men'. Sometimes the day ended peaceably with foot-races, drinking and wagering 'at the bab' (in *Cramond*, p. 119, Wood translated this as 'playing at ball and quoits'). On more memorable occasions there was a violent scrimmage in which each side – which by then might number as many as sixty boys and young men – tried to capture the other's colours. The old man recalled taking part in two such 'bloody battles' on Cramond Muir, perhaps, he thought, in 1734 and 1735. In the second his side forced their opponents to lower their colours, 'and I trampled on them'. As he talked he recollected more names of the long-forgotten heroes of these affrays, two of whom should have their names inscribed on parchment in letters of gold. And there was the married colour-bearer, who had been careful to pocket his cravat lest it became bloodstained and reveal to his wife what he had been up to.

These activities and patterns of association lay quite outside the concerns of the kirk and therefore made no appearance in the session minutes. For various reasons the practice of fostering children, which established other personal connections, did at times attract sessional attention. Janet Paton had nursed a son of Sir James Ritchison. Ritchison's daughter Margaret, married to an absentee Captain Dunbar, had children lodging with Janet and her daughter and son-in-law (Thomas Hamilton) in Granton. While herself staying with the Hamiltons in January 1716, Margaret fell pregnant to a gardener in Granton. Janet Paton undertook to find a nurse for the child. The ties established by fostering were so strong that when she and the Hamiltons were admonished for 'haunting a person of so bad character about their house and concurring with her to conceal her sin', Janet asserted that she was under an obligation to Margaret by virtue of being foster-mother to Margaret's brother. Other Cramond families were charged with breach of sabbath when they received visits from the family of a nurseling. On two successive Sundays in July 1715 a coachful of men and women was seen going to Thomas Paul's house in Nether Cramond at time of morning service. On the second occasion the elders 'heard a whispering of tongues in the house, but when they knocked at the door they all kept silent, not opening to them'. Paul's wife told the minister that the visitors were the parents of the child she nursed and she couldn't tell them to go. 'And further they were Episcopally inclin'd and would not go to church.'[13] Her carriage to the minister when he spoke to her 'was such as gave ground to fear she had no due sense of her sin'. Her husband denied that the party had been offered ale, and said that it was the visitors who would not let his wife open the door. As was now happening with increasing frequency, the case was dropped. Similarly, in April 1725 James Young and his wife were called before the minister and two elders for entertaining strangers in their house during divine worship. The Youngs said they had a nurseling in the house whose relations had come to see it in the morning and been given four pints of ale.

The stress of wider events still affected the comfortable classes of Cramond. The combined menace of Jacobitism, popery and aggression by foreign powers meant that the heritors voting for a new minister in 1710 must take the oath of allegiance to the established crown. There were general fasts 'for the safety of this realm and disappointing the boundless ambition of France', to ward off an expected invasion from Sweden in 1717 'in favours of a popish pretender', and, in 1719, a similar threat from Spain. In September 1713 congregations were generally warned to beware popery and trafficking priests 'and to shun the pretender'.[14]

These fears came to their first head in 1715. On 15 August the Cramond minister and available heritors met to list the 324 'fencible men' in the parish,[15] and on 10 October there was a 'Randevouse' of this militia on Cramond Muir to guard the coast from Cramond Water to Inchbucklar-brae against surprise by the 'rebellious parties in the north'. The rebels did not in fact disturb Cramond, but one incidental victim of the abortive rising was wounded in the arm by Dutch soldiers as they were passing by in June 1716. He was unable to pay the surgeon, one Andrew Anderson, whose account, including the price of drugs when an itemised one was presented to the session, came to 10s. sterling.

These alarms brought Cramond's one Catholic family into prominence. In June 1711 the mason George Clark and his wife, Esther Jackson, were ordered to confer with 'the professor' and two other ministers, but failed to do so. It was then reported that two papist priests had been in the Clarks' house in Sandyhaugh (Muirhouse) baptising their child. In June 1717 invigilating elders found a great number of men and women eating and drinking in the Clarks' house at service-time. As non-members of the kirk they could not be summoned before the session, and Mr Robert Dundas, then living in Muirhouse, was asked to complain to Clark. Then in April 1726 the minister called George and his wife to a private meeting and vainly endeavoured to show Esther 'the evil of her popish principles'. Her husband stoutly 'denied that he was an apostate, [saying] that he was popish as soon as he knew anything, and that when he came from the north he disguised his principles by reason of his poverty. That he had always a remorse during that time, and continued so for several years till his brother came from the north and advised him to join again with those of his own principles'. One daughter was triumphantly reported in the minutes for 17 January 1725 to have turned protestant, but later, in January 1732, the Clarks' son John was irregularly married 'by one of his own way of thinking'. It was contrary to the laws of the kingdom for a popish priest to conduct marriages, and no marriage lines were available 'because their minister uses to give none'.

Worse still, Mrs Clark ran a school. Her religion meant that she was by no means one of those orthodox and well-affected persons who were by now being tolerated as teachers of dame schools, and who offered a more practical education than the parish schoolmaster. All the same, her school was well patronised, and on 14 May 1714 one of the elders themselves had to be admonished for sending his children there and told to look elsewhere. On 1 March 1719 Solicitor Dundas was to be asked for an official order to stop Esther keeping her school. Although on 5 April she was reported to have given it over, in November 1725 she was still teaching and again in April 1726 was promising to desist as soon as her current scholars had finished their terms.

Esther Jackson's school was conveniently situated at some distance from the parish school and it was the taint of popery that was mainly feared by the authorities. Private schools in Nether Cramond itself had more immediate impact on the parish schoolmaster's authority – and income – so that in March 1719 Baillie Inglis was to speak to 'such who teaches private schools in Nether Cramond to desist therefrom'. Agnes Weir then gave a limited undertaking 'to teach neither boys nor girls English, but such who are learning to sew or work stockings, after the quarters of her present scholars are ended'. On 20 July 1722, however, we find the sessioners agreeing to pay Janet Dowie for three quarters teaching George Donaldson's grandchild, a poor scholar, and on 17 January 1725 they reported that the parish contained several private schools for younger children, 'with the teachers of which the session has no reason to be dissatisfied'.

Mr Thomas Forrest's enforced retirement as parish schoolmaster and session clerk in April 1715 marked a significant break with the past. He had served under five ministers of various characters and allegiances when, obviously ailing, he made his last entry in the sessional minute book, relating to the meeting of 13 February 1712. He was noted as sick and unable to bring the roll of examinable persons up to date on 3 December 1714, while the precentor who had been his substitute at services for two months was himself unable to do so by late February 1715. Forrest lived on, at first a burden on his successor Mr John Haldan, who was obliged to allow him part of his own stipend, and then an object of parish charity, until early December 1718. His widow was then maintained at parish expense until, on 10 August 1723, the session noted that she was being boarded with a Cramond family at her brother's expense. She was luckier than the widow of the parish schoolmaster in Ratho, where it was reported on 1 April 1716 that all the heritors who had owed payment of her husband's salary were dead and there was no hope of obtaining the arrears due.

Although in October 1712 there was still £2,000 of the poor's stock and several years' interest owed by Sir Henry Wallace of Ingleston[16] and John Menzies of Cammo owed a further £100 when he was declared bankrupt in 1714, parish funds were now less tight than they had been at various crises in the past. There was some temporary difficulty early in 1713: on 2 January the session deferred a decision on a petition for enrolment 'until there be money in the box to pay the ordinar poor', and on 19 May it cannily put off the question of enrolling an aged and sickly woman in Cockle Mill until it was known whether she would recover. In March the appointment of five constables was called for, in one of the usual efforts to keep sturdy beggars away from the parish. Once the legal processes had been completed, John Strachan's mortification of his estate of Craigcrook for the benefit of the poor, in 1719, must have eased pressures on Cramond's funds.

As always, collections were regularly taken for outsiders recommended by presbytery: in December 1713 Cramond paid the 20s. requested for a young minister going to Carolina, and on 6 September 1724 £4 10s. sterling was collected 'for the Scots congregation in New-York in America'.

Frequently an appeal might be made to private generosity when a parishioner met with disaster: in December 1724 when James Young petitioned for a loan of 40s. sterling to help repair his boat, which had been badly damaged in a violent storm, he was told to apply to well-disposed persons in the parish. An earlier storm, in February 1714, damaged John Elder's coal-boat and demolished Alexander Williamson's. In such cases the session tried to balance the needs of the family with shrewd commercial supervision. Elder was already in debt to the coal suppliers of Fordel, Fife. The session, anxious lest his boat, once repaired, should be seized by his creditors, proposed that he should transfer ownership to their nominees until the debt was cleared. Shortly before the storm, being in a mean case and having many children, he had been given £10: £4 in gift and £6 as a loan so that he could stock his boat. A public collection was taken up for him after the boat was damaged, but he may have decided to leave his debts unpaid and sell it for what it would fetch once some repairs had been done.

In February 1714 Alexander Williamson had wanted £5 sterling to buy a new coal-barque and agreed to repay the session with 40d. each time that he came into Cramond with coals, giving a bond to that effect jointly with John Sim, his father-in-law. No repayments were in fact made and when, in 1719, his wife brought forth twins and was found to be in great want the parish provided her with butter and meal. It reads oddly that on 2 October two of the elders were asked to speak to her husband, to get him to give part of his wages for the maintenance of his wife and family.

Whenever possible, sessions encouraged self-help among the poor. Robert Loudan was twice given money to buy leather so that he could trade as a cobbler, and rather than enrol Edward Moubray's crippled son among the poor, the session offered to put him to a trade. In 1718 the widowed Katherine Couper, whose crippled son, John Young, was one of the enrolled poor, sought help to set him to a trade. She was asked to find him a master and tryst him to discuss arrangements with two of the elders. The boy was then bound apprentice to a tailor in Newhaven for four years, at an annual fee of 26s. sterling. This was more than Katherine could afford, so she was offered 30s. sterling from the poor's box towards the total. A month later, however, the sub-treasurers were told that John had returned home indisposed and his indentures had been cancelled.[17]

Ideals of good management as much as scarcity of resources may have prompted moves to force single pensioners to live together. Three elderly women agreed to do so in May 1714, but the scheme was generally resented. In May 1728 Agnes Walker refused an order to take some of the enrolled poor into the house with her, and had her allowance stopped until she complied.

When the church officer died in November 1722 his widow, Jean Mitchell, maintained herself for six months by taking the emoluments and employing someone else to perform the duties of the job. However, she was hard-pressed by illness and a family of small children. Despite being given the usual wet-nursing fee when she refused to put the youngest to a foster-mother, in July she petitioned 'showing her necessitous condition by reason of weakness of body, great weakness of her sight, and that she hath four young children, and one of them affected with the scrofula in both arms and both feet'. The session agreed to give her 10s. a month for two months. She died about five years later, and, as usual, the session ordered that the 'plenishings' of her house should be rouped (auctioned) for the benefit of her orphaned daughter, now 'cast upon the session'. The total value of her goods was just under 40s. sterling, of which a small amount was owed to various people. John Malcolm's wife also claimed a timber bed, bequeathed to her in gratitude 'for the service she did to her during her long sickness'. It was agreed that Malcolm and his wife should keep the orphan in bed and board at 40d. per month, the session to provide her clothes.

Another mother, the widow of the late smith in Muttonhole, arrived in Dalmeny in December 1717 'in a miserable dying condition', and died two days later, leaving three children. Since the youngest child had been born in Cramond, Cramond session accepted that its maintenance was their responsibility. Five-and-a-half years later, in July 1723, Archibald Lunn was delegated to go to Dalmeny and see whether the child was yet fit to be sent out to service. He reported that she was not. She was only seven years old!

Mary Dick was orphaned at the age of six when her father, James Dick, died in 1723, about a week after his second marriage to one Mary McCaul. Mary's stepmother subsequently complained to the session 'that she thought herself under no obligation to be burdened with the child'. The session allowed her 20d. to keep the little girl on 'until they thought upon some proper course', and enquired how much Margaret Glasgow would take. Eventually Mary's stepmother agreed to keep her for 24d. a month but the session apparently felt some doubts about this arrangement, as on 2 September the elders of the town were instructed 'to take inspection of the child, how she was taken care of'. Perhaps their conclusions were not favourable: next March Mary was boarded with George Marr, the church officer, at 40d. a month. Besides paying for her board, in subsequent years the session bought her a New Testament and sent her briefly to school.

When Mary was nearly eleven-and-a-half, in 1728, the session looked for work for her, and found a woman in Edinburgh who wanted a girl to look after her shop. The minister and clerk were asked to make the best bargain they could for Mary's advantage, and to expend one or two months' allowances 'to put clothes upon her'. It was agreed that if Mary served for three years she should be taught shopkeeping and sewing, that she would go furnished with 'whole clothes' and that her mistress, Mrs Ewan, would provide for her in bed, board and clothes for that time, 'if the said girl shall continue honest during the said space of three years'. George Marr handed over 'what clothes he had that had belonged to Mary's father, James Dick [five years before!], and been in the possession of her step-mother Mary McCaul', and these were made up for Mary's use, at a cost of £6 4s. 6d. Scots. When Mary entered 'home', i.e. into service, she was provided with six shirts, six head cloths, two gowns, a plaiding coat, three aprons, two neck napkins, and her bible. Her mistress said that she left it to the pleasure of the session whether they would give Mary a pair of shoes every year, a decision which they deferred for the time being. The children of the poor could expect to wear made-over clothes. When one of the 'blue-gowns' (licensed beggars) died, in 1728 one of his gowns was given to Katherine Crawford 'to be clothes to her children'.

In this increasingly commercially minded age, a nice question of economics and morality presented itself after a certain John Broun admitted, in 1715, the 'horrid wickedness' of fornication with Helen Duncan, whom he knew at the time to be 'in terms of marriage' with Thomas McAlpine. McAlpine then profited from his wife's fees for fostering a child 'on the child's milk which she brought forth to John Broun'. Should he not, therefore, contribute to the support of her child by Broun? The session decided yes, and McAlpine expressed willingness to give £8 Scots for its maintenance 'if the session would be easy to his wife in respect of her penalty' for fornication.

As ever, the poor must be in genuine need to receive help. Thomas Thomson, who lodged in Andrew Henderson's house in July 1713, was unable to put on his coat without assistance. He had 'his meat made in the house' and paid 16s. a month, which left him only 20d. out of his pension. Baillie Inglis was, however, to investigate the rumour that he had money of his own. In 1713, too, Agnes Simpson, aged eighty-two, who had gone to

Fife for June and July, wanted the pension for those two months to meet her rent. She was allowed only one month's.

As ever, the threat to withhold pensions could be used in an endeavour to bring the enrolled poor to heel. Naturally, it was resented. And one is inclined to agree with the aged Christian Duncan and James Easton, who evidently considered that the session were interfering unwarrantably in their private lives. The offence, which allegedly caused a scandal throughout their district, occurred in 1710, during the ministerial vacancy. The Reverend Mr James Smith might have taken it less seriously. It was reported that on the pensioners' pay day James and Christian drank together in Nether Cramond and then went to Christian's house in the Bridge End where they drank and lay together. The pair said that James had become unwell after drinking between sermons at the baxter's (baker's) house and later at Brigend. Rather than choosing to go to a hostelry, James said, he had sat on a chair in Christian's house till midnight, doing no ill with her. At break of day he went on to see his daughter in Up Craiggie. After further investigations, the session considered that the pair of them had confessed to excessive drinking and being alone together in the night time, and on 15 April 1711 ordered them to be separately rebuked before the congregation. Christian in particular took an obdurate stance, despite having her pension withdrawn: she flatly refused to make the required public appearance at first, and it took her six months to comply.

People like Christian and James would provide a ready audience for the story spread in July 1717 by Margaret Millar (granddaughter of the notorious William Carle) that Baillie Inglis and Claud Wilson had sat drinking in an ale-house at service time when they should have been invigilating in the parish. The elders thus 'calluminiated', as schoolmaster Haldan called it, were two of the more zealous at a time when some of their fellows had been rebuked for failing to attend sessional meetings or collect at the church door. Before the minister, the two maligned elders and Inglis's son, William Inglis in House of Hill, who was her employer, Margaret admitted spreading the story, acknowledged that it was 'grounded on a false report' and apologised.

In a few other cases neighbours were happy to collaborate with the elders. They were carefully examined, however. When rumour spread that Patrick Ballenie and Janet Hall had been seen 'sitting together at the seaside some weeks ago', the unnamed witness told the session in January 1718 that he couldn't tell who the pair were and wouldn't know them again. Nor did he see them lying together.

The widower John Samuel, a weaver in Lennie Muir, created a much more public scandal in 1723. On Saturday 20 April Samuel met a woman on the highway near the moor, took her into his house and shut the door. The neighbours sent for the local elder, Archibald Spotswood, called to the pair to open the door and threatened to break it down when they got no answer. After Samuel had called that they would find him hanged if they did so, they eventually forced it, and saw the woman putting on her 'head clothes' and Samuel standing barefooted. Samuel, who said he had been drunk and could not remember what he said to the neighbours, denied uncleanliness with the woman, 'acknowledged he was in bed but knew not whether she was in it or not, that he was standing barefooted when they broke up the door, and that he only kissed her'. When he was again brought before the session, on 26 May, the minister besought him for a full confession, but Samuel replied 'that he would confess no more than what he had done already'. Later he also denied following the woman to Kirkliston and asking for her there, and told the session to prove it. The session, 'having considered this scandalous behaviour, his disingenuity and breach of former promise of a sober carriage after he had been rebuked some time ago for drunkenness on the sabbath day', ordered him to appear for rebuke before the congregation in a week's time. (He finally did so on 7 July.) The further matter of his suspected guilt was 'to lie open till they see if there be any further discovery about it'. The woman, however, could not be traced.

General views on morality were openly defied in 1716 by George Craw and Agnes Adamson, spouse of Andrew Hill, who continued to converse together despite the minister's admonition and advice, to the extent that Agnes, with her husband's consent, scandalously took a house next to Craw's. Margaret Kello, the feuar of the house (who had, as a widow, cohabited before remarriage herself), was pressured to withdraw their tenancy, and despite stiff resistance from Agnes and her husband, Sir John Inglis eventually made them leave the property. Hill, evidently a most complaisant spouse, had married Agnes when she was pregnant by another man in 1698, as mentioned in Chapter 7.

No accusation of adultery was made against Craw and Adamson. But when on 5 April 1730 Elisabeth Marr, daughter of the church officer, tried to account for her pregnancy by asserting that she had been ravished by a stranger between Cramond and Burnshot 'about the latter end of July' as she was on the way to visit her aunt, the minister recommended her to tell the truth, reminding her that otherwise church discipline demanded that she be treated as an adulteress. Elisabeth stuck to her story, despite being 'put to it' by the midwife and a report from two boys who had seen her 'about the beginning of August last' in a barn with the earl of March's coachman. All she would admit was that 'she had been too merry and light in her carriage'.

Far more seriously, in May 1712 Isobel Aikman, wife of Thomas Short in Nether Cramond, had admitted to her husband, and subsequently to the minister, that she had committed adultery with a John Ogilvie, sergeant in the Master of Elibank's Company, Grant's Regiment. She then tried to retract, 'alleging that she was not in her right wits' when she made the confession. After waiting in vain for Ogilvie to appear before them, the session proceeded to summon witnesses. Margaret Livingston said she had often seen Isobel and the sergeant 'behave unseemly together', sitting alone together in Isobel's house after dark. On the queen's birthday last he had been in her house 'after it was dark night, about seven hours at even', the door being shut. Margaret looked through the lock-hole and saw them both sitting before Isobel's bed. Isobel then lay backward into the bed and he, lifting up her feet, went into it after her, and they stayed like that a good while. Meanwhile Margaret 'cried three several times to her to open, without receiving any answer'. When at last Isobel came out, Margaret accused her, and Isobel 'had not a face to deny' the charge.

Margaret gave her the friendly advice to give up the sergeant's company, and took it upon herself to promise that in that case she would not tell what she had seen. But Isobel refused, since she saw no ill in his company. So Ogilvie continued to be often in her house all the time he was in Cramond. Asked whether she knew whether Isobel was intimate with any other of the soldiers, Margaret said she had seen a man named Moffat frequently in her house, playing at the game of preens with her,[18] sometimes until 10 pm. Another neighbour added that she had often seen Ogilvie in Isobel's house at night. Other soldiers had been there as well, but never alone with her. After rumours spread about Isobel and the sergeant, the other soldiers went to the house less frequently.

After having 'the impudence to deny that she had confessed adultery', on 1 August Isobel was ordained to appear in sackcloth at the church door before service, and then enter the pillar, sit during the morning's sermon, and suffer public rebuke when it ended. After she had done this on twelve occasions, on 2 November the session asked the minister to have her examined, since she was said to be pregnant. On 15 November the minister and three elders interrogated Isobel, and two midwives, Cecile Blair and Isobel Ewin, felt her breast, found milk there and reported that she was with child. Isobel then confessed this to the minister and admitted that Ogilvie was the father. Asked how long she had to go, she said about a month. In fact she gave birth two days later. After 'standing' for the seventeenth time on 8 February 1713 she was finally absolved, with the minister's omnipurpose exhortation 'to seek to the blood of Jesus Christ for her sin' and his injunction to 'consider it was grievous to her to be separated so long and excluded from the fellowship of the congregation'. When her husband returned from sea the two again lived together and had more children.

The attempt to force all parishioners to attend sabbath worship had by now been abandoned. Indeed, employers expected some of the servants to remain in the house to prevent burglary: in December 1729 one of the servants in Royston Mains explained that she had indulged in 'the practice of uncleanness' with a fellow-servant, particularly on the sabbath days when it was their turn to stay at home. Occasionally a zealous elder reported someone – usually in Nether Cramond – for cutting kale or walking down the street without obvious necessity at sermon-time. On 6 December 1712 a soldier who was seen to go down the town in time of sermon was to be reported to his commander, and two months later, when several young women came to the backside of the town on the sabbath afternoon and sat with soldiers, two elders were instructed to visit the town after sermons and 'restrain that abuse'. Perhaps few of Cramond's elders of this time would have gone as far as the country minister of East Carmyllie, who described the practice of selling small goods on Sunday as 'a piece of Atheism which will not fail to draw down wrath both on the buyer and the seller, exposing the place and the congregation to judicial Stroaks from God'.[19] But sessions did try to prevent secular affairs creeping in, as when they complained on 6 April 1712 that the church officer used meetings of the congregation to proclaim matters for which he had no authority from the minister, 'profaning the Lord's day'. And the usual complaints were made about 'the folk of Nether Cramond that convenes after sermons at the doors for clattering on the Lord's days or that goes in companies to the fields', with an injunction 'to go into their houses and read the scriptures'. In the same month of June 1712 there was an attempt to stop William Wright and his wife selling drink in Granton to the many folk who came there from Edinburgh and Leith for Sunday recreation.

Although the Nether Cramond tailor John Sim (or Syme) drew attention to himself on New Year's Day 1714 by extreme intoxication and 'horrid cursing . . . in the minister's own sight and hearing', most cases of drinking had, as usual, to occur on the sabbath to arouse sessional concern. On Sunday 17 March 1717 when Baillie Inglis was patrolling the village, he saw Thomas Paul's wife carrying a pint stoup from her house to another in service-time and rebuked her. Mrs Paul, previously in trouble for entertaining relations of her foster-child, was summoned before the session when she returned from giving birth in Edinburgh, but sent her husband instead. He denied that anyone had been drinking in his house at the time and said the trouble of it 'seized his wife so much that her health is much impaired and the child's life is in danger which she is nursing'. At his request, the minister agreed to call her before him and the Nether Cramond elders for a private rebuke.

On 21 July 1717 the session heard that James Smith in Whiteside had last sabbath entertained a large number of people who were 'cummering', i.e. visiting his wife and new baby.[20] He was censored for encouraging people to visit on Sunday by selling them ale – no more than five 'chapins' among ten of them, Smith said. Some of the elders had met Smith's visitors coming away and thought them drunk, particularly James Gilchrist in Nether Cramond. Summoned before the session, he confessed that 'he was a little mistaken with drink, and begged pardon for any impertinent answer he gave' the elder who had met and rebuked him. He was let off with a warning. Walter Gowan, cook to Sir John Inglis, was reported in August 1717 for drinking in Thomas Anderson's house at sermon time with his wife, who had come from Edinburgh to see him. Gowan denied being drunk and claimed that he had merely happened to stumble as the invigilating elders passed by. Other invigilators on Sunday 2 January 1719 found two strangers sitting in Elspeth Raeburn's house in the afternoon with an empty stoup before them. The elders advised them to go to church, but 'they told they were going further this way' and went off immediately.

On another Sunday afternoon in 1720, 'after the dismissing of the congregation', Archibald Spotswood saw James Samuel lying drunk by the wayside and rebuked him. He was let off with a ministerial rebuke and warning. Similarly, a private rebuke by the minister and three elders was administered to William Hall in the waulk (fulling) mill at Peggy's Mill, when John Dowie brought him to the minister in July 1725 and he confessed to being drunk on a fast day. Hall expressed sorrow, and said that he had never been before a session and would promise never to do the like again if he could be excused from appearing before them.

It was breach of sabbath that concerned the session in April 1727 when John Comb had been seen travelling on the highway at the time of service and looking in at the windows of Granton House, which had caused him to be arrested on suspicion of the burglary committed there that same night. The case, however, became one for the civil authority. And a complaint from Dalgety required Cramond, on 16 July 1721, to send over David Young, skipper in Nether Cramond, to answer for the offence given to the people there 'in sailing his barque loadened with coals out of their harbour in time of divine worship'.

It was also the timing that meant that a great noise in Alexander Williamson's house brought enquiry by the patrolling elders on 2 January 1719. They elicited that Williamson had been contending with his wife and beating her in the time of divine worship. Williamson promised before the session that he would observe the sabbath 'more punctually and carry himself more kindly towards his wife in time coming'. She gave birth to twins six months later, when, as previously mentioned, her husband had to be politely asked to contribute something towards her maintenance.

Apart from some insolence to elders and an increasing indulgence in irregular marriage (usually by the poorer members of the congregation), 'passive resistance' was, as ever, the commonest way of 'slighting' the session's authority. Cornelius Kay had undertaken, in June 1706, to pay a crown to the poor box, in addition to the usual penalty for fornication, for the privilege of performing his penance three times on the one day. Over six years later, when Cornelius absolutely refused to pay, his brother and sister-in-law were approached on the matter without success. Early in 1713 an elder eventually found Cornelius at home, but he ran out of the house when spoken to. The session, 'seeing no probability of recovering that money, resolved not to seek any further after it, but to leave that affair with their declaration that the said Cornelius Kay hath broken his promise to the session'. In future no such promises should be accepted. They had met similar frustration in 1712 when Elisabeth Thomson, widow in Nether Cramond, 'scorned the kirk' when she was publicly proclaimed for marriage with two successive men and failed to proceed with the banns. It was felt reasonable that she should pay £3 Scots penalty to the poor box. After a series of promises to pay, extending over ten months, she was finally told on 31 July 1713 that the matter would be dropped but she was to be 'noted in the session book a mark of infamy'.

It has been observed often enough already that a system of parish discipline that required the cooperation of offenders and, often, the active assistance of another session, had never been wholly efficient. Increasingly, though, minister and sessioners in Cramond tended to abandon prosecutions when difficulties arose. Jonet McMath (see Chapter 7) never was 'purged' from the sin of pretended marriage in 1710. Fewer couples were now pursued for antenuptial fornication. If they alleged that they had been married clandestinely, the claim could be troublesome to disprove. In

1712 a soldier named John Echolm or Axom, who was cohabiting with Christian Henderson in her father's house, said they had been married by one Mr Lockie, though he didn't know whether he was a minister or not. A year later, in November 1713, Baillie Inglis learned that they were shortly going to Ireland and the session felt that they need not trouble with them further, except that it would be reasonable to inspect the testimonial of marriage the couple claimed to possess. The minister then discovered that none existed. Echolm and Christian's father then confessed to Inglis that the pair were not married, although they had been together for twelve months. Echolm offered to perform penance and marry, but the session felt that he was 'of no good character otherways, as also it was unclear whether he had been a single person or not, [and] rather wish'd they might remove from this place, and the baillie promis'd to speak to Sir John Inglis of it'. Sir John promised that if the couple did not leave within the present week he would lock the door against them. Christian's father said this course had his approval, and the two duly went.

Two outsiders were thankfully abandoned after enquiries in 1716. 'Some persons of known credit' had told one of the elders that on Friday 25 May they had seen a man and woman in the fields below Drylaw House in an indecent posture. The man fled at their approach, but they apprehended the woman. At first she refused to give them her name, but they later found that she was Jean Forrest, a domestic servant in Edinburgh. She denied uncleanliness with the gentleman, whom she did not know and had met by accident in James Bruce's house when she was about her master's business. Asked why she had not kept to the highway, she said he had promised to take her a short cut. 'Did he offer any incivility to her by the way?' 'She replied he fash'd her several times, and when going up a balk he threw her down to abuse her, and when she cried there were none to help her.' When at last two men came by, she told them, 'You are well come, to deliver me from this adulterous fellow'. One of them deposed that he had seen the pair in the balk, with the gentleman above Jean a considerable time, until he and his servant came 'within a pennystone cast of them', whereupon the gentleman ran away 'with his breeches among his feet'. He had not heard Jean cry out, nor did she seem to have been weeping.

The man concerned proved to be a certain John Beton, who lived with his mother at Craigleith, West Kirk parish. He acknowledged that he had been walking that way and had met a woman, but, being drunk at the time, 'did not remember if he offered any incivilities to her', and denied throwing her down. She sat down and he sat beside her. He could not identify Jean as the woman involved. Jean identified Beton as the man, but said he had not wronged her. The session thought it difficult if not impossible to prove guilt when both denied it. She was not with child and the scandal was not flagrant throughout the parish. So it would be 'edifying' enough to administer a sessional rebuke to him for being drunk and to both for scandalous conduct. Perhaps the fact that witnesses described Beton as a 'gentleman' also had something to do with this outcome.

If Cramond showed disinclination to be unduly severe on two strangers who behaved indecently within their own bounds, they were happy enough to relinquish responsibility when, in April 1718, one of their own parishioners fell pregnant (her second such sin) to a weaver in Paul's Work after an encounter in the King's Park. The man was now in Berwick and 'the scandal not being as yet flagrant in this parish it belongs to Duddingston to purge it'. Unfortunately the duty was refused because the authorities in Duddingston replied that no part of the park fell within their parish.

In September 1723 rumours flew around the parish in connection with the visit of a woman calling herself Janet Brand, who took lodgings at Bog-End in Lauriston. She was seen there with Muirhouse's coachman, John Mitchell, and Mitchell's fellow-servant John Matheson or Mathewson. She had also been in the kitchen and stable of Lord Advocate Dundas's residence in Upper Cramond, where one of the servants came under suspicion of dealings with her. On the night of Wednesday 25 September Janet and a woman companion met with four men, including Muirhouse's coachman and a groom employed by Dundas. About six o'clock next morning another of Muirhouse's servants, John Nave, was in the house of the Granton gardener John Miller, where Mitchell and Matheson were boasting about their evening's exploits. Three weeks later Nave deposed:

> that the said John Mathewson said to him that yesternight they met with a piper in Granton links, that they had a pleasant spring, that they had all danced round, and after they had done they sent in William Wilson to dance. That . . . William Wilson lost his bonnet there. That he, the declarant, asked where it was. That . . . John Mathewson told it was in the goodwife's of Granton her chaff-house and that the said John Mathewson told in other words that it was with a woman, and a lesser woman with her. That they had agreed with her for fifteen pence. . . . That he told that the little woman asked her neighbour if she had got the money. That she told she had it in her

pocket. That after they came from Granton chaff-house they came to John Miller's, and being refused ale there, they came to Andrew Yeats his house at Slovans and drank Galloway whey.

According to Miller's servant-woman, early the same morning the two women went to Miller's, drank three chopins of ale and asked for the coachman. They then seem to have departed from Cramond. Some time later, when these stories were going the rounds, one of Lord Royston's servants puzzled a servant in Granton Mains by asking jestingly, in reference to the chaff- (alias coal-) house, 'Who keeps the key of your bawdy-house now?'

The five men concerned in these various escapades were summoned before the session, which had first felt obliged to obtain Muirhouse's consent to call his servants. Matheson meanwhile had gone to Edinburgh, and then London. One of Dundas's servants, who said he had not even spoken to Janet Brand, was dismissed failing any contrary evidence. The other three all denied, with some insolence, that they had had any illicit dealings with Janet or her friend. In the absence of any definite proof the matter had to be shelved in the vain hope of obtaining 'clearer light'. In such circumstances Mr Smith resorted to telling suspects that 'though their wickedness be hid from the eyes of men, yet it cannot be hid from the eyes of an all-seeing God'.

Both the difficulty of obtaining hard evidence and, undoubtedly, a desire to protect the reputation of one of their own members influenced the session earlier in 1723 when there was much gossip about the unsuitable behaviour of the elder William Livingston. Until it could be investigated Livingston was to be told, on 25 July, to refrain from serving at the Lord's table at the forthcoming parish communion. Braehead and Livingston's fellow-elder in Upper Cramond, John Dowie, were to speak to Livingston and his wife and any neighbours who could provide information. Dowie (tactfully, perhaps?) was away when Braehead and the Reverend James Smith consulted neighbours. They and Livingston's servants all declared that they knew nothing unsuitable in his carriage with Ann Gillon (or Gelon, daughter and wife of Barnton gardeners), or of 'his unkindness towards his own wife', save that 'one person of good credit' told the minister that one night he had been in Livingston's house when there was a quarrel between Livingston and his wife, 'and several high words passed betwixt them'. Sometimes, too, Livingston was heard to swear and seemed to be 'in drink'. Mr Smith had also spoken bluntly to the Livingstons about their behaviour, admonishing him to guard against passion, intemperance and swearing, and exhorting both to live in peace and quiet together and to bear one another's infirmities. It was felt that nothing was likely to be proved 'anent the grosser things he had been blamed for by the common reports', so William was then called in to a sessional meeting and warned that, all the same, his conduct had been somewhat unbecoming to an elder, 'particularly that by reason of the frequent company he had occasion to keep [as an innkeeper and brewer] he was sometimes overtaken with drink [and] that when in that case, he was ready to give way to his passion to that degree as profanely to swear'.

Livingston acknowledged this with sorrow, but added that the session had been given exaggerated accounts. He was permitted to rejoin the sessioners, and they recommended that the minister should speak as soon as possible to Mrs Livingston 'that she might take care to behave with all due respect to her husband, and particularly to be tender of his reputation, and to beware of spreading anything to his disadvantage which she will not stand to when it comes to be enquired into'. Livingston sulked for a while: on 3 November the session noted that he had not taken his turn in collecting at the church doors or attended sessional meetings since these rebukes, but he appeared on 10 November and promised to obey the minister when exhorted by him 'to abstain from all appearances of evil and to live circumspectly and to perform faithfully all the duties of an elder'. He and Dowie were chosen as sub-treasurers in February 1727.

But ten years after he had been forbidden to keep company with Ann, the old practice of 'privy censure' by the session was revived for Livingston's benefit on 22 April 1733. The minister (now Robert Hamilton) then reported 'that there was a flagrant report of an indecent behaviour in William Livingston'. Livingston had been seen very drunk in Thomas Andrew's garden in company with Andrew's wife Ann Gillon, her father and a ten-year-old girl. Margaret Howison (Mrs William Dawling) was one of six people who gave evidence that Livingston and Ann were lying in the garden, at some distance from each other. When Livingston tried to get up he fell and had to be led home by his servant.[21] He was still not removed from office until, in a temper at sessional censure, he declined to attend further meetings or play any part as an elder, which the session accepted as a resignation. Four years later Livingston, now a tenant in the Colt Muir across the Almond, petitioned for relief because on 15 July 'by an accidental fire his whole household furniture in a few minutes were consumed to ashes, that they had not so much as their body clothes preserved from the flames and that he is reduced thereby to the greatest extremity'. He was enrolled among the poor in May 1741. Mr John

Hamilton, in the late seventeenth century, might have seen that fire as ignited by the hand of God. If his successor in 1737 (Robert Hamilton's brother Gilbert) did so, it is not mentioned in the minutes.

The session's patience with William Livingston was largely due to a desire to protect one of their own. In 1729 it was mainly William Bruce's social position as a merchant (and, again, a male?) that gained him undeserved leniency. On 28 December Mr James Smith had Bruce summoned before the session on the information that 'he had frequently been guilty of horrid cursing and swearing, and of treating his wife very cruelly at diverse times', especially last Thursday night, 'when he stripped her naked and unmercifully beat her with a horsewhip, having charged pistols by him, and shutting the door that none might have access to relieve her'. Bruce confessed all this and professed sorrow. After a ministerial rebuke he was sent out while the sessioners considered his case. They decided that as he was just a young man, and had never been prosecuted for anything before, and 'out of an earnest desire to reclaim him', they would impose no further penalty beyond recording the rebuke already administered and notifying it to the congregation next Sunday. Four years later, however, in November 1733 a baby was found exposed in Royston 'with a line in its bosom declaring it to belong to William Bruce merchant in Sandyhaugh' and in January 1734 Bruce was excommunicated for failing to answer a summons by presbytery on a charge of adultery in an Edinburgh parish. On 28 March 1736 his wife, Marion Miller, who had married him in Cramond in March 1729, some nine months before the assault, asked the clerk to surrender a bond of agreement made between her and her husband some years before, 'upon a difference that fell out between them', because she was now parted from him and meant to take further legal advice.

NOTES

1. *Disputed claims.* Two of the Nether Cramond feuars were alleged to be disqualified because they received charity from the poor box. It was answered that they were not on permanent pensions.
2. *William Law.* In this case opposing lawyers quibbled unsuccessfully that although William held the equivalent of a general power of attorney for his brother (titular laird of Lauriston and future wrecker of the French economy with his financial schemes), it did not specifically mention the right to any say in the nomination of a minister.
3. *Ann Houston.* After the death of Sir James Inglis Ann married Sir William Hamilton of Whitelaw, Lord Justice Clerk, and then, after his death in December 1704, Adam Cockburn of Ormiston, also a Lord Justice Clerk.

4. *James Smith*. Wood MSS, NLS (National Library of Scotland) MS 9885, p. 57.
5. *William Inglis*. The baillie's holding of 17 Scots acres (roughly 21½ English acres or 8 ha) may have been the land known as 'lie Serjand-croft' in 1579, when it was probably held by the steward of the bishop of Dunkeld.
6. *Edinburgh gentlemen*. 1 June – 23 Sept. 1716; 21 Oct., 11 Nov. 1722.
7. *Excise officers*. Baptismal register, 1721, 1729. Had Nether Cramond been a centre for smugglers earlier, one wonders. If so, they were not a concern of the session.
8. *Robert Mitchell*. One of his properties was the acre that became known as Barbara's Croft and is now the site of 'The Old Schoolhouse' in Cramond Glebe Road. The history of Mitchell and his family is retailed in Wood's private papers (NLS MS 9885, p. 79.) Some jealousy is evident, perhaps of Mitchell, perhaps of the Bain White who had acquired some of the properties by marriage at Wood's time. Informants did not fail to mention, disparagingly, that Mitchell's second wife had been housekeeper to Sir John Inglis.
9. *Earl of Lauderdale*. The Statistical Account of Scotland, 21 vols, 1791–99. Reprinted and rearranged in 20 vols., Donald J. Withrington and Ian R. Grant (edd.) (Wakefield, 1977–83). vol. 1, p. 419 (emphasis added).
10. *Folk Customs*. NLS MS 9886 fols. 43r – 44v. See David Simpson, 'The Lammas Feasts in Cramond Parish', *Scottish Studies*, V (1961), pp. 222–28.
11. *Boys*. A reminder that quite young children worked for wages. Because wage-earners below the age of sixteen were not liable to pay the poll tax of 1694 such juveniles do not appear in the return of that year. Wood himself, counting the population of Corstorphine in 1793, considered 'children' to be those aged eight and under: NLS MS 1872 (no pagination).
12. *Awl and thread*. The recorder added the Scots words 'elson' and 'lingle'.
13. *Episcopally inclin'd*. In February 1719, when it was learned that Isobel 'Bog' had had her illegitimate child baptised 'with one of the ministers of the Episcopal communion', she was told to have the child's name entered in Cramond's register and pay the clerk his due of 14d.
14. *Fasts*. French ambition: 6 March 1711; Spain: 5 April 1719; pretender: 5 Sept. 1713.
15. *Fencibles*. Wood, Cramond, p. 110, from the Clerk of Penicuik papers (NAS) Box 138 No. 4137, Return of fencible men and arms (none) in the parish of Cramond.
16. *Poor's stock*. 5 Oct. 1712. Sir James Dick of Priestfield took over this debt when he bought Corstorphine: 13 Feb. 1713.
17. *Self-help*. Cobbler: 5 May 1723, 2 June 1727; cripple: Dec. 1712; Couper: 3 Jan., 11 May, 15 June, 11 July 1718.
18. *Preens*. A game in which the players competed to lift up pins with wetted thumbs.
19. *Carmyllie*. NAS CH2/558/2, May 1722.
20. *Cummering*. 'Cummer', noun or verb, derived from the French *commère* 'godmother'.
21. *Had to be led home*. George Gillon, Ann's father, told the session indignantly that he himself was not as drunk as reported, because he had gone home and sowed a field with corn.

NINE

Victims and Delinquents, 1731–1750

The Reverend James Smith left Cramond in July 1730, to be followed in succession by two sons of William 'the professor' Hamilton: Robert (April 1731 to October 1736) and Gilbert, ordained in March 1737 when he was not quite twenty-two years old. One of their younger brothers, Patrick, attended Cramond parish school and died in 1732 as a result of being run over by a cart while playing with his school-fellows on Cramond Green.[1]

Smith's session had shown inappropriate leniency to the brutal William Bruce. During Robert Hamilton's short ministry a still more serious miscarriage of justice occurred. On 27 February 1733 Isabel Craig confessed to Dunfermline session that she was with child to James Sandilands, change-keeper in Muttonhole, Cramond, a married man in whose employment she had then been for the last half-year (i.e. from Lammas to Candlemas?). The guilt, she repeated to Cramond session on 15 April, was committed about ten weeks before Martinmas (11 November), in his own room when she was making his bed. He had 'attempted to be guilty with her shortly after she entered to his service, but he got not his will'. Before she left his service she told him that she feared she was pregnant, but 'he said, "there is no fear", and bade her, when she went to the town, draw blood and take a vomit'. (Did either of them really suppose that this would produce an abortion?) Sandilands failed to appear before Cramond session to answer this charge on 22 April and had the girl arrested in Cramond, on a warrant from a JP, and taken to prison. A week later he met the session, denied ever having carnal dealings with Isabel, and added that he declined to answer to Cramond session further, not from disrespect, but because he was prosecuting Isabel before the commissary court for calumny.

Confronted with him, Isabel repeated her assertion, adding that she had never 'known' any man other than him, that about twenty days after she went to work for him 'he laid hands upon her, thinking to get his will, but was prevented by a carrier calling for ale at the door. That she threatened to leave his service if he troubled her any more, that he promised to trouble her no more', and that when Mrs Sandilands was told that Isabel was with child to her husband, she offered to give her 9d. a week and take a private room for her until her delivery, 'if she would father the child upon another'. Isabel, however, had said that her sin was too great already, and she would not add to it by fathering the child upon an innocent person.

On 2 July two of the neighbours confirmed that Isabel had had two meetings with Mrs Sandilands at the time she claimed. Both, however, had been scrupulous not to eavesdrop on their conversation. Jean Davidson testified that Mrs Sandilands had come to her house in a passion, asking for Isabel, whom Jean produced on a promise that the girl would not be harmed. Jean then stood at the doorway of a neighbour's house while they conversed alone. On the second occasion, when they met outdoors, she withdrew and Isabel and Mrs Sandilands sat down at a distance. All she heard was Mrs Sandilands' parting cry of 'Well, Isabel, then you will be obliged to find another father to your child'. Perhaps the two women were afraid to get involved in the affairs of a couple of higher local standing. But their discretion meant that Isabel lacked any support for her story.

Consequently, she failed to gain credence from Edinburgh presbytery when she appeared before them. She had no witnesses and there was a discrepancy in her evidence about the date at which the alleged congress with Mr Sandilands had occurred. At first she had said 'about ten weeks before Martinmas'. But when, in labour, she was questioned by the midwife and, at the midwife's request, two of the elders, she said it was 'at the time of his leading in of his late bere [barley], which was at Hallowday'. The child was born in the night between 30 and 31 July. There seems no obvious reason why Isabel should have lied about the date of conception. The day she fixed on was firmly 1 November, expressed either as 'Hallowday' or 'ten days before Martinmas' This fits her statement that shortly before leaving his service she told Sandilands that she thought she was pregnant. The likely explanation for the discrepancy in the dates she gave is that when first faced with a body of sceptical males she stammered 'ten *weeks*' instead of ten *days*. At any rate, the detail in her story seems very convincing, and becomes still more so in the light of later events.

The gentlemen of presbytery, however, assumed that she was lying, pointed out that on her original statement she must have carried the baby nearly two months longer than normal, and on 30 October declared that there was no evidence of Sandilands' guilt, and ordered Isabel to be censured as an adulteress. On Martinmas Day Sandilands came to Cramond session and asked them to find a way to do him justice and retrieve his character, damaged by the way in which Isabel had industriously and persistently defamed him and was still doing. Isabel herself fled Cramond on 8 December, just before she was due to make her first appearance before the congregation, leaving her child 'in the house where she quartered', with Marion Mure. Marion, one of the enrolled poor, had her pension augmented by half-a-crown a month to keep the child. Isabel disappeared. The story illustrates the inflexibility of the system of church justice, its unwillingness to take account of motive and circumstances, and its ability to induce a sense of personal sin in a woman who might have been the innocent victim of rape, or at best 'seduction' by an employer. Moreover, if the man happened to be married, the woman became as much an adulteress as a married woman who conceived a child not her husband's. No distinction was made.

Mrs Sandilands was ill-paid for her loyalty to her husband. On 15 September next year, the session was 'informed of several base and unchristian practices that James Sandilands tenant in Muttonhole is said to be guilty of'. Four of his women neighbours (including Jean Davidson, who had befriended Isabel Craig) testified to seeing him beat his wife and kick her out of doors. Badly bruised, she took refuge in a neighbour's house for several days. A quarrel had arisen because 'he kept too familiar converse with one of his maid-servants', and although he had put the girl away from the house, he still kept company with her in her father's house and could often be seen walking with her in the fields 'in suspected places'.

Next Sunday two elders found Sandilands in John Henderson's change-house in 'Clik-him-In' at service time, in company with Henderson, his wife and their daughter. When asked why he was not at church, Sandilands claimed to be indisposed, and said he was at the house to see a child that had been injured by one of his horses. When it was pointed out that there were similar distances involved, so that he could as easily have attended church as visited an inn, Sandilands replied truculently 'that he would go and not go to church when he pleased'. Spoken to by the minister, he then said that all these reports concerning his familiar converse with his servant were false and groundless, confessed that he had beaten his wife, but had provocation to do it, and that he went to John Henderson's 'for reasons known to himself'.

Sandilands may, however, have spoken truly when he claimed to be 'indisposed'. On 8 December the session learned that he was dead. The case against him therefore lapsed, and it was thought improbable that enough proof could be obtained against Isabel Craig's successor.[2]

If Isabel had been the victim of a successful counter-attack by her employer and his wife, it must be admitted in support of session and presbytery that many Cramond miscreants did display considerable invention in the stories they concocted. This was especially so when a woman wished to make out that she was respectably married.

Elisabeth Ferguson, questioned in December 1733 about the validity of her clandestine marriage to an under-cook at Barnton House, related that about three years earlier she had been married to one Joseph Rutherman (alias Rutherham), a dragoon from Derbyshire. He had got off from the military and started to work for a stockiner (stocking-maker) in Edinburgh. Two weeks later he took on in the regiment then lying in the Canongate. When it went to Berwick he left her and took another woman away with him. Some time later this woman told her he had been shot for thrice deserting. Elisabeth was prohibited from cohabiting with her new husband until she produced better evidence for the death of this first one. To presbytery she confessed on 17 February that although she had been guilty of uncleanness with this Joseph Rutherham, she was not married to him. At the time she had told her employer so in order to leave her service.

Margaret Jack also invented a marriage for her employer's benefit. While working for the now widowed Mrs Sandilands, she encouraged intimacies from the smith in Muttonhole. For example, the smith had gone to Margaret's bedside early one morning before any of the family were up, to borrow a shilling from her to go to the fair. Later she went to his house at night, as he was going to bed, to ask for her shilling back. Although she now denied that she ever had 'any dealing with him [other] than shaking of hands, or a kiss in civility', under pressure from Mrs Sandilands she had told her that she was married to the man and had burnt her marriage lines, intending to keep her marriage secret until Whitsun, when she meant to hold a public wedding – probably including a 'penny bridal'.[3]

Anne, daughter of Thomas Currie, mason in Nether Cramond, had a different reason in May 1741 for claiming marriage – regard for her parents. She alleged unconvincingly that she was married to one John Malloch, a shoemaker and north-country man who was now in the north, putting the date 'about the tail of harvest last', which was too late for a legitimate birth. She could give no details about the wedding. Cited to appear before presbytery, she retracted her story privately to one of the elders and confessed that the father, now abroad, was David McCulloch, a writer to the signet. The guilt had occurred when Anne was a servant in his father's house. While Anne was nursing a child to a carpenter in South Leith, on 28 November 1742 her father came to the session and said that 'she choosed rather to flee the country than appear before this congregation to bring a reproach upon her parents'. She was, however, willing to appear before the congregation in the parish where the sin had been committed.

The widow Elisabeth Robertson was more stiff-necked in January 1749. When the Reverend Gilbert Hamilton asked whether she was with child, she would answer only 'that time would try'. She went off next day, returned on the Saturday night and on Sunday again disappeared, 'having left the management of her house and family to George Monoch, a pedlar'. George said that he had been called to bring a lighted candle to her byre about midnight on Saturday, and found her with a new-born child in her lap. She enjoined him to keep it secret and asked him to accompany her to Edinburgh, where she carried the baby. He then returned to her house. When Elisabeth returned herself on the Monday evening a committee of the session called on her and she produced a certificate of marriage, dated at Edinburgh on 1 March 1748, to a certain John Simson, a sailor in Newcastle, about whom she knew nothing else. The session thought this certificate to be a forgery and in July presbytery recommended that she perform penance as an adulteress. She refused and was laid under the lesser excommunication.

Eight years later, in November 1757, John Lawrie, tenant in Clapper-know, asked for proclamation of his intended marriage with Elisabeth. It was remembered, and confirmed by the session minutes, that she was still lying under an unpurged scandal and the minister replied that he must take advice on the legal aspects of the affair. He was advised that as no charge had been laid against John Lawrie, the marriage could not be barred. The session, however, pointed out that Elisabeth had claimed before to be married to John Simson, and suggested that she had better prove him to be dead – or else confess that the marriage had never existed. John Lawrie and Elisabeth solved their immediate problem by getting quietly and irregularly married in Edinburgh, and in 1758 Elisabeth acknowledged, both to the minister and to two of the elders, 'conversing aside with them' at a sessional meeting, that John Simson had been a figment of her imagination: she was never married to him, 'nor knew of any such man'.

Kirk and state together were unable to stop the increasing popularity of clandestine marriages. One notorious celebrant in Edinburgh was David Strang or Strange. In 1739 the General Assembly passed an act to banish him from Scotland, and resolved to have those who engaged in irregular marriage prosecuted by civil law as well as being disciplined by the church. All the same, some four or five Cramond couples were married by Strang in 1742, and the session's threats of civil action often came to nothing because the parties were so poor – as happened with two couples in early 1736. When Strang eventually ceased to offer his services, others took his place. In November 1748, to take one example, Patrick Douglas married two Cramond couples in Edinburgh. In what later became quite a common arrangement, each pair in turn acted as witnesses for the other.[4]

Sooner or later one or both of the spouses in such a highly informal marriage found it necessary to 'instruct' it to minister and session. As here, it meant producing witnesses. If these could show that some form of marriage had indeed taken place, the kirk was at least ready to accept it as an imperfect 'remedy for sin' and would regularise the situation by getting the couple to make a formal promise before the session to adhere to each other. The marriage would then be entered into the parish register (for the usual fee) and new lines substituted for the invalid ones, which were often confiscated. The minister in his rebuke took care, however, to emphasise their sin – usually with the standard exhortation to fly to the blood of the Lord Jesus Christ for pardon.

Few parishioners felt any sense of sin in the matter. Despite being frequently dealt with, in June 1735 Isabel Forbes steadfastly refused to 'instruct her marriage', despite – or perhaps because of – the respectability of the witnesses: an Edinburgh merchant and the manager of the Canon Mills. After being labelled 'obstinate and contumacious to the good order and discipline of the church', she eventually, however, appeared before the session with her husband.

Two of David Strang's clients were Eupham Berry and David Lundy. They were married in 1738 when both lived in Cramond, and a child was born soon afterwards. Eupham said, however, that at the ceremony Mr Strang was 'so mortally drunk' that she could never look upon herself as married, and her husband had burnt their marriage lines. Subsequently she discovered the reason: he had a wife already. By the time that Cramond session investigated, in May 1740, David Lundy had long left the parish and been reported to be in Jamaica, while the parents of his legal wife, in Argyll, couldn't tell whether she was now alive or not, as she had left their village about six months earlier for an unknown destination. The whole affair was so involved that Cramond session and presbytery were inclined to hope that Eupham wouldn't persist in her application to do penance for her irregular marriage.

Besides encouraging bigamy, clandestine marriage might enable young people to marry without parental approval. The servants threatened with prosecution in 1736 had 'profaned the name of God, in declaring on oath that they had the consent of their families, when they did not'. On the other hand, when Anne Sanders became pregnant to a fellow-servant in Little Barnbougle, she said in November 1743 that they had intended marriage, but her parents 'hindered it, upon account of their being too young'. James had left the country about August and Anne had not heard from him since.

In view of the church's hostility to irregular marriage, when Margaret Auchterlonie sought baptism for the child of her daughter Jean Adamson in May 1739, she went to pains to 'instruct' Jean's marriage to a soldier, Arthur Evans. Evans had sent a letter to a fellow-soldier in the Canongate, recommending Jean to his care and asking him to see that the child was baptised by Mr [Gilbert] Hamilton, minister at Cramond. At the same time, he wrote to Jean, terming her 'his dear and loving wife'. His friend's personal testimony that he had been a witness at the wedding conducted by Mr Strang, along with a sergeant who had since deserted, was taken as final confirmation that the marriage had occurred.

Much less certainty attached to the claims of Sarah Mason, daughter of the weaver Edward Mason, who had a child on 3 October 1741. She claimed that nearly four years before she had been married at Edinburgh, by one of the meeting-house ministers, to one William 'Spedan' (alias Pedden), soldier-servant to Captain Haliburton, Commissioner Burnet's son-in-law. Her husband was now abroad. She had lost her marriage lines, couldn't tell what house she had been married in, and the witnesses were 'not of her acquaintance'. Subsequently she had lived in Edinburgh, for part of the time in the house of a chairman in Baillie's Close. At her next sessional appearance she said that she was not married after all: the father of the child was a soldier, whose name she refused to divulge. When, a week later, she was again asked whether she was married, she claimed that she was, 'and told she was in confusion and knew not what she said at last meeting'. She then produced a letter from London dated 12 May 1740 in which William Pedden frequently termed her his wife and subscribed himself 'her loving husband till death'. The session determined to write to Captain Haliburton and ask him to get Pedden to write and say whether or not he was married to Sarah, and whether he owned her child. A year later she could offer only her father's testimony that the man whom she called her husband had been several times at his house and owned her as his wife. Two years later again, on 2 September 1744, the session were informed that Sarah had gone off to Ireland with her soldier-husband (but was this William Pedden or someone else?). On 26 January 1755 Sarah and a Thomas Lisk told the session that they had been married a year previously.

No matter what the circumstances, the mother of an illegitimate child was under pressure to obtain an admission from the father. Even when a man admitted liability he might readily escape prosecution. When Agnes Young came pregnant to Cramond in February 1733 she named as father a former fellow-servant of the countess of Rosebery's at Barnbougle. She reported in June that she had asked the father, who was now in the duke of Hamilton's service, to appear before Cramond session, but he refused and expressed anger that she had done so. Six months later the session was told that he had said in the hearing of several people that he was indeed the father. He had given Agnes money and paid the midwife, so Agnes's word was accepted and she was permitted 'to start the process of removing the scandal' by penitential appearances. It is noteworthy that the session of Dalmeny had refused to meddle in the affair 'because that the scandal never made any noise in their parish'. Similarly, when Mary Inglis brought a child to Cramond to be nursed and identified the father as Master Bruce of Mill Hall in the parish of Polmand, Cramond session saw no necessity for them to purge the scandal, since the child was neither begotten nor brought forth in Cramond, and the mother's stay there had been brief.[5]

Without an admission from the supposed father, sessions could often do little. In 1737 Mary White, a stranger big with child, was produced from custody in Edinburgh to accuse John Lauriston, gardener at Lauriston, of being the father. Mary had come to Cramond from Fife just after Lammas the previous year, and shorn (reaped) for William Laurie, tenant at Lauriston. When harvest was over she had spun for various people until Martinmas. She had lived at that time – about six weeks – with Jean Hastie and her husband George Thomson. Because George was sick, Jean had given her house room in return for assistance at nights. When it began to be whispered about that Mary was too familiar with John Lauriston, Jean's husband made her remove Mary out of their house.

According to Mary, Lauriston had been guilty with her in his own house and several times when she went to him to buy apples. In December she had told him she was with child, and he agreed that he could be its father. John, however, denied that he had had any dealings with her, except when she came with the rest of the harvesters to buy apples, or that he ever said anything about being the father of her child.

The session clerk (and elder, Mr Haldan) went to talk to Jean Hastie, who said that while Mary was living with them she went out several times about seven or eight at night and did not return till morning. She supposed that at that time of night she would not have gone far. Also, until Mary came to the house John Lauriston had never been there, and he had not been back since she went away. But while she was there he came several times. One particular night he came in very drunk and, as usual, wanted to send for ale. As he was leaving, Mary said to him, 'You have no fire, Johnny. Shall I put on a fire for you?' Mrs Thomson then lighted a 'purle' (piece of dried cattle-dung, used as fuel) and gave it to her, and John and Mary went to his house together. Mary immediately came back with a candle to light, and said John had fallen and 'wristed' his leg. As she was going away Mrs Thomson said to her, 'Mary, do not stay, for we are going to our bed'. She did not return that night, and when she was asked where she had been she said she was in William Laurie's. When enquiries were made this was found to be untrue. George Thomson agreed that when Mary had stayed with them John Lauriston had 'haunted' their house, but was unwilling to admit that Mary, not himself, might have been the attraction.

Neither the girl's accusation nor this circumstantial evidence was thought sufficient for the session to proceed against Lauriston, and in April the session heard from Edinburgh that Mary had fled after stealing her landlady's clothes.

Later in 1737, in September, Mary Cameron, servant to Mr Andrew Lauder at Pilton, accused his son Charles of fathering her child. Both his parents believed her account that Charles had come to her bed without her knowledge, and that when she told him that she was pregnant he threatened to throw an axe at her. Charles, however, had gone to London. He replied to a letter from the session acknowledging that he had had to do with Mary, and saying 'that if no-one else has had to do with her, that he is very ready to take with the child and act the part of a father as soon as it might be in his power'. Mary had to appear thrice, as usual, before the congregation and be rebuked, although on 4 December she was given half-a-crown for her present supply. The errant Charles returned some two years later, again admitting his guilt. But he was shortly leaving again, and was 'not of our communion and unwilling to submit to the censures of this church', so the session decided to forget the affair unless Charles should ask to be admitted to church privileges. Also, it was now some years since the woman had been purged, and the scandal was now 'sopite' (put to rest).

Although two servants of the surgeon, Mr Gibson, were caught *in flagrante delicto* in April 1739, it proved impossible to bring them to book for indecency. William Marr and Agnes Naper were found in bed together in the upstairs room that Agnes shared with sixteen-year-old Betty Camp-bell when Mr Yorston, who was visiting Mr Gibson, heard them whisper-ing. He went upstairs and heard Agnes say 'O my dear Willie!' On entering the room Yorston said either 'What are you doing there, Will?' or 'I wish you good speed, Willie!' He then fetched Mrs Gibson, a forceful lady, who, finding the pair still lying together, pulled Marr out by the hair and beat him round the head.

When first questioned by the sessional committee who took a 'pre-cognition' of the matter, Marr confessed to being in bed with Agnes at the time and added that it was not the first occasion and he hoped it would not be the last. He agreed that he was accustomed to wake the maids in the morning, sometimes with a kiss. (Betty said that he often left his shoes at the foot of the stair when he went up.) Asked whether he was married to Agnes, or intended marriage, Marr said slyly that 'there were here that knew and knew not'. He refused to say more. Agnes flitted to various places in Edinburgh and was then lost to view. When Marr himself went to the Isle of Bute, the session agreed in July that the process should lie open until he became 'more sensible of his offence' and further light was shed upon it.

In all but the more repressive Scottish parishes the stool of repentance would gradually fall out of use during the 1760s. Even public church censure for adultery went out sometime between 1763 and 1783. With 'enlightenment' came the realisation that the open humiliation of sinners was not, after all, edifying for the congregation. And as one minister would put it in 1790, it gave the impression that in the eyes of the kirk fornication was the sole serious crime.[6] (He also described the stool, rather oddly, as 'that relict of Popery'.) Besides, it had never been easy to bring all sinners to repentance in the first place, and the increasing population must have made it all the harder to trace fugitives.

In the increasingly laissez-faire 1730s and '40s, breach of sabbath and drunkenness did almost disappear from sessional notice in Cramond. During a ministerial vacancy, on 10 December 1730 the baker Robert Mennins was accused of having strangers in his house at service time. He said he was not at home himself then, but there was neither bread nor ale in his house to sell, and when the moderator and two elders called on him he 'uttered very indecent and passionate expressions'. John Lunn added that Mennins had accused him of bringing the charge out of personal malice. Mennins in turn had accused Lunn of eating and drinking in a change-house at service-time. At Lunn's request, Mennins was summoned before the session to apologise or else prove this calumny. He apologised. (All the same, it will be suggested at the end of this chapter that Lunn's reputation was not irreproachable.)

As often, it was a sailor who too publicly profaned the sabbath on 2 July 1738. James Flint admitted taking a stranger gentleman out in his boat at service-time. The gentleman had come to him and begged the favour of a sail 'in the length of the island because he was indisposed'. Earlier, in December 1735, some of the elders observed that the church officer, George Marr, was 'the worse of drink' at the funeral of Mrs [Baillie] Inglis's son. Marr (appointed by way of patronage: he was formerly coachman to Baron Clerk) 'confessed that he got a drink, but not so much as to do him harm'. The sessioners, however, took this opportunity to remark that it had often been noticed that 'what had been spoken or done in the session was immediately spread through the parish' and ordered him to remain outside in future whenever the session meetings were underway.

It was sometimes difficult to replenish the session when vacancies occurred. John Cleghorn, tenant in Granton Mains, at first refused an invitation to join the elders, saying in April 1735 'that he was no hearer in our church for want of accommodation of a seat for his family and that he could not accept of that office till that difficulty was removed'. His objection was met after his landlord, Captain Walter Riddell of Granton, provided room. At the same time Archibald Pratts and the schoolmaster and session clerk, John Haldan, were appointed and a backslider, John Wilson, returned by invitation in July. Two elders dropped out for a time for reasons that Haldan was reluctant to record. When George Wright was 'taked with' on 2 May 1736 about absenting himself from the session and neglecting his office, he said he had no mind to return to the session or perform any part of an elder's duties: 'for some frivolous reasons not worth the mentioning', said the clerk. Archibald Pratts and John Black also abandoned their office, and when the Reverend Gilbert Hamilton invited them back, Black 'absolutely refused, for reasons known to himself' (8 January 1738). In June 1749 he expressed his willingness to return if asked, explaining that 'it was an unadvised step and not for any quarrel or disregard of office'. One cannot help wondering whether these dissidents objected to the presence of Haldan as elder – an unusual access of authority for a Cramond schoolmaster.

Some of Haldan's draft reports of sessional meetings survive to throw light on the practice by which the clerk would transcribe, from time to time, his rough notes into the official book, which had to be shown periodically to the clerk of presbytery for approval. The original spelling and language were sometimes improved (i.e. anglicised) in transcription and some of Haldan's draft entries were either abbreviated or cancelled altogether.[7]

Haldan died in March 1746. For a time his wife kept, or employed someone else to keep, the register of marriages and baptisms and drew the fees. His successor, Alexander Comb, died after only five years in Cramond, and the next schoolmaster, William Dawson, had to transcribe both Comb's sessional minutes and some of Haldan's.

Two surgeons practised in Cramond at this period: Mr David Gibson, who lived in Muttonhole, and Mr James Kirkland. Their main services to the Cramond poor involved setting fractured limbs, an operation that often meant supplying spirits by way of partial anaesthetic, as when, according to a draft minute, on 9 May 1742 the session were informed that William Gilchrist had 'got his leg miserably broken and that the surgeon told that it will require a great quantity of spirits'. The parish surgeon sometimes acted as a kind of auxiliary social worker, as Mr Robert Spotswood would later do to a greater extent as an elder. Thus Mr Kirkland was asked on 12 September 1736 to pass on a crown to Janet

Mordoch for assistance while she underwent a cure for her leg. But on 24 November 1745 Kirkland stood on his professional dignity when asked to establish whether Katherine Stewart was pregnant, declining 'because few of their profession choose to be employed in such matters'.

A degree of greater prosperity in the country at large did not remove the problem of beggars and 'poor strangers'. The session remained concerned about blind people and others being brought in barrows at seedtime and harvest, so that local families had to remove them, taking them as much as half a mile away, at a time when they should be at work in the fields.[8] A mother and daughter, whose place of legal settlement was Kirkliston, had been passed north by a chain of churchwardens and overseers of the poor from St Albans in 'South Britain'. The mother fell ill in Cramond in March 1746 and died two days after their arrival. Arrangements were made to transport the daughter to Kirkliston as soon as possible.

As well as extending reasonable Christian charity to such unfortunates, on two occasions Cramond made an unusual contribution to funeral costs. Besides paying for a coffin for a poor stranger who died in the parish in October 1735, one of the elders ordered a quart of ale for the men who carried her corpse for burial because she had died a great distance from the churchyard. Next year the poor box paid not only for James Hog's coffin and three yards of linen for a 'wounding sheet', but also provided some bread and ale 'to the people that sat up all night' at his wake.

Their own poor were given the means of self-support whenever possible. One of Cramond's coal-boat owners, the aged Andrew Short, had his vessel, his sole means of livelihood, damaged. The session lent him 20s. sterling to repair it. At other times they spent 4s. to buy a woman a lint-wheel and gave 20s. to James Clerk, a poor man in Nether Cramond, to help him buy a cow. Earlier, Clerk had been 'encumbered' with his wife's daughter-in-law and her two children. The woman had then gone off for Ireland, leaving him with one of the children, about seven years old. He had difficulty enough in providing for his own family.[9]

To ensure that a collection for the poor could be taken at weddings, the church officer was instructed to tell the elders of Nether Cramond 'when there happens to be any marriage in the church on a weekday'. He must not open the church door until one of them came.[10]

Cold weather and a shortage of grain meant special need for the enrolled poor in the winter of 1740. On 2 November it was agreed that the monthly allowance should be increased by a third during the winter season and each person was to have half a dail of coals, which the skipper John Wilson should bring to Cramond Shore as soon as possible. The elders were to speak to the tenants, hoping they would not refuse to deliver them to the poor. By December there was a scarcity of meal and the poor were to be paid partly with meal and partly with money. Sir John Inglis undertook to procure corn from Edinburgh. A week later Inglis gave notice that the meal was ready in his 'girnel' (meal chest), and the earl of Selkirk's housekeeper arranged to distribute twenty bolls of meal from the Barnton granary, at the rate of two bolls a week, to the poor 'but no idle person'.

No money was available to pay the enrolled poor in November 1745 because the treasurer had left the area on account of 'the present unnatural rebellion' by Prince Charles Edward Stuart and his followers.[11] One of the elders, a miller, offered to advance two pecks of oatmeal to each of the forty-five pensioners. (Just as a specific limit was set on the number of subsidised 'poor scholars', it is possible that at this period the enrolled poor were limited to forty-five.)

A typical petitioner for enrolment was the widow Anne Hall, who said in June 1737 that she had lived in the parish for over thirty years, had 'undergone much trouble, many times in great want of the necessaries of life' and was now incapable of earning a living. She was now waiting upon John Cleghorn and his wife. The wife was 'close confined to her bed' and helpless, while the couple were in no position to maintain or reward Anne for her services.

The 'monthly poor' were always closely monitored to ensure that they really were in poverty. In November 1741 Isabel Ramsay, aged seventy-five, had her pension stopped when it was reported that she had money by her. Her neighbour, Isabel Grieve, who was also a pensioner, had enticed Ramsay's own grandson to steal a guinea and three crowns from her chest. Ramsay told the session that she was keeping the money to defray the costs of her funeral and to pay her house-rent. She happened to leave the key in the chest when she went out one day, and the boy had taken the money and given it to Isabel Grieve. Grieve denied asking him to do it, or giving him some food in return, and claimed that he brought her the coins, which she kept for three days, intending to return them, 'and was so unhappy as not to tell it to any till the boy discovered [i.e. revealed] it'. The session agreed that her month's pension should be withheld to show their displeasure at her very suspicious behaviour. The unlucky victim of the theft also had her pension suspended until she proved to be in greater need. She was 'reponed' to it about eight months later. Such 'asset-testing' of the aged poor was much resented. In due course benevolent societies would become a popular way to avoid the dreaded stigma of a pauper's funeral.

It was often children who needed temporary or permanent help from the poor box. There was a boy who was 'fixed to his bed by reason of several runnings in his body', and another child described variously as an idiot and a changeling.[12] (Was it Down' Syndrome that affected such children?)

Alexander Williamson, one of the coal-boat owners in Nether Cramond, died in late July 1735, in debt to the session and to Isabel Aikman's dead husband. His ill-treated wife, Janet Sim, had evidently died earlier and their three youngest children were left without support. It was agreed to speak to their elder brother, another Alexander, a clothier in Dunfermline, 'to enquire what course he is to take in disposing of them'. Alexander came to the session on 31 August 1735 and offered to free Cramond of the burden, if they would give him 15s. sterling a quarter during the winter season. They agreed.

Next year, on Saturday 5 June, John Williamson, aged just ten, was found 'indisposed' in a field at Corstorphine and taken to Cramond. Since no-one there was willing to take him in because of his illness, one of the poor was paid to look after him until his brother could be summoned to explain why he had allowed John to wander through the countryside.

When Alexander failed to respond, on 20 June the church officer was sent across to Dunfermline with the boy and a letter threatening to sue if Alexander did not take care of his brother and 'free the session of the burden of him' as promised. Alexander was not at home when they arrived, so the beadle gave the letter to his wife and read her the contents. That same evening the boy turned up at the house of Alexander's father-in-law, saying that his brother (evidently a man as short-tempered and violent as their father had been) had responded to the session's complaint by kicking and beating him, had pulled his coat off him, torn his shift and 'sent him away naked under night'. The minister and session, 'much concerned to hear of such unnatural and barbarous treatment', arranged to have Alexander summoned before Pitreavie's Baron Court. Possibly John was then befriended by one of his mother's Sim – Johnston relations. He may be the person meant in a minute of 12 September 1736 recording the plan to ask Mr McDoual in Edinburgh to take in 'John "Willison", a poor boy, to his work'.

John McFarlan, a poor stranger, came to the house of the surgeon Mr Gibson, fell sick and died, leaving a child behind him. The session made arrangements for its care on 9 December 1733, hoping the mother would 'cast up', when they would give her some money to take the child away. She was said to be begging through the country with two other children. She came for it a month later.

The child found exposed in Royston one wintry day in 1733, with a note identifying William Bruce as the father (see previous chapter), was christened Margaret. The woman who brought her to Nether Cramond was given a groat (4d.) and James Young's wife was persuaded to nurse her, with some difficulty. 'Because of the bad condition that the child was in' she required at least £10 Scots a quarter to undertake the task. Margaret survived this poor start in life, and next year, once weaned, was handed on to Isabel Foreman, 'an aged woman in King's Cramond', who was seeking enrolment as one of the poor. It was arranged to give her 20d. a month for herself and 40d. for keeping the child. Unlike some of the parish orphans, the little girl saw some stability of home life for the next eight years. On 9 October 1743 it was noted that 'the female "fundling" that stays with Isabel Foreman stood in need of clothes'. The session were of opinion that she might go to service, being about eleven years of age, and elders should enquire for a place for her. Six months later she was placed in service for a year.

But Margaret was never physically, nor, perhaps, mentally strong enough to lead a normal life. She was ill for a month in 1751, then 1s. was paid to 'the person who carried her to Town' to Edinburgh Infirmary, where 20s. sterling was paid for medicine and her keep. In April 1753 she was again in the infirmary and given 3s. to buy stockings and shoes. When she returned to Cramond, Robert Spotswood, the surgeon, and another elder looked for a woman to care for her. Clothes and bedclothes were supplied in due course.[13] May 1755 saw her once more in the infirmary, with a guinea for maintenance. She had a sore leg and could do nothing to earn her keep. Thirty-seven years later, Spotswood wrote to thank J. P. Wood for the guinea note he had sent for the use of the poor:

> I have not yet seen that innocent honest creature M. Bruce. She has had more sickness and hitherto recovered from [more] dangerous illness than any individual in the parish. When well, as she is at present, I know none more contented. Her house-rent [of] 20s. is a great affair. She has been in use to collect [it] in shillings and leave it here for security and I have 13s. secured against Whitsunday next.[14]

About 9 am on 28 August 1744 one of Widow Peacock's servants found a male child exposed in the east end of Pilton Avenue. He was wrapped only in a woollen cloth, with the name Andrew McDougal in his bosom, and was thought to be five or six days old. He was put out to nurse, but died in Edinburgh seven months later. Next year, in August 1745, another male child was found one night at the door of Mrs Gibson the surgeon's wife. She took him to the minister next morning, and also brought along some north-country women who had spent the night in her barn. Agnes Adamson, now the Nether Cramond midwife, was called to see whether any had recently given birth, but thought not. The child, about six weeks old, was put in the keeping of Katherine Waddell.

More and more, the session's chief role was coming to be the care of the very poor and incapacitated, and the maintenance of orphans. While it long remained important to identify the father of an illegitimate infant, in the hope of obtaining support for it, correcting sinners became largely the minister's job. On rare occasions, however, sessions were still asked to act upon a private complaint.

In August 1742 Thomas Mure applied to the minister and his two local elders for redress against his neighbour, the shoemaker John Collin, whom he suspected of being too familiar with his wife, Margaret Ravelton. On a Monday morning Thomas had gone home to speak to his wife, but found her absent. He went to Collin's house, and as he was entering heard his wife whisper 'Let alone! Someone is coming in!' He then saw his wife sitting on a chest beside Collin's bed, with Collin standing in front of her with both his hands up her coats (i.e. petticoat). Margaret claimed before the session that Collin had tried to interfere with her, and to frighten him she said that someone was coming, not believing that anyone really was. 'To prevent his being rude' she sat down and struggled with him. Collin denied that on this occasion he had done anything wrong, though they both agreed that he had behaved indecently to Margaret at other times. Collin added blithely that she wasn't by any means the only one – 'many a woman's clothes he had lifted up when he was taking the measure of their feet to make shoes to them'. But he had never done any more than that since he became a widower. The session were told that the Mures had made up their difference and were living together again, while the neighbours would swear to Margaret's respectability. But Thomas Mure wanted Collin publicly rebuked for his behaviour. Since the elders thought Collin too stupid and naive to make an 'edifying' appearance before the congregation, and it was sensibly pointed out that publicity wouldn't help Mure and his family either, two elders were sent to ask Mure to drop the case. In return they would try to get Collin removed from Cramond.

The session also told Thomas Edmundston to apply to the sheriff or a JP when he complained in October 1743 that James McAlpine's wife had abused him and his wife, uttering 'imprecations not proper to be mentioned' and threatening to burn them alive. All this abuse, he said indignantly, was offered without the least offence or provocation, as the whole neighbourhood could attest.

Murder was distinctly a matter for the civil arm, but Cramond session was initially involved with the case of Margaret Short, daughter of Thomas Short and the adulterous Isobel Aikman. Margaret had married the sailor Thomas Fairholm in January 1743 and in August 1747 was suspected of being pregnant, although her husband had been serving abroad for several years past. The elders 'got trial made' of her by local women, who found milk in her breasts, but Margaret persisted in her denials. The midwife in Upper Cramond was asked to re-examine her, but in the interim Margaret was thought to have given birth in secret. The neighbours conveyed their supicions to Mr Gilbert Hamilton and one of the elders, who sent once more for the midwife. Upon her confirmatory report, Margaret confessed that after delivery she had sewn the baby up in a cloth and hidden it under a bed. When the corpse was examined, those present judged that it was that of 'a ripe child', i.e. full-term. The midwife in particular detected marks of violence on the body.

Pending action by His Majesty's Advocate, the session obtained a warrant from a JP to have Margaret kept in custody. Guards were set on her house to watch her night and day, but in the morning of 23 August she contrived to steal through a window behind her bed, so quietly that the two Cramond men sitting in the room were unaware of her escape. When they discovered it, they pursued her (they said) a long distance before returning empty-handed.

In Nether Cramond at least, neighbours and even elders seem to have paid less attention to minor sexual irregularity after the early 1730s. One Sunday in March 1731 the invigilating elders found a stranger lying in the bed of Elspeth Cleland, widow of one of the John Sims. They were told that he had been there all night and claimed to be sick. Elspeth, however, was known to them as a woman of bad character, so they turned the man out of the house and reported the incident.

Elspeth told the session that as she was coming out of Edinburgh 'under night' on the Saturday she had lost her staff, and was unable to walk because she had lately broken her leg. On this side of the Dean she met a stranger who was on his way to Queensferry, and asked his help to get to Cramond, in return for a chopin of ale there. He came along to her house, and told her that he had been ill of the ague and was afraid he would not be able to reach the Ferry that night. So out of compassion she offered him her bed, and went herself to share Elspeth Fairie's.

Carelessly, the two women failed to coordinate their stories, so that Fairie did not vouch for Cleland's continuous presence in her house overnight. The session, while unable to prove anything, strongly suspected that the two women had 'concerted together to conceal [Elspeth Cleland's] wickedness'. Cleland was told (optimistically?) that her iniquity would find her out, and the session recommended that Sir John Inglis be asked to remove her from Nether Cramond. Elspeth Fairie was also rebuked for prevarication and told that she 'rendered herself a partaker of her neighbour's wickedness by denying what she knew of or about it'.

In March 1733 Elisabeth Kid, a widow who kept a lodging-house in Nether Cramond, was spied on by a beggar-woman and a young girl and accused of sharing her bed with a visiting chapman who 'haunted' her house. Further, when she was woken from a drunken sleep by the noisy crowd that gathered about her house, she had sworn and spoken disrespectfully of the session. When three elders subsequently interviewed her, Elisabeth said she had been drunk and fallen asleep on a chair at the man's bedside. When she woke she threw off her clothes and lay down beside him, but no harm was done.

The sailor James Finlayson did attract general scandal in Nether Cramond over the period 1745–49, when the session justly described his relations with some of the local women as 'intricate'. Initially, on 11 August 1745, he was accused of 'unsuitable behaviour' towards his wife, Alison Ranald: namely cruelty in beating her unmercifully. He counter-claimed that she made his home life intolerable, and he also expressed doubts about the legality of the marriage, since it had been performed by an Episcopalian.

Having left the matrimonial home, Finlayson was now sleeping 'for ordinary' in Margaret Young's house, with (she said) her brother, who was about eighteen, her husband being away in Newcastle. Finlayson also frequently drank in her house with others when they were 'about business'. When first cited to appear before the session, she refused to attend and evidently abused the church officer who brought the summons. When she later came she was warned against arousing suspicions which were likely 'to break the peace of her own family when her husband should return'.

Finlayson was also reported to frequent the company of Katherine Stewart, a single woman, and the inn-keeper Margaret White, a married woman. Katherine, orphaned daughter of Jean Mitchell and the former beadle William Stewart, had been, with her sister, a 'poor scholar' sent to school at parish expense in 1727. Margaret, the famous 'Meg White' of the scurrilous poem to be quoted below, admitted that Finlayson was often in her house, because she kept a change. But she denied that he ever spent a whole night in her house, and said that she often urged him to go home to his own. Asked whether Katherine Stewart was her servant, she said she was not, but, being out of service, had stayed with her since Whitsun. When prompted, Meg promised in August never to entertain Finlayson alone or at unseasonable hours in her house.

In November there was then a 'flagrant report' that Katherine was pregnant. She denied this. Agnes Adamson, the midwife, and some other discreet women examined her and reported that she had all the symptoms of being with child. The local elders were then recommended to keep an eye on her and stop her leaving the parish if possible. On 22 December the session were told that Katherine, then lying indisposed, had confessed to Margaret White and Margaret's mother Margaret Crie that she was indeed with child.

After the birth Katherine left the parish with the baby, but returned some two years later and formally confessed her adultery. Finlayson, who had already admitted that he was the father, had also left the district. About May 1749 Katherine had another child by Finlayson, who was then 'a soldier in the Castle of Edinburgh'. Having appeared 'several times' in the public place of repentance, Katherine was absolved on 10 September 1749. Her penance for adultery was by no means as long-drawn-out as that suffered by earlier women.

Meg White makes her sole appearance in the kirk-session minutes as hostess and confidante of Katherine Stewart. But by the time of her death in 1782 she enjoyed – or had conferred upon her in some quarters – a certain notoriety. At that time a bawdy epitaph was written for her, possibly by one of those 'writer-blades' – young clerks – who came from Edinburgh to frolic in Cramond at weekends. The author modelled his piece closely on Allan Ramsay's elegy on the ale-wife Maggy Johnston, who died in 1711. Implications that Cramond Meg ran an informal bawdy-house are strengthened by the fact that two lines are adapted from Ramsay's verses of advice from an Edinburgh brothel-keeper, 'Lucky Spens'. Meg White's elegy, with its double-entendres about flesh-kettles and chimney-sweeping, was quite unsuitable for inclusion in Wood's *Cramond*, scrupulously adapted for family reading as it was. Wood, however, preserved the poem among his papers for private enjoyment. It deserves quotation here because it gives a lively idea of Meg's life as change-keeper long before her death, and, once more, Wood's manuscripts illuminate a side of life in Cramond that the session records barely hint at. Moreover, this item is a reminder that respectable eighteenth-century gentlemen frequented bohemian drinking and versifying clubs as much as they did the kirk. It may, indeed, have been presented at such a gathering.

Meg was probably a daughter of James White and Margaret Crie. She married John Grinzlay, Grindlay or Grinlaw in July 1740, and, as we have seen, was running her hostelry by 1745. The John Lun libelled was probably the kirk elder ('in black disguise'?) of that time.

On the much lamented death of Meg White of Cramond

who died on Thursday 28 Novr 1782
in the 67th year of her reign.

	O, Cramond now may greet an' grane,	weep and groan
abundance	Wi' fouth o' tears mak muckle mane,	
	Sin auld Meg White is dead an' gane;	
	Left honest John	
scratch his head	To scarb his pow and claw his wame,	belly
	Ohon, ohon!	alas, alas!

	Meg was a wife that was weel kend,	
reluctant	She was nae sweer her loom to lend.	pot
afraid	But I am fleed I should offend	
	To tell her pranks:	
	Frae mony ane, ye may depend,	
	I'd get sma' thanks.	

	They ne'er do weel that never thrives	
are in fear of	An' am ay fleed for flitting wives,	scolding
	Though it's neither Death nor yet men's lives:	
	The truth to tell,	
	There's mony ane in black disguise	
	Can do't themsell.	

	Meg to the trade fell soon begun	
ewe	Whan a young gimmer, wi' John Lun.	
sweep	He mony times did swoop her lum,	chimney
	His back she'd claw.	
wanton	Weel, glaiked Meg did lo'e sic fun –	love
	But that's awa.	

Whan loon-like chiels cam frae the gouff   golf
Meg's chimley-nuik was ay their houff.   haunt
O' belly-fare Meg ay had routh   plenty
To stegh their wames.   bellies
O' gin or brandy there was scouth   abundance
To sap their banes.   moisten their bones

(margin: rascally fellows)

(margin: cram)

The loons, when on a merry pin,
Meg wad slide out, wi' little din,
An' tip the lasses to come in
Wi' candles lighted.
Meg didna think it ony sin
To have them sighted.

O' what was gaun, Meg had a skair.   share
The fisher chaps she didna spare
But gard them pay weel for her fare.
They ne'er wad settle,
But boil'd their trouts an' ither ware
In her flesh kettle.

Some worthless chiel, a clappit lown,   poxy knave
A writer blade frae Embro Town,   Edinburgh
Plaid Meg a trick that made her gloom
An' cock her nose:
Mix't purging pills, baith black and brown,
In Jonnie's brose.

Wi' dancing, Meg did never fag:
She was ay souple as ony nag;
At penny bridals bore the brag –   was champion
That's kent to a'—
And was a bawdy spoken jade
As e'er ye saw. . . .

There's taylor Tib an' Christy Hill,
Her cronies baith, may greet their fill   weep
And by their lanes a while sit still
Ere Meg appear
To help them to another gill,
Or drink o' beer. . . .

Now, farewell, Meg, sleep till Doomsday!
You're now a lump o' useless clay!
I'm sure your death mak's mony wae!
There's nae remeid.   remedy
In heav'n or hell, there's nane can say:—
We're sure you're deid![15]

NOTES

1. *Patrick Hamilton.* Wood MSS NLS MS 9885, p. 54.
2. *James Sandilands.* 'Sometime wright in Edinburgh', he had his will registered in the Edinburgh Register of Testaments, 17 March 1736.
3. *Margaret Jack.* 30 Jan., 17 Feb. 1737.
4. *Witnesses at irregular marriages.* 23 April 1749. Women frequently acted as witnesses on these occasions, though not at the marriages that took place in the kirk.
5. *Mary Inglis.* 7 Jan. 1733.
6. *Sole serious crime. Stat. Act.*, I, p. 312.
7. *Draft minutes.* NAS CH2/426/11: Draft minutes from March–Dec. 1735 and Dec. 1736 to 5 Feb. 1744. 'The ffunlan', for instance, was changed to 'the fundling' or 'the foundling' and 'the tail of harvest' to 'the end of Harvest'. A new schoolmaster regularly had the task of writing up draft minutes that his predecessor had not fair-copied into the minute book.
8. *People in barrows.* Draft minute for 3 July 1741.
9. *Self-support.* Short: 1 July 1743; lint-wheel: 1 Feb. 1747; James Clerk: 9 June 1749; 4 Sept. 1743.
10. *Collection at weddings.* 1 Feb. 1736. In modern times marriages involved not a collection for the poor but an indiscriminate 'pour oot' to bystanders. In the late 1960s the minister's son used to profit by his special knowledge to tip off his schoolfellows when one was due.
11. *Charles Edward Stuart.* The only reference in the minutes to the Young Pretender's invasion, in which Edinburgh itself was occupied by Highland soldiers for a considerable time. Their advance party had reached Kirkliston, on Cramond's western border, on 15 September 1745.
12. *Poor children.* Runnings: 4 Jan. 1736; changeling: 3 July 1737, 8 Jan. 1738.
13. *Clothes for M. Bruce.* 20 May, 12 June 1753, 5 Feb. 1754.
14. *Spotswood to Wood.* NLS MS 9886 fol. 36: 24 Jan. 1792.
15. *'Now, farewell, Meg . . .'* Ramsay's own elegy ends:

> Then farewell Maggy douce and fell
> Of brewers a' thou boor the bell;
> Let a' thy gossies yelp and yell
> And, without feed,
> Guess whether ye're in heaven or hell,
> They're sure ye're dead.

TEN

Industry, an Evangelist and Disorder

Mr Gilbert Hamilton was Cramond's minister from March 1737 until his death in May 1772. Conformable to the 'moderate' pattern of a comfortable country minister, 'he was', says Wood, 'an affable, easy, plain man, high in the esteem of the superior order of his parishioners' (implying, not that he was disliked by the rest, but that the 'superior order' held the only opinions worth notice).[1] Hamilton's ties with the parish, and with the family of Sir John Inglis, were reinforced when, in March 1754, he took as his second wife Sir John's granddaughter, Margaret Craigie.

Sir John himself died in 1771, aged eighty-eight. In what was an eventful period in parish history, from 1751 to 1785, further continuity would be provided by the clerk and schoolmaster Ninian Paton, who was appointed in November 1764 and remained active until after 1810, and by Robert Spotswood, one of three members of that family to be appointed elders in 1753. The other two were Robert's brother William, a brewer, and Thomas Spotswood, tenant in Lennie Muir. Robert, whose father had also been an elder, had taken his medical degree at Edinburgh University, seen action as a naval surgeon and made enough in pay and prize-money to purchase a small estate as a 'portioner' in King's Cramond and settle as surgeon in the parish. In 1774 he was the first non-heritor to become kirk treasurer, a role he fulfilled for twenty years. Wood no doubt shared the view of the better class in general when he remarked that he was especially suitable for this office because he could prevent fraudulent claims: as parish surgeon he was familiar with all the families in the parish and neighbourhood, 'so as to render all attempts to impose upon the session impracticable and hopeless'.[2]

In one of the clichés applicable to the second part of the eighteenth century, this was an age of exploration, warfare, general territorial aggression and expansion. The careers of several residents in Cramond reflect this. Sir Philip Ainslie inherited Pilton from his father, the Bordeaux merchant George Ainslie, in 1773. Sir Philip had begun his military career in 1754 and served, for instance, as lieutenant-colonel of Portuguese cavalry against Spain in 1762. Between 1763 and 1780 Caroline Park (as Royston had been renamed) was tenanted by Sir James Adolphus Oughton, KB, commander of forces in Scotland 1768–80, who had served at

Culloden and then in Flanders in 1747–8. 'An excellent officer, an universal scholar, and a man of boundless curiosity and unwearied diligence', he was a zealous proponent of the authenticity of *Ossian*[3].

Charles, the youngest Inglis son, entered the Royal Navy in 1745 at the age of fourteen and saw his first service under Captain Rodney. His subsequent career, until he died as a rear-admiral in 1791, took him to various seats of war: the Rochefort expedition of 1757, the bombardment of Le Havre in 1759, the relief of Gibraltar from siege by Spain in 1781 and early next year the operations of Viscount Hood in the West Indies, followed by Lord Rodney's 'glorious victories over the French fleet' in April. He was again in the West Indies in 1788–9.[4] Mr Ninian Paton's son Hamilton, born in 1766, would also become a naval officer and be killed at Gorée, the island facing Dakar, Senegal, in 1804, 'by the natives . . . in storming a small fort', as his sorrowing father took it upon him to insert beside the record of his baptism. John William Law, the exiled heir to Lauriston, also born (in India) in 1766, was a lieutenant in the French navy. In June 1785 he sailed with La Pérouse's two ships on a projected voyage around the world. They disappeared after leaving Botany Bay in March 1788.[5]

Charles Inglis was accompanied on some of his tours of duty by men from Cramond. In registering two births in 1771 the clerk carefully noted how long the fathers had been absent from home: on 3 April 1771 James Ranken, sailor in Cramond, 'now abroad with Captain Inglis', had gone away 'harvest last', and on 1 May William Miles, 'sailor with Captain Inglis, went about half-year from this'. (But one sailor added to Cramond's illegitimacy rate without official notice being taken. In February 1766 the baptism was registered of 'Anne, daughter to Ann Henry in Nether Cramond, the father not known'. Later, however, some gossip added, 'natural daughter to Captain Charles Inglis'.)

Other Cramond men joined the armed forces less willingly. In 1755 four wives needed temporary support from the poor box. One, Anne Campbell, was 'reduced to great distress, her husband being impressed for the service of his majesty's fleet'. She got a loan of half-a-crown a month, which she promised thankfully to repay as soon as her husband's pay should come to hand.[6] In November 1757 Anne Finlayson was similarly accommodated. In 1762 there was a squabble between Cramond and South Leith over which parish was responsible for supporting Helen Comb, whose husband had been impressed and sent to Germany with his regiment, leaving her with three children, one of whom was sick with a fever.

Portions of the 'poor's stock' were still lent out to heritors: among 'desperate' (unredeemable) debts listed in April 1751 was one from the late, 2nd, earl of Rosebery, 'which perhaps may yet be made good'. But treasurers were now diversifying investments and it was then agreed to purchase a feu-duty arising from two properties in the West Kirk parish, Edinburgh, one of them 'the dunghill stead-ground' whose feu was paid (or at least calculated) in barley. By now, money was also placed on deposit with Edinburgh bankers, including Mr John Inglis, over whose account with Sir John Inglis, as kirk treasurer, there was some trouble in April 1757. From 1763 a sum was invested with the trustees of the turnpike roads in the shire of Edinburgh on security of an assignment on the tolls from the Cramond road,[7] and money for the stock was also raised when, from 1756, the body of the kirk was filled with fixed seats to be rented out.

There were occasional emergencies. In late January 1757 a boatload of coals was bought and distributed to the poor 'on account of the severity of the weather' and 'the present straitning times'. Money was also given by Lord Chief Baron Sir John Clerk, Sir John Inglis and others to buy meal or oats and sell them a little below cost 'to proper objects'. The grain was bought from 'Mr Chalmers', at a total cost of £10 1s. 1d. sterling. And in March 1770 the session understood that the poor box was empty and planned to suspend payment of next month's pensions to the forty-five enrolled poor. In the event, David Strachan, the treasurer, found that £3 3s. 3½d. remained in cash, which sufficed for reduced allowances. In June the poor were still 'under scrimp allowance' and the minister offered to pay for carriage of the elements for the forthcoming communion provided it was not taken as a precedent. (Purchase of the bread and wine was a charge upon the patron, but cost of transport was usually met from parish funds.) At the same time, it was reiterated that no more than six scholars should be maintained at parish expense unless the session made a special exception.

The session continued to act as financial managers for parishioners in a variety of situations. In 1764 when Agnes Short's son died in the armed forces, 'Mr Inglis' (the Edinburgh banker or Sir John's son Adam?) held £5 18s. sterling in back-pay which he delivered to the sub-treasurer to be placed to her account. £1 of it had already been given out to buy clothes for her other children. When Anne Steedman, one of their pensioners, died early in 1766 leaving a boy 'not able to do for himself', his uncle, Andrew Bizzet, proposed to roup (auction) her house and take care of the orphan. The session suspected that once the proceeds of the auction were spent he might tire of the boy and throw him upon public expense, so they arranged for an elder to attend the rouping, receive the money for the furniture and take the boy 'under their immediate protection'. Bizzet then agreed to take the boy into his own house, give him clothes and maintain him. The proceeds, £4 5s. ½ d., were given to Bizzet, who agreed to account to the session for his expenditure at the allowance of 2s. 6d. a month. Later the session acknowledged that this was not enough, and allowed 4s. for maintenance and 18d. to buy shoes for the child.

Back in May 1734 George Naughtie or McNaughton had been enrolled as one of the ordinary poor as 'deprived of the use of his reason [and] incapable to provide for himself', while his father was unable to support him, 'being but a work-man'. In 1770 George was bequeathed £150 by an aunt in Edinburgh. The session, asked by George to obtain this legacy on his behalf, instructed their clerk to look back through the records to see how much money George had received from the poor box over the last thirty years. George agreed to repay this amount (£33 4s. 7d.) and mortified £100 to the session, in exchange for £10 annually for life. The session in turn lent out £120 in July 1771 to Mr Adam Inglis, at interest of 5 per cent per annum, and allowed George £16 15s. 5d. in hand.

For at least nine years from January 1755 the parish was burdened with a child abandoned in particularly shameless circumstances. After exposing the infant, the mother went to Bo'ness as nurse, first to a sailor and then to a baker there. The latter agreed to pay her wages to the Cramond box towards expenses over her abandoned child, unless she removed it from Cramond within three weeks. She failed to do so. When, six months later, she was reported to be in Edinburgh, the session voted to prosecute her according to law. However, she absconded before 'diligence could be done against her'. Apparently Cramond made no effort to involve the alleged father, a tenant in North Clermiston, in the child's maintenance.

Sir John Inglis senior probably thought of 'industry' as meaning 'useful employment', as well as offering a means of boosting his own revenues from rent. On 23 July 1752 he drew up a formal contract of feu with partners in a consortium of entrepreneurs, 'The Smith and Wright Work Company of Leith', several of whom had existing local connections. This permitted them to convert the two lower mills on the east bank of the Almond – Niddery's Mill, alias Fairafar, and Cockle Mill – for iron-processing.[8] On 21 December 1759 the two (Fairafar still only a meal- and waulk-mill) were sold to Dr John Roebuck and his co-partners, who were about to start their major ironworking undertaking at Carron. Once the Carron works became operative, the Cockle Mill and Fairafar were run as an offshoot, rolling and slitting bar-iron. In October 1770 William Cadell junior and his brother, sons of one of Roebuck's partners, bought out the rights in the Cramond works.

The Carron Company initially had difficulty getting experienced nailers to move to Cramond, 'as they say there is none of their own country-people dwelling there'.[9] But shortly before the Cadells took sole ownership of the Cramond works, a small number of nailmakers began to set up their individual workshops in Nether Cramond, in association with the company, which provided accommodation and tools. This secondary branch of the manufacture increased the noise and general industrial pollution in the village while adding to the overcrowded conditions. Both the nailmaking and the mills also attracted workers who were little inclined to respect the kirk's attempts at social regulation.

Drunkenness among their workers was a frequent concern to the millowners. The early manager Christopher Bell was several times warned against selling ale at the mill, 'a very bad thing for the workmen'. In September 1762 the manager was told that the mill should be constantly employed, 'for which purpose it is needful that you do everything you can to prevent the men from getting drunk as this will certainly throw everything into confusion'. Next month, however, the owners commented resignedly, 'We suppose you find drink to the men really needful. This expense should be avoided as much as possible'. And drink-money was sometimes used to encourage the workers. On 1 January 1763, when Cramond was to experiment with the cutting of iron made by a new process, the manager was told to give the millmen and firemen a shilling for drink, 'to make them careful in heating and cutting'.[10]

In the 1790s Wood estimated that the rent of the ironworks brought in £260 annually. But already in 1775, when a further forge had been installed at Fairafar, the second Sir John seems to have regretted the advent of this mini-Industrial Revolution to Cramond and took legal action in an attempt to limit the company's activities. In 1787 the earl of Rosebery, annoyed by the presence of industrial works opposite his nice new plantations, by millmen who allegedly poached his fish, and by 'sailors and other disorderly persons' trespassing in his woods, would try to put the company out of business by withdrawing water-rights, and succeeded in having the towpath removed from the west bank.[11] When the forge hammers and furnaces were in operation beside the Almond, Burns's quip on the Carron Works might have applied:

> We cam na here to view your warks
> In hopes to be mair wise,
> But only, lest we gang to Hell,
> It may be nae surprise.[12]

While the mill owners imported many of their skilled hands, they also employed some local men. But much of the work was seasonal. The machinery depended on water power and often water was short. Occasionally, on the other hand, the great wheel became flooded. When work was slack, even the expert slitter might be employed as a blacksmith making hoes or other implements and paid only what he could earn thereby. In 1761 just four men sufficed to run the works except at peak periods when water was plentiful, usually in winter. In 1767 there were eight regular hands and an errand boy, with three more men in winter and some boys on piece work, straightening hoops.[13] Numbers increased in time, however, and children of some of the earlier ironworkers would in turn find employment in the industry.

There was also increased local employment for seamen in crewing or piloting the sloops that could dock at the slit-mill on the lower reach of the Almond with supplies of iron. The work came appositely when Cramond's oyster-dredging activities in the Firth had almost come to an end.[14] Not all workers were incomers. Among the nailers, Robert Russon or Russell, for instance, a frequent witness at the marriages and baptisms of both sailors and nailers, may have been a grandson of Robert Russon and the Elspeth Fairie who connived at Elspeth Cleland's immoral activities (Chapter 9). He himself had married Margaret Mennons or Mennins, daughter of the Nether Cramond baker William Mennons and granddaughter of the baker Robert. And among those employed at the slit-mill in November 1767 was John Grindlay – husband or son of the hostelry-keeper Meg White.[15] A John Grindlay was also master of the sloop *Neptune* in 1762. John McAra, slitter in the iron-mill in 1771, was the son or brother of the Nether Cramond innkeeper Archibald McAra, who witnessed the baptism of John's son in January of that year. And John 'McCurrie', middleman in the mill in November 1767, William McCurrie, furnaceman, and James McCurrie, letter-carrier and errand boy, were members of the (variously spelled) McCurich family. Jean McCurich had been born in June 1750 to a John McCurich and his wife Anne Currie, daughter of the Nether Cramond mason Thomas Currie (for Anne, see Chapter 9).

Among Cramond's seamen and the new small group of nailers it would become the norm to get quietly married in Edinburgh, then notify the marriage to the kirk authorities in Cramond shortly before the birth and baptism of a child. (Russon and his friends patronised a marriage celebrant named Thomas Clerk). Thus on 22 November 1768 Andrew Kilgour and Janet McCurich were married in Edinburgh. The marriage was registered at Cramond on 30 April 1771, and on 18 May John, son of Andrew Kilgour 'on board the *Triumph*', was entered in the register of baptisms. In

February of the same year the mother-in-law paid the kirk dues for registering the marriage of William Marshall, then on board the *Lizard*.

Another, highly irregular, marriage was contracted in Edinburgh on 3 December 1768, between Margaret Mowbray and John Fashion, a black slave whom Captain Charles Inglis had brought to Cramond. The minister was scandalised to discover later that Fashion had not been baptised at the time of his marriage, and 'John, an American black above 25 years of age, belonging to Captain Charles Inglis, son to Sir John Inglis of Cramond, was baptised on Monday the 3 of April 1769, witnesses Captain Charles Inglis and James Fairholm, both in Nether Cramond'. The couple's son John was baptised on 10 September of the same year, followed by a daughter, Ann (of whom more later), on 28 February 1771.

There was nothing remarkable about the circumstances that led to Mary Martial (or Marshall) conceiving an illegitimate child by William Stuart when both were employed by Walter Gowans in Peggy's Mill, where they worked together at the grain mill and about the byre and fields. What distinguishes the affair is William's amusingly ambivalent attitude. He talked obsessively about the birth but at the same time, being a married man with a family, tried to disclaim responsibility.

Mary herself did her best to keep his name secret until the midwife refused any assistance in the birth until she had elicited this information. She first named a number of the men-servants at the mill, all of whom Mary cleared. She then asked whether the father was a young man. 'No', said Mary, 'and that was her grief.' (Evidently 'young' equated with 'unmarried'.) At last William Stuart was named (he was then thirty-four years old to Mary's twenty-seven), and Mary said yes, 'it was to him and to no-one else'.

When the case first came before Cramond session in January 1755 (brought, perhaps, by the surgeon and elder Robert Spotswood, who had heard much gossip about it), William denied any improper dealings with Mary. When Mary was asked whether she could bring any evidence to 'fix the guilt upon him', she replied that 'none but God and themselves knew anything of the matter'. This proved to be a most naive assumption. Various neighbours and fellow-servants gave evidence, both to the session and before presbytery.

Jean Mather (a relation of William's wife, Katherine Mather?) was present when William was told that Mary was in labour. He expressed the greatest concern, saying words to the effect that 'he felt as much pain for her, as if his heart was burning in the fire, and that the account of her uneasiness did him more hurt, than his meat would do him good for eight days to come'. 'He wished the midwife would do what was fair to her' and 'he would give the said Mary Martial a guinea if she would father the child upon him; that he would dree [suffer] all the repentance the session should impose upon him, and wished he could bear her pain too'. At some point he also told Jean that the child was conceived six weeks before Whitsun, that their fellow-servant Thomas Gilmer was not the father, 'but that some damned ruffian was the father of it, and that he himself knew when it was got, as well as the said Mary Martial herself'. Next morning he visited a neighbour and told her that Mary had had a child, and that it was said he was the father.

About a fortnight after the birth, when a number of women were visiting Mary, William also came to see her, and told her 'that he would take her and the child, provided the session would take his wife and children'. He asked her what she intended to do with the child. Mary said she would ask the minister to baptise her, and do whatever the minister and session wanted. William replied that he would take her away to Edinburgh and get her baptised for a shilling, that he would give three shillings to buy a frock for her, and that if Mary had kept her mind to herself he would have given her a guinea. Mary said plaintively that she had 'kept up [concealed] his being the father as long as she could', before being forced to reveal it in order to get help in her labour.

Another of the women present at the meeting commented that William had shown great fondness for both Mary and her child. The interested bystanders had seen him take the baby in his arms and kiss her, and also lay his hands on Mary's shoulders. Although, in disappointment over her admission that the responsibility was his, he withheld the guinea, William kindly promised to send Mary a flank of beef. On the same day he told George Edmundstone that he had given Mary some money the night before, that he intended to take the child and get her baptised for a shilling, and that he was 'free of the child' but knew who the father was. George asked him several times whether he was not the father himself, but 'was always shifted with this evasion, that he knew who was the father of it'.

Despite William's tergiversations, on 6 April the minister announced to the session that one of the elders had written to say that William had confessed to him. Meanwhile, Mary had begun her penance for adultery and the session had agreed to her request for baptism, provided that her father sponsored it. Mary was absolved on 13 April after standing six times, 'the session having judged it not for edification to continue her appearance any longer'. William compeared before the session on 13 April, again admitted guilt, and was told to appear before presbytery. He also asked to have a legitimate child baptised, which was permitted if his wife stood sponsor. (By now, women were doing so in exceptional circumstances.)

William avoided making any penitential appearances for some six months, but eventually stood before the congregation for the first of six times on 12 October, and was absolved in January 1756.

Eupham Ogston was probably telling the truth when in February 1758 she fathered her child on, she said, the son of her former employer, John Prentice, tenant in South Clermiston. But she could bring no effective evidence, the family enjoyed respectable standing, and young James Prentice would make no public admission but countered her accusation by alleging her promiscuity with the male servants. Eupham told the session that one night the previous winter she had sent for James to speak with her at Whitehouse. He came and acknowledged privately that he was the father, gave her 6d. and promised to supply her with money as soon as she left his father's house. James admitted only to going to Whitehouse at 9 pm in bad weather to talk to Eupham, although, according to Eupham, he asked for the child to be named after him if a boy. A few days later he wrote that he was now bound apprentice to a wright in the Canongate and so less at liberty to attend any session, but nominated as 'exculpatory witnesses' two men-servants of his father and his sisters Elizabeth and Margaret. Margaret, aged 'upwards of sixteen years', said she had no reason to suspect her brother. Asked whether she had ever seen any indecent behaviour between Eupham and any manservant, she said she had seen impropriety between Eupham and a Robert Brown.

Whatever the truth of the matter, Eupham made no headway against the united front of this family. A measure of their relative social position is that both the Prentice girls could sign their own names.

A cluster of cases of antenuptial fornication came to sessional notice in January 1757, and in July Alexander Brown in Craighouse confessed to having had sex with a servant-woman whom he had now married. He asked to have the scandal removed and be received again as a member of the established church, after seceding some time previously. He declared that he had no selfish motive for this step, although he wanted his child baptised and was also seeking a testimonial. While a dissenter he had lapsed again and again into fornication and adultery. When presbytery was consulted the matter was referred back to Cramond session, since the scandal was now very old. Brown was absolved on 13 July 1758 and in October 1761 was given a testimonial for the twenty-one years up to Martinmas 1758.

Which dissenting sect Brown had patronised, with little effect on his morals, is not revealed. In Cramond, just as the social results of the new industry were beginning to be felt, a new patron of the kirk arrived, imbued with the fervour of the religious revival that also marks these eighteenth-century decades. The previous spirit of 'moderation' was being replaced by 'enthusiasm', awoken by the preaching of such as Whitefield and Wesley, and Dissent (which had started formally with the formation of Ebenezer Erskine's Original Secession in the '30s), began its fissiparous proclivities with a split between the Burghers and Anti-Burghers in 1747.[16] This convert to Evangelical enthusiasm was Willielma (or Wilhelmina), Viscountess Glenorchy, who in 1769 got her husband to buy Barnton, as part of a strategy to plant suitable ministers in Scottish parishes, in addition to founding chapels, in Edinburgh and elsewhere.[17] Lady Glenorchy thus followed in the reforming steps of the Covenanting Lords Balmerino a century and a half before. After her husband's death at Barnton on 14 November 1771 she seldom resided there herself. But Barnton House had, says Wood, 'the honour of being for some years occupied by her beautiful, amiable, and accomplished niece', that countess of Sutherland made notorious at a later date by the clearances carried out on her Highland estates.[18]

It might be fair to say that in choosing ministers Lady Glenorchy was sometimes actuated by personal benevolence at the expense of more pragmatic considerations. Wood relates that one of her protégés was the Reverend Francis Sherriff. He had been chaplain to the Scots regiments in Dutch service, the only ministerial charge that he could obtain. Possibly it was there that he met Lady Glenorchy's friend and mentor, Robert Walker senior, who had been pastor to a Scots congregation in Rotterdam. In failing health, Sherriff returned to Edinburgh in September 1777 and Lady Glenorchy made him minister of her new chapel in Edinburgh and accommodated him at Barnton. He died there on 12 June 1778, aged 28, and is buried in the Barnton vault of Cramond kirk.[19] Of Lady Glenorchy's three appointments to the Cramond manse, the third was not an unqualified success and the first, her choice of a successor to Gilbert Hamilton, proved an unmitigated disaster. On 1 November 1772 the session were told that their patron had laid a presentation before presbytery in favour of Mr Charles Stuart of Dunearn, together with his letter of acceptance. Stuart, who was ordained to Cramond in April 1773, held his one and only sessional meeting on 27 December that year, but was developing crippling conscientious doubts about the authority of the established church, with its non-scriptural organisation of kirk sessions and presbyteries. Although he apparently continued to preach, without his chairmanship the session could not function for most purposes. When he finally resigned and the church was declared vacant on 19 May 1776, the last parish sacrament had been administered in June 1771. (After that no sessional minutes were kept between July 1771 and February 1772, owing to Hamilton's illness.) It was reported on 11 July 1776 that the beadle, James Fearholm or Fearm, had been 'sometime dead'. The stable, byre and other offices of the manse were in a ruinous condition, though Stuart did make repairs to the manse itself, the churchyard dykes were tumbling down and the schoolhouse and schoolmaster's house were in such bad repair that plans now had to be drawn up for a total rebuilding.

When David Strachan, the treasurer, died the heritors had replaced him by Robert Spotswood, but the acting elders had been reduced to two, Spotswood and John Black, who was old and ill. George Robertson, senior, in Granton, who had previously been an elder in Colinton, had been nominated at Stuart's only session in 1773 but was not appointed until July 1776. In April-June 1777 only Spotswood and Robertson were attending sessional meetings and on 22 August the new minister had to ask two elders from South Leith and two from Corstorphine to assist at the forthcoming communion.

Stuart, the son of a Lord Provost of Edinburgh and a man of varied talents, later joined the Anabaptists, took a medical degree and practised as a successful doctor in Edinburgh. He also edited the *Edinburgh Quarterly Magazine* of 1798–1800.[20] Possibly he continued to live in Cramond for a time, as in the copy of a rent-roll, before 1781, in Wood's papers, 'Charles Stewart of Dunnairn' is listed as holding Barnton Mains from Lady Glenorchy.[21]

Lady Glenorchy's next appointment, in October 1776, was Robert Walker junior. He seems to have been an able and conscientious minister of Cramond, but after some seven years succumbed to the lure of a prestigious pulpit in Edinburgh and became senior minister in the Canongate church. He is the subject of Raeburn's painting of 'the skating minister' in the National Gallery of Scotland, depicting him demurely circling the ice on Duddingston Loch. His other-worldly expression, black clothes and hat and air of constrained clerical decorum would probably not have exculpated him from a charge of unbecoming behaviour in the eyes of some of his seventeenth-century predecessors in Cramond's manse, any more than such public – and permanently publicised – frivolity would seem proper to pious clergy in a later time. Mr Walker's display of innocent worldliness was, however, quite proper to his place in the Edinburgh society of the time. He may well have had little in common with the rough and rootless element among the ironworkers who were entering his parish.

When Sir John Inglis died in 1771 he was succeeded briefly by his eldest son, Sir Adam, and in November 1772 by his next son, Sir John Inglis 2.

The second Sir John kept up the tradition of alliance with families notable in the political and cultural life of Scotland by marrying a daughter of Sir Robert Sinclair of Longformacus.[22] After their father's death, Adam and then John Inglis set about refashioning Cramond House on elegant, modern, lines. In 1778 John took the opportunity to carry out a scheme first mooted by his father in 1747.[23] Having negotiated an exchange with Mr Walker so that the glebe no longer divided parts of his own grounds, Inglis arranged to have a new schoolmaster's house and schoolroom built in a field well away from his mansion. He also demolished the main village road and paid for a new one to be made to the south of the kirk and his estate, enclosed on each side by a four-foot-high stone wall. He could not yet quite emulate the splendid policies of Muirhouse, with their three grand avenues of stately trees and plantations down to the shore of the Forth, because the construction of what is now Cramond Glebe Road did not completely remove the village dwellings from his vicinity and their proximity was made more noisome when nailers began working there from 1769. Lord Rosebery pursued 'improvement' more ruthlessly in 1764 when he instituted a clearance of 360 acres along the west side of the Almond, a beautification that eventually removed thirty-four out of the thirty-seven households there and was reckoned to have diminished Cramond's population by as many as 150 persons.[24]

The social regulation of the parish still depended greatly upon the zeal of minister and session. When the private controls that public opinion, or a well-drilled conscience, imposed on individual parishioners proved insufficient, the kirk had employed a range of sanctions to bring sinners to heel. Each district of the parish had had an 'elder of the bound' to keep a watchful eye on his charges. Now the 'cutty stool' and sackcloth were going out of fashion, to be followed in time by any form of public penance. Of the former sanctions, private rebuke and deprivation of church privileges now chiefly remained. When Janet Ranken had borne an illegitimate child to the overseer at Barnbougle in 1779, Mr Walker told her that 'her future good behaviour would alone recommend her for readmission into the privileges of the church, and unless her deportment pleaded in her favours, he could not admit her [as] sponsor for her child in the sacrament of baptism'. It was not sufficient to deter her from adultery later.

Active elders might be few and literally far between, a trend which, if general, would help explain the breakdown in discipline often descried in late eighteenth-century Scotland as a whole. As for the relaxation in the severity of ecclesiastical discipline, it was sensible in itself and much in tune with the more 'enlightened' attitudes of the new age. Inevitably, though, there were those who scorned an authority that seemed to be weakening, or who, in the case of some of the incomers, had barely recognised it in the first place.

On top of all this, during the five-and-a-half years when first Gilbert Hamilton was dying and then his successor struggled unhappily with a nonconformist conscience, the number of sessioners declined until Robert Spotswood was for a time the sole effective elder. What authority he then retained derived from his position as kirk treasurer and his personal influence as parish surgeon. Without a moderator to authorise meetings, the kirk session was inoperative. By the time that proper sessional government was restored, ground had been lost that was never fully recovered.

After Robert Spotswood was joined by George Robertson, they remained the only active elders until July 1779, when they were joined by David Wilson, boat-owner and feuar in Nether Cramond, and James Gillespie, farmer in Fairafar. In January 1783 Thomas Cleghorn, farmer, and the Nether Cramond residents James Black, spademaker, and James Robb, brewer, and later also baker, were added to the session.

Some of the errant among Mr Walker's parishioners had connections with the ironworks. On 27 June 1779 he informed his session that Jean McCurich, wife of William Marshal, soldier in America, was pregnant in adultery. Jean, whose husband had been a nailer before joining the army, delated as father of her child James Bathgate, principal clerk to Mr Edington, the manager of the slit mill, 'a most hurtful accusation' which Bathgate persistently denied. Jean's story was that congress had occurred when she went to buy herring from Bathgate, on account of Mrs Probert at the slit mill. (Evidently he ran a 'truck-shop' for the workers.) The minister asked Bathgate to show him his daybook, which should have recorded any sale of herrings on what Jean subsequently pinpointed as Monday 11 January. No such entry appeared, but Walker remained suspicious of Bathgate's statement that the record produced was the original and not a falsified copy. Presbytery, when involved, also expressed surprise at the extreme neatness of the document, but in March 1780 Bathgate offered a written explanation to the session, along with a string of 'vague invectives against his accuser and [her] family'. For five years the matter seems to have rested there, unresolved, until on 21 August 1785 Bathgate, wishing to sponsor the baptism of his child by marriage, admitted of his own accord that he had indeed fathered Jean's child. His sponsorship was permitted, after the new minister exhorted him to lead a godly life in future. No penalty was exacted for his former adultery.

One of the open and scandalous pieces of modern immorality noted in

Wood's *History of Cramond* in 1794 occurred on Sunday 27 January 1782, when, presumably on a tip-off, the elder James Gillespie went with others at midnight to the house of the widowed Christian Richmond in Nether Cramond. There they found Christian and her twenty-year-old daughter, Mary Rew, alone with William Probert, a married worker in the slit mill. Mary was in bed, Christian had apparently just risen out of it, and William was trying to conceal himself under the bed, 'all circumstances which tended to confirm a report that an improper connection subsisted between said William Probert and Mary Rew for some time past, to which Christian Richmond her mother was privy'.

When questioned before the session, Mary admitted that she had been guilty of criminal intercourse with William Probert, 'but not often'. She denied that he had been in bed with her on the 27th. When asked what business he had in her mother's house at such an unwarranted hour, Mary replied that she had been so ill-treated by the neighbours on the evening before that she was unable to rise out of bed, and Probert came to ask after her. While she did not name Mrs Probert, it may be suspected that it was the aggrieved wife who had instigated this attack. Mary added that she had been connected with Probert since Martinmas, when she had left her service on his advice. Since then she had lived in a hired room in the Land Market (Lawnmarket) in Edinburgh. William had visited her, 'but not very often', and given her money, 'but very little'. Did her mother know of the connection? – She had never told her of it. Had William frequented her mother's house after she came home at New Year? – Yes, 'but not often'. How often? – Only twice. And she refused to answer when asked whether she did not meet him elsewhere, especially in a house at Lauriston. She thought she was not with child, but was not certain.

Mary's mother testified that William, 'much the worse of liquor', had come to her door wanting to be in for just ten minutes, to find out who had abused Mary 'that he might have amends of them'. Asked why she had let him in at that hour, Christian said simply that she, too, would like to be revenged on Mary's assailants. She denied that William was in bed, he had sat in a chair. And when asked how she could encourage a married man to show any attention to her daughter, Christian replied that 'she never saw any harm in the man'. Nor had she enquired about Mary's situation after she left her employment.

None of those concerned appeared before the next several meetings of session, until on 17 March Christian finally compeared and reported that Mary was now in service with an elderly lady in Edinburgh. In June the session, most tamely by the standards of earlier times, found Probert liable to 'the sentence of contumacy' for not compearing before them, 'but in respect that the scandal hath, in some measure, ceased with regard to this place' (presumably because Mary was in Edinburgh), decided to leave Probert 'under the scandal he hath contracted, reserving to themselves the power of renewing the process if the scandal again becomes flagrant'. Possibly Probert, whose name suggests Welsh extraction, was not officially a member of the congregation in any case.

On the same day, 27 June 1779, that Mr Walker brought Jean McCurich's pregnancy to sessional notice he had also informed the meeting 'that he had heard that Margaret Mowbray (wife of John Fashion, an American Black, who hath been years out of this place) hath brought forth a child in adultery'. Margaret, whose husband was presumed to be still alive, as she had had a letter from him about a month earlier, said unconcernedly that she had had several children in adultery, and cited John McLauchland, now an ensign in the army in America, as father of her latest. The sessioners doubted her veracity on that point, but the minister remained content with administering a general rebuke for her sinful course of life.

At this period Sir John Inglis possibly acceded to a petition to remove from Nether Cramond 'a few persons of notoriously bad fame' – the session probably had Margaret Mowbray Fashion and Jean McCurich in mind. Both, however, were still in the parish six years later.

Other parishioners, mostly of the servant class, exhibited familiar instances of feckless behaviour. On 6 April 1777 Margaret Tennant delated as the father of her child a farm-worker, John Pickhard. He admitted responsibility to the minister, but was going to sea so his sessional appearance was postponed. After he had appeared once it was reported that he 'had made an elopement' and gone to sea again, leaving Margaret with their child. She then 'eloped' too, and left the child with Alexander Pickhard's wife. The session agreed in September that something ought to be done by them for its protection, and arranged for a woman to nurse and care for it. George Gilchrist's wife similarly deserted him and their two infants in 1780.

Understandably enough, Mr Walker's session made little or no effort to investigate a series of vague allegations in November 1782 against the aged heritor John Howison of Braehead when Ann Carmichael accused John Drummond, junior, the tailor in King's Cramond, and James Stevenson or Stevens, the smith at Cramond Bridge, of defaming her and so causing her husband's desertion. The affair was confused at best, and is made more so by Mr Ninian Paton's carelessly written report in the minutes. The smith blamed the tailor for spreading stories about Ann's relations with Mr Howison and thereby alienating her husband's affections. It seems that Ann's husband was himself suspected of improper relations with the maidservant at Braehead House and had left the parish after a tip-off from Drummond, conveyed by Stevenson, that he was about to be summoned before the session. Stevenson also alleged that the first, written, evidence that he had submitted to the minister on Ann's behalf had been falsified at Howison's insistence when Ann showed the draft to the laird.

The deserted Ann, who was now maintaining herself partly by spinning and other casual work and 'partly by assistance from the family at Braehead', explained that her husband, Peter Campbell, had been working for Howison after a period of army service in the Duke of Buccleuch's Fencibles when he suddenly turned against her, accusing her 'of being bad with other men in his absence while a soldier'. In particular he told her that he had received a letter saying that she had borne a child at a time when he could not possibly have been the father. 'The town's talk', she said, 'laid it [the supposed child?] on Mr Howison of Braehead.' Asked who had told her of the rumour, Ann named four neighbouring couples in King's Cramond, all of whom subsequently denied doing so.

A week before Campbell went off, Ann heard him whispering with the tailor, Drummond, who urged him to leave her. When her husband eventually came home – past ten at night – and she called 'Is that you, Peter?', he asked, in effect, what business it was of hers. When he entered the house, 'God Almighty knows what names he gave her'. Asked to specify, Ann said he called her 'a damned whore, bitch and suchlike names'. Asked whether he was drunk, she said that he appeared to have drunk some, but not so much as to be drunk. The slanders about her were the only reason she could think of for his ill-treatment and eventual desertion: while he was in the regiment and when he first came home he had been very kind to her. In the absence of any substantive evidence, however, and bemused by the confusing and largely irrelevant details offered by Stevenson, the session formally absolved Drummond from the charge of slander.

Lady Glenorchy's third and last appointment to Cramond, Mr Archibald Bonar, was thirty when he replaced Robert Walker in 1785. A son of the manse, who married a cousin, the daughter of another minister, and had brothers in banking in Edinburgh, he was a man of feeble health and retiring disposition. He had found the rigours of a Glasgow parish too much for him after a year or so and was thankful to move to Cramond's seemingly more salubrious and peaceful setting. He would serve there for the next thirty-one years, much dismayed at times by the dissolute behaviour of some of his flock.

Lady Glenorchy, having run out of her husband's money, had to sell Barnton in 1785. She died at Edinburgh next year, aged only forty-four. Her personal piety was long respected in the parish. Several Cramond girls were named Wilhelmina in her honour, and at least one unfortunate boy was christened Glenorchy.[25] Whether she ever overcame endemic shyness to engage humble Cramond cottagers in spiritual discourse is not recorded.

If Lord Balmerino's body was disturbed by Cromwell's soldiers, Lady Glenorchy's remains would fall victim to the forces of Mechanical Progress when, in 1844, her chapel in Edinburgh was demolished and her coffin shifted because the ground was required by the North British Railway. For the next fifteen years the remains of this zealous Presbyterian were given shelter by an Episcopalian church.[26]

NOTES

1. *Gilbert Hamilton.* Wood, *Cramond,* p. 82.
2. *Suitability as treasurer. Ibid.,* p. 85 n.
3. *Ainslie and Oughton. Ibid.,* p. 20. Scholarship and a zeal for learning were another characteristic of the time: the first edition of the *Encyclopaedia Britannica* was published in three volumes in Edinburgh in 1771.
4. *Career of Charles Inglis.* Wood, *Cramond,* p. 266; *Dictionary of National Biography.*
5. *John William Law.* Wood, *Cramond,* p. 264.
6. *Impressment.* 11 May, 7 Sept. 1755. Fear of forcible recruitment by the press-gang long persisted. My great-grandfather told that he had been born in Carnoustie around midnight of 31 Dec. 1826 and the birth was ascribed to 1 January, 'to give him a year's respite from impressment'.
7. *Assignment on tolls.* Recorded 27 March 1828. The Cramond District Turnpike Trust improved the road between Nether Cramond and Muttonhole in 1759. Another development saw the Edinburgh to Glasgow stagecoach begin running in 1749, taking only 12 hours for the journey one way (!): G. S. Pryde, *A New History of Scotland,* vol. 2, Edinburgh (1962), p. 89.
8. *Iron Mills.* See, in detail, Basil C. Skinner, *The Cramond Iron Works,* University of Edinburgh Dept. of Adult Education and Extra-Mural Studies, 1965, and Patrick Cadell, *The Iron Mills at Cramond,* Edinburgh University Extra-Mural Association: Studies in Local History, 1973.
9. *Recruiting nailers.* Carron Company Letter books (NAS), June 1769, quoted Skinner, p. 19.
10. *Drinking at the mill.* Patrick Cadell, p. 8; Carron Co. Letter-Bk. 1762–63 (NAS GD 58/1/3) p. 235; ibid., pp. 287, 401.

11. *Legal actions.* Patrick Cadell, p. 22; Basil C. Skinner and Patrick Cadell, 'The Riverside Industries', in *Cramond*, Cramond Heritage Trust, 4th edn 1989, p. 39. See also Barclay S. Fraser, 'The Toun of Nether Cramond, 1792', *ibid.*, p. 30.

12. *Burn's quip.* Robert Burns, 'Impromptu on Carron Iron Works'.

13. *Employment at mill.* Patrick Cadell, pp. 7, 10.

14. *Oyster fishing.* Wood, *Cramond*, p. 93, said that about 1790 four or five dredgers were still operating occasionally, while in 1740 'eleven large boats, belonging to Cramond, were constantly employed, during the season, in dragging for that delicious bivalve'. Much earlier Cramond was celebrated in the (ironical?) reproof, 'Ye are sib to Cramond oysters and pewter vessel, ye are aye clattering', while in 1572 the poem 'The Lamentation of Lady Scotland' contained the lines: 'It is a pietie to se / Folk in a towne for cauld and hounger die; / It is mair schame in Burgh for to se beggers / Nor it is skaith in Crawmont to want dreggers'. ('It is more disgraceful to see beggars in a town than it is damaging to lack oyster-dredgers in Cramond'): *Satirical Poems of the Time of the Reformation*, Scottish Text Society, 2 vols., 1891–93, vol. 1, no. 33.

15. *Iron workers.* The list is reproduced in Patrick Cadell, App. 4, p. 54.

16. *Sects.* It has been estimated that by 1773 there were 190 dissenting congregations in Scotland: Pryde, *New History*, 2, p. 179.

17. *Date of purchase of Barnton.* Lord Glenorchy's body-servant, 'Mr' Peter Robertson (note the respectful title that the clerk, Ninian Paton, accorded him) had a child christened in Cramond in May 1769, which suggests that Barnton was purchased before the date of 1770 usually given. It was bought from the earl of March, whose wife was daughter and heir to John, earl of Selkirk and Ruglen. Her father (Wood, *Cramond*, p. 55 n.) died in Dec. 1744, aged 82, after overheating himself in dancing at an Assembly in Edinburgh.

18. *Countess of Sutherland.* Wood, *Cramond*, p. 55. For the clearances, e.g. Smout, *History of the Scottish People*, pp. 331–7.

19. *Lady Glenorchy's benevolence.* Wood, *Cramond*, pp. 74–5, n.

20. *Stuart's career. Fasti Ecclesiae Scoticanae* I.

21. *Barnton Mains.* NLS MS 9885 p. 73.

22. *Inglis family.* Wood, *Cramond*, p. 57.

23. *Scheme of 1747.* Edinburgh Presbytery Minutes, vol. 16, 24 June 1747, quoted in Joan Crowther, *The 'Old Schoolhouse' of Cramond, Edinburgh, and Education in Cramond, 1653–1875*, Moray House College of Education (Edinburgh), 1965, p. 46.

24. *Clearance.* Spotswood to Wood, 19 Nov. 1789, NLS MS 9886 fol. 33; Wood, *Cramond*, p. 110.

25. *Naming of Cramond children.* A tenant's son was christened Adolphus Oughton Cleghorn in compliment to the general, and the two children of Andrew Reoch, former engineer in Demerara (d. 1854 in Stirling), are named on his tombstone as Wilhelmina Cadell Reoch and John Inglis Reoch (b. 1795): Joan M. Aitken and others, *Gravestones and Memorials in Cramond Churchyard*, rev. edn. by Denise List, 3 vols., typescript (1982), in Edinburgh Public Library, ECH YDA 1818. Later the youngest son of a wright in Nether Cramond was named after the earl of Rosebery's family and christened Primrose Haig.

26. *Lady Glenorchy's remains.* Dean [Edward Bannerman] Ramsay, *Reminiscences of Scottish Life and Character*, 22nd edn (1872), pp. 344–5.

ELEVEN

Liberty, Vice, Stability, 1785–1799

In 1785 the Reverend Mr Archibald Bonar, having been rescued by Lady Glenorchy from a twelve-month ministry in Glasgow, was settled in the rural peace of Cramond. To John Wood the parish indeed exemplified the traditional country virtues. In 1794 he wrote of the landowners (the potential purchasers of his book):

> it may confidently be affirmed, that no other country parish in Scotland of equal extent, contains a greater number of resident heritors more decent in their general deportment, more punctual in attendance on religious ordinances, more ready to promote every measure tending to alleviate the distresses, or to meliorate the situation, of the common people; and, what will appear not a little extraordinary when the splendid fortunes possessed by some of them are considered, more free from luxury, pride and ostentation.[1]

Similarly, the twenty-nine farmers were 'in general industrious, sober, intelligent, and hospitable; few are wealthy, and none of them, happily for their families, entertain the foolish ambition of vying with their superiors in the luxuries of life':[2]

> With respect to the lower classes, I can safely assert, from the observation of several years, that a greater degree of industry, honesty, and content cannot be seen anywhere. No doubt there are exceptions, especially among a particular class, but the before-mentioned character is applicable to a great majority of the common people, particularly those employed in agriculture.[3]

But to Wood's essay on Cramond for the first volume of the *Statistical Account of Scotland*, published in 1791, Mr Bonar had insisted on appending a more splenetic impression. Wood's concluding paragraph reads: '*Miscellaneous Observations.* There are 2 coaches, and 4 four-wheeled chaises in this parish; 7 licensed ale-houses. The corruption among the lower classes, says the Rev. Mr Bonar, the minister, is mournful; as perhaps in few country parishes the liberties and vices of the town are anywhere more accurately copied'.[4]

Fears that the working classes were getting out of hand were, of course, greatly exacerbated by recent events in France and the activities of agitators who organised 'clubs' to discuss possible improvements (some radical, some mild) to the sacred political system in force in the United Kingdom. Unthinkable for the likes of Sir John Inglis, who was chosen to preside at a great meeting of the gentry of Edinburgh and the Lothians, held at Goldsmiths' Hall to oppose French revolutionary ideas.[5]

Wood closely echoed Lord Braxfield's dictum that the British Constitution was 'the best that ever was since the creation of the world',[6] when he thankfully reported that Cramond's lower classes had not so far succumbed to the terrifying new infection:

> they demeaned themselves in a quiet and peaceable manner, well worthy of imitation, during the late ferment that agitated the country. Sensible of the invaluable blessings secured to them by the excellent constitution of this kingdom, which has stood the test of ages, no wish for innovation or alteration found a place in their minds, and no reforming clubs presumed to rear their heads in this district.[7]

Doubtless those thought to be most at risk of catching revolutionary fervour were the inhabitants of Nether Cramond, especially the industrial workers among them. Mr Bonar would have subscribed to the view of his colleague in Corstorphine (if he did not himself inspire it) that such men were incomers who came from all the manufacturing towns in England, Ireland and Scotland, felt no ties with their parish of residence and

> act as if delivered from all the restraints of decency and decorum. In general, they manifest a total disregard to character, and indulge in every vice which opportunity enables them to perform. The influence of their contagious example must spread, and familiarize to crimes persons who formerly considered them with abhorrence.[8]

Mr Bonar would have found ample evidence of moral corruption in some of the scandals that had occurred under his immediate predecessor in the manse (Chapter 10). Wood, after perusing session minute books, was moved to remark that deplorably little was now done to check 'the most open and scandalous irregularities. . . . Emancipation from the intolerable yoke of ecclesiastical tyranny is no doubt to be reckoned among the advantages enjoyed by the present age; but it were much to be wished that great part of the antient discipline was restored'.[9]

It is true that the kirk had greatly alleviated, indeed largely removed, the penances imposed on sinners – now predominantly sexual offenders and couples engaging in irregular marriage. Irregular marriage was an assertion of independence on the part of working-class people, as well as a cheap and easy way of escaping the kirk's heavy-handed system. For the Establishment and the respectable in general it represented a deliberate flouting of the rules of law and order, and there was little that could be done to prevent it. Even counting cases of clandestine marriage, however, it would be hard to argue that the number of Cramond's sinners had increased as the penalties exacted became notably less severe, or the behaviour of occasional individuals become any more outrageous.

Mr Bonar had his own scandals to deal with – often, though not exclusively, among the ironworkers. Three years after the Mary Rew-William Probert affair (previous chapter) and at the very start of Mr Bonar's ministry, on 26 June 1785, a William Probert, 'servant to Mr Edington of the slit mill, Cramond', probably the son of William senior (both Williams are listed as forgemen in the parish survey of 1792), was accused by Margaret Angus of fathering her child. He denied this, while admitting that he had been guilty of uncleanness with her on a single occasion the previous March or April. In October the session, faced with implacable accusation on the one hand, and unhesitating denial on the other, gave up the case as impossible of proof. A few decades earlier Margaret at any rate would have had to 'satisfy' in public. When the child was three years old, Margaret sought to have it baptised. She was told that 'if the moderator found her qualified to instruct her child in the knowledge of religion, there was nothing in her conduct of late to prevent her from obtaining her request' and Bonar duly, if rather lukewarmly, certified on 17 February 1789 that he was 'satisfied that she had a willingness to improve her capacity for the instruction of her child'.

Jean McCurich's husband William Marshal (Chapter 10) returned to Cramond and his former occupation as nailer, and in February 1789 was allowed to sponsor a legitimate child in baptism, with a warning from Mr Bonar that, having been very unfavourably reported for intemperance and cruelty to his wife, 'strict notice would be taken of his future conduct'. In July 1800 the couple's daughter Jean would come to live with her widowed mother, 'with a suckling infant'. It was unclear whether or not she was married, and she was ordered to give security to the parish that she and her child would not become a burden on funds, otherwise her mother would be deprived of her pension if she continued to harbour them.

In October 1788 Margaret Mowbray, the promiscuous wife of the 'American Black' John Fashion (Chapter 10), was again in trouble, this time for contracting an irregular marriage with a labourer named David

Purie. She produced documents to prove that she had been divorced by Fashion for adultery, and presbytery permitted her remarriage. But the session demurred when Purie asked for baptism for the child 'brought to him [by] Margaret Mowbray in consequence of the marriage just now confirmed', and 'considering the particular situation of this family, judged it expedient not to be rash in baptising the child, until such time as Mr Bonar was satisfied of David Purie's Christian knowledge and other requisites becoming [to] a member of the Christian church'. David thereupon 'thought proper' to get the child baptised in Edinburgh by what school-master Paton calls, on 17 February 1789, an 'Espocalian minister'.

'The particular situation of this family' referred not merely to the sexual irregularities of Margaret Mowbray, but also to those of her daughter, Ann Fashion. On 25 December 1788 Ann gave birth in her mother's house at Lauriston. (Can this have been the 'house in Lauriston' where William Probert and Mary Rew sometimes met together?) Ann said that her child had been begotten in Edinburgh, the father being a Mr Reid, watchmaker in Parliament Square, who met with her in a house at the foot of Forrester's Wynd when she was delivering washing to the family there. She had never seen Mr Reid before, and met him only once subsequently. She could not name the mistress of the house, who had employed her as a washerwoman on that single occasion, on the recommendation of 'an old comrade' and former fellow-servant named Biny Calder, now in Galloway. The session noted primly that there was reason to suppose that the house referred to was a House of Bad Fame, that Ann knew it to be so, and was no stranger to it: performing, it seems, the double function of laundrywoman and call-girl. She was, however, 'dismissed for the present' and nothing else is recorded. Perhaps Mr Bonar had Ann Fashion chiefly in mind when he fulminated against the pernicious ways of the city.

Lesser offenders might be 'laid under church censure' and denied the privilege of baptism. John Stuart, junior, and Jean Willis, from an ironwork-ing family, said on 24 October 1791 that they had been privately married in Edinburgh by a minister named John Stuart (who did perform such ceremonies). They produced a certificate to that effect, but 'there being reasons to suspect that the certificate produced was wrote by the parties themselves', the couple were told to return at the next meeting. They then had their marriage confirmed and were permitted to register it, but were laid under church censure for prevarication in falsely claiming to be married and offering a forged certificate. Margaret Angus, David Purie and William Marshal had been permitted baptism for their children only on conditions. Private interviews with the minister were imposed upon a couple who confessed to fornication in April 1790: 'Both parties were suitably rebuked and exhorted by the moderator and desired to converse with him from time to time, that upon their giving signs of repentance he may inform the session and have them absolved from church censure'. The session agreed to restore them two months later and they were formally absolved on 2 August, after exhibiting adequate penitence. In a more serious case, of adultery for instance, offenders might still be called before the session (but not the congregation) for private rebuke. George Grant, having committed adultery with Janet Ranken, came from Liberton on 23 April 1786 seeking 'to be purged of his sin' before the session, but was told to come back in three weeks, since the circumstances were 'aggravating, such as his leaving his own house and carrying the said Janet Ranken along with him'. 'Upon this, George went away much dissatisfied', commented the clerk.

The comparatively relaxed attitude that elders were now taking to sexual licence is suggested by Spotswood's report to Wood of one piece of parish scandal in February 1789. What shocked Spotswood was less the breach of morality than the wanton disregard of financial advantage. 'The news of the day', wrote the Cramond elder, 'is that Mr Ramsay's household servantman who has been with him eight years and got eight guineas to his handsel [initial salary], to be increased one guinea every year while with him, has foolishly forfeited all future favours and [been] discharged the service together with a servant-maid with child by him.'[10]

Like Mr Robert Walker in the case of James Bathgate, Mr Bonar could meet difficulty in bringing a recalcitrant man to book. On 5 March 1791 the authorities in Corstorphine reported that Elisabeth (or Bethia) Duncan had confessed herself with child to Harry Hanna (alias Hannay), blacksmith in Lennie Port. Elisabeth told Cramond session that Hanna had come to her brother's house in Lennie Port when she was living there and intercourse had taken place when he was in the house alone with her for some time between 7 and 10 pm. Before that time he had 'been sometimes in use to sit with her in her brother's house and had frequently solicited her compliance with his criminal desires'. Hanna denied paternity, or ever soliciting her to guilt. He had been alone with her, for no more than three minutes, at the end of October but never sat down then, and had not previously visited her for many months. Elisabeth had asked him to ascertain whether Mrs Johnston in Corstorphine wanted a maidservant. He found that she did, and Elisabeth obtained the post. On returning home she went to Hanna's shop to tell him the news and next day, Hanna continued, he stepped for a moment into her house 'to advise her to behave better for the future than she had done formerly, and to enquire for her brother, who, he found, was not at home'. He further declared that Elisabeth was well known to be of Bad Character and had earlier threatened to do him an ill turn.

Further investigation was then delayed until 25 September, when the session heard that Elisabeth had given birth in Edinburgh infirmary some three months earlier – at a date consistent with Hanna's admitted visit to her. For the past two months she had been reduced to the most miserable straits and obliged to sell her clothes to procure food and lodging. 'If any other person but Harry Hanna had been the father of her child she would have applied to that other person for some support in her great straits', she told the session, 'but that she never could, nor would, give up any other than Harry Hanna as the father of her child.' The session disbelieved Hanna's reiterated denial, and laid him under church censure. Both Hanna and Elisabeth were therefore suspended from church privileges. Three years later, on 4 October 1794, having given Hanna plenty of time 'to weigh matters with himself' – time in which he had never admitted Bethia Duncan's charge, 'nor sought to be absolved from the imputation' – the session took steps to prosecute Hanna. He seems to have left the parish by 1792.

Hanna had skilfully impugned Bethia's reputation in his explanation of why he had visited her at the crucial time. William Horsbrugh, who in May 1792 lodged in Muttonhole while working in Lauriston stone quarry, disputed paternity of Nanny Paterson's child on the grounds of her bad character, although he freely confessed guilt with her. At his insistence she swore on the bible that she had never had carnal knowledge of any other man. Whatever the case with Nanny, Johanna Pickhard, a farm-servant, did become notorious, with three children by different fathers (at least two of them also farm-servants) between 1794 and 1804.[11]

Any increase in industry from the ironmills did not, of course, bring permanent prosperity to all members of the community. Incomers became old and incapable of earning, like the nailer William Kilgour, or died, like the nailer William Ruddiman, leaving an impoverished widow. The session had to lend money to the families of James McCurich (master of *The Four Brothers* in 1791), and the nailer John Jamison,[12] while Jean McCurich also received support at various times. John Forrest, wright, and Claud Douglas, mason, the father and husband of Isobel Forrest (both from old families in Nether Cramond) successfully claimed that they were too poor to maintain Isobel in the Edinburgh asylum when she became insane. The session agreed on 30 November 1794 to support her there for a quarter year, 'if she has to be kept in Bedlam so long'. An earlier session had agreed on 11 October 1777 to settle Euphan Young, illegitimate daughter of James Dick, with some pensioner when she became 'distracted in mind' after her mother's death and attempted to strangle herself. In November 1796 fifty-five people were getting assistance from the poor funds, almost all so needy that they required extra payment over winter. A Friendly Society had been set up in 1773 to provide death and other benefits for subscribers, but by 1793 an increase in the number of pensionable widows was seriously depleting its funds.[13]

The session was so short of money in December 1796 that it was thought desirable to cut down the number of places offered to poor children at the parish school. Education for the very poor was a privilege. In June next year it was noted that all except one of the existing 'poor scholars' had already had three years of schooling. It was thought unfair to keep them there longer at the expense of other deserving candidates, so they must leave at the end of the week in which their quarter-year was up and be considered to have received all the education necessary. The new admissions were to be kept 'close' at school by their parents, and if the schoolmaster complained about bad attendance to the session they would be removed again. Andrew Baverage (Chapter 7) may have been typical in starting his three years of free education in January 1695, when he had recently turned ten.

Poor scholars would not have taken any 'extra' subjects. On his appointment as schoolmaster in November 1764 Ninian Paton had been allowed to charge fees at an increased level. Pupils taking the basic course in reading English would pay 16d. sterling a quarter, and for Latin or arithmetic 3s. By a curious-sounding arrangement it was agreed that instruction in writing would be free if given, at the parent's request, in school hours in place of an English or Latin lesson, but would also cost 3s. if Paton chose to teach it outside the usual school time.

In December 1786, having achieved a measure of isolation by moving the school and village road away from his estate, absorbing the green and rehousing some of the villagers, Sir John Inglis was perhaps anxious to control mischievous village children who were still running wild about his property on sabbath evenings and so offered to fund a Sunday school,

> which might not only be the means of bringing the children together at six in the evening, or any other hour that shall be thought most convenient, and keep them from strolling idly about, but of bringing them to attend the church by their being interrogated and show [sic]

how they had spent the preceding part of the day, and be reproved when necessary.

For this purpose Mr Paton was to receive the annual interest on an endowment of £25. What was on offer was some routine drilling in the elements of religion. Participants were to read a portion of sacred scripture and repeat part of the single catechism and proofs, with part of a psalm or sacred hymn as paraphrased. Parents could attend if they chose. The session acclaimed the scheme, thinking it of great utility, especially (significantly) 'in the village of Nether Cramond'. Like that much earlier plan of Mr John Hamilton's for edifying the Nether Cramonders by a special service, the Sunday school does not seem to have aroused much enthusiasm. Two years later, on 4 May 1789, the session agreed that each member should take a month's turn and 'endeavour to cooperate with Mr Paton to cause the children in and near Nether Cramond to attend the Sunday school regularly'.

When Marjory Fleming, aged seven, was staying with the family at Braehead in the summer of 1810 she noted in her journal the message of 'the sarmon preached by Mr Bonner it was that we sould ofer ourselves to God morning and evening and then we will be happy with God if we are good'. The religious teaching of Mr Bonar and his contemporaries was not as benign as this might suggest: young Marjory was not always good and a little earlier had written in anguish, 'O what would become of me if I was in danger and God not friends with me I must go to unquenchiable fire'.[14]

Wood put part of the blame for what he saw as a recent relaxation of general morals on 'the non-attendance of the landed proprietors on the meetings of the Kirk Session, and their not enforcing its decrees', adding, with some exaggeration, that during the seventeenth and early eighteenth centuries 'even the most considerable heritors, peers of the realm not excluded', had regularly attended meetings.[15] It is certainly true that now even the occasional meetings of heritors were being poorly attended. But few of the landowners had ever consistently enforced sessional decrees. Wood also forebore to mention that no more than seven heritors were now to be found residing in the parish, four of them well advanced in years. Many of the great houses were now let to such tenants as Sir John Stewart in Caroline Park or William Keith, accountant, in Lauriston Castle – 'gentlemen not heritors'.

Some of the gentry were, in any case, 'Episcopally inclined', though not necessarily stand-offish with regard to the national church. Marjory Fleming wrote when on a visit early in 1811, 'An annibabtist is a thing I am not a member of: – I am a Pisplikan just now & a Prisbeteren at Kercaldy my native town'.[16] In 1792 Cramond had at least nine Episcopalians of various ranks, from Sir John Stewart and some of his household to the ironworker Richard Squires. In the six out of twelve districts where the parish survey of that year noted dissenters the total, including Episcopalians, comes to 29 (persons or families?): besides three unspecified 'seceders' there were six Antiburgher seceders, nine Anabaptists, one French Calvinist and one Glassite. (Wood, whose figures are often unreliable, made the total only 21.) Naturally, these adherents of other religious bodies were not amenable to the discipline of the Established Kirk. And while, by a process of simple subtraction, Wood claimed that 1,464 Cramonders (from infants upwards) were members of the Kirk, the reality was that the size of the regular congregation was not keeping pace with growth in the parish population as a whole. Ministers could exercise no discipline over an increasing number of uncommitted parishioners who were insufficiently imbued with the dread of 'unquenchiable fire'.

NOTES

1. *Wood on the heritors.* Cramond, p. 119.
2. *Wood on the farmers.* Ibid., p. 120.
3. *Wood on the lower classes.* Ibid..
4. *Mournful corruption.* Statistical Account I, 76.
5. *Revolutionary ideas.* Meeting in Edinburgh: Barclay Fraser, 'John Wood's Cramond', in *Cramond: An Introduction to the Life of the Village and Parish Throughout the Centuries*, privately printed for Cramond Kirk, revised (2nd) edn., 1976, p. 19. Radical agitators: some were tried, and in some cases transported to Australia, on a new Scottish charge of sedition: Mitchison, *A History of Scotland*, pp. 363–66.
6. *British Constitution.* Braxfield as quoted in Thomas Johnston MP, *The History of the Working Classes in Scotland*, 2nd edn, Glasgow 1929, p. 221.
7. *'Demeaned themselves in a quiet manner'.* Wood, Cramond, p. 120.
8. *Minister of Corstorphine.* Statistical Account I, p. 157 n.
9. *Intolerable yoke.* Wood, Cramond, p. 87.
10. *News of the day.* Spotswood to Wood, 27 Feb. 1789, NLS MS 9886 fol. 32.
11. *Johanna Pickhard's bastards.* 23 March 1794, 9 Feb. 1800, 11 March 1804.
12. *Loans to poor.* Dec. 1794 and Jan. 1795, entered with other payments from the poor fund at the back of vol. 10 of the session minutes.
13. *Friendly Society.* Wood, Cramond, p. 86 n.
14. *Marjory Fleming on a sermon by Mr Bonar.* The Complete Marjory Fleming: her Journals, Letters and Verses, ed. Frank Sidgwick, 1934, pp. 71, 81.
15. *Heritors' attendance at meetings.* Wood, Cramond, p. 87.
16. *'An annibabtist'.* The Complete Marjory Fleming, p. 99.

TWELVE

Surveys and Surveyors of the Parish, 1785–1794

In 1755 the Reverend Dr Alexander Webster had collected population figures from the parishes of Scotland. The same spirit of enquiry inspired Sir John Sinclair's great project of publishing a statistical and topographical account of Scotland as it was in 1790. Most commonly it was the minister or schoolmaster who was invited to contribute the essay on his parish for the multi-volumed *Statistical Account of Scotland*. For Cramond the honour fell to Wood, not Bonar, because Wood had submitted an extensive manuscript account of the parish, as yet unpublished and suitable for summarisation.[1] Cramond would appear in the first volume, which was to be issued in 1791.

Lack of reliable data made Wood's task of tracking the size of the parish population at previous periods almost impossible. He was unaware of the existence of the poll-tax return of 1694,[2] and expended much energy on a futile counting of baptisms and such deaths as were indicated in the accounts for the hire of mortcloths, then listing the respective totals for each twenty-year period between 1680 and 1779. His other attempt at estimating population size, for 1715, was to take the number of men summoned for the local militia in August that year (324) and deduce a possible total population of about 1,600. He does not explain his basis for this calculation.

When it came to providing a contemporary count of the parish for his essay, the project met a series of disasters. Wood relied on a survey undertaken for him by James Bathgate in 1785, which updated a (now lost) survey that Bathgate had made in 1782. From these data Wood compiled and published two impressive tabulations, one giving the number of people in various occupations and the other listing the number of 'families' (meaning households) in ascending order of size, from fourteen single-person households to the one that contained sixteen members. It was discovered too late that Bathgate had accidentally included one small area (with nine households and 33 people) that fell outside the parish boundaries.[3] The error did not make much difference to Wood's analyses: Wood had anyway done some miscounting and then adjusted figures to make them tally. Most notably, where the entries in

Bathgate's extant survey add up to 321 households and 1,354 persons, Wood made the totals 319 and 1,340.

Mr Bonar then introduced a complication. Evidently in November 1790 the text of Wood's essay had been shown to him for comment. Perhaps the minister was piqued that his function had been usurped by a layman. As we have seen, he inserted his own addendum about Cramond's lamentable morals. On 6 December 1790 he wrote to Sir John Sinclair complaining that Bathgate's population figures were inaccurate and putting forward his own estimate of the current size of the parish.[4] Despite his own (justified) doubts about Mr Bonar's accuracy, Wood was forced to rewrite a portion of his account and suggest possible reasons for the supposed loss of over 200 people within the last five years.

In the summer of 1792 Wood asked Dr Robert Spotswood to organise a further and more careful survey of the parish. The enumerators found a total of 319 households and 1,485 people. This time Wood correctly counted the number of people but managed to produce 330 households in the tables that he produced for his book and reproduced in shortened form as an update published in the final volume of the *Statistical Account*.[5] Again, some of his itemised entries were awry. In his breakdown of householders according to marital status, for example, Wood numbered 27 widows where the survey had counted 42, and 35 'bachelors and unmarried women housekeepers' (i.e. householders), where only 15 persons in this category had been specified.

From the point of view of the social historian, all this arid head-counting means that the dead hand of the statistician had fallen crushingly upon Cramond, and just at a time when comparisons might otherwise be made between conditions in 1694, in 1785–1792 and in 1841–1851 as shown in the national censuses. In their edited form the surveys of the late eighteenth century, with their over-processed data, fail to answer questions about, for instance, the composition of households. James Spotswood was singled out for mention in 1792 as living with (a son-in-law?) Thomas Cleghorn because he was thought to be the oldest parishioner at that time. How many other elderly people lived with an adult child, or themselves housed grandchildren, with or without the parents? How many tradesmen and artisans could now afford to take apprentices or employ one or more adult assistants – a son, perhaps? Few could do so in 1694. And what local family connections did the never-named wives of 1785 and 1792 have? What we are given are the names of householders, occupation, marital status ('married' is assumed in the absence of any other indication, but Bathgate had trouble defining Margaret Mowbray's status and resorted to a row of meaningful crosses) and size of household. Spotswood's survey went further, giving the number of males and females in each household and adding a rough division by age, but not sex: under 10, 10 to 20 and so on. His assistants also counted the total numbers of people in different occupations in their assigned area and were asked to record the number of dissenters with their affiliations. It is not altogether certain that this was done for all areas. While much more specific detail about the individuals who composed the population would be very welcome, the historian is reduced to accepting, what good John Wood apparently felt, that any figures are better than none. Once or twice, however, Wood's friends Robert Spotswood and George Robertson do show us something of the human being who existed behind a statistical entity.

George Flint was a labourer living on Spotswood's property in Over Cramond. On 24 January 1792 Spotswood reported to Wood that he had given Flint 2s. 6d. at New Year, part of the guinea (£1 1s.) that Wood had donated for him to disburse among deserving cases. 'He is a truly honest man, laborious for his family, an useful member of the community. His wife has no foible, is no waster, but wants that activity of head and hands which many people have. I likewise gave in some old clothes, [they] being for many years principally supplied with body-clothes from myself and son'.[6] Flint appears in still sparser detail in the surveys: in 1785 as a labourer with a household containing five others. In the summer of 1792, by which time his wife had died, he is 'lab. wid.' with one male and two females in the household, one aged between ten and twenty years, one between twenty and fifty, and one (Flint himself?) over seventy. With a daughter and grand-daughter? Who can tell. The surveys are uninformative on such matters.

To obtain an example of the income of a typical farmworker's family and the taxable items in the household budget, Mr George Robertson questioned one of his employees, the barnman James Fullarton.[7] Fullarton was one of ten cottagers on Robertson's farm at Royston Mains (mains = home farm), and lived with his wife, two daughters, aged about eighteen and thirteen, and a grandson of nine or ten. There were also two sons, sailors, who often lodged with their parents, bringing 'enough soap for their own washing'. (There had been eight people in the household in 1785.) The boy was 'boarded with them at a moderate charge', as Robertson believed. Fullarton and the two girls were in continuous employment on the farm, at a wage of 10s. 6d. per week for the three, with additional payment for reaping at harvest time – in all there was a family income of about £30 per annum. 'I believe the mother does not gain much, her chief employment being to take charge of the house – the meal-making and the washings.' They paid only 10s. in rent for the house and had their fuel (coals) brought carriage-free.

The incomplete annual budget, on taxable articles only, that Robertson ascertained from what his barnman was willing to tell him, came to £3 13s. 6d: 14 pairs of shoes at 4s. 6d. each (the leather was taxed); 5 pecks of salt at 8d, 12 lbs of soap at 6½d; 4 lbs of candle at 6½d. and 1½ gallons of small beer at 1s. per gallon. The beer, he believed, was 'only used when milk cannot be had' (a reminder that a year-round supply is a modern phenomenon). Robertson had not enquired what spirits, tea (that deplorable luxury of the working class) or sugar was consumed, 'for I am certain I would not have got a fair account'. The shoes were mainly for the girls and boy, so the price per pair was probably overstated, though the father's ones would cost considerably more than theirs. The number was probably overstated, too, 'for I know that in their line they are commonly restricted to two pairs each per annum'.

It will have become amply clear in the preceding pages that no-one can write about Cramond before 1794 without drawing on John Philp Wood's book, *The Antient and Modern State of the Parish of Cramond*, a minor monument to the spirit of enquiry that characterises the later eighteenth century.

Wood, born in Cramond on 9 March 1762 to Captain John Wood and his wife and hurriedly baptised the same day, was profoundly deaf. He was educated at the special school run by the Edinburgh teacher (and mathematician) Thomas Braidwood. There, in the words of one of Wood's contemporaries:

He learn[ed] to utter such uncouth sounds as are employed by dumb persons who have been instructed in the art of speech. By his mother (whose attentions to him were unremitting) those sounds were commonly understood; but rarely so by strangers, to whom they were extremely disagreeable.

His quickness of comprehension was truly marvellous, and from the motion of the mouth aided by a word or two described with the fingers in the usual way he could generally understand what was said to him. I have seen his mother employ her fingers nearly as fast as she spoke, and she would do the same while another person was speaking. Hence he was able to understand pretty well the conversation which was passing in the room.[8]

Others besides Wood's mother acquired the skill of signing or finger-spelling. Sir James Foulis of Colinton, inviting Wood to call on his family, wrote in 1785, 'though I cannot talk with you, my daughters can, and I may say that as well as you they have tongues at their fingers' ends'.[9] Acutely conscious of being cut off from ready communication with the run of people, Wood as a young man had begun to engage in what Sir James rather patronisingly called 'the harmless and agreeable amusement you have chosen for yourself': historical research, especially into the genealogy of Scotland's landowning families, a field in which he became an acknowledged expert. He also became an assiduous collector of miscellaneous facts and figures relating to Cramond and its neighbouring parishes.

While Wood's overriding interest was in the genealogy and doings of the various families ever associated with Cramond as landowners, so that he filled out his book with over a hundred pages containing his previously printed account of the activities of John Law of Lauriston in France as author of the Mississippi Scheme and the subsequent history of Law's family, his work incorporated valuable information about Cramond at his time, much of it contributed by his friends Dr Robert Spotswood, George Robertson and James Bathgate, clerk at the ironworks in the 1780s.

James Bathgate was the son of the gardener at Craigiehall, just across the Almond from Cramond, one of those who took advantage of a sound Scottish education and the opportunities offered by industrialisation to become a white-collar worker. As clerk at the ironworks he enjoyed the respectworthy status that he went to lengths to protect against Jean McCurich in 1779 (Chapter 10). Some time after 1785 he moved south and in November 1793 was employed at saltworks near Guisborough in Yorkshire. After compiling a survey of the inhabitants of Nether Cramond and its environs in 1782, Bathgate, as previously mentioned, updated it and extended it to cover the whole parish at Wood's request in 1785. In October that year he also answered a query about the minister's glebe, elucidating that it had formerly extended from the south wall of the churchyard down to the river, with part of it on the east side of the church where the old manse had stood before 1745 and part 'where Sir John's garden now occupies', and he sent Wood a list of the more than twenty 'accidental deaths and murders that have happened in this parish. You'll have a paragraph from the Magazine relating to Lamont's death and the manner of Mann's death at Cocklemill (now Slittmill)'.[10] This material (now apparently lost) failed to make Wood's book: Wood confined himself to the notorious murder of John Strachan's housekeeper at Craigcrook in

1707 by two Edinburgh men in pursuit of burglary and the much earlier crimes of the last two Oliphants of Muirhouse.[11] Bathgate also supplied Wood with information about the flourishing activities of the Cramond ironworks. (Wood himself married one of the Cadell family.)

To Wood, living in Edinburgh where he was employed in the Excise Office, the parish surgeon and elder Robert Spotswood would write to regale him with bits and pieces of local gossip and comments on the assistance to the poor that Wood contributed. His report on Margaret Bruce was quoted in Chapter 9. (She appears in the 1785 survey as 'a foundling, aged' – being in fact fifty-one years old.) In February 1789 he mentioned that Thomas Hodge, farmer on the Inglis property of Southfield and a hero of the Lammas battles between the herdboys some fifty years earlier (Chapter 8), was thought to be close to death. Pleasantly, he reported his casual observation of some crockery women, 'ragg'd and bare legg'd, with their heavy shops on their backs', encountered as he (in his seventies) and his mount Donald were 'prosecuting our ambulatory course of life' around the district.[12]

One anecdote concerned

> David Murray, a sailor going to Jamaica in the Roselle, who lives with his aunt at Cramond. [Murray] being from home, a porter brought a letter in his name with plausible reasons demanding his new clothes, shirts, etc. The aunt demurred, porter showed his badge and name. They were sent. Murray coming home soon after discovered the deceit. Found out the porter, who carried him to the house where he'd delivered them. The rascal escaped at the back window – from description suspected an old shipmate. Apprehended and recovered the clothes. Had two letters of the same handwriting upon him to the same effect. The swindler was incarcerated.[13]

Spotswood also gave his professional services outside Cramond and as medical attendant had an entrée to Craigiehall and Hopetoun Houses. It was with glee that he described to Wood the scene at Hopetoun House when, shortly before midnight on Sunday 8 July 1792, Lady Anne Hope, daughter of the earl of Hopetoun, married Lieutenant William ('Billy') Hope in the bedchamber of her distracted mother and in defiance of her parents' wishes. 'The skeely bodies or connoissours [sic] are a little staggered in their conjecture concerning pregnancy, which is reckoned [to reach] the fifth month the 13th Instant.'[14]

George Robertson, as tenant of the large combined farm at Granton and Royston and himself a writer on agricultural and local matters, provided a great deal of information on such questions as crops and prices, land use, rents and wages.[15] It was surely Robertson who furnished an unusual amount of detail when he came to describe his area of Caroline Park/ Royston/ Granton in 1792. (Who but Robertson would have scrupulously counted the number of dogs in the district – ten?) The district, he reported, contained 16 married couples, two widowers, four male house-servants, 14 female ditto, 13 male farm servants (of the householders among them, five are specified as ploughmen, four as labourers), nine female farm servants, one gardener (a widower, employed at Granton House, which was otherwise empty), one schoolmaster, with 30 scholars attending his school, one tailor and one mason. In all there were 18 households and 88 people. Besides the ten dogs, Robertson accounted for five swine, 40 sheep, seven black cattle and seven cows. Forrest Wilson in Pennywell is down as 'straw-seller' (was the straw for stabling or the use of milliners?) and David Ready as simply 'invalid: insane', aged between 50 and 70 and living with a woman (wife?) in the same age range. Lizy Henry, described as a farm labourer, lived at Caroline Park lodge and probably doubled as lodge-keeper. At a later date most large houses employed one, often an elderly woman, at their entrance or entrances.

One question debated at the time was whether or not the amalgamation of some farms (like that about fifty years previously which gave Robertson some 228 (statute?) acres) and a switch from tillage to pasture had meant a loss in farmworkers. Robertson argued that on balance the changes had increased rather than diminished overall numbers because on the larger farms – the fourteen that contained over 100 Scots (127 statute) acres – married cottagers with their families were now greatly preferred to single, live-in hands. He regarded the latter, who had to be fed within the farmhouse but slept in the stables so that they could attend to the stock, as a troublesome appendage of smaller farms.[16] By contrast, the three farmers who had occupied Robertson's land in 1694 had housed between them nine unmarried male farmworkers and a herdboy. The only other employee was a married hind with a live-in male worker.

Whatever the case with farm labourers, small farms were gradually disappearing. While Thomas Forrest had designated over sixty people as 'farmer' in 1694, only twenty-nine were thus labelled in 1792, and only nineteen would be so in 1851. Hinds, too, were disappearing as a specific class: the thirteen in 1694 decreased to eight in 1785, and in 1792 only two remained: one on the baillie's holding in Nether Cramond, the other on Spotswood's estate. (Two of those in the 1785 survey were now called 'grieves'.) One or two graziers, however, represented a new class in Cramond.

Disappointingly, Wood offered only scanty and scattered details about the living conditions of 'the common people'. On their diet, he described a healthy if limited regime of oatmeal for breakfast and supper, with milk in season. The working class, he said, 'seldom taste flesh, fish, butter or cheese, and during the winter months live chiefly on potatoes, prepared in different ways'.[17] The inhabitants of Nether Cramond also ate a large quantity of shellfish of various sorts. (But what has happened to the ubiquitous kale in this menu?)

When asked to estimate the average budget of a common labourer, Mr George Robertson contented himself with listing the expenditure on taxable articles by one family – that of his barnman. The more highly skilled ploughmen and carters could earn a minimum of £13 a year when perquisites and allowances were included.[18] Skilled ironworkers might be paid far more than that but for various reasons their employment could be irregular.

In return for his scanty information Robertson proposed to give Fullarton 2s. 6d: 'unimportant as it is or as he is, he was exceedingly shy about it [and I] could hardly get him convinced that no ill was intended to him'. The barnman's distrust of his employer indicates the gulf that existed between agricultural worker and tenant-farmer, and, perhaps, a more general fear of the taxman. Fullarton's reluctance to part with potentially damaging information was shared by some of the Cramond heritors when Wood sought to obtain details of their landholdings and valuations for statistical purposes.[19]

Taxation was biting hard, although Wood played down the effects on the income of working families. Apparently on the basis of Robertson's single sample, Wood deduced that 'each individual in the families of the common people of this parish pays no more than 1s. 5½d. yearly in indirect taxes for necessary articles'. In a still-familiar argument, he justified this surcharge on everyday items by citing the crippling burden that the rich carried. Resident heritors and 'a few other gentlemen and farmers' paid no less than £410 per annum in direct duties on such things as windows, horses, carriages and servants, and well above £1,000 in indirect taxes on consumption.[20]

Robertson seems to have thought it a little surprising that Mrs Fullarton earned no wages from 'out-work' – except possibly at busy periods like harvest, when even the local tailor, mason and private schoolmaster took part. It was commented that there was now much more employment available to women than formerly, as they could earn for at least six months in the year by hoeing, weeding and picking.[21] The extensive plantings of potatoes (increasingly common from mid-century) would provide one such means of employment. Backbreaking work, but possibly welcome to the women as a means of boosting family income at a time of inflation and of standards of living that had risen sufficiently for farm-workers like the Fullartons to buy candle and soap instead of making their own, or aspire to purchase that new consumer desirable, a wag-at-the-wa' clock. But as Wood also acknowledged, few workers earned enough to support them in illness or old age.

In assessing the economic impact of Lord Rosebery's clearance of thirty-four families from his land in Cramond, Spotswood offered some other details on cost of living.[22] He calculated the cost of marriage as 4s. (3d. in government tax, the 2s. payment to the poor box that was now a standard exaction, 1s. 2d. to the clerk for registration and 7d. to the beadle). Burial costs could vary between just under 6s. for hire of the mortcloth and payment to the beadle for attending the funeral and digging the grave (given elsewhere as 20d. for an adult and 12d. for a young person), with another 3d. in tax, and 9s. if the beadle turfed over the grave and tolled the kirk bell. Another government tax of 3d. was payable for (registering?) baptism, and the clerk was paid 6d. for the certificate for anyone leaving the parish (Spotswood reckoned that two persons, or families, from thirty-four families might do so annually). It cost 4s. per annum for a child at the parish school, and Spotswood estimated that each family would give a modest 1s. annually in collections at the church door. He assumed, for polemical purposes, that the thirty-four dispossessed families, thirty-one of them cotters, would have contained an average of 4.5 persons each, and that five births and five deaths would have occurred among them annually.[23]

Just what Wood meant by the 'particular class' that he exempted from his eulogies he left unstated, but like Bonar in 1790 he probably had the new industrial workers chiefly in mind. The parish had always had its comple-ment of scattered wrights, blacksmiths, masons, quarriers and so on. There had been maltings in the village beside the River Almond and grain mills and kilns strung along its banks. The ironworks, however, were far larger in scope, and more dirty and noisy. Their activities did not improve the amenities of the area. Although Wood praised Cramond's delightful situation and healthy air, he observed that the parish school had lost favour with the gentry who once chose to board their sons there. This was possibly a reflection on the calibre of recent teachers, but more likely a reaction to the industrial pollution now occurring.[24]

Apart from a few families housed at the slit mill itself, most of the mill hands and nailers at first settled in Nether Cramond, which grew steadily to accommodate them – and the nailers' workshops. Like those of their predecessors in the village whose activities were described in Chapter 7, they intermarried and witnessed each others' (typically clandestine) marriages and baptisms. They would be distinctive by virtue of occupation and included a proportion of immigrants, some short-time, of the sort 'collected', as the minister of Corstorphine put it, 'from all the manufacturing towns in England, Ireland and Scotland'.

In the parish as a whole the number of wrights and masons alone approximately doubled between 1694, when very few tradesmen could afford to employ a son or paid assistant, and 1785. Among the new artisans were no doubt some of those sons of agricultural workers who, as George Robertson observed, were now becoming 'mechanics' where formerly the sons of tradesmen were sent to the plough.[25] Thanks to the new opportunities for tradesmen, to the carrying work provided by the iron mills, which could support as many as twenty-three seamen,[26] and the influx of ironworkers themselves, Nether Cramond's population may well have doubled between 1694 and 1792. In 1792 there were 343 inhabitants, forty-five per cent of them under twenty.

In 1694 the village had contained sixty-eight occupied dwellings – ranging from the laird's house to single-room units. By 1785 there were seventy-eight. Two years later work began on new housing, including some along the shore with the Forth, where excavation turned up a portion of the paving from the Roman bath-house.[27] Sixteen more dwellings were built in 1791–2. By summer 1792, when Spotswood's survey was made, there were eighty-seven 'houses'. Details in a list in Wood's papers, of slightly earlier date, specified, besides Cramond House with its grounds of 65 Scots acres and the manse and schoolhouse, James Robb's brewery, bakehouse and private house, William Young's public house and stables, sixty-six houses rented at 20s. each per annum and seventeen at 15s., besides granaries, cellars and workshops.[28] Two of the houses were occupied by Sir John Inglis' gardener and one of the two remaining parish hinds. Robb, who was Inglis' baillie in addition to his other occupations, farmed the smallholding of 17 Scots acres earlier worked by Baillie William Inglis. By 1792 a second inn in the village was being run by James Falconer, who was not in the 1785 survey but described as shipmaster in the marriage register in October 1789, when he married one of the shipowning Wilson family. The third 'licensed alehouse' of 1792 must have been James Robb's.[29]

The thirty-three village properties held in feu from the laird of Nether Cramond in 1694 had long since returned to the hands of the Inglis family, enabling Sir John Inglis 2 to build the still-existing (but much restored and modernised) three-storey block of dwellings to rehouse thirty-six families among his village tenants, who were dispossessed when he took over the area of the village green, around which many houses had previously clustered. Only four properties in the village were still held by feu in 1785. Ironworkers – tenants of Messrs Cadell and Edington – predominated among their inhabitants, but the shipowner David Wilson had one, housing his own family as well as two further families. In Messrs Cadell and Edington's feu John Grindlay, widower of the celebrated hostelry-keeper Meg White?, lived next to Meg's old crony Kirsty Hill. In Nether Cramond in 1792 was still Katherine Stewart, 'spinster' ('widow' in 1785), former friend of Meg White and intimate of James Finlayson (Chapter 9).

Spotswood numbered, in the total village population of 343 – not just the 87 named householders – 18 seamen, Sir John's gardener and an assistant or apprentice, seven masons, 14 wrights (only three of them householders) and one turner or wheelwright. There was enough work to support three tailors, two shoemakers and one weaver. Besides the brewer James Robb there was a baker, evidently lodging with and working for Robb, who had taken over the bakery since Thomas Nimmo held it in 1785. Robb, whom the clerk Ninian Paton honoured with the title Mr, was an entrepreneur like the earlier brewer Robert Mitchell.

As a port, Cramond had a resident customhouse officer. In 1785 James Bathgate had lived in the village. By 1792 his successor as chief clerk at the ironworks had joined the growing community upriver at the slit mill. No beadle was listed in 1792. In June 1794 it was noted that the previous occupant of the office, John Marr or Mawers, had been dead for 'some years'. His widow had taken the emoluments to support her children and perhaps performed the duty of sweeping the church, but had to hire a man to dig graves and ring the church bell. When her employee died she was unable to get another man and had to resign.

Spotswood or his enumerator omitted to count the total number of labourers, smiths, nailers and other ironworkers living in the village and directly employed by Cadell and Company. Of householders there were five smiths, including Richard Squires, who had come from Newcastle as a skilled spademaker and was notably an Episcopalian, and James Crokat, alias Crookshanks. There were seven nailers and six other ironworkers.[30] Many more must have lived at home or lodged with other families, on a pattern made very clear in the census return of 1851. Members of the group of ironworkers and seamen will appear in the next chapter, giving some later justification for the view of moral decline expressed by Mr Bonar in 1790.

Parish surveys taken in 1785 and 1792 still divided Cramond into the estates of different landowners and Wood still saw the heritors as the mainstay of a stable community. But they were really a slowly dying breed. When Wood wrote of their readiness to alleviate the distresses of the common people he probably had chiefly in mind their contributions to the poor funds, on which the aged and unfortunate depended. When Craigcrook mansion house was let as a lunatic asylum, the session lamented on 8 December 1796 that the poor thus lost the benefit of the Sunday collections previously given by its private tenants. In 1785 it was occupied by a Mrs Billingsley, boarding-school mistress. Rather than the heritors, it was now the likes of Thomas Edington, Spotswood and Robertson who provided vigorous leadership in parish affairs. It had been Thomas Edington – who counted as a heritor because he was a working partner in the ironworks and lived in Cramond until the late '80s – who helped out the session when meal was bought to be resold cheaply to the poor in the terrible winter of 1782–3. He lent them £45 19s. 4d. to cover the shortfall. Subsequently he offered to collect and disburse £88 due from his fellow-heritors for various church expenses and to draw up a scheme of assessment and division without fee or reward.[31]

Major changes in landholding had been taking place. In 1776 Muirhouse was sold to William Davidson, formerly a prominent merchant in Rotterdam, who spent winter and spring amid elevated company in his villa at Highbury or his London house in Red Lion Square. On John Howison's death in 1787 Braehead was inherited by his daughter and her husband, the Reverend James Moody, alias James Howison Moody Crawfurd. (And in 1799 Sir John Inglis would die, leaving his estate entailed on his daughter Anne, who had married Lord Torphichen in 1795.) In 1786 poverty forced the last Loch of Drylaw to sell Drylaw to William Ramsay, the Edinburgh banker who had succeeded Lady Glenorchy in Barnton. Ramsay, who came to live in Cramond in 1788, would also acquire Pilton, the Hope-Weir land in Gogar and Whitehouse. He embarked on the extensive rebuilding of the old mansion house of King's Cramond, for many years occupied by Wood's father (and already annexed to the Barnton estate), which eventually took over status and name from the decaying Old Barnton House to the east, especially once the village of Over Cramond had been demolished to extend the Ramsays' new grounds.[32]

Possibly Ramsay was chief among those heritors who withheld information from Wood lest he publish 'commercially sensitive' material about their landholdings. Was Wood's emphasis on the modest lifestyle of even those heritors possessed of splendid fortunes meant as an oblique criticism of him? Certainly in 1792 Ramsay had the largest household among the resident gentry – thirty-one persons. A director of the Royal Bank of Scotland, newspaper proprietor, sportsman and entrepreneur, Ramsay was a new phenomenon among Cramond heritors and not always popular with Wood's circle. While most of his improvements to transport and roads may have been appreciated, he aroused Spotswood's determined and successful opposition to a proposal in 1790 to close Double Dykes Road, thus imposing a detour of several miles for travellers between Upper Cramond and Lauriston.[33] 'In my opinion', wrote Spotswood, 'the lieges, like a brave general, should dispute every inch of the road *cum vi et armis.*'

With genteel pretensions of his own, Wood took a deferential – or at the least, discreet – attitude to Cramond's current landowning families. But he was capable of mordant criticisms of past representatives, and was well aware that many earlier heritors had made and kept their fortunes by dubious means. Three at least had profited from a position as farmer of the customs and excise, and many had died leaving their affairs 'involved', as he delicately put it.[34] Until judges and other officials received a salary, most had customarily expected bribes and other perquisites of office. While praising an uncle who had eschewed such sources of income, Wood sadly remarked that his unusual probity had cost his family a fortune.[35]

Dr Robert Spotswood, that son of a tenant-farmer, was more robust in his attitudes to the upper class. In particular, the enclosure of land started by Lord Rosebery in 1764 rankled with him. Although he (and Wood) wrote as though thirty-four families, comprising perhaps 150 persons, had been expelled in that year, there were still seven small households in the area in 1785. By 1792 they had decreased to only three, and it may have been the final losses that caused Spotswood, in 1789, to furnish Wood with painstaking estimates of the monetary effect of the clearance. George Robertson had his difficulties with his absentee landlord, the duchess of Greenwich, or more specifically her factor. On New Year's Day 1796 he told Wood not to be surprised if this was the last year he spent in Cramond: 'indeed, I would almost as soon carry a musquet [sic] as submit much longer to the domination of the ruffian with whom I have at present to do'.[36]

After much early discouragement and some changes of plan, Wood gradually put his collected materials on Cramond into shape, with help from the Edinburgh bibliophile and antiquary George Paton. The book achieved publication in 1794. Handsomely, and expensively, produced, it includes specially made engravings depicting some of the grand mansions of the parish and inserted family trees. Wood had intended to give the profits to the Cramond poor fund, but in November 1796 he wrote to the Revd Mr Bonar, 'I now find that in consequence of a very limited sale, so far from any profits accruing, I will sustain no small loss by that undertaking, notwithstanding the liberal support I have met with from some of the heritors'. Instead he donated thirty copies of the book for the minister to sell as opportunity offered. Even these failed to find many purchasers. One was given, at Spotswood's tactful suggestion, to the schoolmaster Ninian Paton, who had done something to assist Wood's researches – mainly, perhaps, by giving him access to the parish registers and minute books. James Robb sold two copies in 1803 at 10s. 6d. apiece, whereas the original price had been 15s.[37] But Wood would doubtless have been gratified to know that Lord Rosebery gave the copy now in my possession to his son, then Lord Dalmeny, perhaps as a birthday present, in August 1822. He may indeed have known – he died at a good age in 1838.[38]

NOTES

1. *Wood's submission of existing MS.* Intro. to *Cramond*, p. v.
2. *Tax return of* 1694. Thomas Forrest did not list all the younger inhabitants of Cramond or those in extreme poverty so that only a guesstimate can be made about the total size of the parish. But this suggests that it is unlikely that the winter population in that year much exceeded 1,200. That being so, if the estimate given to Webster in 1755 was accurate (Wood reported it variously as 1,458 and 1,468), the parish had certainly not experienced the large downturn in population over the intervening period that Wood postulated.
3. *Error in* 1785 *survey.* Wood, *Cramond*, p. 111.
4. *Bonar's survey of Cramond. Statistical Account* I, p. 174; Wood, *Cramond*, p. 112.
5. *Wood's population figures for* 1792. Cramond pp. 112–13; *Statistical Account* vol. 21 (1799), p. 177. Bathgate's and Spotswood's surveys, in processed form, are preserved among Wood's surviving papers, NLS MS 9885. Patrick Cadell, *Iron Mills*, App. 6 p. 64, miscounted some entries in Spotswood's survey (e.g. by counting in one area twice) to offer totals of 339 households and 1,491 persons in 1792.
6. *George Flint.* NLS MS 9886, fol. 36.
7. *Fullarton.* Robertson to Wood, 5 June 1793: NLS MS 9886, fols. 17–18v. In September 1782 Robertson had nominated Fullarton to receive a share of the cheap meal to be issued to the poor, but his case was adjudged doubtful.
8. *Wood's speech.* MS note, signed only with the initials J. W. and inserted in a copy of Wood's book formerly in the possession of Barclay Fraser. Printed (with original capitalisation and punctuation) in *Cramond: An Introduction*, 1976, p. 35.
9. *Foulis to Wood.* NLS MS 9886, fol. 4: 24 Oct. 1785.

10. *Bathgate's list of murders.* Ibid., fol. 2.

11. *Murders.* Sir James Oliphant was a baronet and Lord of Session but expelled from the bench in 1632, 'having murdered his gardener by shooting him with a hagbut'. His son and heir stabbed his mother to death 'with a sword, in her own house', when drunk and died wretchedly in exile in Ireland: Wood, *Cramond*, pp. 25–6.

12. *Casual observation.* NLS MS 9886, fol. 36, 24 Jan. 1792.

13. *Theft of sailor's clothes.* Ibid.

14. *Conjecture of pregnancy.* Ibid., fol. 38. Apparently a child was not in fact born until the following May: Wood, *Cramond*, p. 160. On 5 January 1793 Spotswood reported that Lady Anne 'is in every respect improven since her marriage': NLS MS 9886, fol. 39.

15. *Writer on agricultural matters.* Robertson published *A General View of the Agriculture of the County of Midlothian* in 1795, among other works.

16. *Robertson on housing of farmworkers.* Wood, *Cramond*, pp. 110–11 n.

17. *Workers' diet.* Ibid., p. 114.

18. *Earnings of ploughmen and carters.* They might get allowances of £1 in lieu of milk, butter, small beer, etc., 10s. for two pairs of shoes, $6\frac{1}{2}$ bolls of oatmeal, meals at harvest time, a free house and garden, carriage of coal and cash wages between £4 and £5: *Statistical Account* I, p. 168. Wood counted about 100 men in these two categories.

19. *Uncooperative heritors.* Wood, *Cramond*, p. vii.

20. *Wood on distribution of taxation.* Ibid., p. 120.

21. *Employment of women.* Ibid., p. 108.

22. *Costs of living.* NLS MS 9886, fols. 33–34v, 19 Nov. 1789. In 1694 there had been 25 families in this area.

23. *Cleared area.* The trans-Almond part of the parish did, in time, become repopulated, though less densely than before. At the date of the 1851 census there was again a farm at East Craigie, of 227 acres, and the area as a whole contained 19 households and 102 people, including workers in the quarry that now operated near the river.

24. *Parish school.* Wood, *Cramond*, p. 83. Dalmeny's school was now among those favoured.

25. *'Mechanics'.* Ibid., p. 111 n.

26. *Seamen.* About 1790 Nether Cramond was home to seven sloops: the *Mary and Ann*, master John Wilson, was the largest at 80 tons and a crew of six. The others were *Nanny and Jean* (James Falconar), *Friendship* (Alex. Anderson), *Peggy* (William Wilson), *Diligence* (William Young senior), *Nanny* (William Young jnr.) and *Christian* (David Wilson): NLS MS 9885, p. 38.

27. *Roman bath-house.* Letter from G. Paton to Wood, 9 Nov. 1793. Wood, *Cramond*, p. 12, describes a (medieval?) lime-kiln found at the spot.

28. *Houses in Nether Cramond c.* 1790. NLS MS 9885, p. 73.

29. *Location of houses.* It is difficult to correlate the surveys of 1785 and 1792 in terms of where in the village individuals lived, partly because of Sir John Inglis' further relocation of tenants in the interim, partly because the enumerators proceeded in different directions. James Robb's premises are 14th in Bathgate's list, last, at no. 87, in Spotswood's. The two almost coincide with Margaret Bruce: 65th in 1785, 66th in 1792.

30. *Number of Ironworkers.* A list in Wood's papers, perhaps compiled about 1790, names 56 men and adds 22 boys employed either at the mills or working as spademakers or nailers: NLS MS 9885, p. 27. According to Wood, *Cramond*, p. 112, there were also three clerks.

31. *Edington's assistance*, KSM 26 Nov. 1782.

32. *Houses in Over Cramond.* 37 cottages and their occupiers are listed, c. 1782?, in an item in Wood's MSS, NLS MS 9885, p. 46.

33. *Double Dykes Road.* NLS MS 9886, fol. 35 (26 March 1790). The road ran through the policies of King's Cramond House to connect the two main roads between Edinburgh and Cramond. George Ramsay tried again to close it in 1806.

34. *Dubious means.* In 1682 Robert Miln of Barnton and Sir William Binny were brought before the Privy Council. On behalf of a consortium of fellow-farmers of the revenues of custom and excise they had offered a bribe to the Treasurer Depute. When it was refused, they double-crossed the other contributors by pretending that the money had been accepted, and pocketed it themselves: Wood, *Cramond*, p. 54 n.

35. *Wood's upright uncle.* Ibid., p. 58 n. Places in the civil services were, of course, conferred through patronage. A son of Cramond's former minister Robert Hamilton was a colleague of Wood's in the Edinburgh Excise office and, Wood privately noted, 'a sort of idiot': NLS MS 9885, p. 57.

36. *Ruffian factor.* NLS MS 9886, fol. 22.

37. *Wood's sales.* KSM 29 Nov. 1796, 28 Feb. 1799, 10 April 1803.

38. *End Note.* Wood's papers have been gradually reassembled in the National Library of Scotland. Among its Advocates' Library collections are, besides scattered letters from Wood, six volumes of material 'chiefly genealogical' presented by Wood's great-granddaughter Marguerite Wood in 1938 (Adv. MSS 1872–78). NLS MS 9885 (materials relating to Cramond) and MS 9886 (correspondence) were purchased by Dr and Mrs David C. Simpson and bought for the library in 1983, having been deposited there in 1968.

THIRTEEN

Erring Sheep and Earnest Pastors

Wood, picturing a Cramond based upon a stable and law-abiding rural people and a group of benevolent landowners, and Mr Bonar, emphasising a growing group of disorderly industrial workers, saw Cramond from different but complementary perspectives. Both men were conscious that the kirk had gradually moved from an oppressive moral tyranny to something closer to benevolent paternalism. Not only had the session lost many of the sanctions that had formerly given it a precarious means of enforcing its moral authority, but fewer and fewer Cramonders now recognised that authority. In 1835 a roll of male communicant heads of household would list 129 men. There had been almost twice as many male householders in 1792, and the total population of the parish had since risen by some 500 persons – from 1,485 to 1,984 in 1831.[1] Relatively few on the list of communicants were industrial workmen, as distinct from tradesmen and farmworkers.

Nor, at least until it was enlarged in 1811, could the church itself now serve as a physical meeting point for the community at large. In November 1810 it was reported that the various private pews of the heritors left space for no more than half the rest of the people, so that, even when crowded, 600 people at most could be seated, whereas the parish contained (it was alleged) more than 1,300 potential communicants. The building was also so cold in winter that 'tender and aged persons' attended services only at the expense of their health. Non-attenders thus had a ready excuse for absence from services.

Despite his gloomy view of parish morality, Mr Archibald Bonar refused calls to move elsewhere and died at Cramond, after a very long illness, in August 1816, having served the parish for thirty-two years. A month later he was followed by Ninian Paton, aged eighty, parochial schoolmaster for the past fifty-two years – nominally at least: his son John had assisted him in the school and effectively took over as parish clerk in November 1810. His father, failing, recorded John's appointment as joint clerk on 21 October, fulsomely rehearsing in the minutes the session's commendations on his son. John remained as schoolmaster and parish clerk for no more than a year after his father's death. John Gourlay then provided new continuity as schoolmaster and clerk between October 1817 and his eventual resignation in 1848.

Mr Bonar's successor as minister was the Reverned George Muirhead, at fifty-two an older man than many of his predecessors had been on appointment. He was presented by Mrs Ramsay of Barnton, exercising that lay patronage that would be a prime reason for the ecclesiastical rebellion of 1842–3 and his own prompt retreat to the Free Kirk.

It was a long time since sessions had met weekly to discuss current scandals and receive reports from those elders who had invigilated their bounds at service-time to detect evidence of ungodliness. Meetings were by now fewer and irregular. On more than one occasion they were held in one of the inns: at the New Inn on 6 December 1808; at 'Village of Cramond Publick House' to induct John Paton as joint clerk on 26 December 1810; and on 20 July 1813, when 'sundry important matters' had arisen, the session arranged to dine at the Falconers' inn. Either because no meetings were held or because draft minutes were lost, there are sometimes lengthy gaps in the record; for instance nothing is entered between 14 December 1817 and 29 November 1818, and there is a shorter gap between 30 October 1821 and 13 January 1822. Despite his ill-health, Mr Bonar exercised a very conscientious stewardship of his flock, upholding the conservative evangelical principles of the much-revered Lady Glenorchy. Fewer delinquents appear in the session minutes after his death, but one reason could be that his two successors preferred to deal with the errant in private and without involving elders and recording clerk.

Between 1783 and 11 January 1801 no additions to the session were thought necessary. Mr Bonar then, reverting to tradition, nominated six farmers: another George Robertson, James and Alexander Hodge, John Binnie, John King, and David Flint. Six-and-a-half years later, two elders had to be recruited from Bonar's family in Edinburgh to assist at the parish communion. Numbers were brought up to strength again with the appointment in February 1808 of three more farmers: John Millar, Thomas Binnie and Alexander Binnie, who thus kept up the tradition of family membership. Active members of the session decreased to only two or three at meetings in 1811, and in June 1813 John Millar gave up his eldership 'for reasons he will explain to the minister in private'.

Some time between 19 November 1820 and 30 October 1821 the next minister, George Muirhead, recruited James Curror or Currier and Dr James Robertson as sessioners. By 13 January 1822 William Brown had been added. But the long-serving treasurer John King died in 1828 and

Robertson resigned in 1831. For some length of time before October 1836 sessional meetings consisted only of the minister and Alexander Binnie. When three more men were finally chosen, from the roll of 129 possibilities, on 2 October 1836, William Gray in Braehead Mains was another farmer, but William Chesser or Chisser was a house-carpenter and James Simpson one of the two remaining linen handloom weavers in the parish. Mr Muirhead's last sessional meeting was held on 15 May 1842. Next year all his elders accompanied him into the fold of the Free Kirk.

The Cramond ironworks were never large enough to be really profitable to their owners, and underwent a serious financial crisis in 1797, followed by a redistribution of shares among members of the Cadell family.[2] Philip Cadell, who took over the immediate management in 1808, was a classic manic depressive. He thought of selling in 1809, but in November 1810 was in exuberant mood when he told the session that the works had been considerably extended of late. Although he estimated that at present there were only some nineteen families in his employment, three or four more from the Dalnotter Works were expected to arrive the following week, and he anticipated that within six or eight months he might well be building houses to accommodate twelve or fifteen more. New workers' cottages did indeed spring up along the River Almond: at the Cockle Mill there were three in 1785, seven in 1792 and by 1841 twenty-three. About 1815 Cadell diversified into a business with which he was more familiar and started paper works at Peggy's Mill. In 1845 the two industries between them employed about a hundred hands.[3] The village of Nether Cramond itself was by then much diminished in size because in 1826 Lady Torphichen had completed her father's work and removed the last of the houses that encroached upon her private grounds.[4] Rather impressionistically, the village could still be described in the 1841 census return as 'chiefly inhabited by workmen employed at Mr Cadell's iron works'.

There were always a few among this industrial proletariat who might serve to justify Mr Bonar's 1790 prophecy of disintegrating order and creeping immorality. Size for size, however, it seems unlikely that the Cramond village of his time was any more sinful than it had been a century before. The clerk did not specify exactly what 'extremely irregular, riotous and offensive' conduct made Robert Russon or Russel, son of John in Nether Cramond, 'to business a nailer', unworthy of admission to Christian privileges, such as baptism for his child in June 1806. Russon promised repentance and reformation, 'with much earnestness', was conditionally promised admission in due course, dependent on his behaviour, and had his irregular marriage ratified and registered a year later.

When notable instances of antisocial behaviour came to sessional attention it was usually because of complaints by neighbours of the same social background. In February 1810 the nailer Charles Burtley, Birkly or Barclay, his wife Margaret McUrich and the turner John Murdoch and his wife accused the ironworker Charles Probert and his wife, along with the seaman James Dodds and his wife Bethia Crookshanks (probably a daughter of James Crookshanks, formerly slitter at the iron mill), of 'haunting in their houses wild and dissipated persons, male and female, at untimeous hours', to the great annoyance of their neighbours. They had been particularly 'clamorous, troublesome and offensive' the previous weekend, when the wild females concerned had been Janet Hill and Mary Jamison, daughter of the nailer John Jamison. These had been carousing and drinking in the Proberts' house (tenement apartment?) with some young men. When the various parties came before the session Dodds and his wife 'begun a rude and clamorous speech in exculpation'. In May Mrs Dodds proposed to sue her detractors in the civil court for defamation and pressed the minister to provide her with a certificate of good moral character, but the session thought it quite inappropriate to issue one in such circumstances.

Mary Jamison and her sister Elisabeth had long been notorious. In 1797 their mother had applied for a pension but was told that she was ineligible as long as she kept at home a daughter who was fit for service. Elisabeth did leave home but returned in September 1801, pregnant by a sailor now serving in the Royal Navy. Six years later, in September 1807, Mr and Mrs Jamison were one of two village couples who were strongly suspected of operating disorderly houses, as 'harbour[ing] in their house women who do not work and, it is thought, cannot give a proper account of themselves'.

Mary Jamison then, in May 1808, produced a child in fornication to an Edinburgh jeweller and the session endeavoured to procure sufficient guarantees for its maintenance. Mary's father was not an adequate guarantor, 'he being seemingly a poor man upon the decline of life' who might soon be asking for parish aid for himself and his family.

The Jamisons indeed came almost annually to sessional notice. Next August Mr Bonar told John and his wife that they could not be unaware of the reason for their new summons: there were many reports of improper behaviour by the two daughters whom they retained in their house, who were not only idle themselves but 'make their house a haunt to idle and dissipated fellows, to the great disturbance of their sober and industrious neighbourhood'. The Jamisons 'did not deserve the appellation of Christian parents to wink at so offensive and disorderly behaviour in their children'. Moreover, their daughters' illegitimate children could easily become a burden on the parish.

Consequently, if the daughters and children remained, the session would have to call the civil magistrate to assist them in expelling the whole family: since the parents had shared their daughters' sin it was only just (or, as the schoolmaster Ninian Paton accidentally wrote, 'unjust') that they should share in the penalty. Under this threat, the Jamisons gave a written undertaking to comply. It seems, however, that they failed to observe their undertaking and that the family were forcibly uprooted, only to return almost immediately and in December 1809 take up residence, along with the daughters' 'spurious race', in the accommodation that Margaret 'Square' (Squires) had rented until her death. Neither the owner of the property, Lord Torphichen of Nether Cramond, nor his factor, Mr Mathew Sandilands, had been aware of this. Lord Torphichen, he said, would readily concur in their renewed expulsion.

Another ironworker, Alexander White, a spademaker, and his wife, a Probert, were reported in 1807 to be harbouring a woman of Bad Fame named Mrs Lashan, together with her child by Mr John Robertson junior, son of the landowner of Clermiston. He had visited her in the Whites' house, but spent only one whole night with her there. Nothing more needed saying: White was admonished for encouraging vice and 'turning his house, where decency and piety should be strictly maintained, into a receptacle of lewdness and fornication, as setting at defiance the good laws of the land and the sacred commands of scripture'. But White was as rude to Mr Bonar as the Dodds, repeatedly interrupting his reproof 'very insolently', before being laid under church censure.

Presumably it was one of the onlookers who spread abroad a flagrant report that members of the two branches of the McAra family – James McAra and Alexander McAra in Nether Cramond, Thomas McAra in Fairafar Mill and James McAra in the slit mill – had got intoxicated at Muttonhole on 20 June 1801 and quarrelled 'to such a degree as [to] proceed from high words and abusive language to blows'. All confessed and promised not to transgress again and in view of their seeming penitence were dismissed after admonition from the minister. Nine years later, in another drunken quarrel, the forgeman James McAra killed his brother Alexander with a pair of forge tongs and was sentenced to transportation for life.

Although marriage and unregulated sex were still prime areas of attention, it is hard to avoid the conclusion that illegitimate births were now censured as much for financial as ethical reasons. On the rather rare occasions when either antenuptial fornication or irregular marriage was brought to notice, the minister and session saw their function mainly as a tidying-up process. A meeting was held by Mr Bonar on 20 September 1812 specifically 'to confirm marriages', including one between Robert Henderson, spademaker at Cramond Iron Works, and Ellis Smith, presently servant to Mr Philip Cadell. In the old terms, in February 1809 another couple were 'assoilyed and admitted *de novo* as members of the visible church'. James Lowther, girdlemaker at the slit mill, admitted prenuptial intercourse in August 1812, and in October 1817 James Bell and his wife, on doing so, were told to bring their child to the manse to be christened that same evening.

When the nailer William Baillie and Jean Rodger were reported in February 1826 to be living together as man and wife they claimed to be married but couldn't recollect the day on which the ceremony had been performed or produce the marriage certificate. Their position was regularised when they acknowledged themselves as man and wife in presence of the session. Baillie is listed as a communicant in 1835. Another man was, it seems, sincere but naive. James Drummond, a regular attender at the Cramond kirk when he was not working in Corstorphine, thought it 'proper and expedient to give up himself and his wife (presently in Abercorn) to have his marriage confirmed and produced a written document which he called his marriage lines'. The session of 1805 expressed themselves much shocked by his do-it-yourself methods, and told the pair to have themselves proclaimed in their respective parishes of residence. They were also intrigued enough to have the document recorded in their minutes. It ran:

> Echloan [sic]. February 2nd 1805. I take Ann Linn to be my lawful married wife and do, in the presence of God and before this session or congregation, promise and swear to be a loving and affectionate husband unto her until it shall please God to separate us by death. Signed James Drummond (and the mark of Ann Linn).

In the 1841 census return, Samuel Conway, roller at the Cockle Mill, aged sixty-four, was reported to have living with him a granddaughter aged four, his daughter Mary (aged thirty-five) and her husband Samuel Wright, an Irish-born hawker aged fifty. Subsequently doubts arose about the existence of any marriage between Mary and Wright, and in March next year (Mary's father having died?) the session accused Mary of continuing to cohabit with the man, and supplying him with money. Evidently she was receiving help from the poor box, because they now offered her 2s. 6d. a week in maintenance for the next fortnight, and another 1s. per week for room rent, but after that she must provide for herself.

Promise of marriage was offered in mitigation by some women, like Isabella Proverb (or Probert?), with child to William Allison, unmarried nailer at Cramond Iron Works, in November 1829. Or the pregnant and unfortunate Mary Middlemist, who, on 3 July 1814, had told the session that David Marshall, son of William Marshall, wright in Davidson's Mains, had deceived her with promises of marriage, and then, only a few weeks before, had married another woman. Mr Bonar pointed rather to the 'peculiar enormity' of her guilt, since she had been admitted as a communicant just a year before.

Some fathers admitted paternity but denied suggestions that they had made any offer of marriage, as did James McAra junior in the slit mill when Euphan Clark, formerly of the parish, came of her own accord and accused him of fathering her child some two years previously. On 24 March 1805 she brought James along with her to confront the session, 'thinking he would recollect what then he promised and perform it accordingly'. James, however, said the matter was under the consideration of a civil judge, and he 'never did promise her marriage and was convinced in his own mind never would'. Another ironworker, James Aitkenhead, agreed that he had had intercourse with Widow Murdie between Cramond village and the slit mill on 14 May 1821. When she found herself pregnant she had, she said, spoken to him about her situation and he promised marriage. James, however, denied both promise of marriage and paternity, as he claimed that the times failed to match.

If a marriage could not be forced (in 1842 the father of Janet Jack's child made Janet a promise of marriage 'in presence of her parents'), sessions, supported by the civil authority, did what they could to obtain financial assistance for the woman – and more important, maintenance for the child – from the father. That public interest was their chief incentive is illustrated by the willingness with which Cramond session in January 1804 abrogated all responsibility for Jean Hill, who had borne a child to a student of physic from Ireland. Since the child had died, 'there is no purpose in seeking after the father'.

Jean Falconer, daughter of the innkeeper in Nether Cramond, may well have been the victim of rape by a drunken customer. If so, her case was not distinguished as such, and the concern was still simply to obtain an admission from the man and support for the child. In September 1806 Jean accused the spademaker Robert Henderson of coming to her mother's house on the morning after Handsel Monday, getting her alone in one of the rooms and having carnal dealings with her. He admitted to being in Mrs Falconer's house at the time, and to being intoxicated, but at first denied that intercourse had taken place. After the birth he acknowledged paternity, took the child home, procured a nurse for it and expressed his resolve to ensure that it was properly brought up. Subsequently, in frequent private conversations with the minister he seemed 'more sorry for his transgression than any other case that had come to [Bonar's] notice'. He was duly received back into the congregation and permitted to sponsor the child.

Archibald Rogers admitted guilt with Marrion Reid in October 1817 but denied paternity, saying that she had been seen under night with other men. As he could prove nothing of this, he was told to set about at once to provide for the child in question. Possibly this was the same Marrion Reid, a young woman residing at Muttonhole, who in March 1825 was reported to have had a child in fornication to her lodger, a mason. Her mother was also a woman of dubious character.

Costs of maintenance are illustrated in the written declaration extracted in 1827 from a wright, who undertook to pay the mother of his child £6 per annum if she was willing to keep it, and otherwise to share costs of nursing with her. He would then pay half its maintenance up to the age of twelve.

While John Jamison of notorious family was not considered a reliable guarantor for a grandchild, Caleb Atkinson, forgeman at Fairafar forge, was accepted in 1811 in the case of his unmarried daughter's child, as long as his promise was recorded in the session minutes. Possibly he took the responsibility at his wife's insistence: she appeared before the session in lieu of her daughter, saying that she had been unable to prevail upon Mary to answer their summons.

Less formally, Peter Fenton, tailor in Davidson's Mains, had for some time supported the two natural children of his stepdaughter, Alison Murdie (or Murdoch), when the session agreed to his request for assistance on 28 March 1842. A year or so later Alison produced a third child, the father being James Dalrymple, aged about twenty-two, recently residing in the village of Cramond but now at Monkland Iron Works. (In 1841 he lived in the household of Alexander Dalrymple.)

Alison was by no means the only Cramond woman of lax behaviour this time. Early in Mr Muirhead's ministry, on 24 November 1816, Rachel

Forrest was laid under sentence of excommunication and dismissed for the present, having been found to be with child for the second time to William Paton at Gibbet Toll. At the same date Lilias Dods obstinately refused to answer a charge of unmarried pregnancy and was laid under church censure for contumacy, and so, on 21 May 1820, was a woman who persisted in withholding details about the Edinburgh man by whom she had had a child. By then, however, the session had given up on Janet Aitkenhead. In April 1815 she confessed herself pregnant by the White-house tollkeeper. The session clerk, John Paton, recorded tersely, in an incomplete sentence: 'But owing to her scandalous and infamous char-acter, this being no less than the eight time that she has been in her present state'. Apparently she had a ninth child, by a carrier operating between Edinburgh and Linlithgow, in December the following year. In 1851 Janet, aged seventy-four, 'pauper, former domestic servant', was living in Cra-mond with one of her illegitimate sons. Few people, men or women, now fled the parish when faced with sessional disapproval, though some unmarried fathers might do so to escape their practical responsibilities, like Mr George Ramsay's new dogkeeper, who abruptly left his service and took flight when named by a pregnant women in 1808.

Mixed emotions towards one 'fallen woman' were displayed, in special circumstances, by the Reverend Dr Simpson in Slateford. In August 1815 he wrote with shock of his hitherto respectable woman servant who had that very morning revealed that she was some eight months pregnant. His letters on the subject are a mingling of condemnation (for the woman's wilful loss of respectability and failure of loyalty as much as for her sin itself) and compassion for her situation. Naturally she had been dismissed forthwith and dispatched to her relations in Stockbridge. These included an infirm old mother whom Margaret had supported from her earnings. It would have been out of the question for a minister's family to continue the woman's employment, but she had been 'for many years entitled to the respect and confidence of this family and we should be vexed to think that even in her present degraged [sic John Paton] state she should be exposed to further misery from the obstinacy or hard heart of the man she accuses as her partner in guilt'. Would Mr Bonar therefore do his best to obtain some support from the alleged father, a gardener in Cramond?

The man proved 'more penitent and submissive and open to advice' than the ministers had expected. Although he denied paternity, he regretfully admitted to having been alone in Margaret's company on various occasions, and in order to avoid the expense of legal prosecution agreed to give her £1 sterling per month until she was delivered and able to return to service. He further promised to undertake the expenses of nursing and rearing her child.

The expense of maintenance was no doubt one incentive for men to deny their responsibility for a child. A married man had still more reason. William Brown said on 14 November 1824 that he thought Barbara Macdonald's accusation against him of fathering her child was 'nothing but revenge and ill-will to him and his family'. When he had earlier asked whether she was with child she had said not, 'and that it was none of my business if it was the case, that it was none of mine, that she would make me rue it and that she would do the thing she never intended'. Barbara admitted denying that she was pregnant when he asked her in March. It is not said whether this was the same William Brown who was accused of adultery with Catherine Jack when they were returning one early morning in June 1821 from viewing the illuminations in Edinburgh (to celebrate the coronation of King George IV?). As both parties persisted in their conflicting stories (though Brown claimed that Catherine had admitted guilt with him on a previous occasion), on 31 March 1822 the session agreed to drop the matter for the present, 'hoping that some circumstance will happen to put the matter in its proper light'.[5]

An adulterer was still seen as unequivocally 'unworthy of any religious privileges whatever and deserving of the highest censure'.[6] And Mr Bonar adhered to the old insistence that when a woman could not identify the father of her child she must be supposed guilty of adultery. This happened in the case of Christian Lowrie or Laurie, who said in June 1803 that her child was begotten on the highway between Edinburgh and Stockbridge by some gentleman's servant whose name she didn't know and whom she had never seen before or since. There may have been some justified doubts about Christian, in view of her later fall in 1816 with the married William Hosie and, as she admitted, the nailer James Guild, also a married man. Guild had confessed to Hosie before witnesses that he had had connexion with Christian between Muttonhole and Lauriston some time before Hosie was involved with her. The session's chief reaction seems to have been to help Christian prosecute for an aliment before the sheriff.

Another married man and communicant, Maxwell Irvine, declared to the session that he had committed adultery with Elisabeth Robertson on 1 January 1836. When his declaration was read to her she agreed that it was true: originally she had named another father at Irvine's request, because of his family. Irvine confirmed this, but said he was willing to support the child. Elisabeth denied the report that she had used means to destroy the baby before birth – the last of the (rare) instances of such accusations in the minutes. The case was taken to presbytery, which remitted it back, and Cramond further delayed it 'because of unfavourable reports respecting Maxwell Irvine'.

A case of alleged adultery that came before the session in 1820 illustrates the pattern for servant accommodation at farmhouses where unmarried men were employed. The traditional practice was for women servants to sleep within the house proper while the men had separate quarters. An outside 'bothy' for unmarried men is specifically mentioned in the 1851 census on the Barnton House estate, which had a stable bothy for one man and a gardeners' bothy for the undergardeners. In October 1820 Mrs Catherine Sharp declared that one night James Allan and his fellow-servants were in the house. When it got late and she wished to go to bed, she sent them out. After locking the door she retired, thinking they were all outside. But Allan, having hidden in the passage, came into her bed. She immediately rose (she said) and went into the bed occupied by the other women servants. After repeatedly calling on the women to get up and open the door, Allan escaped through a window. He counter-claimed that his sister and another woman had once looked through a hole in the shutter of the kitchen window and seen Catherine and a certain Brodie Campbell come out of the kitchen bed together.

It has been argued that breaches of Sunday observance become less frequent in session records of the later eighteenth century because they seldom occurred: people in general were now keeping the Lord's Day with scrupulous piety.[7] The evidence adduced seems unconvincing. In 1813, however, Mr Bonar was inclined to believe that standards had recently fallen, telling his sessioners that he

> had with grief to state that there seemed to be increasing in the parish a general relaxation of conduct on the Lord's Day, occasioned by a selling of sundry family articles on that day, a sailing in the evening near the harbour in pleasure boats and tippling in public houses on that day.

As a last-ditch attempt to restore old proprieties Bonar proposed to read the 1787 Royal Proclamation against sabbath breakers, with suitable exhortations that all such offenders would be cut off from church privileges and, if persisting, be prosecuted before the civil magistrate. His elders dutifully expressed the pious hope that 'these provisions would suffice to bring back the good old way of sanctifying the sabbath'. But no specific prosecutions appear in subsequent minutes, apart from an accusation in 1825 that two women in Davidson's Mains had acted in a disorderly manner on the night of the last parish communion. They were told that until they appeared penitent they couldn't be readmitted into communion with the church.

Other allegations aired were also kept vague in the minutes, to the regret of later students, as when Mr Bonar had 'heard with deepest grief of several instances of very improper conduct of late' in November 1815 and proposed to summon James Mann, innkeeper at Muttonhole, with his servant and daughter, 'if the *fama* continues against them'. Alexander Dalrymple was rebuked in July 1838 for occasional irregular conduct and failing to attend church consistently. And for unstated reasons the session declined in December 1814 to give a certificate of good character to Widow Reed, mother of 'Marrion' and lately residing in Muttonhole. She had 'very boldly demanded' one and evidently threatened to sue, since they added that they were ready to defend their refusal in any court. With equal vagueness, when Mrs Betty Middlemass wanted baptism for her two children in September 1824, 'in consequence of a letter received relating to her she was told that dispensing of the ordinance would be delayed'.

A temporary suspension from church privileges was used on 28 October 1838 to mark the session's disgust with the millwright John Douglas, son of Claud, when he claimed an honorarium of 17s. from the sum he had collected from the inhabitants of Cramond for the benefit of the late Widow White and her family. A hard-nosed businessman, Douglas still had £1 17s. in hand and promised to pay the £1 but insisted on keeping the rest, the equivalent, he said, of a week's lost wages. The session felt that he was acting in a very unchristian manner.

Sessions might still be obliged to deal with cases of persistent drunkenness, though they now did so very seldom. James Shade (evidently a descendant of the earlier Shedds) was charged on 30 May 1819 with having gone to great excess in drinking on a former night and promised to do so no more. Mr Muirhead asked him to call at the manse next Wednesday for the purpose of serious conversation. Alexander Shade was also summoned but failed to appear. Alexander Wright, who had for some time been 'under church scandal' for frequent drinking, having again been found intoxicated was rebuked and restored on 22 July 1827. And in September 1840 Janet Young expressed contrition for her sinful conduct in frequently indulging in intoxicating liquors to excess. In 1826 the session refused to support James Falconer junior when he sought a licence to sell spirits. In 1841, however, Nether Cramond had three premises selling spirits: those of Mrs Isabella McAra and her daughter in New Street, of Euphemia Gloag in Old Street and the two Gibson sisters in Shore

Street. Some grocers also stocked them, and in April 1853 the session's efforts were directed to supporting Mr Forbes Mackenzie's parliamentary bill to prohibit grocers from selling ardent spirits to drink on the premises and to have all houses that sold them shut entirely on the Lord's Day.

Squabbles over rights to the limited seating in the church before 1811 twice came to sessional notice, though they no longer concerned rival heritors as they had in the late seventeenth century. On 31 August 1806 some members 'noted the flagrant indecency committed' when Mr Thomas Cleghorn junior prevented Mrs Thomas Cleghorn in Lennie Muir from bringing into her seat the two young nephews who usually sat there when staying with her. Mr Paton the schoolmaster, who had complained in 1763 that his wife had no pew allotted to her, reported in July '1810' (i.e. 1809) that the elders' rent-free seat had been lately filled by persons who had no manner of right to it, and were depriving his family of their share. When his own family could not attend a service they might permit 'decent-looking strangers' to use their place, but James Falconer and his wife Margaret Wilson were claiming some heritable property in it. The session directed that a lock should be put on the door and two keys kept by the schoolmaster and beadle.

For various reasons, three cases of theft found their way into session minutes. In one, in 1806, Cramond's poor fund received fines to a total of £9 imposed in the sheriff court on several young men of the parish who had been found guilty of breaking into the gardens and orchards of Dr Davidson of Muirhouse and Mr Ramsay of Barnton. The money was used to give each enrolled family an extra 5s. to buy coal for the winter. Philip Brodie was a member of a communicant family when summoned before the session in November 1831 for stealing potatoes from Mr Curror, presumably the elder James Currier. But it is not clear why, on 23 June 1833, the session summoned for rebuke Alexander Erskine, residing in Kirkliston, who had been caught poaching on the grounds of Craigiehall and had aggravated his offence 'by a concealment of the truth'.

Only once do foundlings appear in the minutes of this period, when two infants were exposed at Neal Heath's door in Crummielands, on the highway between Edinburgh and Linlithgow, on New Year's Eve 1809. The session voted to give some reward for the trouble caused to Neal and his wife and those who diligently pursued the unknown mothers.

On three particular occasions in the 1820s the session were called upon to act as a tribunal to hear a private dispute. Like the family quarrel between the McAras, two involved violent altercation.

A few years before Cramond village lost almost all its workshops to redevelopment Mrs Ann Ruddiman (Ann Symons), widow of a nailer, complained to the minister about an assault by her brother-in-law, Thomas Hardie, carpenter in the village, where both had houses at the Forth end of the settlement.[8] When Mr Muirhead brought the matter before the session, some six weeks later, in July 1820, it appeared that the quarrel was one of fairly long standing. Ann had allowed Hardie to use part of her house as a workshop but later apparently changed her mind and removed the key, whereupon he procured a substitute. Ann twice attacked his wife and child, and Hardie annoyed her by dropping off pieces of timber at her door about 1 am, then returning to put the wood in his workshop. When she refused to let him in he forced open the door, damned her, said he would drive her ribs together, struck her with a stick which he broke upon her shoulder and was beating her with another when David Moodie came in and took him away. Nelly (alias Helen) Baillie, wife of the seaman James McUrich and another of the neighbours, then came in and bound up Ann's head, which was bleeding. Hardie, while denying that he had taken wood to the back of the house, agreed that he had broken a stick on Ann's shoulder, but she had torn the coat off his back in ejecting him from the house, flown into a passion when he asked why she had attacked his family, and given him abusive language. When Nelly failed to appear at a further sessional meeting, and David Moodie said he had not seen any blows struck, Mr Muirhead contented himself with reiterating 'an impressive address' to Ruddiman and Hardie alike.

In September 1824 the precentor and tailor James Rae was accused by Thomas Mason's wife of making her eldest son drunk. Rae denied being with James Mason on the night alleged (which was some two months before the date of the sessional hearing), nor had he seen him since they were at the kirk's singing school that he conducted, on the Thursday before. Now Mrs Mason and her son had come to his house when he was in bed, used the most opprobrious language towards him and spread their unfounded reports over town and country. At the next sessional meeting Mrs Mason, her husband and two sons appeared and unanimously declared that Rae was the person who had led James Mason astray, so that he had often come home tipsy from his company. When her son arrived home drunk on the occasion in question, Mrs Mason had assumed, wrongly as she now recognised, that he had again been with Rae. Rae received a sharp admonition as to his future conduct.

On 28 October 1826 Mr Muirhead and two elders met at night in Davidson's Mains schoolroom to calm a quarrel between James Marshall and Alexander Leggit and their wives over a pathway between their respective gardens, which a Mr Sommerville had marked out with thorns to the annoyance of Mrs Marshall, who had repeatedly changed the boundaries. According to Mrs Leggit, she had then walked over the Leggits' kale, at which Mrs Leggit had said to her, 'You stupid ass, what do you mean by going through my kale? You know that is not a road'. She then got Sommerville to redraw the line of the path, the husbands were drawn into the argument, and Leggit swore at the Marshalls and hit James, shouting 'You'll tramp a' my kale'. Marshall took him by the napkin around his throat and struck him in the face. Without offering any opinion on the question of the pathway, Mr Muirhead exhorted both parties to live peaceably and in future be more careful of their language. Whether the session had summoned the warring neighbours on their own initiative, or had been asked to intervene by one of the couples, is not recorded. No issue was made of the fact that one of the incidents complained of had occurred on a Sunday.

In the 1830s the parish had a sum of £600 to invest, on security, with private short-term borrowers. It was made up of the £500 bequeathed to the poor by Colonel Robert Spotswood of the East India Company, a native of Cramond, who had died suddenly at Portobello on 4 September 1828, and a loan of £100 made, at different times, by Mrs Gourlay, the schoolmaster's wife, and Dr Robertson, the current surgeon. In March 1842 the parish received the bequest of £200 for the education of the poor of the parish from Mrs Baillie of Drylaw, then living in Edinburgh. This was banked with Archibald Bonar junior. Smaller legacies had been received at various times from heritors like Charles Hope Weir in 1800 (£20 sterling) and Lord Torphichen in 1815 (£10). In early 1850 Lady Torphichen (Ann Inglis) would leave the parish £99 7s. 6d.

Early in the century finances had fluctuated greatly, according to weather conditions and, less directly, the costs of war. In early January 1800 the heritors, meeting at John's Coffee House in Edinburgh, raised a special subscription of £79 4s. in view of the 'unexampled dearness of meal and fuel and necessity of assisting workmen and artificers and for supporting the real poor'. In November that year George Ramsay of King's Cramond, William Ramsay of Barnton (the treasurer) and the session clerk assessed a special rate to total £180 sterling because of the unexampled high prices of provisions. The number of those needing aid was reduced in the following autumn, 'things being greatly reduced in price and harvest employment bringing them supplies of cash and their victuals'. Mr Bonar waited until May 1802 and, as was then thought, the end of the Napoleonic wars, to ask the heritors for repairs to the manse that had been outstanding since 1794. The manse had not been properly finished when built: the roof and garret were unplastered and unfloored and the nursery should be lathed, plastered and given a wooden floor-at present it was paved with flagstones 'and is uncommonly damp'. He also wanted a brick porch added on the north side.

In 1803 the heritors also expanded the opportunities for poor children to attend the parish school. The session had long supported six 'poor scholars', for whom they paid 18d. a quarter from the funds. Now a further twelve children, to be termed 'Gratis Scholars', could be selected from the most needy families at the beginning of each year. They might be rechosen if making progress and attending punctually, but only with the consent of the heritors or presbytery. Their schooling in English, writing and the principles of religion was to be free.

The session had a considerable surplus in the funds in October 1806 and their treasurer, Ramsay, wanted to put £1,000 sterling in the hands of the Trustees for the Public Roads at 5 per cent per annum. The session thought the proposal very inadvisable: the funds were a temporary accretion, since most of the money was unexpended from the last assessment on heritors and tenants. They also needed an emergency fund. Provoked, perhaps, by his insistence, they then pointed out that Ramsay had held a surplus for years without paying any interest. Although they could not expect as much from him as the trustees for roads paid, they were, they said, 'persuaded their treasurer will cheerfully allow them the interest commonly paid for money lying in his hands' as a banker. Their reluctance to tie up funds was vindicated in August-September 1812 when another scarcity of food meant that money was almost exhausted and a special collection had to be taken at the church door.

William Ramsay had succeeded our old friend Robert Spotswood as kirk treasurer in 1794. Despite the criticism of 1806, he continued in the office until his death the following year, when he was replaced by John King, farmer and son of a farmer in Silverknowes. King had been a member of the session for twenty-six years and treasurer for twenty-one when he died on 2 March 1828. He was succeeded briefly by the parish surgeon, James Robertson, who wrote, however, in November 1831 to say that after mature consideration he had resolved to resign his seat as an elder and to have nothing further to do with the management of the church funds.

The earlier surgeon, Spotswood, had apparently treated the parish poor at his own expense. When Mr David Landale came to Cramond as his successor he found himself expected to follow suit, but after four years protested that this free service was costing him at least £5 a year, which he could ill afford. The session, after seeking approval from the heritors, agreed on 17 December 1804 to pay his future accounts. In 1816, however, when Landale submitted, from Edinburgh, two bills for a total of £9 6s. the session would pay only £2 15s. and laid down that in future he should be paid for attending one of the poor only with an order from an elder or the parish clerk.

As ever, the session and sub-treasurer (who did the ordinary work of distributing money) took careful cognisance of the material and moral circumstances of their pensioners. James Philp was once docked half-a-month's payment, in November 1803, for keeping with him an idle daughter, and when Janet Yule, widow of a former parish beadle, came to the schoolhouse on a Sunday in January 1815 to collect her monthly pension, 'evidently in a state of intoxication', she was summoned to be rebuked and perhaps have her pension taken from her. The widow of a former precentor, it was noted on 26 December 1811, was to lose her pension after the next payment provided she had then started her new service as housekeeper to the dowager Mrs Ramsay of Barnton.

Careful shepherding of the funds meant enforcement of the rule that a pensioner's effects were the property of the poor box. John Forrest, a former elder and father of the Isabel afflicted by insanity in 1794, died on 11 October 1799, 'an enrolled pensioner upon the funds of the poor of this parish'. The sub-treasurer who attended the funeral learned that Forrest had evidently been imposing on the session by pretending poverty, because he left cash and moveables to a considerable value. The session resolved to recoup as much as possible of the £7 10s. that Forrest was estimated to have received from the poor box, but his family refused to pay and carried off the key of his house. On behalf of the parish, James Robb took Forrest's daughter Elisabeth to court and obtained a sheriff's order to roup (auction) as many of the effects as would meet the debt. If they were insufficient, Forrest's son-in-law Claud Douglas was to be 'called for his interest'.

In the event the session obtained £5 11s. and a guinea from Douglas for a feather bed that he had appropriated, and gave the guinea and 9s. 10d. to their clerk and the church officer in recompense for their trouble. They then enacted, on 30 November 1800, that to prevent the relatives of dead paupers from secreting or carrying off any goods to the detriment of the surviving poor, everyone admitted to a pension was to sign an agreement, submitting anything left at death to the management of the session.

Margaret Falconer circumvented sessional control eighteen months later when she sent them £4 sterling, the proceeds from auctioning the effects of her mother, née Margaret Wilson and by recent remarriage Mrs William Young senior, after paying funeral charges. The session objected that relatives ought not to conduct a sale without warning the session, unless they were prepared to repay all the money given from the poor fund. Mr David Wilson, the representative of the deceased, was to be asked for an inventory, the roup roll and vouchers for the expenditure on the funeral.

Care for the unfortunate included a loan of 10s. to Mrs David Wilson senior, widow of a former elder, shipowner and manager of the poor's funds. Mr Bonar, happening to pass in April 1809, had called on her, found her very frail and noted her mention of her poor circumstances. Practical assistance was given to the widow of Alexander Stuart in Old Smiddy when the session agreed on 21 February 1813 to let her occupy the wooden booth that they had erected for her husband so that he could sell gingerbread and other small articles in the daytime. And when they were told that Elisabeth Donaldson had for months in that same year waited almost constantly on her next-door neighbour, a pensioner who had 'long been in great distress with a dropsical complaint' and was quite unable to give Elisabeth the smallest recompense, they granted Elisabeth 5s. for her past services and 1s. a week to look after her neighbour, prepare her food and keep her clean.

The standard rules on eligibility for parish relief were often imposed: a newcomer to the parish must remain there for at least three years, without burden to the parish, before receiving aid. Anyone already a pauper on arrival, or reduced to that state within three years, was ineligible. A badly timed move therefore led to disaster, unless one of the parishes concerned was willing to show generosity. In January 1800, when 'Widow Binnie' returned to Cramond, inspection of the poor roll showed that she had been out of the parish for at least three years. She failed to meet the criteria for relief from Kirkliston, despite Cramond's recommendation that she had been 'a woman of decent deportment whilst under their inspection', and the session, considering her great age, decided it was easiest to go on paying her. Early in 1803 it was found that Janet Liston was still classed among the 'extraordinary poor', having received a subvention while nursing her father in his last illness. She had emigrated from the parish after his death. But 'at the beginning of the last dearth' she had solicited supply and been given some assistance because she had not been long enough in her new parish to receive help there. As a young woman able to work she was now removed from Cramond's list.

The nailer William Kilgour and his wife had left Cramond ten or eleven years before 1803 and for a few years afterwards had received occasional help from the Cramond poor box, the last time being in October 1796. They were now in the charity workhouse in the West Kirk parish, both 'bad of a fever' and in very distressed circumstances. The workhouse managers were expecting Cramond to support the couple. Eventually, on 25 August 1805, Cramond agreed to allow Kilgour and his wife 4s. monthly, on condition that he made them a monthly report on his circumstances. Ten years later one of the Edinburgh baillies informed the session that he had found William Kilgour begging in the street. The authorities had confined him all night and had now sent him out of the city 'and devolved him on our care'. Cramond objected strongly that he should be supported by the session of St Cuthbert's.

When John Crumbie and his wife came from Newcastle in July 1806 to apply in person for assistance, Cramond responded. Crumbie said he was a native of the parish and had been a soldier for some years until discharged for almost total blindness. As a disabled soldier he had a pension of £7 sterling per annum but nothing else to live on save what little he could make by going about the towns and villages near Newcastle as a travelling chapman. As it was 'inconvenient' to send him any monthly supply in England, the session gave him £1 in return for a declaration by the couple that they would be satisfied with that until the same time next year.

But the overseer of the poor in Lewisham, Kent was making a desperate attempt to shift responsibility in February 1815 when he tried to get help for a woman who was in great distress, having been turned out of hospital as incurable. Her husband, a seafaring man named Fletcher Dun from whom she had not heard for some time, was thought to be a parishioner of Cramond, where he had a grandfather, surnamed Young, still living. Unless Cramond would assist the woman, Lewisham would have to send her up to them. After diligently searching parish records, Mr John Paton was able to absolve Cramond of responsibility by reporting that Dun's mother had taken him, when a mere infant, to join his father in Portsmouth.[9]

Another former seaman and *bona fide* resident of Cramond received little more sympathy when George Gilchrist, now aged eighty, petitioned for help two months later. He had been born and brought up in the parish but went to sea early in life. 'After leaving of the seafaring life he engaged himself with Mr Thomas Edington at his iron works upon Clyde and has resided there for the most part since the year 1792.' The session would do no more than pay his expenses back to Barony parish.

Hugh Dryburgh had no formal claim on anything more than Cramond's humanitarian impulses. He had been born in Corstorphine and came to Cramond about 1823, having worked in Currie for some fifteen years before that as an unmarried farm servant. Initially he had earned £5 or £6 a year, but towards the end of that time he received no wages and his work scarcely repaid his employer for his daily food. When he went to live in Cramond with his sister and her husband Robert Haig he was almost destitute except for £9 which had been left him by his mother, on the grounds that he was weakly and paralytic on one side and unlikely ever to earn an adequate living. For eighteen months he had been entirely maintained and clothed by his brother-in-law (a tailor), apart from drawing occasional sums from his legacy. For a further eighteen months he herded for Mr Trotter at Cramond Bridge in return for two meals each weekday, while the Haigs provided his bed, clothes and Sunday meals. But for the last two years he had made nothing whatever towards his own support and the money from his mother had run out. 'In consequence of his destitute condition we gave him 5s.', noted the clerk on 21 March 1828.

In 1845 four of those dependent on parish support would be inmates of the Edinburgh asylum in Morningside. In 1815, at the urgent request of the inhabitants of Nether Cramond, the sheriff had John Hill, son of Gavin Hill late tailor in Cramond, confined in the Edinburgh Bedlam, after John had 'become quite deranged, very outrageous and alarming to the neighbourhood'. The law required that the session should agree to pay for his confinement. The minister and three elders expressed reluctance to expend much money on him, and John was an ex-soldier, so his widowed mother was asked to sign over to them his Chelsea Hospital pension of £9 per annum in part payment and they would make up the difference if they found that the country was not obliged to support him. In May 1817 the minister got £22 from the Chelsea fund.

When, in 1843, another of Scotland's ecclesiastical upheavals occurred, Cramond's minister, with his four elders and many of the congregation, went over to the new Free Kirk, which built a church in Davidson's Mains. His successor in Cramond's manse was left to rally a diminished following. In due course further immigration helped to raise their numbers, but by 1851 a population of 2,284 included incomers of a variety of religious persuasions, some of them Irish Catholics, and the session of the Established Church had necessarily ceased to take effective responsibility for the behaviour of all Cramond's inhabitants. With their restricted roll of communicant heads of family in 1835 and their reliance on an eldership composed predominantly of farmers, there is room for suspicion that ministers and sessions had begun to lose touch with many elements in a changing community much earlier in the century.

NOTES

1. *Population 1831*. The *New Statistical Account of Scotland*, 15 vols. Edinburgh and London, 1845, vol. 1, p. 599.
2. *Ironworks*. Patrick Cadell, *Iron Mills*, pp. 25–6.
3. *Workers at iron and paper mills*. New Statistical Account 1, p. 601.
4. *Torphichen*. Sometimes given the pronunciation spelling 'Torphine', as Muirhouse had in the past been written 'Murrays' on occasion.
5. *Catherine Jack*. In 1841, aged about 40, she was sharing a house in Corbie Hill with Marion Reid and Thomas Reid, Marion's son by her former lodger. There was also Michael Jack, aged 8 – an illegitimate son born to Catherine c. 1833?
6. *Censure for adultery*. Bonar, 2 May 1813.
7. *Sabbath observance*. For this view, see Leah Leneman, ' "Prophaning" the Lord's Day: Sabbath Breach in Early Modern Scotland', *History*, vol. 74 (1989), pp. 217–32. Later, Victorian and Edwardian piety did bring renewed rigour in some quarters. In the Free Church family of Barclay Fraser's childhood any necessary domestic conversation on the sabbath was conducted in whispers.
8. *Premises in village*. Plan by John Leslie of part of Cramond village with names of landholders, January 1821 with later update, belonging to the Cramond Heritage Trust.
9. *Fletcher Dun*. The clerk's researches must have been complicated by the fact that Fletcher was a name given to both males and females. A William Young had married a Flecher Dunn in 1791 and another bride in 1794 was named Fletcher Tiviotdale. In August 1786 a James Dunn had married an Elisabeth Young, which may be the connection referred to.

FOURTEEN

Cramond after the Disruption

In past periods Cramond's kirk session minutes have afforded occasional glimpses of the social circumstances of the offenders whom sessioners chased up. After 1843 the offenders against morality have all but disappeared from these records. Their misbehaviour was by now treated either as a civil offence or a matter to be addressed in private by the minister or one of the elders. So Cramond's sinners – the delinquent members of the kirk's remaining constituency – are lost to view just when the national censuses of 1841 and 1851 would supply personal details of the sort that were previously hard to find.

After Mr Muirhead and his sessioners joined the Free Church in 1843, Mr (later Dr) Walter Colvin took his place in Cramond's manse and obtained new elders from those who remained faithful to the Established Kirk.[1] He continued as minister until 1877. Although the concern of sessions was now almost exclusively with such sexual offences as members of a reduced congregation might confess to, on rare occasions they dealt with some of the other old preoccupations. An old remedy was resorted to when a general Day of Public Humiliation and Fasting was held on 14 December 1848 'on account of the present afflictive dealings of Providence, more especially in the renewed attack of pestilential disease', namely cholera. One preacher in Glasgow is said to have attributed the outbreak to God's displeasure at an attempt to get a Deceased Wife's Sister's Marriage bill through parliament.[2] (In 1868 seventeen-year-old Henrietta Lindsay, illegitimate daughter of Anne Brown and granddaughter of Grace McPherson in the slit mill, would have a child by a Charles Lindsay, a joiner living at the main gate of Cramond House. Charles meant to marry her but this course was 'inconsistent with the Confession of Faith and the laws of the land' because Henrietta was the daughter of his deceased wife's sister.)

Despite Wood's boast in the early 1790s that Cramond's poor were exceptionally well cared for by voluntary contributions (the system greatly preferred by the heritors), in 1845 a legal assessment system was instituted by act of parliament, and the sum of £382 was expected to be set for that year.[3] The number of paupers on the roll was then averaging sixty, and some twenty more people received occasional relief. (But in the census return of 1851 only twenty-nine men, women and children are described as 'paupers'.)

Mr Colvin's 1845 report on the current state of Cramond in the *New Statistical Account of Scotland* reveals a somewhat backward-looking stance on the part of its author.[4] He devoted some space to relating how, in 1822, William Howison Crawford of Crawfordland (alias William Keith), who had acquired Braehead through marriage to a descendant of the legendary Jock Howison – believed to have been given the land as a reward for rescuing James V from attack at Cramond Brig – performed the supposed feudal service for the lands by presenting a basin of water and a napkin to George IV at a banquet in Edinburgh.[5] The holy relics thus sanctified were carefully preserved by the Howison-Crawfords and the minister added, with utmost solemnity, 'The rose water then used has ever since been hermetically sealed up, and the towel which dried the hands of Majesty on that occasion has never since been used for any other purpose'. Perhaps the Reverend Mr Colvin had the urge to record this trivial, not to say comic, information from a general desire to legitimise the historic standing of the Established Church in the face of claims on behalf of the 'Free Seceders' who now possessed a rival place of worship and school at Davidson's Mains. Perhaps for such a reason, too, 'we cannot forbear alluding to the fact that the estate of Barnton was once the property of Viscountess Glenorchy, a lady pre-eminently distinguished for her piety and good works' – patron saint of the Establishment that still countenanced lay patronage.

The heritors and their fine mansion-houses received their accustomed emphasis in Colvin's account. Of more appropriate symbolic significance to the new age was the 'noble' pier for the use of steam-boats recently built by the Duke of Buccleuch at Granton. The previous existence of a harbour at Granton could scarcely be guessed from the kirk session minutes. Granton, which 'has lately become a very populous district in the parish', had a rail link with Edinburgh by 1851, when it would contain forty-nine houses, with eight more under construction, and hold a population of 262. The parish as whole had by then grown to contain 2,284 people.[6]

With the growth in population – the figure was 1,986 in 1841 – the various parts of the parish were acquiring separate identities. This was notably so in the case of Granton. Granton, with its pier master and customs officer, its dock area, its rail link with Edinburgh and the associated railway workers, commuters such as 'George G. Goldie, commercial traveller (fine arts)' and a substantial residential hotel, had only one householder born in Cramond; its connections lay with Edinburgh, not the rest of the parish, and the area was well on the way to becoming formally integrated with Edinburgh.

Apart from the booming activities of Granton, the most important industrial development was now quarrying, with quarries in operation in several parts of the parish, some of which had formerly provided ashlar and 'battellings' for the Palace of Holyrood in 1535–6.[7] By 1851 quarry workers outnumbered the employees of the ironworks. While some were Cramonders, most came from outside the parish and the majority were single men, living in lodgings. Few of the married men among them had brought wife or family, so they were probably in short-term work and their rent constituted their largest return to Cramond's economy. The ironworks along the Almond might still be carried on, as Mr Colvin wrote in 1845, 'with much spirit', but the technology was outdated. Although William Cadell, the managing partner, claimed in the census return of 1851 that the company employed fifty men, eight women and twenty boys, some of them must have worked on a very casual or peripheral basis. Further industrial activity, like the paper, spade and spade-handle making, extended upstream to Peggy's and Dowie's Mills and Cramond Bridge and employed fourteen families in those areas. Seventeen people were engaged in the production of the cartridge paper for hosiery manufacturers that the paperworks specialised in.

Newer avenues of employment were provided for a few people by the post office and the police force. The post office employed, not only the accountant to the General Post Office, Edinburgh, who lived in Easter Drylaw house, but also a letter-carrier, a twelve-year-old postboy and a post-office runner. The 'penny post' had improved communication enormously. In 1815 the minister in Slateford had had no means of conveying a letter to his counterpart in Cramond, so sent it to one of Mr Bonar's brothers at the Bank in Edinburgh. Earlier still, in 1692, the kirk treasurer had paid 2s. Scots when a letter was carried 'by the post' to the minister in Culross. (This was only 2d. sterling, but a penny bought much more in those days.) The official postal service did not, however, entirely eliminate private enterprise by the elderly. In 1851 Joanna (Symons) Wallace or Willas, a widow of sixty-four living in the grounds of Cramond House, gave her occupation as message-carrier (in either the English or the Scottish sense of 'message'). Half a century later Willie

Henderson acted as general message-carrier, dressed in the minister's old black coat and 'lum' ('chimney') hat.

By 1841 policemen were stationed in Davidson's Mains and Granton. In 1851 Davidson's Mains had an Irish-born rural district constable and Granton had four officers, two of them from Shetland.

While some settlements were well on the way to suburbanisation, much of the parish still retained its old rural character. Where George Robertson had run a combined holding in the 1790s, in Granton Mains Alexander McDougal farmed 182 acres and employed nine labourers, two of whom (aged seventeen and sixteen) lived in the house, contrary to Robertson's former preference. In East Pilton a tenant born in Barbados held 100 acres, and in West Pilton George Stenhouse farmed 160 acres and employed sixteen labourers. Only one of the total of nineteen farmers of 1851 had been born in Cramond.

Farmworkers still formed the largest single group in the male labour force: some 186 men as well as a significant number of women labourers and 'out-workers'. The men among the farm-workers were designated either 'agricultural labourers' (i.e. casual farmworkers) or 'farm-servants', in permanent employment and typically younger than the labourers and rather less likely to be Cramond-born. (The enumerator in the Granton district made a further distinction, where a 'farm labourer' was living with his mother, widow of a 'farm servant', and his brother, an 'agricultural labourer'.)

Domestic service was still the most common occupation for wage-earning women, 154 of them in 1851. Next came agricultural labour (43) and dressmaking (16). Ten women and girls were employed in a menial capacity in the paperworks.

The amount of child labour was comparatively small by some standards of the time. It is not possible to make any comparisons with Cramond at an earlier period. In 1851 only seven girls under the age of fifteen were employed as housemaids or nursemaids. Four of these were fourteen years old and three were thirteen. Another three girls aged fourteen were in farm work.

More boys than girls under fifteen were working for wages. Four of the boys employed on farms were fourteen, one was thirteen and one twelve. A further nineteen boys had a variety of occupations. One twelve-year-old was an apprentice railway clerk, one a gardener's apprentice, one a postboy, one a boiler-boy at the ironworks and the fifth was employed at the paperworks. Some thirteen- and fourteen-year-olds were also apprentices and there was a fourteen-year-old following his grandfather's occupation as a seaman in Cramond village. Of the nine thirteen-year-olds, Alfred Prince was a page in Cramond House, and like the rest of the staff, imported from outside the parish. Another boy of thirteen was a pigkeeper, one a quarryman's labourer and two were errand boys. The enumerator (the schoolmaster?) thought it necessary to note, however, that one thirteen-year-old boy in an Irish family was 'not at school'.

The number of people living alone had fallen since 1792 (6.6% of householders in 1851 compared to 9% in 1792). By modern, Western, suburban standards housing was grossly overcrowded, and by 1851 conditions were made worse by the number of lodgers, often enough quarryworkers, who were crammed in.[8] Doubtless lack of privacy was endemic and unremarkable to observers like Wood and Spotswood. Almost certainly, in 1851 the four quarrymen who lodged with the farm servant Alexander Brown in Craigie Mill shared the kitchen-cum-living-cum-sleeping-room with Brown, his wife and their year-old daughter. In the industrial housing at the slit mill, the smith Alexander Dalrymple lived in a single room, rented from the iron company at £1 10s. per annum, with his second wife, five children of his own and three stepchildren, the eldest in the combined family being fifteen and the two youngest mere babies. Adam White, forgeman, paid the same rent but had two rooms for himself, his wife and eight children. That the families rented rooms, not individual cottages, is shown in a sale-bill of 1860, when, for example, a row of three houses contained sixteen 'apartments'.[9] Such crowded conditions were notoriously a standard feature of working-class housing of the time.[10] Families emigrating to the United States or 'the Colonies' cannot have found the cheek-by-jowl accommodation in steerage so very different from what they had left.

By contrast, the 'middle-class' house of Almond Bank contained, in 1860, dining and drawing rooms, a parlour, four bedrooms and kitchen, cellars and garret room. In March 1851 Mrs Clementina Phipps, widow of a partner in the ironworks, lived there with a son and two women servants. As a relatively well-to-do woman she was rather unusual in having no further relations, friends or paying guests in her household. The poor could not afford privacy, the rich did not like it, and there were long-term visitors in almost all of Cramond's 'big houses'. In 1841 Lady Torphichen shared Cramond House with four relations or acquaintances described as 'independent', along with the nine-month-old daughter of one of them, and ten women servants.

Some of those in tight living conditions were immigrants from Ireland, part of the general influx that began before 1841. In 1851 there were sixteen Irish householders and further people in lodgings. Most were unskilled labourers, many of whom had come in a family party, like Thomas McGovern in Peggy's Mill, a labourer at the ironworks. His wife and fourteen-year-old niece were farm outworkers, his eldest son (aged sixteen) was a paper sorter, and they lodged another ironworks labourer and a married couple and the brother of one of them, all agricultural labourers. The widowed Bridget Donoughue housed two sons, two married daughters, a daughter-in-law, a year-old grandson and, as lodgers, a widow aged twenty-four and three men, two of them brothers and two of them married. One party of five unmarried young women, three of them sisters, shared accommodation as 'comrades'. Perhaps it was among some of these miserably poor incomers in a rural area that an observer in 1854 found (in 'Cramond, an agricultural village near Edinburgh') houses built of whinstone and roofed with decaying thatch 'covered with bright green fungoid vegetation' and floored with raw clay lying a foot below the level of the adjacent soil.[11]

Muttonhole, by now more commonly known as Davidson's Mains, was closer than Cramond village to the main road between Edinburgh and Queensferry (and so to the city itself), had room to expand and was generally a more convenient commercial centre for the parish as a whole. It is thought that the 'Mutton' in the old name was a corruption of 'Meeting', which would suit its geographical situation. It was the former Nether Cramond that, dropping the 'Nether', arrogated the name Cramond to itself, but Davidson's Mains had outstripped it in size, with ninety-three houses counted in 1841, compared to perhaps forty-two in Cramond Village as by then defined. Besides the rural district constable and the Free Church minister and school, Davidson's Mains contained a wide variety of people, not excluding the usual complement of 'cotters and servants' – and quarryworkers. In 1851 the area as a whole was large enough to support two tailors and two shoemakers with their employees and, among others, a blacksmith with enough work for his four sons. The spinster Christian (or Christina) Warden, a grocer in 1851 and a schoolteacher ten years earlier, was assisted in her shop by a niece of seventeen and also housed a nephew of nineteen who was a solicitor's clerk (presumably he commuted to work in Edinburgh) and two female boarders, both at school. The elder of these, aged eleven, was an orphan pauper, born in England, and the younger, aged seven, a pauper born in Cramond. Two further householders supplemented their income by boarding pauper children – a scavenger, aged sixty, boarded two boys of six and five, and a man of sixty-four, with his wife, had an orphaned brother and sister. Two 'nurselings' may have been the only ones still fostered in the parish. As well as agricultural labourers there were a few men employed as labourers on either the parish or the turnpike roads, and so, probably, was one 'stone-breaker'.

Here, as in Granton, keeping a grocer's shop offered a new means of livelihood for women. There were three women grocers in this area and three men, one of whom also sold spirits. (One was the Cramond native Thomas Shade, of an old and sometime notorious family – aged fifteen he had been a letter-carrier in 1841). Another man was in business as a potato merchant. In 1841 residents had included the Keeper of Council Records, Edinburgh, a saddler (lodging a parochial missionary), a linen-handloom weaver (who by 1851 had turned grocer), a woman salt dealer and a road surveyor. The two butchers, both members of the Jack family (in 1851 the Scots word 'flesher' was used), represented another new occupation: at earlier periods any meat would be home-killed, not 'shop-bought'. In 1851 middle-class occupations were represented variously by an architect, a clerk to the Poor Law Board and a solicitor's clerk. The Parliament House messenger had his workplace in Edinburgh, as would the Writers to the Signet in Broomfield and Silverknowes Houses. Davidson's Mains and the adjacent areas like Lauriston and Corbie Hill were in train to provide a combination of commercial centre for the parish and a commuter suburb for Edinburgh. A century later the village would offer locals a variety of shops, including a supermarket, churches, a pub, a bank and a branch of the public library system.

Cramond village had no similar room for physical expansion. It was squeezed between the Almond and the Forth on two sides, the ironworks occupied land along the bank of the Almond to the south, and on the east of the road built by Sir John Inglis in 1778 stood the kirk, the kirkyard, the manse and the landlord's private estate. Sir John had demolished the former heart of the village, with its main settlement around the green, and in 1841 the census enumerator placed in a separate district the manse and the Cramond House estate, with its walled grounds containing nine cottages or lodges for estate workers. In the census of 1851 this district was also deemed to embrace the two premises by then marooned from the rest of the village, which occupied the west side of the road. Standing in 'Cramond [Fore]-Shore' (known in 1841 as 'Old Street') were the Cramond Inn, now run by Mrs Margaret Lumley, and the house inhabited by the seaman Robert Russell or Russon.

In 1792 the village had contained eighty-seven dwellings and 343 people, including twelve living in the household of the widowed Sir John Inglis 2. Among the village householders were all but six of those employed as hands in the ironworks. Fifty years later there had been an exodus to Cockle Mill and Fairafar, where in 1841 there was accommodation for over twenty. Many of the same families were still represented there in 1851. Despite that relocation, there remained the view that Nether Cramond was, in the words of the census return of 1841, 'chiefly inhabited by workers employed at Mr Cadell's Iron Works'. The ironworkers still stood out as the most conspicuous group. In 1851, among the 159 inhabitants of the village at its narrowest definition there were still twelve employees of the ironworks (including the commercial traveller Laurence Dow, who despite his luxurious managerial accommodation of six rooms was to be sacked for dishonesty in 1854). They were now outnumbered by the nineteen quarry workers. The former nailers of the village were now represented only by Charles Barclay, now aged sixty-five and living with a widowed daughter, while at Cramond Bridge Thomas Hill aged fifty still followed the trade (and family tradition with a son named Gavin, who was, however, an agricultural labourer). Charles Willis, a nailer in 1841, was now in Cramond village, aged eighty and described as 'labourer at iron works'.

In a far older Nether Cramond occupation there were still seamen in 1851: Robert Russon or Russell, James McUrich and John Murdoch or Murdie, at sixty-nine, and his son-in-law William Scott. Lachlan Hutton was a retired seaman. There was also a sailmaker next the inn on 'Shore Street' beside the Almond. At the slit mill, from still older seafaring families, were John Young, sailor, and Robert Young, skipper. Besides servicing the ironworks the Youngs may have transported the stone from the quarry at East Craigie that was taken by sea to build new docks at Leith, after being railed along the opposite bank of the Almond.

Robert Russon or Russell, aged sixty-four, and living on the Cramond foreshore in the household of his daughter and son-in-law, may in his youth have been the ironworker who was censured in 1806 for his irregular marriage and notoriously irregular conduct. His neighbour in 1841, Euphemia Gloag, 'spirit dealer', probably represented the family who once operated the ferry across the Almond and, in days of harsher kirk discipline, sometimes used their occupation as an excuse for not attending church. As a coal-dealer, James Marshall stood as historical representative of those earlier men, like John Elder and Alexander Williamson (Chapter 8), who had made their living by bringing coal across the water from collieries in Fife. Nether Cramond had, however, lost its resident excise officer again.

By 1851 Euphemia's premises (evidently what is now the 'Old Cramond Inn' on the eastern side of Cramond Glebe Road, with part dating from the 1670s) had been taken over by Mrs Margaret Lumley. The other inn-keeper, Isabel McAra, widow of James McAra and 'spirit dealer' in 1841, in fact ran the 'Royal Oak Inn', a two-storey public house on the riverside. (It is a measure of how much the village had retreated westwards that in 1852 the inn was described as 'near the centre of Cramond'.)[12] Her brother was the wright John Douglas who had so offended the session in 1838 when he took a commission on money collected for charitable purposes. They were children of Claud Douglas and the Isabel Forrest who had had to be taken at parish expense to the insane asylum in Edinburgh, and their grandfather was that John Forrest who was found, on his death in 1779, to have taken a pension under false pretences. By 1851, however, the parish no longer contained bearers of such names as Cleghorn, Harrower, Pargellis, Pillans, McMath or Spotswood.

A few familiar names still remain in the kirkyard, although space there was crowded and residence usually impermanent even in death. In 1796 it was ordained that when no heirs remained in the parish, a family's right to a grave-site should lapse 'after a reasonable time for the dissolution of the corpse and its being mouldered into earth'. The heritors, who enjoyed rights over the ground, tried to prevent any permanent enclosure of the graves of non-heritors and disliked potentially proprietary inscriptions on headstones, such as the 'thurgh stone' put up to the Gillons, market gardeners in Barnton, who included John, persistent non-attender at church, who died aged ninety in 1715.[13] In May 1679 Thomas Wells in 'Charmistoun' (Clermiston) paid £1 16s. Scots in return for erecting a headstone on his wife's grave and this survives in damaged condition, with the record that his wife, Isbel Cleghorn, died on 18 February 1667 (after less than six years of marriage). It also commemorates John Wells of Peggy's Mill, who died on 10 September 1699 – the John who adamantly refused in 1687 to join the session of the episcopalian Mr John Somerville and was not always a satisfactory member of Mr John Hamilton's. The headstone that Jean Smith the midwife put up to her husband John Harrower in 1684, on a promise to pay 14s. to the poor box, has long gone. But Margaret Wright, 'the goodwife of Grotthill' with her succession of ungracious servants, has a memorial together with her husband, George Shiell, who predeceased her by sixteen years. The innkeeper Isabel McAra, née Douglas, was buried in 1853 next her husband James McAra, who had died in 1810, and her father is commemorated on the stone erected by John Douglas. An earlier innkeeper, Robert Mitchell, appears in inscription along with his first wife Isobel Gloag, eight children and his second wife, the former housekeeper to Sir John Inglis. They were an unlucky family as far as their children were concerned. Robert Spotswood, who counted only six deceased children, noted that of three grandchildren, one boy was blinded in infancy by smallpox and Robert, who died soon after his grandfather in 1740, was 'choked by a piece of beefsteak getting into the *trachea anteria*'.[14] Numerous children are included on other gravestones, such as John, son of Richard Hutton, forgeman at the slit mill in 1841, who died in February 1844 aged eleven, 'in an attempt to cross the adjacent rivulet on the treacherous ice'. It is, however, vain to look for any memorial to those many fosterlings for whom mortcloths had once been hired.

In the village of 1851, by now at some distance from the kirkyard, forty-one per cent of the householders and/or their wives had been born in the parish – a much higher proportion than obtained in other areas. As in the previous two centuries, Cramond village also housed a disproportionate number of widows (eleven), widowers (five) and parish paupers: one man and seven women. As always, there was a mix of ages, though there were rather fewer babies, children and young adults under the age of twenty (36%) than in 1792, when the figure was 45%. That roughly half the householders of 1851 had come to the village since 1841 was probably much in line with mobility in earlier periods.

Creating a park-like estate meant removing houses. After 1792 the Ramsays of Barnton had produced a magnificent, 'beautifully wooded' park of nearly 400 acres at the cost of demolishing the village of Upper Cramond with something between twenty-seven and thirty-one cottages. In the late 1770s Sir John Inglis 2 had taken the first major steps towards a similar improvement in Nether Cramond. In 1826 his daughter and sole heiress, Lady Torphichen, completed this privatisation by demolishing any houses that still stood on her land eastwards of Sir John's new road (where the medieval village had also lain). The clearance may have been gradual, achieved partly by the relocation of the iron company's sub-tenants and partly by the gradual removal of houses as their elderly tenants died or tenancies otherwise lapsed. (About 1790 the village of Upper Cramond had also housed a proportion of elderly widows.) The sketch-plan of 1821, showing the eastern part of the village, notes the deaths of some of the tenants of that date. It also shows a carpenter's woodyard in the north, some small gardens, a library and, to the south, the entrance to a tanyard. The removal of the last must at least have meant a welcome cessation of noisome odour.

Local historians have castigated Lady Torphichen for 'halving' or 'mutilating' the village and attributed to her what Robert Spotswood had described as 'public expediency yielding to private pleasure and interest'. There are arguments to be put against this view, not least that it could also be seen as a useful exercise in slum clearance. Like other landowners – notably Lord Rosebery and the Ramsays in Barnton – Lady Torphichen offered some compensation for the loss of 'cotters' accommodation' by dotting her boundaries with lodges and providing other housing for estate workers. In 1841 thirty-two people (including some families with small children) were thus housed on her land. Her successor in 1851 had only nineteen.

Intentionally or not, the various alterations made by members of the Inglis family improved the amenities of the village at the same time as they reduced its population, and they ensured that the surviving parts would retain much of their late eighteenth-century aspect. As the industrial activities petered out, Cramond's very isolation strengthened its reputation as an attractive seaside resort. Thanks, too, to Lady Torphichen and her successors, the grounds of Cramond House did not become a crowded area of 'estate housing' in the modern sense, so that from the 1950s onward it was possible for archaeologists to excavate part of the Roman legionary structures that lay below.

When the Reverend Walter Colvin reported on the current state of the parish for the *New Statistical Account of Scotland* he was following precedent in giving a prominent place to Cramond's diminishing number of heritors. 'Few parishes in Scotland', he wrote, 'can boast of a greater variety of beautiful mansion-houses than Cramond.' But by 1841 most, like Caroline Park, West Pilton or Mr Thomas Davidson's fine new mansion of Muirhouse, were occupied by tenants on a semi-permanent basis.[15] The Treasurer of the Bank of Scotland lived in Drylaw House, along with his son-in-law, a Writer to the Signet. Craigcrook Castle had always housed tenants since John Strachan mortified it in 1719. Two of the most notable had been Archibald Constable, a founder of the *Edinburgh Review* and publisher of Walter Scott, and, after 1814, Francis Jeffrey, also a founder of the *Review*, judge of the Court of Session whose decision supported the establishment of the Free Church in 1843, and friend of literary figures from Scott to Dickens. Cramond had always served as a pleasant dormitory suburb for some of Edinburgh's élite. Queen Victoria's mother, the Duchess of Kent, was a tenant of Cramond House for three years. The queen visited her there in 1860 and the chair occupied by the royal bottom at service-time is carefully preserved in the kirk. In 1885 the tenant was a Count A.P. Bobrinskay. Later a more famous, but fictitious, short-term visitor would be Miss Jean Brodie, in full enjoyment of her prime.

At the Disruption Mr Colvin had been nominated to the manse by one of Lady Glenorchy's successors in Barnton, William Ramsay Ramsay, grandson of William Ramsay, First of Barnton. The Ramsays died out in the male line when, William Ramsay Ramsay having died in March 1850, in December 1865 his heir was accidentally killed soon after attaining his majority. In 1841 the Hon. Mrs William Ramsay Ramsay, née the Hon. Mary Sandilands (a member of Lord Torphichen's family), had living with her a granddaughter named Jean Maitland. The family would continue after 1865 as Maitland-Gibsons and then Steel-Maitlands, but Barnton House (rebuilt from the earlier King's Cramond) has disappeared, like its predecessor to the east.

William Ramsay Ramsay's widow played some part in parish life: a school for some fifty females in Lauriston was under her patronage in 1852[16] and in 1856, according to the kirk session minutes for 11 February, she 'intimated a wish that measures should be taken for the permanent improvement of the singing of the congregation'. Her husband made a wider mark as stagecoach owner with his partner Captain Barclay of Ury, sometimes driving their showpiece, *Defiance,* which ran from Edinburgh to Aberdeen, while the *Tallyho* covered the Stirling run. Ramsay was also an MP of distinctly conservative frame (he voted against the Reform Bill of 1832) and, following his father George Ramsay, Second of Barnton, was Master of Fox Hounds. When George died in 1810 we are told, indeed, that 'the hunting world was wrenched into contortions of grief'.[17]

As a widow Anne Inglis, Lady Torphichen, lived, at least part of the time, in Cramond House. By 1851 it had passed to her cousin Susan Craigie Halkett, whose husband took the name Halkett Craigie Inglis. The surname, after sometimes appearing, phonetically, as Hacket Englis, eventually settled down as Craigie Halkett. Some of the family were Episcopalians. Colonel John Cornelius Craigie Halkett married a Davidson who was a devout Catholic, as were some of their seven daughters. For both denominations churches were built at Davidson's Mains. At Colonel Craigie Halkett's death in 1912 the estate devolved on six of the daughters.

The last representative of the family to live in Cramond House, from 1924 to January 1959, was Dorothy Pearl Lily Harvey, who adopted the name Craigie Halkett and kept some paying guests and, more enthusiastically, large numbers of Pekinese dogs. The house subsequently became the property of Edinburgh Corporation and then of Cramond Kirk.[18] One link with the James Inglis who first settled as feudal superior in Nether Cramond in 1622 survived in the later twentieth century when owners of the modern houses that had gone up in Cramond Glebe Road (still segregated on the opposite side from Cramond House) continued to pay feu-duty to the legal representative of his various remote heirs.

Gradually the congregation acquired more of a say in the affairs of their parish kirk. The list of male communicant heads of families surviving from 1835 would have been produced in response to the Veto Act, narrowly passed by the General Assembly in 1834, which permitted a majority from this sector of the congregation to veto the nomination of a minister, without offering reasons.[19] The 'enfranchisement' of congregations continued, in a limited way, when in 1844 male communicants were formally invited to approve nominations for the selection of new elders. In the early 1870s even the most humble (and in a few cases illiterate) members of the congregation, both men and women, could have their say in a famous row that became known as 'The Great Cramond Harmonium Case'. The parish schoolmaster had long since ceased to act as precentor and that function had been transferred to people like the tailor James Rae, who in 1824 was conducting a singing-school in the interests of maintaining musical standards in worship. When Mrs Ramsay of Barnton complained about these in 1856, the session highly approved of her proposals and 'Mr Hay was taken bound to conduct a class of sacred music on the Saturday of every week in the schoolroom of Davidson's Mains'. In a further attempt to improve matters, it was mooted in 1870 that a harmonium be introduced. Objections were initially led by James Watson, labourer in Dalmeny Park, seconded by the clerk at Craigleith quarry and supported by ten others (one of whom immediately returned to say that he had voted mistakenly, 'for instead of disapproving, he highly approved of the use of a harmonium in public worship'). Two more apparent dissentients wrote to disavow that stance and two others said they objected to a harmonium but would not mind an organ.

Eventually some 400 parishioners petitioned presbytery to permit instrumental music in their services. A harmonium was introduced, whereupon 105 people, including many of the original signatories to the petition and a few who seldom entered the church, objected to its use, opposed by 136 who considered the harmonium 'a very great improvement indeed'. The battle raged on for some years and was taken to the highest level, amid allegations of vote-rigging and other irregularities that were reminiscent of those mustered on both sides in the heritors' bitter, Old Tory versus New Whig, dispute over the choice of a new minister in 1710. In January 1875, after the existing precentor had been told by Dr Colvin that his services were dispensed with because he did not live in the parish – 'which communication was not received in a courteous spirit' – the teacher Mr John Smith took over and was asked to train a choir 'and to improve the psalmody of the congregation by all the means in his power'. In 1911 the installation of an organ chamber and a more musical 'kist o' whustles' may have improved the instrumental offering and perhaps also the singing.

Lay patronage fell into disuse and was finally abolished by parliament in 1874, after the General Assembly had petitioned for the change. And in 1929, after long negotiations, the two major presbyterian church bodies reunited. In the wake of the reorganisation the original Cramond parish, which had already lost some portions of its former area, was further divided for ecclesiastical purposes. It now lies compactly between Silverknowes, Davidson's Mains, Blackhall, Clermiston, Cammo and the Almond.

In 1920 all the geographical area of the original Cramond parish, save for the part lying on the Dalmeny side of the river Almond, was incorporated for administrative purposes in a new Greater Edinburgh. Two locally famous golf clubs and a private preparatory school for boys took over much of the Ramsays' old parkland, although many of the fine trees remained and it was observed in 1926 that 'intruding villas and bungalows have broken through the [former] enclosure without essentially destroying the beauty of this sylvan scene'.[20] Barnton's attractions as a residential area were increased when a rail-line from Edinburgh opened in 1894. (It closed again in 1960.)

In 1811 the village of Cramond was already capitalising on its recreational attractions, especially the modish pastime of sea-bathing, when the following advertisement appeared in the *Edinburgh Advertiser* of 30 April:

To let for the summer season, a genteel furnished house in Nether Cramond consisting of three rooms and kitchen, well accommodated for the sea bathing, and commands a most pleasant and delightful prospective view. 'For particulars apply to Jas Gibson, at Black Bull, Calton Street Edinburgh or Henry Newton, on the spot, Cramond Shore.

Alas, Mr John Keith, brother of Mr James Keith Esq. of Edinburgh, fell victim to the fashion and the kirk session minutes record his drowning on 8 April 1814.

In 1926 it could be said that 'Cramond of today chiefly lives and grows on the summer visitor'.[21] In the 1960s old residents, recalling that inter-war period, described how poor families from Edinburgh would spend their summer holidays encamped by the shore to the east of Cramond village. They came by rail to Barnton, where Mum and the equipment took Harry Baillie's wagonette on to Cramond (at a cost of 4d.). On arrival she picked a tent-site and boiled up the kettle while the children walked from Barnton station. Some Cramond residents walked further than that. Like Cramonders of generations before – like the bibulous little party that contained David Pillans and Mrs Margaret Etrick in 1703 (Chapter 7) – groups of neighbours would join together at the West End in Edinburgh to make the five-mile walk home in company, especially after dark.

Eventually the former Royal Oak Inn became a cafe, and at one time there was an Italian ice-cream shop beside the Almond as well as a general shop. The inn on the other side of Cramond Glebe Road remained in the hands of the Lumley family until 1938. Run by the Misses Lumley, aunt and niece, it was remembered for its strawberry teas and sedate entertainments of whist drives, darts and dominoes. Some of the houses in the village belonged to weekenders, who came out by pony and trap and stabled their horses along from the village by the shore of the Almond. Further upriver there were only a few ruined remnants of the ironworks and some cottages to be seen where the City Corporation established a leafy walkway in 1935. (This is now a feature of Cramond's 'Heritage Park'.)

A flourishing boat club was started in 1934. In the second half of the century summer Sundays regularly saw what Mr Bonar had termed 'a sailing near the harbour in pleasure boats'. The residents of 'Nether Cramond' might be disturbed by persons coming out from the city for their recreation, but it was not the desecration of the sabbath that distressed them: before a public car park was constructed it was the blocking of their driveways.

Cramond had always offered desirable living conditions to a few of the well-to-do. Their numbers steadily increased as new houses were built in the Cramond-Barnton-Whitehouse-Braehead areas, although a commentator in 1966 regretted that 'the new Cramond houses many young executives whose length of stay in the area varies inversely with their rate of promotion'.[22] Within the new, restricted, boundaries of the parish poverty-stricken residents were few and far between. Consequently in 1989 the session had to tackle a problem that had seldom troubled previous sessions – how to find suitable recipients for the interest on substantial funds accumulated for 'the poor of the parish'. At that date the session contained one hundred elders, including–it was now unnecessary to say – women. Nor, by then, did the ordination of women occasion debate within the kirk.

In other respects one may well imagine the astonishment with which Messrs William Dalgleish, John Somerville, John Hamilton and the rest would have viewed developments. What, for instance, would they have thought on hearing the reaction of the last resident heritor of Nether Cramond to the information that the kirk building unfortunately covered an important part of the Roman fort then being excavated? Herself an Episcopalian, she declared unhesitatingly, 'Pull the church down, then!' What would they have made of a minister who was a Highlander, a man acquainted with play-actors, an observer of the pagan rite of first footing and, strangest of all, a preacher who mixed entertainment with instruction in his (now extraordinarily brief) sermons. True, in the late 1960s a fornicator was once more denounced from the pulpit. This culprit, however, was accused of fathering puppies on the minister's young collie bitch. Mr Campbell Maclean reported the sequel with relish the next Sunday. The suspect's owner, a very proper gentlewoman, had faced up to him, saying 'If it was my dog you had in mind, that canna be'. 'But they were seen together', objected the minister. 'He is a verra well behaved dog, who is never allowed to stray', she said firmly. And, after a pause, 'Forby, he's no a "he", he's an "it" '. Laughter in the kirk of the Covenant?[23]

NOTES

1. *Elders*, 1843. The replacement elders after the Disruption were formally elected by those male communicants still loyal to the established church. Five were nominated, including William Phipps, bookkeeper and then partner in the Iron Mill Company, but Phipps declined appointment and three more farmers were admitted, along with George Whittet in Whitehouse, the Ramsays' factor. After two deaths in 1850, one further farmer was added to the session. It is curious that none of the parish's professional inhabitants seems to have been in the running. They were, however, a mobile group: relatively few of those living in Cramond in 1841 were still there ten years later.

2. *Cholera as divine punishment.* Johnston, *Working Classes in Scotland*, p. 293.
3. *Care of the poor. New Statistical Account* I (1845), p. 605. The Act of 1845 spread the responsibility for poor relief beyond the kirk session by setting up 'parochial boards of managers of the poor'. In 1851 Granton House was occupied by the chairman of the Board of Supervision for the Poor in Scotland and his household. There was a clerk to the Poor Law Board in Davidson's Mains and in Cramond village an Inspector of the Poor, a former shoemaker.
4. *1845 report. New Statistical Account* I, pp. 589–606.
5. *Banquet for George IV.* This was a great pseudo-historical extravaganza. Even the Lord Mayor of London was rigged out in tartan for the occasion, and Sir Walter Scott, contemplating some of those present, was surely reminded of how his Glaswegian Bailie Nicol Jarvie had envisaged himself derisively in *Rob Roy* a few years earlier: 'wi' my fat wame in a short Hieland coat and my puir short houghs gartered below the knee, like ane o' your long-legged gillies' – 'a daft-like thing to see'. The Howison charade was quite of a piece with the rest. Wood had found and published a charter of 1470 confirming the conveyance of land to a Howison (but not Jock and not issued by the crown) by *servitium lavacri in nomine albae firmae* – 'blench ferm', here the payment of a basin or ewer if one was ever demanded by the superior, which like the payment of a silver penny or a red rose was a purely nominal condition of tenure. Nothing was said about a towel or the washing of hands: Wood, *Cramond*, pp. 61–2.
6. *Population 1851.* By my count and excluding those whom the census return designates as visitors.
7. *Stone for Holyrood. Masters of Works Accounts*, vol. I (1529–1615), ed. Henry M. Paton, Edinburgh 1957, pp. 138–9, 144, 146. Quarriers included the pleasingly named John Merilyone, while the boatman John Bulcrag ('Bull-neck') and his fellows ferried 155 pieces of ashlar to Leith from Nether Cramond and Granton.
8. *Modern housing standards.* When 26 dwellings were modernised, under the auspices of Edinburgh Corporation, in 1959, they produced only 16 renovated houses.
9. *Housing at Slit Mill.* List of houses occupied by workmen at Cramond Iron Works, Feb. 1851, Cadell Papers; Skinner, *Cramond Iron Works*, p. 47.
10. *Working-class housing.* The census return for 1861 showed that one-third of the population of Scotland (which was then something over three million) lived in single-room houses, 7,964 of them with no window: Johnston, *Working Classes in Scotland*, p. 294.
11. *Hovels in Cramond. Ibid.*, quoting *Courier*, 28 Jan. 1854.
12. *Royal Oak Inn.* Description in the *Original Name-Book of the Ordnance Survey*, 1852.
13. *Memorials in Cramond Kirkyard.* Aitken, *Cramond Gravestones and Memorials.*
14. *Spotswood on the Mitchell family.* Wood MSS NLS MS 9885, fol. 79.
15. *New mansion of Muirhouse.* Mr Colvin noted that all that remained of the old house, built in 1690, was two staircases. The towers containing them were still standing in isolation in the early 1920s, when a sketch was included in John Geddie, *The Fringes of Edinburgh*, London and Edinburgh (1926), p. 31. One might speculate that Robert Louis Stevenson, who was a friend of Colvin's, saw them on one of his visits to Cramond and put the image to dramatic effect in David Balfour's adventure at the House of Shaws in *Kidnapped.*
16. *Mrs Ramsay as patron of Lauriston School. Original Name-Book*, 1852.
17. *'Contortions of grief'.* J. H. Rutherfurd, *History of the Linlithgow and Stirlingshire Hunt*, 1911.

18. *Cramond House.* In the 1960s a new kirk hall was built on the site of the old stables. In 1966 the Dunfermline College of Physical Education moved from Aberdeen to new buildings and sports facilities on and about Sir John Inglis' south avenue. (Later it was renamed in accordance with changes in scope and administration.)

19. *Veto Act.* Mitchison, *History of Scotland*, p. 383.

20. *Barnton's sylvan scene.* Geddie, *Fringes of Edinburgh*, p. 37.

21. *Living on summer visitors. Ibid.*, p. 25.

22. *Young executives.* [Dr] Alastair G. Donald, 'Suburb by the Sea', *Cramond: An Introduction*, Cramond Association 1966, p. 28.

23. *Unattributed information* in the latter part of this chapter derived mainly from various members of the Cramond Association, especially the late Barclay Fraser, when an exhibition on the history of Cramond was in preparation in 1966. Much has subsequently appeared in essays in the excellent booklets put out at intervals by, initially, the Cramond Association and then its successor, the Cramond Heritage Trust. One or two items came from 'personal communication' and some, particularly the final anecdote, depend on my own recollection.

Index

Abbotshall, 88
Abercorn, 226
  minister of, 46
Aberdeen, 253
Aberdour, 95
abortion, 31–2, 34, 156, 230
Act Rescissory, 41
Adamson Agnes, 114–5, 145, 171, 174
  husband of. *See* Hill Andrew
Adamson Archibald, 106, 108–9
  wife of. *See* Hogg Jean
Adamson Jean, 161–2
Adamson Jonet, 29
Adamson Robert of Craigcrook, 38
Adamson Thomas, 73, 102
  wife of. *See* Baxter Helen
adultery, 3, 14, 33, 48, 53, 57, 145–6,
        154, 156, 158, 160, 165, 172,
        184, 186, 190, 192, 199, 200, 230
African Indian Company, 100
Aikin Jean, 96
Aikman Isobel, 146–7
  daughter of. *See* Short Margaret
Aikman James, 68
Aikman John, 72, 87
Ainslie George of Pilton, 178
Ainslie Sir Philip of Pilton, 178
Aire Jonet, 113
Aitkenhead James, 227
Aitkenhead Janet, 229
Alexander Ann, 114–5
  husband of. *See* Crie William
Alison Margaret, 31–2
Allan James, 231
Allen Jean, 61, 103–4
  son of. *See* Hume Alexander
Allison William, 227
Alvis Elisabeth, 124–5, 128–9
America, British forces in, 190, 192
Anderson Alexander, 219
Anderson Andrew, 138
Anderson David, 44
Anderson Elisabeth, 55, 82, 135
Anderson James, 45
Anderson Jean, 13–4, 79
Anderson Jonet, 29, 54, 82
Anderson Katherine, 59
Anderson Margaret, 71–2, 99
Anderson Thomas, 101, 148

Anderson William, 24, 131
Andrew Thomas, 153
  wife of. *See* Gillon Ann
Angus James, 73, 74, 76
Angus Margaret, 198
Annand Robert, 44
Argyll Countess of, 89
Argyllshire, 161
Arniston, 134
Arthur Margaret, 97–8
Atholl, 68
Atkinson Caleb, 228
  wife of, 228
Atkinson Mary, 228
Auchinleck Elisabeth, 29
Auchterlonie Margaret, 161
  daughter of. *See* Adamson Jean

Baillie Harry, 256
Baillie Mrs of Drylaw, 235
Baillie Nelly, 234
Baillie William, 226
Balfour Mr James, 38
Ballantyn John, 70, 132
  wife of. *See* Rae Bessie
Ballantyn Thomas, 99
Ballenie Patrick, 144
Balmerino, Barons. *See* Elphinstone
Bane Anna, 78
Baptie James, 99
  wife of. *See* Thomson Margaret
Baptie Jonet, 49
baptism, 3, 15, 16, 17, 60, 80, 155, 161,
        185, 186, 189, 198, 199, 213,
        223, 232
Barbados, 245
Barclay. *See also* Burtley
Barclay Captain, 253
Barclay Charles, 249
Barclay Rev. John, 129, 130, 132
Barnbougle, 162, 189
  lairds of. *See* Rosebery
Barnton, lairds of, 9, 17
Barony, 239
Bartan William, 55
Bartleman Henry
  wife of, 132
Barton Katherine junior, 33–4
Barton Katherine senior, 33

Barton Matthew, 28
  mother of. *See* Cranston Jean
  wife of. *See* Corston Margaret
Barton William, 104
Batherston Elisabeth, 58
Batherston James, 25
Bathgate James, 190, 205–6, 209, 215
bathing wells, 108
Baverage Andrew, 119–20, 202
Baverage Margaret, 88, 119
Baxter George, 130
Baxter Helen, 73, 131
  husband of. *See* Adamson Thomas
Baxter John, 102
Beg John, 26, 28
  wife of. *See* Cochran Rachel
Bell Agnes, husband of. *See* Nimmo Hugh
Bell Christopher, 182
Bell John, 58
benevolent societies, 202
Berry David, 26
Berry Eupham, 161
Berwick, 151, 159
Beton John, 150–1
bigamy, 59, 96, 161
Billingsley Mrs, 216
Binks Elisabeth, 46–7
Binnie Alexander, 222, 223
Binnie John, 222
Binnie Thomas, 222
Binnie Widow, 238
Binny Sir William, 220
Bishop Margaret, 76
Bizzet Andrew, 180–1
Black James, 190
Black John, 166, 188
Blair Cecile, 146
blasphemy, 25, 93, 153
Bleckie Jonet, 78
  father of, 78
Boag David, 34, 36
Boag Isobel, 34–6, 53, 155
Boag Robert, 56
Boag William, 62, 98
Bobrinskay Count A. P., 253
Bonar Archibald junior, 235
Bonar Rev. Archibald, 193, 196–204, 205,
    206, 218, 221, 222, 224–6, 227,
    229, 230, 231, 232, 235–9
Bordeaux, 178
Borrowstouness, 74
Botany Bay, 179
Bothwell Bridge, 68
Bowie Robert, 34–6, 91, 105
Braidwood Thomas, 208
Braithwit George, 51
Brand Janet, 151–2
Braxfield Lord, 197
breach of promise, 29, 81, 128, 227
breach of sabbath, 2, 14, 23, 26, 43, 53–4,

    68, 70, 82, 90–2, 119, 122, 124,
    129, 130, 138, 147–9, 165, 231
Brodie Miss Jean, 253
Brodie Philip, 233
Broun Bessie, 47–8, 54
Broun David, 24
Broun Grissell, 113
Broun Isobel, 99
Broun James, slater, 73
Broun James, officer, 116
Broun James, weaver, wife of, 3
Broun John, 143
Broun Jonet, 96
Broun Lieutenant Gilbert, 89
Broun Robert, 100
Broun William, 56–7
Brown Alexander, 186
  family of, 246
Brown Anne, 242
Brown Robert, 186
Brown William, 230
Brown William, kirk elder, 222
Bruce James, 150
Bruce Margaret, 170, 210, 219
Bruce Master of Mill Hall, 163
Bruce William, 154
  wife of, 154
Bryce Agnes, 95–6
Buccleuch Duke of, 243
Buchan Mr Alexander, 102
Bulcrag John, 258
Burges Margaret, 39
Burnet Commissioner, 162
Burnshot, 145
Burnton William, 72
  wife of, 72
Burtley. *See also* Barclay
Burtley Charles, 224
Bute, 38, 165

Cadell and Edington Messrs, 215
Cadell Philip, 223
  servant of, 226
Cadell William, 244
Cadell William junior, 181
Cairns Robert, 113
Calder Biny, 199
Callendar Thomas, 58
Cameron Mary, 164
Campbell Anne, 179
Campbell Betty, 164
Campbell Brodie, 231
Campbell Peter, 192–3
Cardross, 111
Carle Margaret, 72, 73, 88, 90, 115–6
Carle William, 70, 73, 84, 104, 115–6
Carmichael Ann, 192–3
Carmyllie East, minister of, 147
Carolina, 141
Carriden, minister of, 101

Carron, iron works at, 181
Carson Robert, 30
Cassilis 6th Earl of, 50
Castle Drummond, 73
Chalmers Mr, 180
Chapman Isobel, 30
Charity James, 61, 113
Charity Jonet, 58
Charlemont, siege of, 30
Charles I, 18, 22
Charles II, 7, 22, 41, 50
Charley William, 108–9
Cherry Moses, 68
Chesser William, 223
Chisholm Patrick, 48
Chisholm William, 98
Chrystie Andrew, 93
church officer, duties of, 23, 46, 69, 83, 102, 120, 167, 169, 213, 215
Clark Euphan, 227
Clark George, 90, 139
  brother of, 139
  daughter of, 139
  wife of. *See* Jackson Esther
Clark John, 139
clearances, 213, 216, 217, 219, 223, 248, 251–2
Cleghorn Adolphus Oughton, 195
Cleghorn Isbel, 250
Cleghorn Jean, 54
Cleghorn John, 166–8
  wife of, 168
Cleghorn Jonet, 82
Cleghorn Mrs Thomas, 233
Cleghorn Robert, 93
Cleghorn Thomas, 190, 206
Cleghorn Thomas junior, 30, 233
Cleland Elspeth, 172–3
Clelands James, 121
Clemat John, 74
Clerk James, 167
Clerk John, 131
Clerk John, shipwrecked sailor, 63
Clerk Rev. Thomas, 183
Clerk Sir John of Penicuik, 110, 134, 180
Cochran Rachel, 26, 28, 72
  husband of. *See* Beg John
Cockburn Adam of Ormiston, 134
Cockburn John, 134
Cockburnspath, 132
Colinton, 188
Colinton Mains, 127
Collin John, 171
Colvill Rev. William, 18
Colvin Rev. Walter, 242–3, 252–5
Comb Alexander, 166
Comb Helen, 179
Comb John, 148
Comrie, 59, 60
Constable Archibald, 252

contumacy, 34, 47, 56, 83, 98, 146
Conway Mary, 226–7
Conway Samuel, 226
Corse Mistress, of Whitehouse, 81
Corston family, 26
Corston Isobel, 31
Corston Margaret, 28, 39–40
  husband of. *See* Barton Matthew
Corstorphine, 38, 59, 80, 89, 90, 98, 127, 137, 169, 188, 200, 240
  minister of, 197
Couper Katherine, 102, 108–9, 141
  son of, 141
Couper Margaret, 91, 104, 116, 120, 132
  daughter of. *See* Ramsay Alison
Court Christian, 28
Cowan Agnes, 76
Cowan Thomas, 119
  wife of, 101
Craig Isabel, 156–8
Craigie Halkett Colonel John Cornelius, 253
Craigie Halkett Dorothy, 257. *See also* Harvey Dorothy
Craigie Halkett Susan, 253
Craigie Margaret, 178
Craigiehall, 209, 233
Cramond
  census returns from, 223, 242–50
  Irish families in, 247
  iron industry in, 181–3, 190, 213, 215, 219, 223, 244, 249
  oyster dredging in, 183, 195
  population of, 205–6
  population of (1694), 9
  population of (1792), 221
  population of (1831), 221
  population of (1841), 243
  population of (1851), 240, 243
  quarrying in, 99, 201, 244, 258
  Roman remains in, 214, 252, 257
  ships belonging to, 219
  survey of (1785), 205–6
  survey of (1792), 198, 206–7, 211, 215
  tax return for (1694), 205, 211, 214, 218
Cramond Harmonium Case, 254–5
Cramond Jonet, 101
Cramond Lady, 84. *See also* Houstoun Ann
Cranford Saint John, 89
Cranston Jean, 28, 33, 39
Cranstoun Rev. Michael, 17, 20, 21
Crauford Agnes, 76–7
  husband of. *See* White John
Crauford Alexander, 102
Crauford Thomas, 62
Craw George, 145
Crawford Katherine, 143
Crawfurd James Howison Moody, 216
Crie Elisabeth, 70, 77, 90, 104

Crie Margaret, 174–5
Crie Marjorie, 37, 70
Crie Thomas, 114
  wife of. *See* Raeburn Elisabeth
Crie William, 131
Crokat. *See also* Crookshanks
Crokat James, 215
Cromwell Oliver, 22, 41
Crookshanks. *See also* Crokat
Crookshanks Bethia, 224
Crumbie John, 239
  wife of, 239
Culloden, 179
Culross, 244
Cumber, 66
Cumin James, 82
Currie, 81, 84, 240
  minister of, 85
Currie Anne, 159, 183
  daughter of. *See* McCurich Jean
Currie Thomas, 159
Curror James, 222, 233
cursing, 23, 39, 94, 99, 104, 105, 130,
  147, 154
Cuthell Jonet, 76

Daingill William, 93–4
Dalgety, 120, 149
Dalgleish Rev. William, 18, 21, 22–42
Dalkeith, 96
Dalmeny, 63, 98, 111, 124, 142, 163
  minister of, 33
Dalnotter Iron Works, 223
Dalrymple Alexander, 228, 232
  family of, 246
Dalrymple James, 228
Davidson Dr of Muirhouse, 233
Davidson Jean, 157–8
Davidson John, 71, 95
  wife of, 71, 92
Davidson Mr Thomas of Muirhouse, 252
Davidson William of Muirhouse, 216
Dawling William, 135
  wife of, 153
Dawson Mr William, 166
death, proof of, 30
Demerara, 195
Denny, 111
Derbyshire, 159
Derry, 68
Dick James, 53, 142, 202
  natural daughter of. *See* Young Euphan
Dick Mary, 142–3
Dick Sir James of Priestfield, 155
Dickson Rev. James, 133
Dinboge, 30
divorce, 199
Dobie Agnes, 118
Dobie Alexander, 118, 132
Dobie Isobel, 54

Dodds James, 224
  wife of, 224
Dods Lilias, 229
Doe Katherine, 57–8
Dollar, 102
Donaldson Elisabeth, 238
Donaldson George, grandchild of, 140
Donaldson James, 53, 58, 118
  wife of. *See* Lawrence Christian
Donaldson Patrick, 117, 118, 119, 120,
  126
  wife of. *See* Robison Christian
Donoughue Bridget, family of, 247
Douglas Claud, 201, 237, 250
  wife of. *See* Forrest Isobel
Douglas John, 232, 250, 251
Douglas Rev. Patrick, 160
Dow Laurence, 249
Dowie Charles, 135
Dowie Janet, 140
Dowie John, 135, 152, 153
Drummond James, 226
Drummond John, 192–3
Drummond Jonet, 56
Drummond Margaret, 73–6
Dryburgh Hugh, 240
  family of, 240
Drylaw Lady (Isobel Foulis), 71, 85, 134
Duddingston, 46, 151
Duddingston Loch, 188
'Dumbar Father, a popish priest', 78
Dun Fletcher, 239
  mother of, 239
  wife of, 239
Dunbar, battle of, 22, 30
Dunbar Captain, 137
Duncan Christian, 23, 144
Duncan Elisabeth, 200–1
Duncan Helen, 143
Duncan John, 29
  mother of, 29
  wife of, 29
Duncan Margaret, 47, 82
Duncan William, 31
Dundas James in Southfield, 37, 72, 87, 91
Dundas Robert of Arniston, 134, 135, 139,
  151
Dundee John Viscount, 69
Dundonald Earl of, 87
Dunfermline, 156, 169
Dunkeld
  bishops of, 17, 18, 51
  commissioner of, 51
Dunn Flecher, 241
Dunn James, 241

Easington, 96
East India Company, 235
Easton James, 144
Echolm John, 150

Edgar Mr, surgeon, 55
Edict of Toleration (1657), 41
Edie Thomas, 94
Edinburgh, 10, 33, 35, 46, 58, 59, 77, 91,
    95, 98, 106, 107, 143, 147, 148,
    160, 174, 185, 192, 199, 255
  banquet for George IV in, 243, 258
  Bedlam of, 201
  bishops of, 43, 50
  Braidwood's school in, 208
  burning of, 100
  Canon Mills in, 161
  Castle of, 78, 126, 174
  House of Correction in, 84, 102
  Infirmary of, 170, 201
  integration with, 244, 248, 255
  John's Coffee House in, 235
  Lord Provost of, 19, 188
  ministers of, 45
  Morningside Asylum in, 240
  North East parish of, 105
  North West parish of, 32, 37
  Palace of Holyrood in, 244
  presbytery of, 5, 30, 33, 46, 47, 48, 49,
    51, 52, 57, 58, 67, 83, 85, 92, 97,
    105, 109, 123, 124, 129, 132,
    133, 157, 186, 190, 231, 236
  Saint Cuthbert's parish in, 63
  Scott's House in, 89
  University of, 90, 110, 135, 178
    Principals of, 110, 135
    professors of, 110
  West Kirk parish in, 39, 45, 68, 79,
    111, 115, 129, 135, 150
  charity workhouse in, 239
Edinburgh Advertiser, 255
Edinburgh Quarterly Magazine, 188
Edinburgh Review, 252
Edington Mr Thomas, 190, 198, 216, 239
Edmundston Thomas, 171
Edmundstone George, 185
Elder John, 126, 141
Elder John junior, 82
  wife of. *See* McCulloch Mary
Elder William, 128
elders, abuse of, 44, 53, 58, 60, 77, 82,
    98, 126, 148, 165
Elphinstone John 2nd Baron Balmerino, 18,
    19, 21, 39
Elphinstone John 3rd Baron Balmerino, 18,
    37, 42, 43, 46, 50, 51
Elphinstone Sir James of Barnton, 17, 20
England, 4, 19
Erskine Alexander, 233
Erskine Ebenezer, 187
Etrick Thomas, 63
Etrick William, 120–2, 128
  wife of. *See* Forbes Margaret
Evans Arthur, 161–2
Ewan Mrs, 143

Ewin Isobel, 146
expulsion from parish, 6, 61, 72, 83, 90,
    115, 116, 145, 150, 173, 192, 225

Faape Margaret, 27
Fairholm Agnes, 70
Fairholm James, 184
Fairholm Jean, 127
Fairholm Jonet, 26
Fairholm Marion, 125, 127
Fairholm Thomas, 172
Fairie Elspeth, 172–3, 183
Falconer James, 214, 219, 222, 227, 233
  wife of. *See* Wilson Margaret
Falconer James junior, 232
Falconer Jean, 227–8
Falconer Margaret, 238
Falconer Rev. David, 43–50
Falkirk, 111
Fashion Ann, 184, 199
Fashion John, 184, 192
Fashion John junior, 184
Fashion Mr Donald, 69
Fearholm James, 188
Fenton Peter, 228
Ferguson Elisabeth, 158–9
Fife, 84, 144, 163
Finlayson Anne, 179
Finlayson James, 173–4
Flanders, 102, 179
Fleggum the piper, 20
Fleming Marjory, 203, 204
flight from parish, 45, 48, 76, 81, 181,
    192, 229
Flint David, 222
Flint George, 207
Flint James, 165
Flookheart Alexander, 31
Flookheart James, 25, 48, 62
Forbes Arthur, 2–4
Forbes Isabel, 161
Forbes Jean, 80–1
Forbes Margaret, 120–2, 128
Fordel, 141
Foreman Isabel, 170
fornication, 13, 22, 106, 143, 149, 163,
    179, 200, 224, 229
  by laird, 106
  premarital, 13, 30, 54, 65, 69, 82, 115,
    149, 186, 226
Forrest Elisabeth, 237
Forrest Isabel, 201, 250
  husband of. *See* Douglas Claud
Forrest James, 62
  son of, 62
Forrest Jean, 150–1
Forrest John, 201, 237, 250
Forrest Mr Thomas, 2, 4, 45, 49, 50, 64,
    66, 77, 87–8, 112, 140, 211, 218
  widow of, 140

Forrest Rachel, 229
Foulis Sir James of Colinton, 209
 daughters of, 209
foundlings, 59, 60, 81, 101, 170, 181, 233
France, 18, 138, 209
 revolution in, influence of, 197
Frazer John, 79, 92
 wife of, 79
Frazer Mr, 135
Fullarton James, 207, 212
 family of, 207
 wife of, 212
Fulton Mr, 115

Galloway, 18, 199
Garvie Mary, 117, 118, 119, 124–5, 130–1
Gellon. *See also* Gillon
Gellon family, 70
George IV
 banquet for, 243, 258
Germany, 179
Gibb Helen, 45
Gibraltar, 179
Gibson Alexander, 91
 wife of, 91
Gibson Dorothy, 3, 78
 husband of. *See* Wilson Francis
Gibson Euphemia, 232
Gibson James, 256
Gibson Janet, 232
Gibson John, 82
Gibson Margaret, 72
Gibson Mr David, surgeon, 164, 166, 169
 wife of, 164, 170
Giffard George, 96
Giffin. *See* Given
Gilbert John, 90
Gilchrist George, 239
 wife of, 192
Gilchrist James, 148
Gilchrist Nicolas, 45
Gilchrist William, 166
Gilcrise John, 81
Gillespie Alexander, 136
Gillespie James, 190, 191
Gillies Marion, 45, 78
Gillon. *See also* Gellon
Gillon Ann, 152–3
Gillon George, 155
Gillon John, 250
Gilmer Thomas, 185
Given James, 49
Glasgow, 63, 193
 archbishop of, 51
Glasgow Margaret, 142
Glenorchy Viscount, 187
Glenorchy Willielma Viscountess, 187, 188,
 193–4, 222, 243
 chapels of, 187, 194
Gloag Euphemia, 232, 249

Gloag family, 70
Gloag Isobel, 90, 125, 132
 husband of. *See* Mitchell Robert
Gloag John, 54–5, 90, 91
 first wife of, 54–5
Gloag John junior, 128
 John son of, 128
Goldie George G., 244
Gordon Duke of, 78
Gordon Elisabeth, 2–3
Gordon William of Easter Pencaitland, 80
Gorée, 179
Gourlay Mr John, 222
 wife of, 235
Gowan Walter, 148
 wife of, 148
Gowans Walter, 184
Grant George, 200
Granton, goodwife of, 151
Gray James, 33–4
Gray John, 119
Gray Thomas, 74–6
 wife of, 76
Gray William, 82
Gray William, kirk elder, 223
Greenwich Duchess of, 217
Gribb Jean, 87–8
 child of, 88
 mother of, 88
Grieve Isabel, 168
Grieve John, 111
Grindlay John, 183, 215
Grinton Alexander, 73
Grinzlay. *See also* Grindlay
Grinzlay John, 175
Grotthill, goodwife of. *See* Wright Margaret
Guild James, 230
Guisborough, 209
Guthrie Jean, 63

Haddan William, 126–7
 wife of, 127
Haig Primrose, 195
Haig Robert, 240
Haistie Agnes, 91, 98
Haldan Mr John, 140, 144, 163, 166
 wife of, 166
Haliburton Captain, 162
Haliday John, 47
Halkett Craigie Inglis Mr, 253
Hall Anne, 168
Hall Janet, 144
Hall William, 148
Hallyards laird of, 83
Hamilton Duke of, 162
Hamilton Lord John of Barnton, 134, 195
Hamilton Patrick, 156
Hamilton Patrick of Cammo, 10
Hamilton Rev. Gilbert, 154, 156, 159–74,
 178, 188, 190

Hamilton Rev. Henry, 85
Hamilton Rev. John, 1–7, 66–85, 86, 106, 112
Hamilton Rev. John (Episcopalian minister), 43
Hamilton Rev. Robert, 153, 156–9
  son of, 220
Hamilton Rev. William, 85, 86, 87–110, 112, 123, 125, 130, 133
  sons of, 156. *See also* Hamilton Rev. Gilbert, Hamilton Rev. Robert
Hamilton Sir George of Barnton, 6, 85
Hamilton Sir William of Whitelaw, 154
Hamilton Thomas, 137
Hanna Harry, 200–1
Hardie Thomas, 234
Hardy John, 119
Hardy William, 55, 82, 119
  wife of, 3
Harrower Elisabeth, 84
  husband of, 84
Harrower James, 3, 5
Harrower Jean, 70, 98, 102, 108, 109
  husband of. *See* Hill William
Harrower John, 3, 5, 7, 71, 98, 113–5, 126, 133
Harrower John senior, 2, 250
Harrower Robert, 111
Harvey Dorothy Pearl Lily, 254. *See also* Craigie Halkett Dorothy
Harvie John, 122–3
Harvie John senior, 122, 123
Hastie Jean, 163
Hastie Thomas, 116
Hastings Jean, 31
Hay Mr, 254
Heath Neal, 233
Henderson 'Phoebe', 136
Henderson Andrew, 117, 131, 143
  wife of, 81
Henderson Bessie, 39
Henderson Christian, 150
Henderson John, 158
  daughter of, 158
Henderson Robert, 226–8
Henderson Willie, 245
Henry Agnes, 72
Henry Ann, 179
Henry Lizy, 211
Heriot Mr David, 38
Higgins Elisabeth, 50
Hill Alison, 30
Hill Andrew, 109, 115, 145
Hill Christian, 215
Hill Christy, 176
Hill Gavin, 249
  son of, 240
Hill James, 84
Hill Janet, 224
Hill Jean, 227

Hill John, 240
Hill Thomas, 249
Hill William, 102
Hodge Alexander, 222
Hodge George, 48
Hodge James, 222
Hodge John, 72
Hodge Thomas, 210
Hodge William, 72
Hog James, 167
Hogg Jean, 108–9
Holland, 68, 88, 129, 187
Hood Admiral Viscount, 179
Hope Lady Anne, 210, 219
Hope Lieutenant William, 210
Hope Sir Alexander of Granton, 43, 46, 50, 51, 84
  wife of, 51
Hope Sir Thomas of Craighall, 18, 19
Hope Weir Charles, 235
Hopetoun Earl of, 210
Horsbrugh William, 201
Hosie William, 230
Houston laird of, 32
Houstoun Ann, 65, 86, 134. *See also* Cramond Lady
  husbands of. *See* Inglis Sir James, Hamilton Sir William of Whitelaw, Cockburn Adam of Ormiston
Howat Helen, 71
Howat Mary, 71
Howison Alexander of Braehead, 4, 83, 87, 100–1, 132
Howison Crawford William of Braehead, 243
Howison David, 128–9, 132
Howison James of Braehead, 38, 41
Howison Jock, 243, 258
Howison John, 82–3, 124, 125
  father of, 83
  wife of. *See* Cleghorn Jonet
Howison John of Braehead, 192–3, 216
  daughter of, 216
Howison Margaret, 153
Howison William of Braehead, 152
Huguenots, 68
Hume Alexander, 61, 104
Hume James, 61
Hume Marion, 90
Hunter Alexander of Muirhouse, 60
Hunter James of Muirhouse, 50, 51, 85
Hutson Helen, 70, 81
Hutton David, 36
Hutton Lachlan, 249
Hutton Richard, John, son of, 251

impressment, 179
incest, 53, 242
Inchbucklarbrae, 138
Inchmickery, 133
infanticide, 31, 59, 172

Inglis Baillie William, 87, 88, 135, 139,
    143, 144, 147, 150
    son of, 144, 165
    wife of. *See* Mercer Janet
Inglis Charles, 179, 184
    natural daughter of, 179
Inglis James I of Nether Cramond, 18
Inglis Janet, 134
Inglis John I of Nether Cramond, 19, 31,
    40, 43, 50, 51
Inglis John in Over Cramond, 27
Inglis John, servitor, 31
Inglis Margaret, 46
Inglis Mary, 163
Inglis Mr Adam, 181
Inglis Mr John, 180
Inglis Sir Adam, 188
Inglis Sir James, 50, 86
    wife of, 65
Inglis Sir John, 86, 111, 123, 134, 145,
    150, 168, 173, 178, 180, 181, 188
    cook of, 148
Inglis Sir John II, 182, 188–9, 192, 197,
    202, 209, 215, 216, 219, 248, 251
    Anne daughter of. *See* Torphichen Lady
Inglis William in Craigcrook, 79–80
    wife of, 80
Inglis William in House of Hill, 144
insanity, 63, 102, 201–2, 211, 240
Inverkeithing, 23, 99
Inverleith Mains, 105
Ireland, 1, 85, 150, 162, 167, 227, 245
    refugees from, 68
    Scottish forces in, 3, 30
Irvin Mr, change-keeper in Edinburgh, 78
Irvine Maxwell, 230–1

Jack Catherine, 230, 241
Jack family, 248
Jack Janet, 227
Jack Margaret, 159
Jack Michael, 241
Jackson Esther, 139
Jackson Margaret, 89
Jamaica, 161, 210
James VI and I, 18, 20
James VII and II, 1, 7, 50, 51, 52, 63
Jamison Elisabeth, 224
Jamison James, family of, 224–5
Jamison John, 224
Jamison Mary, 224
Jeffrey Francis, 252
Jersey, 69
Johnsto(u)n Adam, 74, 75, 76, 117, 118,
    132
    children of, 74, 75
Johnston Agnes, 39, 58, 118, 119, 132
    daughter of. *See* Dobie Isobel
    granddaughter of. *See* Garvie Mary
    wake for, 116

Johnston Andrew, 98
Johnston Archibald, 97
Johnston Bessie, 55, 72, 118
    husband of. *See* Sim John
Johnston Cecile, 114, 116–7, 118, 120,
    122, 126, 128
Johnston James, 63, 70, 118, 132
    wife of. *See* Mungell Rebecca
Johnston John, 55, 68, 82, 102
    wife of. *See* Anderson Elisabeth
Johnston John the piper, 16, 54, 71,
    118
Johnston Jonet, 117, 118
Johnston Maggy
    elegy on, 174, 177
Johnston Margaret, 71, 72, 117, 118
    husband of. *See* Temple John
Johnston Marion, 114, 116, 117, 118
Johnston Mrs, 200
Johnston Samuel, 95–6
Johnston Thomas, 70
Johnston William, 68, 129, 132
Johnstoun. *See also* Johnston
Johnstoun John, 73, 74, 75
Johnstoun Richard, 73, 74, 76
    wife of. *See* Drummond Margaret

Kay Cornelius, 95–6, 149
Kay James, 68, 74, 90, 98
Keith Mr James, 256
Keith Mr John, 256
Keith William, 203. *See also* Howison
    Crawford, William of Braehead
Kello Agnes, 55
Kello Margaret, 73, 77, 93, 133, 145
Kenlay Margaret, 102
Kennedy Janet, 24
Kent Barbara, 28
Kent Duchess of, 253
Kent Humphrey, 28
Ker Deacon Andrew, 60
Ker Elisabeth, 77, 122, 132
Ker Jonet, 78, 118, 119, 122, 123
    husband of. *See* McMath John
Ker Lord Charles of King's Cramond, 99,
    134
Ker Margaret, 25
Kid Elisabeth, 173
Kidd Jonet, 62
Kilbucho, minister of, 36
Kilgour Andrew, 183
Kilgour John, 183
Kilgour Robert, 46, 65
Kilgour William, 201, 239
    wife of, 239
Killiecrankie, battle of, 69
Kincaid John, 29
King John, 222, 236
Kinglassie, minister of, 88
Kinneil, 111

kirk session
  complaints to, 14, 29, 39, 58, 72–3, 99,
    233–5
  duties of, 2, 12, 14, 40, 60, 62–3, 66,
    67, 90, 171, 233
  fine for non-attendance at, 67
  privy censures of, 67, 153
Kirkcaldie James, 100
Kirkcaldy, 204
  presbytery of, 88
Kirkland Mr James, surgeon, 166–7
Kirkliston, 88, 145, 167, 233, 238
Kneelands James, 119
Kneelands John, 119–20
Kneelands Robert, 57–8, 119
  wife of. *See* Rankin Isobel
Knight John, 71, 90, 99, 131
  wife of, 71, *See* Broun Isobel

La Pérouse, Comte de, 179
Lachlan John, 81, 92, 118, 129
  1st wife of. *See* More Margaret
  2nd wife of. *See* McMath Jonet
Lachlan John junior, 130
Ladley John, 98
Landale Mr David, surgeon, 236
Larbert, 53
Largo, 37
Lashan Mrs, 225
Lauder Charles, 164
Lauder Mr Andrew, 164
Lauderdale Earl of, 136
Laurie. *See also* Lowrie
Laurie William, 163
Lauriston Jean, 56–7
Lauriston John, 163–4
Lauriston Lady, widow of William Law (1),
    85
Law John of Lauriston, 133, 209
Law John William, 179
Law William (2), 133
Lawrence Christian, 58, 116, 118
Lawrie John, 160
lay patronage, 6, 17, 42, 110, 133–4, 180,
    186–7, 193, 222, 243, 253, 255
Le Havre, 179
Lees James, 44, 90, 92, 93, 94, 95
Leggit Alexander, 235
  wife of, 235
Leichman Marion, 58
Leith, 33, 124, 147, 249, 258
  Cromwellian governor of, 22
  minister of, 76
Leith South, 159, 188
  minister of, 133
Leslie Elisabeth, 81
Lewisham, 239
Liberton, 200
  laird of, 59
Lindsay Charles, 242

Lindsay Henrietta, 242
Lindsay John, 29
Lindsay John junior, 53
Linlithgow, 102
  minister of, 101
Linn Alexander, 89
Linn Ann, 226
Linn George, 87, 125
Linn Jonet, 92, 112–3, 127–8
Linton, 96
Lisk Thomas, 162
Liston Janet, 238
Lithgow Elspeth, 49
Little Blanch, 34
Livingston Margaret, 146
Livingston Robert, 135
Livingston William, 135, 152–3
  wife of, 152–3
Loch George of Drylaw, 134, 216
Loch James of Drylaw, 40, 51, 53, 59,
    64
  widow of. *See* Drylaw, Lady
Loch Tay, 59
Lockie Mr, 150
Logan Archibald, 86
Logan Margaret, 94
London, 31, 162, 164, 216
  Chelsea Hospital in, 240
  Lord Mayor of, 258
Longniddry, 89
Loudan Robert, 141
Loury James, 93
Low Mr, preacher, 96
Lowdon Margaret, 29
Lowrie. *See also* Laurie
Lowrie Christian, 230
Lowther James, 226
Lumley Mrs Margaret, 248, 250
Lumley the Misses, 256
Lumsdale John, 29
Lun(n) John, 165, 175
Lundy David, 161
Lunn Archibald, 89, 136, 142

Macdonald Barbara, 230
Macintosh John, 78
Mackenzie Mr Forbes, 233
Mackenzie Sir George of Royston, 51, 85,
    108, 133
  son of, 133
Mackenzie Sir James of Royston, 133
Maclean Rev. Campbell, 257
Maitland Jean, 253
Malcolm John, wife of, 142
Malloch John, 159
Mann James, 232
March Earl of, 195
  coachman of, 146
Marr Elisabeth, 145–6
Marr George, 143, 165

Marr James, 101
  wife of, 101
Marr John, widow of, 215
Marr William, 164–5
marriage, 12, 16, 69, 88, 92, 94, 98, 129,
    143, 161, 213
  disorderly, 30, 84, 89–90, 128–30, 149,
    160–2, 173, 183, 198–9, 224, 226
  forged certificate of, 199
  purported, 78, 96, 149, 158, 159
Marshal Jean, 198
Marshal William, 190, 198
Marshall David, 227
Marshall James, 234–5, 249
  wife of, 235
Marshall John, 30
Marshall William, 90, 184, 227
Martial Mary, 184–5
Martin David, 92–5
Martin Finlaw, 79
Martin Thomas, 97–8
  mother of. *See* Wells Margaret
Mason Alison, 72, 101
Mason Edward, 162
Mason James, 234
Mason Sarah, 162
Mason Thomas, 234
  wife of, 234
Mather Jean, 184
Mather Katherine, 184
Mathewson John, 151–2
Matthie Isobel, 58–9
Matthie John, 62
McAlpine James, wife of, 171
McAlpine Thomas, 143
McAra Alexander, 225
McAra Archibald, 183
McAra Isabel, 232, 250
McAra James, 225, 250
McAra James (2), 225
McAra James junior, 227
McAra John, 183
McAra Thomas, 225
McBaith Jean, 79–80
McCaul Mary, 142
McClaren Robert, 125
McCleish John, 115
McClelland John, 46
McCrabbie William, 95
McCulloch David, 159
McCulloch Hugh of Pilton, 51
McCulloch Mary, 82
McCurich. *See also* McCurrie, McUrich
McCurich James, 201
McCurich Janet, 183
McCurich Jean, 183, 190, 192, 198, 201,
    209
McCurrie. *See also* McCurich, McUrich
McCurrie James, 183
McCurrie John, 183

McCurrie William, 183
McDonald John, 46
McDoual Mr, 169
McDougal Alexander, 245
McDougal Andrew, 170
McFarlan John, 169
McFarlane Andrew, 78–9, 83, 84
  sons of, 84
  widow of, 84
McFarlane John, 84
McGill Sir James of West Drylaw, 10
McGovern Thomas, family of, 247
McGowan Elspeth, 24
McKenzie Colin, 89
McKenzie Daniel, 89
McKenzie Donald, 90
McKenzie Murdo, 90
McKie Robert, 56
McKynnell Mr Robert, 49
  son of, 49
McLauchland John, 192
McMath Dorothy, 118, 122–3, 129
McMath John, 59, 118, 122
  wife of. *See* Ker Jonet
McMath John junior, 118
McMath Jonet, 78, 82, 86, 92, 118, 122,
    129–30, 149
  husband of. *See* Lachlan John
McPherson Grace, 242
McUrich. *See also* McCurich, McCurrie
McUrich James, 234, 249
McUrich Margaret, 224
Meane John, 30
Mennons Margaret, 183
Mennons (Mennins) Robert, 165, 183
Mennons William, 183
Menzies John of Cammo, 4, 80, 84, 85,
    87, 100, 106, 110, 129, 134, 136,
    140
  Dr John, son of, 134
Mercer Janet, 135
Merilyone John, 258
Methven, 55
Middlemass Mrs Betty, 232
Middlemist Mary, 227
Miles William, 179
Millar. *See also* Miller
Millar Agnes, 29
Millar Alexander, 92, 98
Millar Ann, 114–5
Millar Daniel, 59, 70, 72, 92, 99, 100
Millar Elisabeth, 104–5
  son of, 105
Millar family, 53, 72
Millar Henry, 70, 72, 90, 116
  wife of. *See* Carle Margaret
Millar Hugh, 100
Millar Isobel, 114
Millar James, 31, 49
  wife of. *See* Steinson Elspeth

Millar John, 72, 104, 105, 115
Millar John, kirk elder, 222
Millar Jonet, 59–60, 125, 126, 127
Millar Margaret, 144
Millar Robert, 108, 109, 117
Millar Thomas, 25, 29, 62
Miller James, gardener, John son of, 128
Miller John, 151–2
Miller Marion, 154
   husband of. *See* Bruce William
Miller Mary, 106
Miln Robert of Barnton, 220
Mississippi Scheme, 209
Mitchell Agnes, 91
Mitchell Jean, 142
   daughter of. *See* Stewart Katherine
Mitchell John, 151–2
Mitchell Robert, 90, 92, 129, 132, 136,
     155, 215, 251
   1st wife of. *See* Gloag Isobel
   2nd wife of, 155
   family of, 251
Moffat, soldier, 146
Monck General George, 41
Monkland Iron Works, 228
Monmouth James Duke of, 68
Monoch George, 160
Monro General Robert, 30
Moodie David, 234
Mordoch. *See also* Murdie, Murdo,
   Murdoch
Mordoch Agnes, 128
Mordoch Janet, 167
More Margaret, 81
More William, 78, 82
Morham, minister of, 133
Morison Alexander in Lauriston, 24, 25
Mosse George, 96
Moubray Edward, 92, 94
   son of, 141
   wife of, 92
Moubray James, 34
Moubray John of Cammo, 10
Moubray Robert, 25
Moubray Robert at Cramond Brig End, 27,
   36
Moubray Thomas, 24
Mowat Rev. Samuel, 89, 90
Mowbray Margaret, 184, 192, 198–9, 206
Muir James, 113
   wife of. *See* Purvis Mary
Muirhead Rev. George, 222, 228, 232,
     234, 240, 242
Mungell Margaret, 118, 129
Mungell Rebecca, 70, 118, 120, 122, 127
   husband of. *See* Johnston James
murder, 209, 219, 225. *See also* infanticide
Murdie. *See also* Mordoch, Murdo,
   Murdoch
Murdie Alison, 228

Murdie Widow, 227
Murdo James, wife of, 101
Murdoch John, 224, 249
Mure George, 95–6
Mure Marion, 157, 158
Mure Thomas, 171
   wife of. *See* Ravelton Margaret
Murray David, 210
Murray Hugh, 15, 62
   wife of, 15
Murray Mr Andrew, surgeon, 89
Murray Rev. John, 89
   father of, 89
Mutter Rev. Robert, 133
Mylne William, 76, 100

names, spelling of, 42, 136
Naper Agnes, 164–5
Naper Margaret, 113
Napier John of Merchiston, 15
Napier Sir Alexander of Lauriston, 15
National Covenant, 17, 18, 41
Naughtie George, 181
Nave John, 151
neighbours, prying by, 1, 14, 73, 78, 94,
     114, 123, 144, 146, 150, 173, 231
Neilson William, 62
New Statistical Account of Scotland, 243, 252
New York, the Scots congregation in, 141
Newcastle, 88, 96, 160, 173, 239
Newhaven, 75, 141
Newlands, 106
Newton Henry, 256
Nicoll Thomas, 11
Nimmo Archibald, 112
Nimmo Hugh, 88, 93, 126
   wife of, 93
Nimmo James, 122–3
Nimmo John, 71, 112–3
   wife of. *See* Pillans Barbara
Nimmo Thomas, 215
Nisbet Anne, 89
Nisbet Rebecca, 88–9

Ochiltree George, 56
Ogilvie Sergeant John, 146
Ogston Eupham, 186
Oliphant Sir James of Muirhouse, 210, 219
   son of, 210, 219
Ormiston, 134
Ormiston David, 125
Ormiston James, 93
   wife of. *See* Smith Susannah
orphans, 180. *See also* Dick Mary,
    Williamson John
Ossian, 179
Oughton Sir James Adolphus of Caroline
    Park, 178–9
Oxon John, English scholar, 63

Paisley, 87
Pargillies. *See also* Purgillies
Pargillies William, 93
Parke Thomas, 56
Paterson John, 108, 109
  wife of, 109
Paterson Mrs Christian, 135
Paterson Nanny, 201
Paterson Sir William of Granton, 7, 51,
    84–5, 106–9
  son of. *See* Paterson John
Paton George, 218
Paton Hamilton, 179
Paton Janet, 137–8
Paton Margaret, 54, 102
Paton Mr John, 221–2, 229, 239
Paton Mr Ninian, 178, 179, 192, 195,
    199, 202–3, 215, 218, 221, 225,
    233
Paton William, 229
Paul Thomas, 138, 148
  wife of, 147–8
Peacock Andrew, 101
Peacock Widow, 170
Pedden William, 162
Penicuik, 134
Perth, 7
Philp James, 237
Phipps Mrs Clementina, 246
Phipps William, 257
Pickens John, 105
Pickhard Alexander, wife of, 192
Pickhard Johanna, 201
Pickhard John, 192
Pillans David, 92, 112–3, 117, 120–2, 127
Pitreavie, Baron Court of, 169
Pollock George, 87
Pollock John, 102
Pollock William, 102
  son of, 102
Polmand, 163
poor relief, 12, 40, 60, 61–3, 68–70, 100,
    102, 104–5, 140–2, 167–9, 180,
    201–2, 237–40, 242–3
  financing of, 12, 19, 41, 50, 52, 69,
    100, 179–80, 235–6
Portobello, 235
Potter John, 87
Pratts Archibald, 166
Pratts Isobel, 78
Pratts Robert, 93
Prentice Elizabeth, 186
Prentice James, 186
Prentice John, 186
Prentice Margaret, 186
Pretender, the Old, 138
Pretender, the Young, 168
Pride David, 45
Primrose James of Whitehouse, 37, 46
Prince Alfred, 246

Probert Charles, 224
Probert William, 191–2, 198
  wife of, 190, 191
Professor the. *See* Hamilton Rev. William
Proverb Isabella, 227
Punton George, 130
Punton, Skipper Robert, 96
Purgillies John, 60
Purie David, 198–9
Purvis Mary, 99, 113

Queensferry, 172

Rae Archibald, 53
Rae Bessie, 14, 70, 118, 126, 132
Rae Christian, 104
Rae James, 234, 254
Rae John, 48
Raeburn Elisabeth, 90, 125, 126, 132, 148
  husband of. *See* Crie Thomas
Raeburn Henry, 188
Raeburn James, 27
Ramsay Alison, 116
Ramsay Allan, 174
Ramsay Charles Ramsay of Barnton, 253
Ramsay George of Barnton, 220, 233, 235,
    253
  dog keeper of, 229
  widow of, 222
Ramsay Hon. Mrs William Ramsay of
    Barnton, 253, 254
Ramsay Isabel, 168
  grandson of, 168
Ramsay Isobel, 124
Ramsay John, 55, 91
Ramsay Jonet, 49
Ramsay Richard, 120
Ramsay William, 3, 63, 66, 77, 121, 133
  wife of, 120
Ramsay William of Barnton, 216, 217,
    235, 236
  servant of, 200
Ramsay William Ramsay of Barnton, 253
Ranald Alison, 173
Ranken James, 179
Ranken Janet, 189, 200
Rankin Isobel, 57
Rankin Thomas, 73, 80
Rankin William, 58
rape, allegations of, 14, 46, 79, 145
Ratho, 140
  minister of, 136
Ratho Byres, 111
Ravelton Margaret, 171
  husband of. *See* Mure Thomas
Ready David, 211
Reed Jonet, 44
Reed Widow, 232
Reid Barbara, 116
Reid David, 95

Reid James, 16, 62, 76–7, 90
Reid John, 86, 124
  wife of, 86
Reid Marion, 228, 241
Reid Mr, 199
Reid Thomas, 241
Renny Margaret, 71
Reoch Andrew, 195
Reoch John Inglis, 195
Reoch Wilhelmina Cadell, 195
Restalrig, 20
Rew Mary, 191–2
Richmond Christian, 191
Riddell Captain Walter of Granton, 166
Ritchie Alexander, 93, 102
Ritchison Bessie, 45
Ritchison Margaret, 137–8
Ritchison Sir James, 137
Robb James, 190, 214, 215, 218, 219, 237
Robertson. *See also* Robison
Robertson David, 14
Robertson Elisabeth, 159–60, 230
Robertson George, 207, 208, 209, 210,
  211, 212, 214, 216, 217
Robertson George (3), 222
Robertson George senior, 188, 190
Robertson Mr James, surgeon, 222, 235,
  236
Robertson Mr John junior, 225
Robertson Peter, 195
Robison. *See also* Robertson
Robison Bessie, 62
Robison Christian, 116, 117, 118, 125–7,
  129
  husband of. *See* Donaldson Patrick
  mother of. *See* Rae Bessie
Robison Elisabeth, 55, 101, 122
Robison James, 48
Robison John, 47, 69
Rochefort expedition, 179
Rodger Jean, 226
Rodney Captain George, 179
Roebuck Dr John, 181
Rogers Archibald, 228
Ronald Alexander, 126, 130
Rosebery Countess of, 162
Rosebery Earl of, 111, 134, 180, 182, 189,
  213, 217, 218
  son of, 218
Ross, bishops of, 43, 51
Rotterdam, 187, 216
Royal Bank of Scotland, 217
Royston Lord. *See* Mackenzie Sir James of
  Royston
Ruddiman Mrs Ann, 234
Ruddiman William, 201
Ruglen Earl of. *See* Hamilton Lord John of
  Barnton
Russell. *See* Russon
Russon John, 223

Russon Robert, 183, 223, 248, 249
Russon Robert senior, 183
Rutherford Rev. Samuel, 18
Rutherman Joseph, 159

St Albans, 167
St Andrews
  archbishop of, 52
  archdeacon of, 43
  bishops of, 51
  St Leonard's College, 43
St Kilda, 103
St Ninians, 111
Samuel James, 148
Samuel John, 144–5
Sanders Anne, 161
Sandilands James, 156–8, 177
  wife of, 156, 157, 158, 159
Sandilands Mr Mathew, 225
Sawers William, 98, 111
schoolmaster, duties of, 19, 21, 24, 26, 45,
  83, 166, 202, 236, 254
Scot Jean, 73, 74, 75
Scott Sir Walter, 136, 258
  father of, 136
Scott William, 249
Scugall Margaret, 26
Seatoun Mrs Margaret, 89
sects, 41, 186, 187, 204
Selkirk Earl of. *See* Hamilton Lord John of
  Barnton
Shade. *See also* Shedd
Shade Alexander, 232
Shade James, 232
Shade Thomas, 248
Sharp James, 45
Sharp Mrs Catherine, 231
Shedd Agnes, 45, 96–7
  mother of. *See* Gillies Marion
Shedd Alexander, 26–7
Shedd Thomas, 45, 78
Shedd William, 100
shelly coat, 92
Sherriff Rev. Francis, 187
Shetland, 245
Shiell George, 250
Short Agnes, 180
  son of, 180
Short Andrew, 167
Short Charles, 91
Short Margaret, 172
Short Thomas, 146, 169
Sim James, 80
Sim Janet, husband of. *See* Williamson
  Alexander
Sim John, 55, 72, 118, 122, 141, 147
  son of, 55
  wife of. *See* Johnston Bessie
Sim Jonet, 127
Simpson Agnes, 14, 143–4

Simpson Dr and Mrs David C., 220
Simpson James, 223
Simpson John, 14
Simpson Rev. Dr, 229
    servant of, 229
Simpson Sir James Young, 132
Simson John, 160
Sinclair Sir John, 205, 206
Sinclair Sir Robert of Longformacus, 189
slander, 29, 34, 72, 109, 144, 193, 224,
    234
Slateford, 229
Smith Ellis, 226
Smith James, 148
Smith Jean, 1, 3–7, 55, 70–1, 108, 133,
    250
    children of. See Harrower
Smith John, 71
Smith Jonet, 45
Smith Mr John, 255
Smith Rev. James, 133–54, 156
Smith Sir John of Grotthill, 19, 51
Smith Susannah, 93
Solemn League and Covenant, 19, 41
Somerville Rev. John, 43, 50–64, 66, 84
    maidservant of, 52
    widow of, 51
Sommerville Mr, 235
Spain, 138, 178
Spotswood Archibald, 145, 148
Spotswood Colonel Robert, 235
Spotswood Eupham, 81
Spotswood James, 206
Spotswood Mr Robert, surgeon, 166, 170,
    178, 184, 188, 190, 200, 206,
    207, 209, 210, 216, 217, 218,
    236, 251, 252
    horse of, 210
Spotswood Thomas, 178
Spotswood William, 178
Squire Agnes, 28
Squire Widow, 54
Squires Margaret, 225
Squires Richard, 204, 215
Stalker Donald, 60
Stalker John junior, 22
Stalker John of East Drylaw, 10
Statistical Account of Scotland, 196, 205,
    206
Steedman Anne, 180
Steill Christian, 86
Steinson. *See also* Stevenson
Steinson Catherine, 30
Steinson Elspeth, 31
Stenhouse George, 245
Stevenson. *See also* Steinson
Stevenson James, 192–3
Stevenson Robert Louis, 258
Stewart. *See also* Stuart
Stewart Jonet, 39

Stewart Katherine, 167, 173–4, 215
Stewart Mary, 68
Stewart Patrick, 93
    alleged niece of, 93
Stewart Sir John, 203, 204
Stewart William, 121, 173
Stirlin Jonet, 7
Stirling, 253
Stockbridge, 229, 230
Story Eupham, 71
Story George, 58
Strachan David, 180, 188
Strachan Helen, 99–100
Strachan John, 140, 252
    housekeeper of, 209
Strang Rev. David, 160, 161, 162
Strathbrok (Uphall), 32
Stuart. *See also* Stewart
Stuart Alexander, widow of, 238
Stuart James, 60
Stuart John, 29
    wife of. *See* Auchinleck Elisabeth
Stuart John junior, 199
Stuart Katherine, 29
Stuart Rev. Charles, 187–8
Stuart Rev. John, 199
Stuart William, 184–6
Succession Act, 51
Sutherland Countess of, 187
Swan Margaret, 56
Sweden, 138

Tailor Andrew, 56
Tailor James, 90
Tailor John, 53, 76–8
Tarbat Viscount. *See* Mackenzie Sir George
Tarves, 88
Taylor Jean, 71
Taylor John, 55
Temple John, 118, 120, 127, 132
Temple William, 116, 117, 118, 119–20,
    122–4
Tennant Margaret, 192
Tennant Mr Jacob, 63
Test Act of 1681, 51
testimonials, 5, 6, 12, 23, 29, 32, 37, 44–
    5, 60, 61, 75–6, 78, 83, 88–9, 90,
    150, 186, 213, 224, 232
theft, 75, 100, 104, 120, 148, 168, 233
Thomson Elisabeth, 149
Thomson George, 163
Thomson Helen, 49
Thomson James, smith, 101, 104
    sister of, 101
Thomson Margaret, 99
Thomson Mr David, 68
Thomson Thomas, 143
Tib, tailor, 176
Tillicoultry, 111
Tiviotdale Fletcher, 241

Tolin Mr, 68
Torphichen Lady, 223, 235, 246, 251–2, 253
Torphichen Lord, 216, 225, 235
Torryburn, 45
Trotter Mr, 240
Tuedy Barbara, 103
Turner Edward, 104
  wife of, 104
Tyninghame, 39
Tynron, minister of, 89

Ulster, 30
United Kingdom
  parliament of, 110, 111, 134
  superior constitution of, 197
Uphall, 32, 111

Veto Act, 254
Victoria, Queen, 253
violence, 70, 74, 75, 92, 99, 121, 130, 164, 225, 235
  domestic, 7, 29, 53, 54, 72, 122, 149, 154, 158, 169, 173, 198, 234
Virginia captain
  sale of girl to, 49

Waddell Katherine, 171
Waddell William, 71, 81
  wife of, 71, 81, 113
Waker. See also Walker
Waker Agnes, 128
Waker Grissell, 48
Waker James, 40, 53, 86
Waker James junior, 92
Waker Marjorie, 36
wakes, 16, 34, 62, 116, 167
Walker. *See also* Waker
Walker Agnes, 142
Walker Rev. Robert, 188, 189, 190–3
Walker Rev. Robert senior, 187
Wallace. *See also* Willis
Wallace Isobel, 39, 40
Wallace Joanna, 244
Wallace Jonet, 103
Wallace Sir Henry of Ingleston, 140
Walmser Katherine, 59
Warden Christian, 247
Wardie, 119
Waterston Anna, 82
Watson James, 254
Watson John of Muirhouse, 152
  coachman of, 151
Watson Robert of Muirhouse, 134
Wauchop Marion, 32–3
Wauchop Robert, 62, 69
Webster Rev. Dr Alexander, 205, 218
Webster Rev. James, 88
Weems William, 46
Weir Agnes, 139

Wells John, 63, 67, 68, 84, 98, 100, 250
  wife of. *See* Logan Margaret
Wells Margaret, 97
Wells Thomas, 67, 87, 250
  wife of, 250
Wemyss, minister of, 88
Wesley Rev. John, 187
West Indies, 179
wet-nursing, 4, 13, 14, 32, 80, 88–9, 97, 101, 102, 113, 131, 135, 137, 143, 181, 230, 248
White Adam, family of, 246
White Alexander, 225
White Bain, 155
White James, 175
White John, 77
White Margaret, 173, 174. *See also* White Meg
White Mary, 163–4
White Meg, 174, 183
  elegy on, 174–7
White Widow, 232
Whitefield Rev. George, 187
Whittet George, 257
Wibert Augustus Rodolphus, 63
Wight George, 97
Wigton Earl of, son of, 44
William and Mary, 1, 52, 64
William of Orange, 68
Williamson Alexander, 141, 149, 169
  wife of, 141, 149
Williamson Alexander junior, 169
Williamson John, 169
Willis Charles, 249
Willis Jean, 199
Wilson Alexander, 32–3, 46, 54
Wilson Archibald, 48
  sons of. *See* Wilson John, Wilson Alexander
Wilson Claud, 54, 95, 105, 107, 144
Wilson David, 190, 215, 219
Wilson David senior, 238
  wife of, 238
Wilson Elisabeth, 56
Wilson Forrest, 211
Wilson Francis, 76, 108–9, 132
Wilson George, 79
Wilson Jean, 94
Wilson John, 54, 68, 72, 166, 167, 219
Wilson Jonet, 92, 93–5
Wilson Margaret, 233, 238
Wilson Mr David, 238
Wilson Robert, 62
Wilson Thomas, 25, 40
Wilson William, 151, 219
witchcraft, 39, 42, 61, 71, 99
Wood Captain John, 208, 216
Wood John Philp, 7, 9, 18, 51, 52, 106, 136, 170, 174, 178, 196–7, 200, 203, 204, 205–18, 221

mother of, 208
The Antient and Modern State of the Parish of Cramond, 208, 217
uncle of, 217
Wood Marguerite, 220
Worcester, battle of, 22
Wright Alexander, 232
Wright Christian, 88
Wright George, 166
Wright Laurence, 79
Wright Margaret, 58, 65, 70, 72–3, 74, 75, 250
  husband of, 250
  servants of, 72, 73–5
  son of, 75
Wright Samuel, 226
Wright William, 147

Yeats Andrew, 152
Yorston Mr, 164
Young Agnes, 162
Young Alexander, 52

Young David, 149
Young Elisabeth, 241
Young Euphan, 202
Young James, 138, 141
  wife of, 170
Young Janet, 232
Young John, 63, 70, 77, 108–9, 141, 249
  wife of. *See* Couper Katherine
Young John in Currie, 81
Young Jonet, 32
Young Margaret, 173
Young Matthew, 68
Young Rev. Alexander, 43, 45
Young Robert, 2–6, 249
  wife of, 2–6
Young Sir John of Lennie, 51, 52, 56, 59
Young William, 214, 241
Young William junior, 219
Young William senior, 219
  wife of. *See* Wilson Margaret
Yule Janet, 237